Hands-On Image Pro with Python

Expert techniques for advanced image analysis and effective interpretation of image data

Sandipan Dey

BIRMINGHAM - MUMBAI

Hands-On Image Processing with Python

Copyright © 2018 Packt Publishing

All rights reserved. No part of this book may be reproduced, stored in a retrieval system, or transmitted in any form or by any means, without the prior written permission of the publisher, except in the case of brief quotations embedded in critical articles or reviews.

Every effort has been made in the preparation of this book to ensure the accuracy of the information presented. However, the information contained in this book is sold without warranty, either express or implied. Neither the author, nor Packt Publishing or its dealers and distributors, will be held liable for any damages caused or alleged to have been caused directly or indirectly by this book.

Packt Publishing has endeavored to provide trademark information about all of the companies and products mentioned in this book by the appropriate use of capitals. However, Packt Publishing cannot guarantee the accuracy of this information.

Commissioning Editor: Pravin Dhandre
Acquisition Editor: Devika Battike
Content Development Editor: Unnati Guha
Technical Editor: Dinesh Chaudhary
Copy Editor: Safis Editing
Project Coordinator: Manthan Patel
Proofreader: Safis Editing
Indexer: Pratik Shirodkar
Graphics: Jisha Chirayil
Production Coordinator: Shraddha Falebhai

First published: November 2018

Production reference: 1301118

Published by Packt Publishing Ltd.
Livery Place
35 Livery Street
Birmingham
B3 2PB, UK.

ISBN 978-1-78934-373-1

www.packtpub.com

I dedicate this book to my beloved parents.

```
mapt.io
```

Mapt is an online digital library that gives you full access to over 5,000 books and videos, as well as industry leading tools to help you plan your personal development and advance your career. For more information, please visit our website.

Why subscribe?

- Spend less time learning and more time coding with practical eBooks and Videos from over 4,000 industry professionals

- Improve your learning with Skill Plans built especially for you

- Get a free eBook or video every month

- Mapt is fully searchable

- Copy and paste, print, and bookmark content

Packt.com

Did you know that Packt offers eBook versions of every book published, with PDF and ePub files available? You can upgrade to the eBook version at `www.packt.com` and as a print book customer, you are entitled to a discount on the eBook copy. Get in touch with us at `customercare@packtpub.com` for more details.

At `www.packt.com`, you can also read a collection of free technical articles, sign up for a range of free newsletters, and receive exclusive discounts and offers on Packt books and eBooks.

Contributors

About the author

Sandipan Dey is a data scientist with a wide range of interests, covering topics such as machine learning, deep learning, image processing, and computer vision. He has worked in numerous data science fields, working with recommender systems, predictive models for the events industry, sensor localization models, sentiment analysis, and device prognostics. He earned his master's degree in computer science from the University of Maryland, Baltimore County, and has published in a few IEEE Data Mining conferences and journals. He has earned certifications from 100+ MOOCs on data science, machine learning, deep learning, image processing, and related courses/specializations. He is a regular blogger on his blog (sandipanweb) and is a machine learning education enthusiast.

> *I am grateful to the excellent online courses provided by top schools across the globe over the last few years. Few of them are: Image processing (@Coursera by Duke, Northwestern), Computer vision and image analysis (@edX by Microsoft), Computational photography (@Coursera by Georgia Tech), Machine learning (@Coursera by Stanford, University of Toronto; @edX by UCSD), Deep learning (@Coursera by deeplearning.ai; @Udacity by Google).*

About the reviewer

Nikhil Borkar holds a CQF designation and a postgraduate degree in quantitative finance. He also holds the certified financial crime examiner and certified anti-money laundering professional qualifications. He is a registered research analyst with the **Securities and Exchange Board of India** (**SEBI**) and has a keen grasp of the Indian regulatory landscape pertaining to securities and investments. He is currently working as an independent FinTech and legal consultant. Prior to this, he worked with **Morgan Stanley Capital International** (**MSCI**) as a global RFP project manager.

Packt is searching for authors like you

If you're interested in becoming an author for Packt, please visit `authors.packtpub.com` and apply today. We have worked with thousands of developers and tech professionals, just like you, to help them share their insight with the global tech community. You can make a general application, apply for a specific hot topic that we are recruiting an author for, or submit your own idea.

Table of Contents

Preface   1

Chapter 1: Getting Started with Image Processing   7
  What is image processing and some applications   8
    What is an image and how it is stored on a computer   8
    What is image processing?   10
    Some applications of image processing   11
  The image processing pipeline   11
  Setting up different image processing libraries in Python   13
    Installing pip   14
    Installing some image processing libraries in Python   14
    Installing the Anaconda distribution   15
    Installing Jupyter Notebook   16
  Image I/O and display with Python   16
    Reading, saving, and displaying an image using PIL   17
      Providing the correct path to the images on the disk   18
    Reading, saving, and displaying an image using Matplotlib   18
      Interpolating while displaying with Matplotlib imshow()   20
    Reading, saving, and displaying an image using scikit-image   21
      Using scikit-image's astronaut dataset   22
      Reading and displaying multiple images at once   23
    Reading, saving, and displaying an image using scipy misc   23
      Using scipy.misc's face dataset   23
  Dealing with different image types and file formats and performing basic image manipulations   25
    Dealing with different image types and file formats   25
      File formats   25
        Converting from one file format to another   26
      Image types (modes)   26
        Converting from one image mode into another   27
      Some color spaces (channels)   28
        Converting from one color space into another   28
      Data structures to store images   29
        Converting image data structures   30
    Basic image manipulations   30
      Image manipulations with numpy array slicing   31
        Simple image morphing - α-blending of two images using cross-dissolving   32
      Image manipulations with PIL   33
        Cropping an image   34
        Resizing an image   34
        Negating an image   36
        Converting an image into grayscale   36
        Some gray-level transformations   37

Table of Contents

Some geometric transformations	38
Changing pixel values of an image	40
Drawing on an image	41
Drawing text on an image	42
Creating a thumbnail	43
Computing the basic statistics of an image	43
Plotting the histograms of pixel values for the RGB channels of an image	43
Separating the RGB channels of an image	44
Combining multiple channels of an image	45
α-blending two images	45
Superimposing two images	46
Adding two images	47
Computing the difference between two images	48
Subtracting two images and superimposing two image negatives	49
Image manipulations with scikit-image	49
Inverse warping and geometric transformation using the warp() function	50
Applying the swirl transform	51
Adding random Gaussian noise to images	51
Computing the cumulative distribution function of an image	52
Image manipulation with Matplotlib	52
Drawing contour lines for an image	53
Image manipulation with the scipy.misc and scipy.ndimage modules	53
Summary	**53**
Questions	**54**
Further reading	**56**
Chapter 2: Sampling, Fourier Transform, and Convolution	**59**
Image formation – sampling and quantization	**60**
Sampling	60
Up-sampling	61
Up-sampling and interpolation	62
Down-sampling	65
Down-sampling and anti-aliasing	67
Quantization	70
Quantizing with PIL	70
Discrete Fourier Transform	**72**
Why do we need the DFT?	73
The Fast Fourier Transform algorithm to compute the DFT	74
The FFT with the scipy.fftpack module	74
Plotting the frequency spectrum	75
The FFT with the numpy.fft module	76
Computing the magnitude and phase of a DFT	76
Understanding convolution	**80**
Why convolve an image?	81
Convolution with SciPy signal's convolve2d	81
Applying convolution to a grayscale image	82
Convolution modes, pad values, and boundary conditions	83
Applying convolution to a color (RGB) image	83
Convolution with SciPy ndimage.convolve	85
Correlation versus convolution	87
Template matching with cross-correlation between the image and template	90

Summary	92
Questions	92
Further reading	93
Chapter 3: Convolution and Frequency Domain Filtering	**95**
Convolution theorem and frequency domain Gaussian blur	**95**
Application of the convolution theorem	96
Frequency domain Gaussian blur filter with numpy fft	97
Gaussian kernel in the frequency domain	98
Frequency domain Gaussian blur filter with scipy signal.fftconvolve()	101
Comparing the runtimes of SciPy convolve() and fftconvolve() with the Gaussian blur kernel	103
Filtering in the frequency domain (HPF, LPF, BPF, and notch filters)	**105**
What is a filter?	105
High-Pass Filter (HPF)	106
How SNR changes with frequency cut-off	111
Low-pass filter (LPF)	112
LPF with scipy ndimage and numpy fft	112
LPF with fourier_gaussian	112
LPF with scipy fftpack	114
How SNR changes with frequency cutoff	118
Band-pass filter (BPF) with DoG	118
Band-stop (notch) filter	119
Using a notch filter to remove periodic noise from images	120
Image restoration	122
Deconvolution and inverse filtering with FFT	123
Image deconvolution with the Wiener filter	127
Image denoising with FFT	128
Filter in FFT	130
Reconstructing the final image	131
Summary	**132**
Questions	**133**
Further reading	**133**
Chapter 4: Image Enhancement	**135**
Point-wise intensity transformations – pixel transformation	**136**
Log transform	137
Power-law transform	139
Contrast stretching	141
Using PIL as a point operation	142
Using the PIL ImageEnhance module	144
Thresholding	145
With a fixed threshold	146
Half-toning	148
Floyd-Steinberg dithering with error diffusion	149
Histogram processing – histogram equalization and matching	**150**
Contrast stretching and histogram equalization with scikit-image	151
Histogram matching	156

Histogram matching for an RGB image	158
Linear noise smoothing	**160**
Smoothing with PIL	160
Smoothing with ImageFilter.BLUR	160
Smoothing by averaging with the box blur kernel	162
Smoothing with the Gaussian blur filter	163
Comparing smoothing with box and Gaussian kernels using SciPy ndimage	164
Nonlinear noise smoothing	**165**
Smoothing with PIL	166
Using the median filter	166
Using max and min filter	168
Smoothing (denoising) with scikit-image	168
Using the bilateral filter	169
Using non-local means	171
Smoothing with scipy ndimage	173
Summary	**174**
Questions	**175**
Further reading	**175**
Chapter 5: Image Enhancement Using Derivatives	**177**
Image derivatives – Gradient and Laplacian	**178**
Derivatives and gradients	178
Displaying the magnitude and the gradient on the same image	181
Laplacian	182
Some notes about the Laplacian	183
Effects of noise on gradient computation	184
Sharpening and unsharp masking	**185**
Sharpening with Laplacian	186
Unsharp masking	187
With the SciPy ndimage module	187
Edge detection using derivatives and filters (Sobel, Canny, and so on)	**190**
With gradient magnitude computed using the partial derivatives	190
The non-maximum suppression algorithm	192
Sobel edge detector with scikit-image	193
Different edge detectors with scikit-image – Prewitt, Roberts, Sobel, Scharr, and Laplace	196
The Canny edge detector with scikit-image	198
The LoG and DoG filters	200
The LoG filter with the SciPy ndimage module	204
Edge detection with the LoG filter	205
Edge detection with the Marr and Hildreth's algorithm using the zero-crossing computation	206
Finding and enhancing edges with PIL	207
Image pyramids (Gaussian and Laplacian) – blending images	**209**
A Gaussian pyramid with scikit-image transform pyramid module	210
A Laplacian pyramid with scikit-image transform's pyramid module	212

Constructing the Gaussian Pyramid	214
Reconstructing an image only from its Laplacian pyramid	218
Blending images with pyramids	220

Summary — 223
Questions — 223
Further reading — 224

Chapter 6: Morphological Image Processing — 227
The scikit-image morphology module — 228
Binary operations — 228
- Erosion — 228
- Dilation — 229
- Opening and closing — 230
- Skeletonizing — 232
- Computing the convex hull — 232
- Removing small objects — 234
- White and black top-hats — 236
- Extracting the boundary — 236

Fingerprint cleaning with opening and closing — 237
Grayscale operations — 239

The scikit-image filter.rank module — 241
- Morphological contrast enhancement — 241
- Noise removal with the median filter — 242
- Computing the local entropy — 243

The SciPy ndimage.morphology module — 245
- Filling holes in binary objects — 245
- Using opening and closing to remove noise — 246
- Computing the morphological Beucher gradient — 248
- Computing the morphological Laplace — 249

Summary — 250
Questions — 251
Further reading — 252

Chapter 7: Extracting Image Features and Descriptors — 253
Feature detectors versus descriptors — 253
Harris Corner Detector — 255
With scikit-image — 255
With sub-pixel accuracy — 256
An application – image matching — 258
Robust image matching using the RANSAC algorithm and Harris Corner features — 258

Blob detectors with LoG, DoG, and DoH — 262
- Laplacian of Gaussian (LoG) — 263
- Difference of Gaussian (DoG) — 263
- Determinant of Hessian (DoH) — 263

Histogram of Oriented Gradients — 265

Algorithm to compute HOG descriptors	265
Compute HOG descriptors with scikit-image	265
Scale-invariant feature transform	**266**
Algorithm to compute SIFT descriptors	267
With opencv and opencv-contrib	267
Application – matching images with BRIEF, SIFT, and ORB	269
Matching images with BRIEF binary descriptors with scikit-image	269
Matching with ORB feature detector and binary descriptor using scikit-image	271
Matching with ORB features using brute-force matching with python-opencv	273
Brute-force matching with SIFT descriptors and ratio test with OpenCV	275
Haar-like features	**277**
Haar-like feature descriptor with scikit-image	277
Application – face detection with Haar-like features	279
Face/eye detection with OpenCV using pre-trained classifiers with Haar-cascade features	279
Summary	**281**
Questions	**282**
Further reading	**282**
Chapter 8: Image Segmentation	**285**
What is image segmentation?	**285**
Hough transform – detecting lines and circles	**286**
Thresholding and Otsu's segmentation	**290**
Edges-based/region-based segmentation	**292**
Edge-based segmentation	293
Region-based segmentation	295
Morphological watershed algorithm	295
Felzenszwalb, SLIC, QuickShift, and Compact Watershed algorithms	**299**
Felzenszwalb's efficient graph-based image segmentation	299
SLIC	303
RAG merging	304
QuickShift	305
Compact Watershed	307
Region growing with SimpleITK	308
Active contours, morphological snakes, and GrabCut algorithms	**313**
Active contours	313
Morphological snakes	315
GrabCut with OpenCV	317
Summary	**321**
Questions	**322**
Further reading	**322**
Chapter 9: Classical Machine Learning Methods in Image Processing	**323**
Supervised versus unsupervised learning	**324**
Unsupervised machine learning – clustering, PCA, and eigenfaces	**325**

K-means clustering for image segmentation with color quantization	325
Spectral clustering for image segmentation	328
PCA and eigenfaces	331
Dimension reduction and visualization with PCA	331
2D projection and visualization	332
Eigenfaces with PCA	333
Eigenfaces	337
Reconstruction	337
Eigen decomposition	339
Supervised machine learning – image classification	**340**
Downloading the MNIST (handwritten digits) dataset	341
Visualizing the dataset	342
Training kNN, Gaussian Bayes, and SVM models to classify MNIST	344
k-nearest neighbors (KNN) classifier	344
Squared Euclidean distance	344
Computing the nearest neighbors	345
Evaluating the performance of the classifier	346
Bayes classifier (Gaussian generative model)	347
Training the generative model – computing the MLE of the Gaussian parameters	348
Computing the posterior probabilities to make predictions on test data and model evaluation	350
SVM classifier	350
Supervised machine learning – object detection	**352**
Face detection with Haar-like features and cascade classifiers with AdaBoost – Viola-Jones	353
Face classification using the Haar-like feature descriptor	354
Finding the most important Haar-like features for face classification with the random forest ensemble classifier	358
Detecting objects with SVM using HOG features	360
HOG training	360
Classification with the SVM model	361
Computing BoundingBoxes with HOG-SVM	362
Non-max suppression	363
Summary	**364**
Questions	**365**
Further reading	**366**
Chapter 10: Deep Learning in Image Processing - Image Classification	**367**
Deep learning in image processing	**368**
What is deep learning?	368
Classical versus deep learning	369
Why deep learning?	371
CNNs	**371**
Conv or pooling or FC layers – CNN architecture and how it works	371
Convolutional layer	372
Pooling layer	374
Non-linearity – ReLU layer	374
FC layer	374
Dropout	374

Table of Contents

Image classification with TensorFlow or Keras — 375
- Classification with TF — 375
- Classification with dense FC layers with Keras — 383
  - Visualizing the network — 385
  - Visualizing the weights in the intermediate layers — 386
- CNN for classification with Keras — 388
  - Classifying MNIST — 388
  - Visualizing the intermediate layers — 391

Some popular deep CNNs — 393
- VGG-16/19 — 393
  - Classifying cat/dog images with VGG-16 in Keras — 395
    - Training phase — 395
    - Testing (prediction) phase — 402
- InceptionNet — 404
- ResNet — 405

Summary — 407
Questions — 407
Further reading — 408

Chapter 11: Deep Learning in Image Processing - Object Detection, and more — 409

Introducing YOLO v2 — 410
- Classifying and localizing images and detecting objects — 410
- Proposing and detecting objects using CNNs — 412
- Using YOLO v2 — 413
  - Using a pre-trained YOLO model for object detection — 413

Deep semantic segmentation with DeepLab V3+ — 421
- Semantic segmentation — 421
- DeepLab V3+ — 422
  - DeepLab v3 architecture — 422
  - Steps you must follow to use DeepLab V3+ model for semantic segmentation — 423

Transfer learning – what it is, and when to use it — 426
- Transfer learning with Keras — 427

Neural style transfers with cv2 using a pre-trained torch model — 432
- Understanding the NST algorithm — 432
- Implementation of NST with transfer learning — 433
  - Ensuring NST with content loss — 434
  - Computing the style cost — 434
  - Computing the overall loss — 435
- Neural style transfer with Python and OpenCV — 435

Summary — 438
Questions — 439
Further reading — 439

Chapter 12: Additional Problems in Image Processing — 441

Seam carving — 441
- Content-aware image resizing with seam carving — 442

Object removal with seam carving	446
Seamless cloning and Poisson image editing	447
Image inpainting	450
Variational image processing	453
Total Variation Denoising	454
Creating flat-texture cartoonish images with total variation denoising	456
Image quilting	457
Texture synthesis	457
Texture transfer	457
Face morphing	458
Summary	460
Questions	460
Further reading	460
Other Books You May Enjoy	463
Index	467

Preface

This book covers how to solve image processing problems using popular Python image processing libraries (such as *PIL, scikit-image, python-opencv, scipy ndimage,* and *SimpleITK*), machine learning libraries (*scikit-learn*), and deep learning libraries (*TensorFlow, Keras*). It will enable the reader to write code snippets to implement complex image processing algorithms, such as image enhancement, filtering, restoration, segmentation, classification, and object detection. The reader will also be able to use machine learning and deep learning models to solve complex image processing problems.

The book will start with the basics and guide the reader to go to an advanced level by providing Python-reproducible implementations throughout the book. The book will start from the classical image processing techniques and explore the journey of evolution of the image processing algorithms all the way through to the recent advances in image processing/computer vision with deep learning. Readers will learn how to use the image processing libraries, such as PIL, scikit-image, and scipy ndimage in Python, which will enable them to write code snippets in Python 3 and quickly implement complex image processing algorithms, such as image enhancement, filtering, segmentation, object detection, and classification. The reader will learn how to use machine learning models using the scikit-learn library and later explore deep CNN such as VGG-19 with TensorFlow/Keras, use the end-to-end deep learning YOLO model for object detection, and DeepLab V3+ for semantic segmentation and neural-style transfer models. The reader will also learn a few advanced problems, such as image inpainting, gradient blending, variational denoising, seam carving, quilting, and morphing. By the end of this book, the reader will learn to implement various algorithms for efficient image processing.

This book follows a highly practical approach that will take its readers through a set of image processing concepts/algorithms and help them learn, in detail, how to use leading Python library functions to implement these algorithms.

Disclaimer

The images used in this book as inputs and the outputs can be found at https://www.packtpub.com/sites/default/files/downloads/9781789343731_ColorImages.pdf.

Preface

Who this book is for

This book is for engineers/applied researchers, and also for software engineers interested in computer vision, image processing, machine learning, and deep learning, especially for readers who are adept at Python programming and who want to explore various topics on image processing in detail and solve a range of complex problems, starting from concept through to implementation. A math and programming background, along with some basic knowledge of machine learning, are prerequisites.

What this book covers

Chapter 1, *Getting Started with Image Processing*, covers image processing and its applications, different Python libraries, image input/output, data structures, file formats, and basic image manipulations.

Chapter 2, *Sampling, Fourier Transform, and Convolution*, covers 2D Fourier transform, sampling, quantization, discrete Fourier transform, 1D and 2D convolution and filtering in the frequency domain, and how to implement them with Python using examples. You will learn the simple signal processing tools that are needed in order to understand the following units.

Chapter 3, *Convolution and Frequency Domain Filtering*, demonstrates how convolution is carried out on images using Python. Topics such as filtering in the frequency domain are also covered.

Chapter 4, *Image Enhancement*, covers some of the most basic tools in image processing, such as mean/median filtering and histogram equalization, which are still among the most powerful. We will describe these and provide a modern interpretation of these basic tools.

Chapter 5, *Image Enhancement using Derivatives*, covers further topics associated with image enhancement, in other words, the problem of improving the appearance or usefulness of an image. Topics covered include edge detection with derivatives and Laplacian, sharpening, and pseudo coloring. All the concepts will be described with the help of examples involving Python.

Chapter 6, *Morphological Image Processing*, covers binary operations and the use of filter rank module to perform operations such as morphological contrast enhancements, noise removal, and computing local entropy. We will also see how a morphology module is used.

Chapter 7, *Extracting Image Features and Descriptors*, describes several techniques for extracting features from images/compute image descriptors.

Chapter 8, *Image Segmentation*, outlines the basic techniques for partitioning an image, from a simple threshold to more advanced graph cuts.

Chapter 9, *Classical Machine Learning Methods in Image Processing*, introduces a number of different machine learning techniques for image classification and object detection/recognition.

Chapter 10, *Deep Learning in Image Processing – Image Classification*, describes why the image processing/computer vision community gradually transitioned from the classical feature-based machine learning models to deep learning models.

Chapter 11, *Deep Learning in Image Processing - Object Detection, and more*, describes a number of remarkable applications of the CNNs for object detection, semantic segmentation, and image style transfer. A few popular models, such as YOLO and object proposals, will be demonstrated. How to use transfer learning to avoid learning a very deep neural net from scratch will also be outlined.

Chapter 12, *Additional Problems in Image Processing*, describes a number of additional image processing problems and various algorithms for solving them. Problems include seam carving (for context-aware image resizing), image quilting (for image resizing with non-parametric sampling and texture transfer), poisson (gradient) image editing (blending) to seamlessly blend one image within another, image morphing (to transform one image to another), image inpainting (to restore a degraded image), and some variational image processing techniques (for image denoising, for example).

To get the most out of this book

1. A basic knowledge of Python is required to run the codes, along with access to image datasets and the GitHub link.
2. A basic Math background is also needed to understand the concepts.

Download the example code files

You can download the example code files for this book from your account at www.packt.com. If you purchased this book elsewhere, you can visit www.packt.com/support and register to have the files emailed directly to you.

You can download the code files by following these steps:

1. Log in or register at www.packt.com.
2. Select the **SUPPORT** tab.
3. Click on **Code Downloads & Errata**.
4. Enter the name of the book in the **Search** box and follow the onscreen instructions.

Once the file is downloaded, please make sure that you unzip or extract the folder using the latest version of:

- WinRAR/7-Zip for Windows
- Zipeg/iZip/UnRarX for Mac
- 7-Zip/PeaZip for Linux

The code bundle for the book is also hosted on GitHub at https://github.com/PacktPublishing/Hands-On-Image-Processing-with-Python. In case there's an update to the code, it will be updated on the existing GitHub repository.

We also have other code bundles from our rich catalog of books and videos available at https://github.com/PacktPublishing/. Check them out!

Download the color images

We also provide a PDF file that has color images of the screenshots/diagrams used in this book. You can download it here: http://www.packtpub.com/sites/default/files/downloads/9781789343731_ColorImages.pdf.

Conventions used

There are a number of text conventions used throughout this book.

CodeInText: Indicates code words in text, database table names, folder names, filenames, file extensions, pathnames, dummy URLs, user input, and Twitter handles. Here is an example: "Mount the downloaded WebStorm-10*.dmg disk image file as another disk in your system."

Preface

A block of code is set as follows:

```
viewer = viewer.ImageViewer(im)
viewer.show()
```

When we wish to draw your attention to a particular part of a code block, the relevant lines or items are set in bold:

```
[default]
exten => s,1,Dial(Zap/1|30)
exten => s,2,Voicemail(u100)
exten => s,102,Voicemail(b100)
exten => i,1,Voicemail(s0)
```

Any command-line input or output is written as follows:

```
>>> pip install numpy
>>> pip install scipy
```

Bold: Indicates a new term, an important word, or words that you see on screen. For example, words in menus or dialog boxes appear in the text like this. Here is an example: "Select **System info** from the **Administration** panel."

Warnings or important notes appear like this.

Tips and tricks appear like this.

Get in touch

Feedback from our readers is always welcome.

General feedback: If you have questions about any aspect of this book, mention the book title in the subject of your message and email us at customercare@packtpub.com.

Errata: Although we have taken every care to ensure the accuracy of our content, mistakes do happen. If you have found a mistake in this book, we would be grateful if you would report this to us. Please visit www.packt.com/submit-errata, selecting your book, clicking on the Errata Submission Form link, and entering the details.

Piracy: If you come across any illegal copies of our works in any form on the internet, we would be grateful if you would provide us with the location address or website name. Please contact us at copyright@packt.com with a link to the material.

If you are interested in becoming an author: If there is a topic that you have expertise in, and you are interested in either writing or contributing to a book, please visit authors.packtpub.com.

Reviews

Please leave a review. Once you have read and used this book, why not leave a review on the site that you purchased it from? Potential readers can then see and use your unbiased opinion to make purchase decisions, we at Packt can understand what you think about our products, and our authors can see your feedback on their book. Thank you!

For more information about Packt, please visit packt.com.

1
Getting Started with Image Processing

As the name suggests, image processing can simply be defined as the processing (analyzing and manipulating) of images with algorithms in a computer (through code). It has a few different aspects, such as storage, representation, information extraction, manipulation, enhancement, restoration, and interpretation of images. In this chapter, we are going to give a basic introduction to all of these different aspects of image processing, along with an introduction to hands-on image processing with Python libraries. We are going to use Python 3 for all of the code samples in this book.

We will start by defining what image processing is and what the applications of image processing are. Then we will learn about the basic image processing pipeline—in other words, what are the steps to process an image on a computer in general. Then, we will learn about different Python libraries available for image processing and how to install them in Python 3. Next, we will learn how to write Python codes to read and write (store) images on a computer using different libraries. After that, we will learn the data structures that are to be used to represent an image in Python and how to display an image. We will also learn different image types and different image file formats, and, finally, how to do basic image manipulations in Python.

By the end of this chapter, we should be able to conceptualize image processing, different steps, and different applications. We should be able to import and call functions from different image processing libraries in Python. We should be able to understand the data structures used to store different types of images in Python, read/write image files using different Python libraries, and write Python code to do basic image manipulations. The topics to be covered in this chapter are as follows:

- What image processing is and some image processing applications
- The image processing pipeline

- Setting up different image processing libraries in Python
- Image I/O and display with Python
- Image types, file formats, and basic image manipulations

What is image processing and some applications

Let's start by defining what is an image, how it is stored on a computer, and how we are going to process it with Python.

What is an image and how it is stored on a computer

Conceptually, an image in its simplest form (**single-channel**; for example, binary or monochrome, grayscale or black and white images) is a two-dimensional function $f(x,y)$ that maps a coordinate-pair to an integer/real value, which is related to the intensity/color of the point. Each point is called a **pixel** or **pel** (picture element). An image can have multiple channels too (for example, colored RGB images, where a color can be represented using three channels—red, green, and blue). For a colored RGB image, each pixel at the (x,y) coordinate can be represented by a three-tuple $(r_{x,y}, g_{x,y}, b_{x,y})$.

In order to be able to process it on a computer, an image $f(x,y)$ needs to be digitalized both spatially and in amplitude. Digitization of the spatial coordinates (x,y) is called **image sampling**. Amplitude digitization is called **gray-level quantization**. In a computer, a pixel value corresponding to a channel is generally represented as an integer value between (0-255) or a floating-point value between (0-1). An image is stored as a file, and there can be many different types (formats) of files. Each file generally has some metadata and some data that can be extracted as multi-dimensional arrays (for example, 2-D arrays for binary or gray-level images and 3D arrays for RGB and YUV colored images). The following screenshot shows how the image data is stored as matrices for different types of image. As shown, for a grayscale image, a matrix (2-D array) of *width x height* suffices to store the image, whereas an RGB image requires a 3-D array of a dimension of *width x height x 3*:

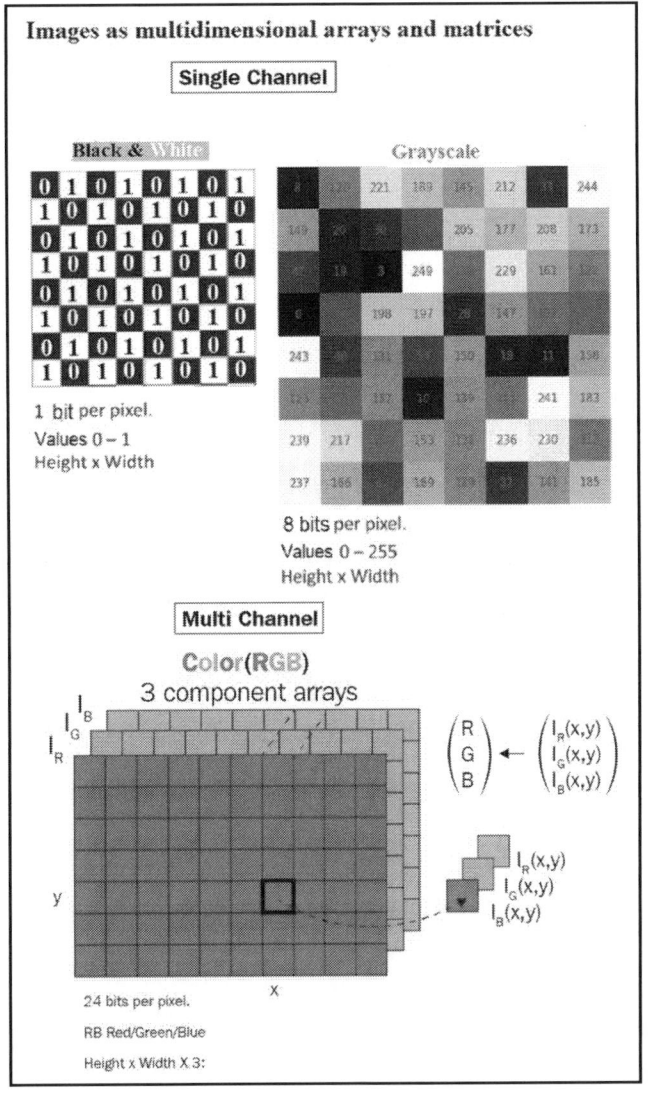

The next screenshot shows example binary, grayscale, and RGB images:

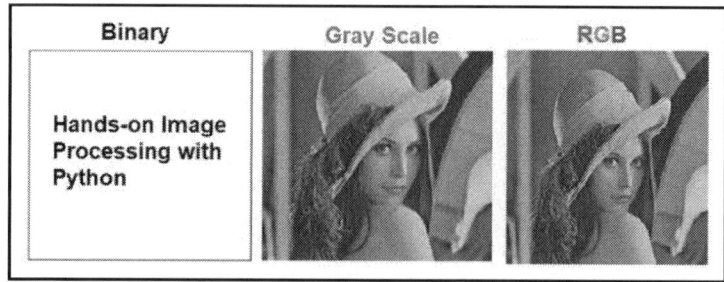

In this book, we shall focus on processing image data and will use Python libraries to extract the data from images for us, as well as run different algorithms for different image processing tasks on the image data. Sample images are taken from the internet, from the Berkeley Segmentation Dataset and Benchmark (https://www2.eecs.berkeley.edu/Research/Projects/CS/vision/bsds/BSDS300/html/dataset/images.html), and the USC-SIPI Image Database (http://sipi.usc.edu/database/), and many of them are standard images used for image processing.

What is image processing?

Image processing refers to the automatic processing, manipulation, analysis, and interpretation of images using algorithms and codes on a computer. It has applications in many disciplines and fields in science and technology such as television, photography, robotics, remote sensing, medical diagnosis, and industrial inspection. Social networking sites such as Facebook and Instagram, which we have got used to in our daily lives and where we upload tons of images every day, are typical examples of the industries that need to use/innovate many image processing algorithms to process the images we upload.

In this book, we are going to use a few Python packages to process an image. First, we shall use a bunch of libraries to do classical image processing: right from extracting image data, transforming the data with some algorithms using library functions to pre-process, enhance, restore, represent (with descriptors), segment, classify, and detect and recognize (objects) to analyze, understand, and interpret the data better. Next, we shall use another bunch of libraries to do image processing based on deep learning, a technology that has became very popular in the last few years.

Some applications of image processing

Some typical applications of image processing include medical/biological fields (for example, X-rays and CT scans), computational photography (Photoshop), fingerprint authentication, face recognition, and so on.

The image processing pipeline

The following steps describe the basic steps in the image processing pipeline:

1. **Acquisition and storage**: The image needs to be captured (using a camera, for example) and stored on some device (such as a hard disk) as a file (for example, a JPEG file).
2. **Load into memory and save to disk**: The image needs to be read from the disk into memory and stored using some data structure (for example, `numpy ndarray`), and the data structure needs to be serialized into an image file later, possibly after running some algorithms on the image.
3. **Manipulation, enhancement, and restoration:** We need to run some pre-processing algorithms to do the following:
    - Run a few transformations on the image (sampling and manipulation; for example, grayscale conversion)
    - Enhance the quality of the image (filtering; for example, deblurring)
    - Restore the image from noise degradation
4. **Segmentation**: The image needs to be segmented in order to extract the objects of interest.
5. **Information extraction/representation**: The image needs to be represented in some alternative form; for example, one of the following:
    - Some hand-crafted feature-descriptor can be computed (for example, HOG descriptors, with classical image processing) from the image
    - Some features can be automatically learned from the image (for example, the weights and bias values learned in the hidden layers of a neural net with deep learning)
    - The image is going to be represented using that alternative representation

6. **Image understanding/interpretation:** This representation will be used to understand the image better with the following:
    - Image classification (for example, whether an image contains a human object or not)
    - Object recognition (for example, finding the location of the car objects in an image with a bounding box)

The following diagram describes the different steps in image processing:

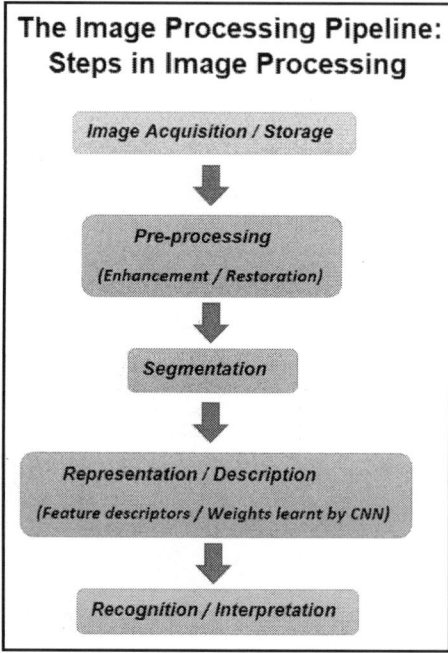

The next screenshot represents different modules that we are going to use for different image processing tasks:

Image I/O, Display, Draw, Mode, Stats

(scikit-image io, external, util, viewer, color, exposure, draw, measure modules,
PIL Image, ImageFile, ImageColor, ImageDraw, ImageMath, ImageStat modules,
Matplotlib image module)

Image Manipulation/Transformation /Morphology

(scikit-image transform, util, morphology modules,
PIL Image, ImageMorph, ImageChops modules)

Image Enhancement/Filter/Restoration/Segmentation / Feature extraction

(scikit-image filters, filters.rank, restoration, segmentation, graph, future.graph, feature modules,
PIL ImageEnhance, ImageFilter modules)

Apart from these libraries, we are going to use the following:

- `scipy.ndimage` and `opencv` for different image processing tasks
- `scikit-learn` for classical machine learning
- `tensorflow` and `keras` for deep learning

Setting up different image processing libraries in Python

The next few paragraphs describe to install different image processing libraries and set up the environment for writing codes to process images using classical image processing techniques in Python. In the last few chapters of this book, we will need to use a different setup when we use deep-learning-based methods.

Installing pip

We are going to use the pip (or pip3) tool to install the libraries, so—if it isn't already installed—we need to install pip first. As mentioned here (https://pip.pypa.io/en/stable/installing/#do-i-need-to-install-pip), pip is already installed if we are using Python 3 >=3.4 downloaded from python.org, or if we are working in a Virtual Environment (https://packaging.python.org/tutorials/installing-packages/#creating-and-using-virtual-environments) created by virtualenv (https://packaging.python.org/key_projects/#virtualenv) or pyvenv (https://packaging.python.org/key_projects/#venv). We just need to make sure to upgrade pip (https://pip.pypa.io/en/stable/installing/#upgrading-pip). How to install pip for different OSes or platforms can be found here: https://stackoverflow.com/questions/6587507/how-to-install-pip-with-python-3.

Installing some image processing libraries in Python

In Python, there are many libraries that we can use for image processing. The ones we are going to use are: NumPy, SciPy, scikit-image, PIL (Pillow), OpenCV, scikit-learn, SimpleITK, and Matplotlib.

The matplotlib library will primarily be used for display purposes, whereas numpy will be used for storing an image. The scikit-learn library will be used for building machine-learning models for image processing, and scipy will be used mainly for image enhancements. The scikit-image, mahotas, and opencv libraries will be used for different image processing algorithms.

The following code block shows how the libraries that we are going to use can be downloaded and installed with pip from a Python prompt (interactive mode):

```
>>> pip install numpy
>>> pip install scipy
>>> pip install scikit-image
>>> pip install scikit-learn
>>> pip install pillow
>>> pip install SimpleITK
>>> pip install opencv-python
>>> pip install matplotlib
```

There may be some additional installation instructions, depending on the OS platform you are going to use. We suggest the reader goes through the documentation sites for each of the libraries to get detailed platform-specific installation instructions for each library. For example, for the `scikit-image` library, detailed installation instructions for different OS platforms can be found here: http://scikit-image.org/docs/stable/install.html. Also, the reader should be familiar with websites such as stackoverflow to resolve platform-dependent installation issues for different libraries.

Finally, we can verify whether a library is properly installed or not by importing it from the Python prompt. If the library is imported successfully (no error message is thrown), then we don't have any installation issue. We can print the version of the library installed by printing it to the console.

The following code block shows the versions for the `scikit-image` and `PIL` Python libraries:

```
>>> import skimage, PIL, numpy
>>> print(skimage.__version__)
# 0.14.0
>>> PIL.__version__
# 5.1.0
>>> numpy.__version__
# 1.14.5
```

Let us ensure that we have the latest versions of all of the libraries.

Installing the Anaconda distribution

We also recommend to download and install the latest version of the Anaconda distribution; this will eliminate the need for explicit installation of many Python packages.

More about installing Anaconda for different OSes can be found at https://conda.io/docs/user-guide/install/index.html.

Installing Jupyter Notebook

We are going to use **Jupyter** notebooks to write our Python code. So, we need to install the `jupyter` package first from a Python prompt with `>>> pip install jupyter`, and then launch the Jupyter Notebook app in the browser using `>>> jupyter notebook`. From there, we can create new Python notebooks and choose a kernel. If we use Anaconda, we do not need to install Jupyter explicitly; the latest Anaconda distribution comes with Jupyter.

More about running Jupyter notebooks can be found at http://jupyter-notebook-beginner-guide.readthedocs.io/en/latest/execute.html.

We can even install a Python package from inside a notebook cell; for example, we can install `scipy` with the `!pip install scipy` command.

For more information on installing Jupyter, please refer to http://jupyter.readthedocs.io/en/latest/install.html.

Image I/O and display with Python

Images are stored as files on the disk, so reading and writing images from the files are disk I/O operations. These can be done using many ways using different libraries; some of them are shown in this section. Let us first start by importing all of the required packages:

```
% matplotlib inline # for inline image display inside notebook
import numpy as np
from PIL import Image, ImageFont, ImageDraw
from PIL.ImageChops import add, subtract, multiply, difference, screen
import PIL.ImageStat as stat
from skimage.io import imread, imsave, imshow, show, imread_collection, imshow_collection
from skimage import color, viewer, exposure, img_as_float, data
from skimage.transform import SimilarityTransform, warp, swirl
from skimage.util import invert, random_noise, montage
import matplotlib.image as mpimg
import matplotlib.pylab as plt
from scipy.ndimage import affine_transform, zoom
from scipy import misc
```

Reading, saving, and displaying an image using PIL

The PIL function, `open()`, reads an image from disk in an `Image` object, as shown in the following code. The image is loaded as an object of the `PIL.PngImagePlugin.PngImageFile` class, and we can use properties such as the width, height, and mode to find the size (*width* x *height* in pixels or the resolution of the image) and mode of the image:

```
im = Image.open("../images/parrot.png") # read the image, provide the correct path
print(im.width, im.height, im.mode, im.format, type(im))
# 453 340 RGB PNG <class 'PIL.PngImagePlugin.PngImageFile'>
im.show() # display the image
```

The following is the output of the previous code:

The following code block shows how to use the PIL function, `convert()`, to convert the colored RGB image into a grayscale image:

```
im_g = im.convert('L')                           # convert the RGB color image to a grayscale image
im_g.save('../images/parrot_gray.png')           # save the image to disk
Image.open("../images/parrot_gray.png").show()   # read the grayscale image from disk and show
```

The following is the output grayscale image:

Providing the correct path to the images on the disk

We recommend creating a folder (sub-directory) to store images to be used for processing (for example, for the Python code samples, we have used the images stored inside a folder named `images`) and then provide the path to the folder to access the image to avoid the `file not found` exception.

Reading, saving, and displaying an image using Matplotlib

The next code block shows how to use the `imread()` function from `matplotlib.image` to read an image in a floating-point `numpy ndarray`. The pixel values are represented as real values between 0 and 1:

```
im = mpimg.imread("../images/hill.png")   # read the image from disk as a numpy ndarray
print(im.shape, im.dtype, type(im))       # this image contains an α channel, hence num_channels= 4
# (960, 1280, 4) float32 <class 'numpy.ndarray'>
plt.screenshot(figsize=(10,10))
plt.imshow(im) # display the image
plt.axis('off')
plt.show()
```

The following screenshot shows the output of the previous code:

The next code snippet changes the image to a darker image by first setting all of the pixel values below 0.5 to 0 and then saving the numpy ndarray to disk. The saved image is again reloaded and displayed:

```
im1 = im
im1[im1 < 0.5] = 0      # make the image look darker
plt.imshow(im1)
plt.axis('off')
plt.tight_layout()
plt.savefig("../images/hill_dark.png")          # save the dark image
im = mpimg.imread("../images/hill_dark.png") # read the dark image
plt.screenshot(figsize=(10,10))
plt.imshow(im)
plt.axis('off') # no axis ticks
plt.tight_layout()
plt.show()
```

The next screenshot shows the darker image saved with the preceding code:

Interpolating while displaying with Matplotlib imshow()

The `imshow()` function from Matplotlib provides many different types of interpolation methods to plot an image. These functions can be particularly useful when the image to be plotted is small. Let us use the small 50 x 50 `lena` image shown in the next screenshot to see the effects of plotting with different interpolation methods:

The next code block demonstrates how to use different interpolation methods with `imshow()`:

```
im = mpimg.imread("../images/lena_small.jpg") # read the image from disk as a numpy ndarray
methods = ['none', 'nearest', 'bilinear', 'bicubic', 'spline16', 'lanczos']
fig, axes = plt.subplots(nrows=2, ncols=3, figsize=(15, 30),
 subplot_kw={'xticks': [], 'yticks': []})
fig.subplots_adjust(hspace=0.05, wspace=0.05)
for ax, interp_method in zip(axes.flat, methods):
  ax.imshow(im, interpolation=interp_method)
  ax.set_title(str(interp_method), size=20)
```

```
plt.tight_layout()
plt.show()
```

The next screenshot shows the output of the preceding code:

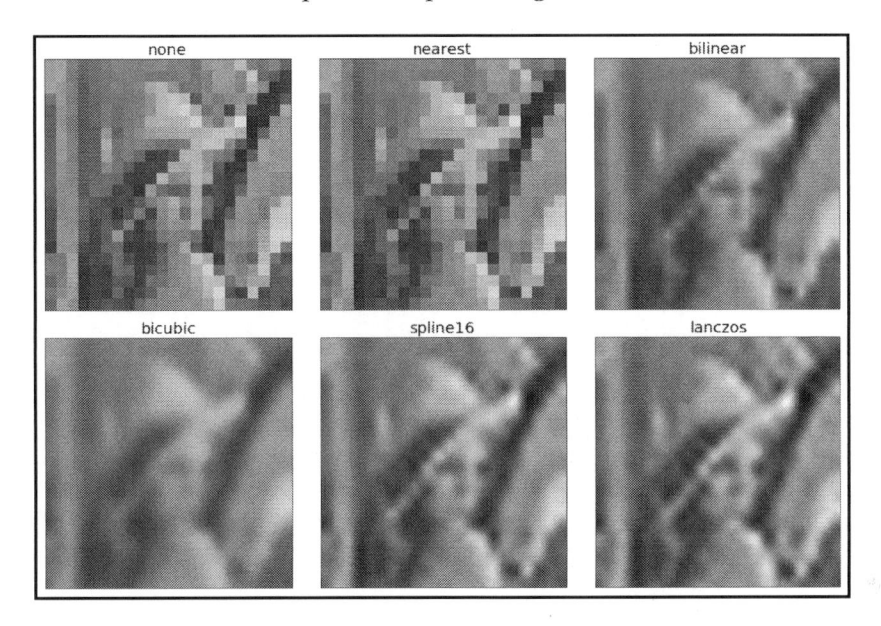

Reading, saving, and displaying an image using scikit-image

The next code block uses the `imread()` function from `scikit-image` to read an image in a numpy `ndarray` of type `uint8` (8-bit unsigned integer). Hence, the pixel values will be in between 0 and 255. Then it converts (changes the image type or mode, which will be discussed shortly) the colored RGB image into an HSV image using the `hsv2rgb()` function from the `Image.color` module. Next, it changes the saturation (colorfulness) to a constant value for all of the pixels by keeping the hue and value channels unchanged. The image is then converted back into RGB mode with the `rgb2hsv()` function to create a new image, which is then saved and displayed:

```
im = imread("../images/parrot.png")    # read image from disk, provide the
correct path
print(im.shape, im.dtype, type(im))
# (362, 486, 3) uint8 <class 'numpy.ndarray'>
hsv = color.rgb2hsv(im) # from RGB to HSV color space
hsv[:, :, 1] = 0.5 # change the saturation
```

```
im1 = color.hsv2rgb(hsv) # from HSV back to RGB
imsave('../images/parrot_hsv.png', im1) # save image to disk
im = imread("../images/parrot_hsv.png")
plt.axis('off'), imshow(im), show()
```

The next screenshot shows the output of the previous code—a new image with changed saturation:

We can use the scikit-image `viewer` module also to display an image in a pop-up window, as shown in the following code:

```
viewer = viewer.ImageViewer(im)
viewer.show()
```

Using scikit-image's astronaut dataset

The following code block shows how we can load the `astronaut` image from the `scikit-image` library's image datasets with the `data` module. The module contains a few other popular datasets, such as cameraman, which can be loaded similarly:

```
im = data.astronaut()
imshow(im), show()
```

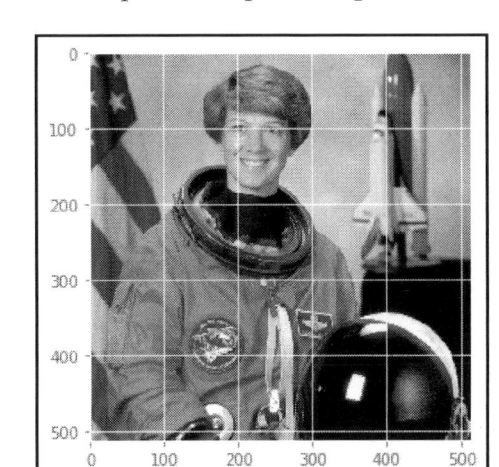

The next screenshot shows the output of the preceding code:

Reading and displaying multiple images at once

We can use the `imread_collection()` function of the scikit-image `io` module to load in a folder all images that have a particular pattern in the filename and display them simultaneously with the `imshow_collection()` function. The code is left as an exercise for the reader.

Reading, saving, and displaying an image using scipy misc

The `misc` module of `scipy` can also be used for image I/O and display. The following sections demonstrate how to use the `misc` module functions.

Using scipy.misc's face dataset

The next code block shows how to display the `face` dataset of the `misc` module:

```
im = misc.face() # load the raccoon's face image
misc.imsave('face.png', im) # uses the Image module (PIL)
plt.imshow(im), plt.axis('off'), plt.show()
```

Getting Started with Image Processing

The next screenshot shows the output of the previous code, which displays the `misc` module's `face` image:

We can read an image from disk using `misc.imread()`. The next code block shows an example:

```
im = misc.imread('../images/veg.jpg')
print(type(im), im.shape, im.dtype)
# <class 'numpy.ndarray'> (225, 225, 3) uint8
```

The I/O function's `imread()` is deprecated in SciPy 1.0.0, and will be removed in 1.2.0, so the documentation recommends we use the `imageio` library instead. The next code block shows how an image can be read with the `imageio.imread()` function and can be displayed with Matplotlib:

```
import imageio
im = imageio.imread('../images/pepper.jpg')
print(type(im), im.shape, im.dtype)
# <class 'imageio.core.util.Image'> (225, 225, 3) uint8
plt.imshow(im), plt.axis('off'), plt.show()
```

The next screenshot shows the output of the previous code block:

Dealing with different image types and file formats and performing basic image manipulations

In this section, we will discuss different image manipulation functions (with point transformation and geometric transformation) and how to deal with images of different types. Let us start with that.

Dealing with different image types and file formats

An image can be saved in different file formats and in different modes (types). Let us discuss how to handle images of different file formats and types with Python libraries.

File formats

Image files can be of different formats. Some of the popular ones include BMP (8-bit, 24-bit, 32-bit), PNG, JPG (JPEG), GIF, PPM, PNM, and TIFF. We do not need to be worried about the specific format of an image file (and how the metadata is stored) to extract data from it. Python image processing libraries will read the image and extract the data, along with some other useful information for us (for example, image size, type/mode, and data type).

Converting from one file format to another

Using PIL, we can read an image in one file format and save it to another; for example, from PNG to JPG, as shown in the following:

```
im = Image.open("../images/parrot.png")
print(im.mode)

#   RGB

im.save("../images/parrot.jpg")
```

But if the PNG file is in the RGBA mode, we need to convert it into the RGB mode before we save it as JPG, as otherwise it will give an error. The next code block shows how to first convert and then save:

```
im = Image.open("../images/hill.png")
print(im.mode)
# RGBA
im.convert('RGB').save("../images/hill.jpg") # first convert to RGB mode
```

Image types (modes)

An image can be of the following different types:

- Single channel images—each pixel is represented by a single value:
  - Binary (monochrome) images (each pixel is represented by a single 0-1 bit)
  - Gray-level images (each pixel can be represented with 8-bits and can have values typically in the range of 0-255)
- Multi-channel images—each pixel is represented by a tuple of values:
  - 3-channel images; for example, the following:
    - RGB images—each pixel is represented by three-tuple (r, g, b) values, representing red, green, and blue channel color values for every pixel.
    - HSV images—each pixel is represented by three-tuple (h, s, v) values, representing *hue* (color), *saturation* (colorfulness—how much the color is mixed with white), and *value* (brightness—how much the color is mixed with black) channel color values for every pixel. The HSV model describes colors in a similar manner to how the human eye tends to perceive colors.

- Four-channel images; for example, RGBA images—each pixel is represented by three-tuple (r, g, b, α) values, the last channel representing the transparency.

Converting from one image mode into another

We can convert an RGB image into a grayscale image while reading the image itself. The following code does exactly that:

```
im = imread("images/parrot.png", as_gray=True)
print(im.shape)
#(362L, 486L)
```

Note that we can lose some information while converting into grayscale for some colored images. The following code shows such an example with Ishihara plates, used to detect color-blindness. This time, the rgb2gray() function is used from the color module, and both the color and the grayscale images are shown side by side. As can be seen in the following screenshot, the number **8** is almost invisible in the grayscale version:

```
im = imread("../images/Ishihara.png")
im_g = color.rgb2gray(im)
plt.subplot(121), plt.imshow(im, cmap='gray'), plt.axis('off')
plt.subplot(122), plt.imshow(im_g, cmap='gray'), plt.axis('off')
plt.show()
```

The next screenshot shows the output of the previous code—the colored image and the grayscale image obtained from it:

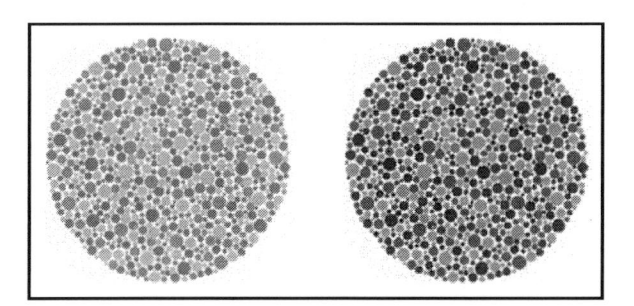

[27]

Some color spaces (channels)

The following represents a few popular channels/color spaces for an image: RGB, HSV, XYZ, YUV, YIQ, YPbPr, YCbCr, and YDbDr. We can use Affine mappings to go from one color space to another. The following matrix represents the linear mapping from the RGB to YIQ color space:

RGB to YIQ

$$\begin{bmatrix} Y \\ I \\ Q \end{bmatrix} = \begin{bmatrix} 0.299 & 0.587 & 0.114 \\ 0.596 & -0.274 & -0.322 \\ 0.211 & -0.523 & 0.312 \end{bmatrix} \begin{bmatrix} R \\ G \\ B \end{bmatrix}$$

YIQ to RGB

$$\begin{bmatrix} R \\ G \\ B \end{bmatrix} = \begin{bmatrix} 1 & 0.956 & 0.621 \\ 1 & -0.272 & -0.647 \\ 1 & -1.106 & 1.703 \end{bmatrix} \begin{bmatrix} Y \\ I \\ Q \end{bmatrix}$$

Converting from one color space into another

We can convert from one color space into another using library functions; for example, the following code converts an RGB color space into an HSV color space image:

```
im = imread("../images/parrot.png")
im_hsv = color.rgb2hsv(im)
plt.gray()
plt.figure(figsize=(10,8))
plt.subplot(221), plt.imshow(im_hsv[...,0]), plt.title('h', size=20),
plt.axis('off')
plt.subplot(222), plt.imshow(im_hsv[...,1]), plt.title('s', size=20),
plt.axis('off')
plt.subplot(223), plt.imshow(im_hsv[...,2]), plt.title('v', size=20),
plt.axis('off')
plt.subplot(224), plt.axis('off')
plt.show()
```

The next screenshot shows the h (*heu or color: dominant wave length of reflected light*), s (*saturation* or *chroma*) and v (*value* or *brightness/luminescence*) channels of the parrot HSV image, created using the previous code:

Similarly, we can convert the image into the YUV color space using the `rgb2yuv()` function.

Data structures to store images

As we have already discussed, PIL uses the `Image` object to store an image, whereas scikit-image uses the `numpy ndarray` data structure to store the image data. The next section describes how to convert between these two data structures.

Converting image data structures

The following code block shows how to convert from the PIL `Image` object into `numpy ndarray` (to be consumed by scikit-image):

```
im = Image.open('../images/flowers.jpg')  # read image into an Image object with PIL
im = np.array(im)                         # create a numpy ndarray from the Image object
imshow(im)                                # use skimage imshow to display the image
plt.axis('off'), show()
```

The next screenshot shows the output of the previous code, which is an image of flowers:

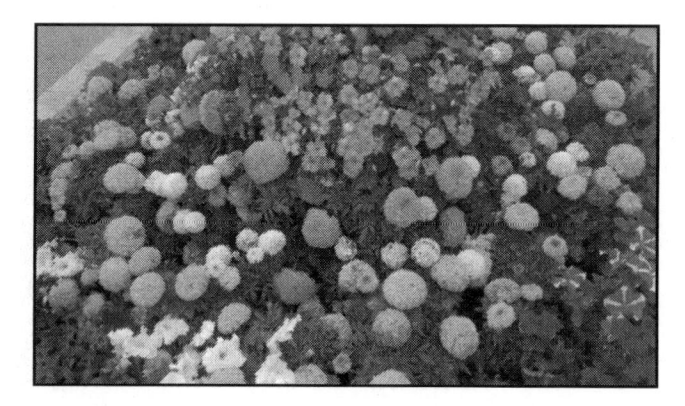

The following code block shows how to convert from `numpy ndarray` into a `PIL Image` object. When run, the code shows the same output as the previous screenshot:

```
im = imread('../images/flowers.png')  # read image into numpy ndarray with skimage
im = Image.fromarray(im) # create a PIL Image object from the numpy ndarray
im.show() # display the image with PIL Image.show() method
```

Basic image manipulations

Different Python libraries can be used for basic image manipulation. Almost all of the libraries store an image in `numpy ndarray` (a 2-D array for grayscale and a 3-D array for an RGB image, for example). The following screenshot shows the positive *x* and *y* directions (the origin being the top-left corner of the image 2-D array) for the colored `lena` image:

Image manipulations with numpy array slicing

The next code block shows how slicing and masking with numpy arrays can be used to create a circular mask on the lena image:

```
lena = mpimg.imread("../images/lena.jpg") # read the image from disk as a
numpy ndarray
print(lena[0, 40])
# [180  76  83]
# print(lena[10:13, 20:23,0:1]) # slicing
lx, ly, _ = lena.shape
X, Y = np.ogrid[0:lx, 0:ly]
mask = (X - lx / 2) ** 2 + (Y - ly / 2) ** 2 > lx * ly / 4
lena[mask,:] = 0 # masks
plt.screenshot(figsize=(10,10))
plt.imshow(lena), plt.axis('off'), plt.show()
```

The following screenshot shows the output of the code:

Simple image morphing - α-blending of two images using cross-dissolving

The following code block shows how to start from one face image (*image₁* being the face of Messi) and end up with another image (*image₂* being the face of Ronaldo) by using a linear combination of the two image `numpy ndarrays` given with the following equation:

$$(1 - \alpha) \cdot image_1 + \alpha \cdot image_2$$

We do this by iteratively increasing α from 0 to 1:

```
im1 = mpimg.imread("../images/messi.jpg") / 255 # scale RGB values in [0,1]
im2 = mpimg.imread("../images/ronaldo.jpg") / 255
i = 1
plt.screenshot(figsize=(18,15))
for alpha in np.linspace(0,1,20):
 plt.subplot(4,5,i)
 plt.imshow((1-alpha)*im1 + alpha*im2)
 plt.axis('off')
 i += 1
plt.subplots_adjust(wspace=0.05, hspace=0.05)
plt.show()
```

The next screenshot shows the sequence of the α-blended images created using the previous code by cross-dissolving Messi's face image into Ronaldo's. As can be seen from the sequence of intermediate images in the screenshot, the face morphing with simple blending is not very smooth. In upcoming chapters, we shall see more advanced techniques for image morphing:

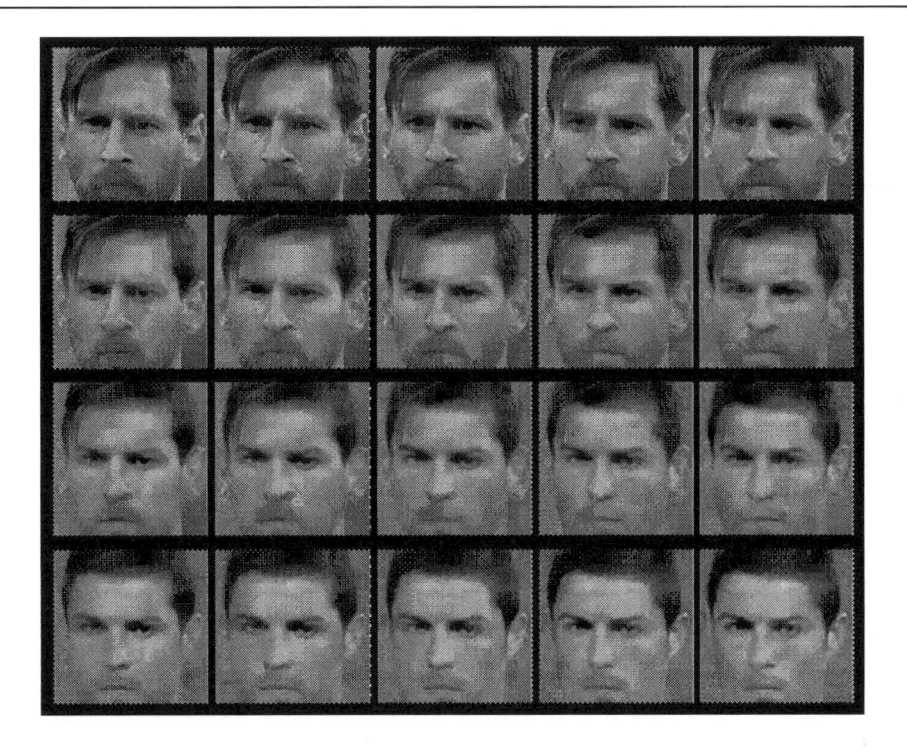

Image manipulations with PIL

PIL provides us with many functions to manipulate an image; for example, using a point transformation to change pixel values or to perform geometric transformations on an image. Let us first start by loading the parrot PNG image, as shown in the following code:

```
im = Image.open("../images/parrot.png")       # open the image, provide
the correct path
print(im.width, im.height, im.mode, im.format) # print image size, mode and
format
# 486 362 RGB PNG
```

The next few sections describe how to do different types of image manipulations with PIL.

Cropping an image

We can use the `crop()` function with the desired rectangle argument to crop the corresponding area from the image, as shown in the following code:

```
im_c = im.crop((175,75,320,200)) # crop the rectangle given by (left, top,
right, bottom) from the image
im_c.show()
```

The next screenshot shows the cropped image created using the previous code:

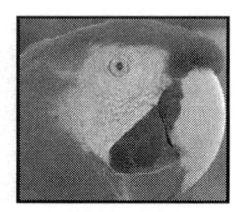

Resizing an image

In order to increase or decrease the size of an image, we can use the `resize()` function, which internally up-samples or down-samples the image, respectively. This will be discussed in detail in the next chapter.

Resizing to a larger image

Let us start with a small clock image of a size of 149 x 97 and create a larger size image. The following code snippet shows the small clock image we will start with:

```
im = Image.open("../images/clock.jpg")
print(im.width, im.height)
# 107 105
im.show()
```

The output of the previous code, the small clock image, is shown as follows:

The next line of code shows how the `resize()` function can be used to enlarge the previous input clock image (by a factor of 5) to obtain an output image of a size 25 times larger than the input image by using bi-linear interpolation (an up-sampling technique). The details about how this technique works will be described in the next chapter:

```
im_large = im.resize((im.width*5, im.height*5), Image.BILINEAR) # bi-linear
interpolation
```

Resizing to a smaller image

Now let us do the reverse: start with a large image of the Victoria Memorial Hall (of a size of 720 x 540) and create a smaller-sized image. The next code snippet shows the large image to start with:

```
im = Image.open("../images/victoria_memorial.png")
print(im.width, im.height)
# 720 540
im.show()
```

The output of the previous code, the large image of the Victoria Memorial Hall, is shown as follows:

The next line of code shows how the `resize()` function can be used to shrink the previous image of the Victoria Memorial Hall (by a factor of 5) to resize it to an output image of a size 25 times smaller than the input image by using anti-aliasing (a high-quality down-sampling technique). We will see how it works in the next chapter:

```
im_small = im.resize((im.width//5, im.height//5), Image.ANTIALIAS)
```

Negating an image

We can use the `point()` function to transform each pixel value with a single-argument function. We can use it to negate an image, as shown in the next code block. The pixel values are represented using 1-byte unsigned integers, which is why subtracting it from the maximum possible value will be the exact point operation required on each pixel to get the inverted image:

```
im = Image.open("../images/parrot.png")
im_t = im.point(lambda x: 255 - x)
im_t.show()
```

The next screenshot shows the negative image, the output of the previous code:

Converting an image into grayscale

We can use the `convert()` function with the `'L'` parameter to change an RGB color image into a gray-level image, as shown in the following code:

```
im_g = im.convert('L')    # convert the RGB color image to a grayscale image
```

We are going to use this image for the next few gray-level transformations.

Some gray-level transformations

Here we explore a couple of transformations where, using a function, each single pixel value from the input image is transferred to a corresponding pixel value for the output image. The function `point()` can be used for this. Each pixel has a value in between 0 and 255, inclusive.

Log transformation

The log transformation can be used to effectively compress an image that has a dynamic range of pixel values. The following code uses the point transformation for logarithmic transformation. As can be seen, the range of pixel values is narrowed, the brighter pixels from the input image have become darker, and the darker pixels have become brighter, thereby shrinking the range of values of the pixels:

```
im_g.point(lambda x: 255*np.log(1+x/255)).show()
```

The next screenshot shows the output log-transformed image produced by running the previous line of code:

Power-law transformation

This transformation is used as γ correction for an image. The next line of code shows how to use the `point()` function for a power-law transformation, where γ = 0.6:

```
im_g.point(lambda x: 255*(x/255)**0.6).show()
```

The next screenshot shows the output power-law-transformed image produced by running the preceding line of code:

Some geometric transformations

In this section, we will discuss another set of transformations that are done by multiplying appropriate matrices (often expressed in homogeneous coordinates) with the image matrix. These transformations change the geometric orientation of an image, hence the name.

Reflecting an image

We can use the `transpose()` function to reflect an image with regard to the horizontal or vertical axis:

```
im.transpose(Image.FLIP_LEFT_RIGHT).show() # reflect about the vertical
axis
```

The next screenshot shows the output image produced by running the previous line of code:

Rotating an image

We can use the `rotate()` function to rotate an image by an angle (in degrees):

```
im_45 = im.rotate(45)   # rotate the image by 45 degrees
im_45.show()            # show the rotated image
```

The next screenshot shows the rotated output image produced by running the preceding line of code:

Applying an Affine transformation on an image

A 2-D Affine transformation matrix, T, can be applied on each pixel of an image (in homogeneous coordinates) to undergo an Affine transformation, which is often implemented with inverse mapping (warping). An interested reader is advised to refer to this article (https://sandipanweb.wordpress.com/2018/01/21/recursive-graphics-bilinear-interpolation-and-image-transformation-in-python/) to understand how these transformations can be implemented (from scratch).

The following code shows the output image obtained when the input image is transformed with a *shear* transform matrix. The data argument in the `transform()` function is a 6-tuple *(a, b, c, d, e, f)*, which contains the first two rows from an **Affine transform matrix**. For each pixel *(x, y)* in the output image, the new value is taken from a position *(a x + b y + c, d x + e y + f)* in the input image, which is rounded to nearest pixel. The `transform()` function can be used to scale, translate, rotate, and shear the original image:

```
im = Image.open("../images/parrot.png")
im.transform((int(1.4*im.width), im.height), Image.AFFINE,
    data=(1,-0.5,0,0,1,0)).show() # shear
```

The next screenshot shows the output image with shear transform, produced by running the previous code:

Perspective transformation

We can run a perspective transformation on an image with the `transform()` function by using the `Image.PERSPECTIVE` argument, as shown in the next code block:

```
params = [1, 0.1, 0, -0.1, 0.5, 0, -0.005, -0.001]
im1 = im.transform((im.width//3, im.height), Image.PERSPECTIVE, params, Image.BICUBIC)
im1.show()
```

The next screenshot shows the image obtained after the perspective projection, by running the preceding code block:

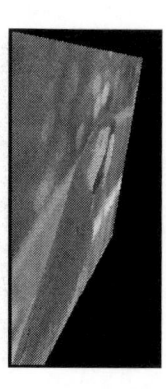

Changing pixel values of an image

We can use the `putpixel()` function to change a pixel value in an image. Next, let us discuss a popular application of adding noise to an image using the function.

Adding salt and pepper noise to an image

We can add some **salt-and-pepper noise** to an image by selecting a few pixels from the image randomly and then setting about half of those pixel values to black and the other half to white. The next code snippet shows how to add the noise:

```
# choose 5000 random locations inside image
im1 = im.copy() # keep the original image, create a copy
n = 5000
x, y = np.random.randint(0, im.width, n), np.random.randint(0, im.height, n)
for (x,y) in zip(x,y):
  im1.putpixel((x, y), ((0,0,0) if np.random.rand() < 0.5 else (255,255,255))) # salt-and-pepper noise
im1.show()
```

The following screenshot shows the output noisy image generated by running the previous code:

Drawing on an image

We can draw lines or other geometric shapes on an image (for example, the `ellipse()` function to draw an ellipse) from the `PIL.ImageDraw` module, as shown in the next Python code snippet:

```
im = Image.open("../images/parrot.png")
draw = ImageDraw.Draw(im)
draw.ellipse((125, 125, 200, 250), fill=(255,255,255,128))
del draw
im.show()
```

The following screenshot shows the output image generated by running the previous code:

Drawing text on an image

We can add text to an image using the text() function from the PIL.ImageDraw module, as shown in the next Python code snippet:

```
draw = ImageDraw.Draw(im)
font = ImageFont.truetype("arial.ttf", 23) # use a truetype font
draw.text((10, 5), "Welcome to image processing with python", font=font)
del draw
im.show()
```

The following screenshot shows the output image generated by running the previous code:

Creating a thumbnail

We can create a thumbnail from an image with the `thumbnail()` function, as shown in the following:

```
im_thumbnail = im.copy() # need to copy the original image first
im_thumbnail.thumbnail((100,100))
# now paste the thumbnail on the image
```

The screenshot shows the output image generated by running the preceding code snippet:

Computing the basic statistics of an image

We can use the `stat` module to compute the basic statistics (mean, median, standard deviation of pixel values of different channels, and so on) of an image, as shown in the following:

```
s = stat.Stat(im)
print(s.extrema) # maximum and minimum pixel values for each channel R, G, B
# [(4, 255), (0, 255), (0, 253)]
print(s.count)
# [154020, 154020, 154020]
print(s.mean)
# [125.41305674587716, 124.43517724970783, 68.38463186599142]
print(s.median)
# [117, 128, 63]
print(s.stddev)
# [47.56564506512579, 51.08397900881395, 39.067418896260094]
```

Plotting the histograms of pixel values for the RGB channels of an image

The `histogram()` function can be used to compute the histogram (a table of pixel values versus frequencies) of pixels for each channel and return the concatenated output (for example, for an RGB image, the output contains 3 x 256 = 768 values):

```
pl = im.histogram()
plt.bar(range(256), pl[:256], color='r', alpha=0.5)
plt.bar(range(256), pl[256:2*256], color='g', alpha=0.4)
plt.bar(range(256), pl[2*256:], color='b', alpha=0.3)
plt.show()
```

The following screenshot shows the R, G, and B color histograms plotted by running the previous code:

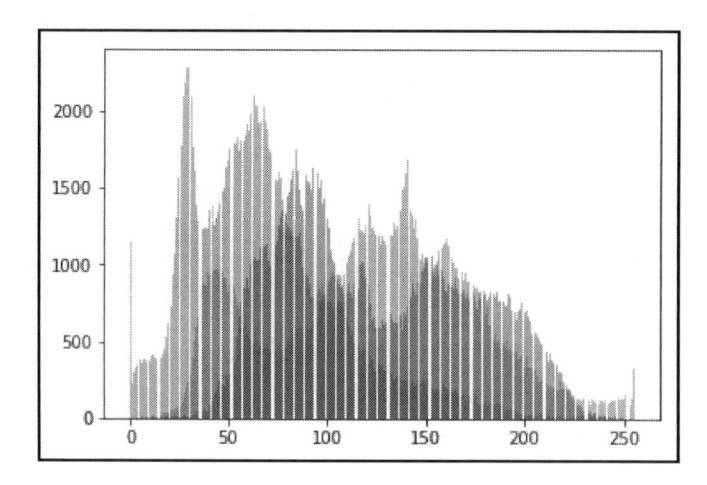

Separating the RGB channels of an image

We can use the `split()` function to separate the channels of a multi-channel image, as is shown in the following code for an RGB image:

```
ch_r, ch_g, ch_b = im.split() # split the RGB image into 3 channels: R, G
and B
# we shall use matplotlib to display the channels
plt.screenshot(figsize=(18,6))
plt.subplot(1,3,1); plt.imshow(ch_r, cmap=plt.cm.Reds); plt.axis('off')
plt.subplot(1,3,2); plt.imshow(ch_g, cmap=plt.cm.Greens); plt.axis('off')
plt.subplot(1,3,3); plt.imshow(ch_b, cmap=plt.cm.Blues); plt.axis('off')
plt.tight_layout()
plt.show() # show the R, G, B channels
```

The following screenshot shows three output images created for each of the R (red), G (green), and B (blue) channels generated by running the previous code:

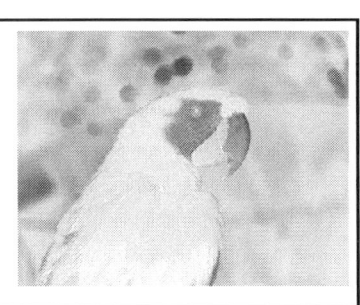

Combining multiple channels of an image

We can use the `merge()` function to combine the channels of a multi-channel image, as is shown in the following code, wherein the color channels obtained by splitting the parrot RGB image are merged after swapping the red and blue channels:

```
im = Image.merge('RGB', (ch_b, ch_g, ch_r)) # swap the red and blue
channels obtained last time with split()
im.show()
```

The following screenshot shows the RGB output image created by merging the B, G, and R channels by running the preceding code snippet:

α-blending two images

The `blend()` function can be used to create a new image by interpolating two given images (of the same size) using a constant, α. Both images must have the same size and mode. The output image is given by the following:

$$out = image_1 * (1.0 - \alpha) + image_2 * \alpha$$

If α is 0.0, a copy of the first image is returned. If α is 1.0, a copy of the second image is returned. The next code snippet shows an example:

```
im1 = Image.open("../images/parrot.png")
im2 = Image.open("../images/hill.png")
# 453 340 1280 960 RGB RGBA
im1 = im1.convert('RGBA') # two images have different modes, must be converted to the same mode
im2 = im2.resize((im1.width, im1.height), Image.BILINEAR) # two images have different sizes, must be converted to the same size
im = Image.blend(im1, im2, alpha=0.5).show()
```

The following screenshot shows the output image generated by blending the previous two images:

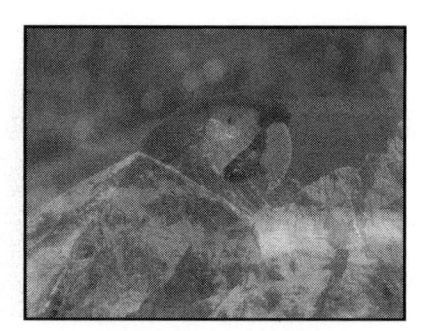

Superimposing two images

An image can be superimposed on top of another by multiplying two input images (of the same size) pixel by pixel. The next code snippet shows an example:

```
im1 = Image.open("../images/parrot.png")
im2 = Image.open("../images/hill.png").convert('RGB').resize((im1.width, im1.height))
multiply(im1, im2).show()
```

The next screenshot shows the output image generated when superimposing two images by running the preceding code snippet:

Adding two images

The next code snippet shows how an image can be generated by adding two input images (of the same size) pixel by pixel:

```
add(im1, im2).show()
```

The next screenshot shows the output image generated by running the previous code snippet:

Getting Started with Image Processing

Computing the difference between two images

The following code returns the absolute value of the pixel-by-pixel difference between images. Image difference can be used to detect changes between two images. For example, the next code block shows how to compute the difference image from two successive frames from a video recording (from YouTube) of a match from the 2018 FIFA World Cup:

```
from PIL.ImageChops import subtract, multiply, screen, difference, add
im1 = Image.open("../images/goal1.png") # load two consecutive frame images
from the video
im2 = Image.open("../images/goal2.png")
im = difference(im1, im2)
im.save("../images/goal_diff.png")

plt.subplot(311)
plt.imshow(im1)
plt.axis('off')
plt.subplot(312)
plt.imshow(im2)
plt.axis('off')
plt.subplot(313)
plt.imshow(im), plt.axis('off')
plt.show()
```

The next screenshot shows the output of the code, with the consecutive frame images followed by their difference image:

First frame

Chapter 1

Second frame

The difference image

Subtracting two images and superimposing two image negatives

The `subtract()` function can be used to first subtract two images, followed by dividing the result by scale (defaults to 1.0) and adding the offset (defaults to 0.0). Similarly, the `screen()` function can be used to superimpose two inverted images on top of each other.

Image manipulations with scikit-image

As done previously using the PIL library, we can also use the `scikit-image` library functions for image manipulation. Some examples are shown in the following sections.

Inverse warping and geometric transformation using the warp() function

The scikit-image `transform` module's `warp()` function can be used for inverse warping for the geometric transformation of an image (discussed in a previous section), as demonstrated in the following examples.

Applying an Affine transformation on an image

We can use the `SimilarityTransform()` function to compute the transformation matrix, followed by `warp()` function, to carry out the transformation, as shown in the next code block:

```
im = imread("../images/parrot.png")
tform = SimilarityTransform(scale=0.9,
rotation=np.pi/4,translation=(im.shape[0]/2, -100))
warped = warp(im, tform)
import matplotlib.pyplot as plt
plt.imshow(warped), plt.axis('off'), plt.show()
```

The following screenshot shows the output image generated by running the previous code snippet:

Applying the swirl transform

This is a non-linear transform defined in the scikit-image documentation. The next code snippet shows how to use the `swirl()` function to implement the transform, where `strength` is a parameter to the function for the amount of swirl, `radius` indicates the swirl extent in pixels, and `rotation` adds a rotation angle. The transformation of `radius` into `r` is to ensure that the transformation decays to ≈ 1/1000th ≈ 1/1000th within the specified radius:

```
im = imread("../images/parrot.png")
swirled = swirl(im, rotation=0, strength=15, radius=200)
plt.imshow(swirled)
plt.axis('off')
plt.show()
```

The next screenshot shows the output image generated with swirl transformation by running the previous code snippet:

Adding random Gaussian noise to images

We can use the `random_noise()` function to add different types of noise to an image. The next code example shows how Gaussian noise with different variances can be added to an image:

```
im = img_as_float(imread("../images/parrot.png"))
plt.screenshot(figsize=(15,12))
sigmas = [0.1, 0.25, 0.5, 1]
for i in range(4):
  noisy = random_noise(im, var=sigmas[i]**2)
  plt.subplot(2,2,i+1)
  plt.imshow(noisy)
```

[51]

```
    plt.axis('off')
    plt.title('Gaussian noise with sigma=' + str(sigmas[i]), size=20)
plt.tight_layout()
plt.show()
```

The next screenshot shows the output image generated by adding Gaussian noises with different variance by running the previous code snippet. As can be seen, the more the standard deviation of the Gaussian noise, the noisier the output image:

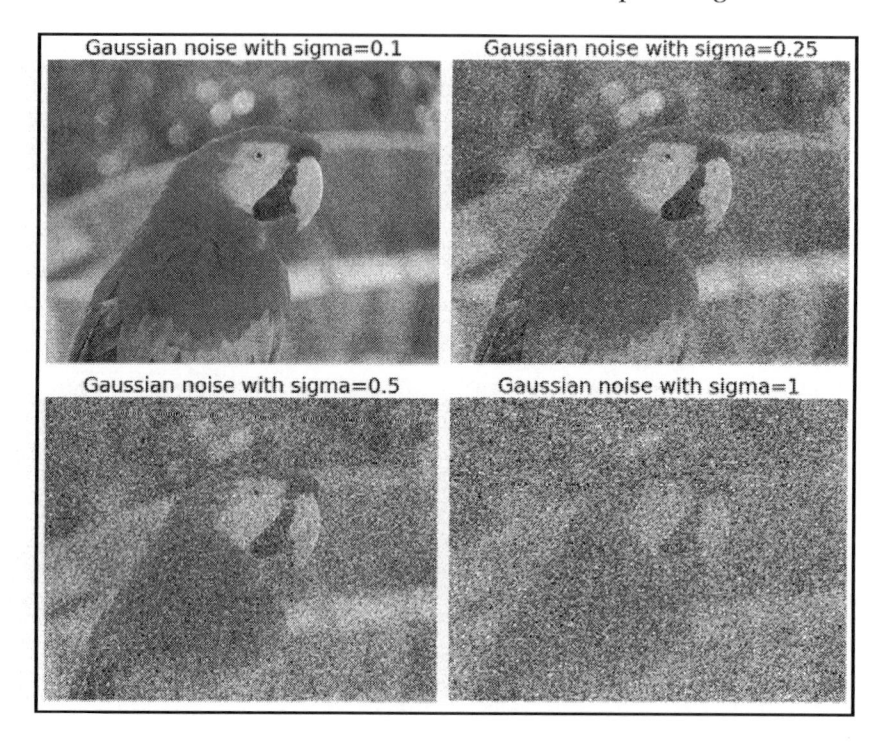

Computing the cumulative distribution function of an image

We can compute the **cumulative distribution function** (**CDF**) for a given image with the `cumulative_distribution()` function, as we shall see in the image enhancement chapter. For now, the reader is encouraged to find the usage of this function to compute the CDF.

Image manipulation with Matplotlib

We can use the `pylab` module from the `matplotlib` library for image manipulation. The next section shows an example.

Drawing contour lines for an image

A **contour line** for an image is a curve connecting all of the pixels where they have the same particular value. The following code block shows how to draw the contour lines and filled contours for a grayscale image of Einstein:

```
im = rgb2gray(imread("../images/einstein.jpg")) # read the image from disk as a numpy ndarray
plt.screenshot(figsize=(20,8))
plt.subplot(131), plt.imshow(im, cmap='gray'), plt.title('Original Image', size=20)
plt.subplot(132), plt.contour(np.flipud(im), colors='k', levels=np.logspace(-15, 15, 100))
plt.title('Image Contour Lines', size=20)
plt.subplot(133), plt.title('Image Filled Contour', size=20),
plt.contourf(np.flipud(im), cmap='inferno')
plt.show()
```

The next screenshot shows the output of the previous code:

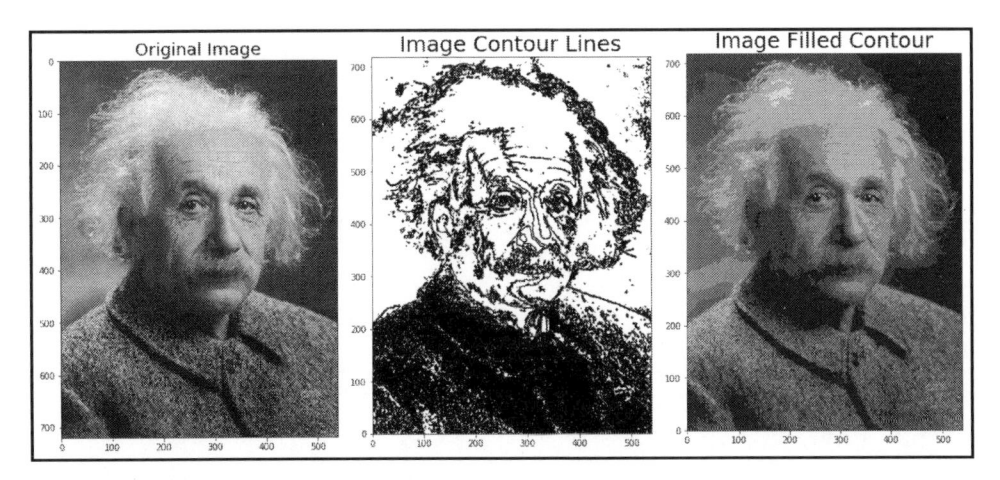

Image manipulation with the scipy.misc and scipy.ndimage modules

We can use the `misc` and `ndimage` modules from the `scipy` library too for image manipulation; it is left as an exercise for the reader to find the relevant function and get familiar with their usage.

Summary

In this chapter, we first provided a basic introduction to image processing and basic concepts regarding the problems that we try to solve in image processing. We then discussed different tasks and steps with image processing, and the leading image processing libraries in Python, which we are going to use for coding in this book. Next, we talked about how to install different libraries for image processing in Python, and how to import them and call the functions from the modules. We also covered basic concepts about image types, file formats, and data structures to store image data with different Python libraries. Then, we discussed how to perform image I/O and display in Python using different libraries. Finally, we discussed how to perform basic image manipulations with different Python libraries. In the next chapter, we will deep dive into sampling, quantization, convolution, the Fourier transform, and frequency domain filtering on images.

Questions

1. Use the `scikit-image` library's functions to read a collection of images and display them as a montage.
2. Use the `scipy ndimage` and `misc` modules' functions to zoom, crop, resize, and apply Affine transformation to an image.
3. Create a Python remake of the Gotham Instagram filter (https://github.com/lukexyz/CV-Instagram-Filters) (hint: manipulate an image with the PIL `split()`, `merge()`, and `numpy interp()` functions to create a channel interpolation (https://www.youtube.com/watch?v=otLGDpBg1EAfeature=player_embedded)).
4. Use scikit-image's `warp()` function to implement the swirl transform. Note that the `swirl` transform can also be expressed with the following equations:

$$x(u,v) = (u - x_0)cos(\theta) + (v - y_0)sin(\theta) + x_0$$
$$y(u,v) = -(u - x_0)sin(\theta) + (v - y_0)cos(\theta) + y_0$$
$$r = \sqrt{(u - x_0)^2 + (v - y_0)^2}$$
$$\theta = \frac{\pi r}{512}$$

5. Implement the wave transform (hint: use scikit-image's `warp()`) given by the following:

$$x(u, v) = u + 20.sin\left(\frac{2\pi v}{64}\right)$$
$$y(u, v) = v$$

6. Use PIL to load an RGB `.png` file with a palette and convert into a grayscale image. This problem is taken from this post: https://stackoverflow.com/questions/51676447/python-use-pil-to-load-png-file-gives-strange-results/51678271#51678271. Convert the following RGB image (from the VOC2012 dataset) into a grayscale image by indexing the palette:

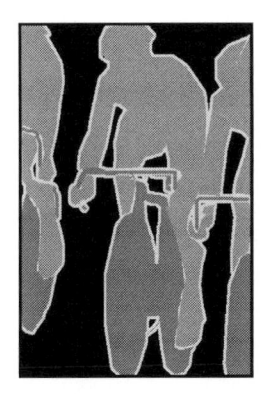

7. Make a 3D plot for each of the color channels of the parrot image used in this chapter (hint: use the `mpl_toolkits.mplot3d` module's `plot_surface()` function and NumPy's `meshgrid()` function).

8. Use scikit-image's `transform` module's `ProjectiveTransform` to estimate the homography matrix from a source to a destination image and use the `inverse()` function to embed the Lena image (or yours) in the blank canvas as shown in the following:

Input Image **Output Image**

First try to solve the problems on your own. For your reference, the solutions can be found here: `https://sandipanweb.wordpress.com/2018/07/30/some-image-processing-problems/`.

Further reading

- *Digital Image Processing*, a book by Rafael C. Gonzalez and Richard E. Woods for image processing concepts
- The lecture notes / handouts from this (`https://web.stanford.edu/class/ee368/handouts.html`) course from Stanford University and this (`https://ocw.mit.edu/resources/res-2-006-girls-who-build-cameras-summer-2016/`) one from MIT
- `http://scikit-image.org/docs/dev/api/skimage.html`
- `https://pillow.readthedocs.io/en/3.1.x/reference/Image.html`
- `https://docs.scipy.org/doc/scipy-1.1.0/reference/ndimage.html`
- `https://matplotlib.org/gallery`
- `http://members.cbio.mines-paristech.fr/~nvaroquaux/formations/scipy-lecture-notes/advanced/image_processing/index.html`

- http://www.scipy-lectures.org/
- https://web.cs.wpi.edu/~emmanuel/courses/cs545/S14/slides/lecture09.pdf
- http://fourier.eng.hmc.edu/e161/lectures/e161ch1.pdf
- http://www.eie.polyu.edu.hk/~enyhchan/imagef.pdf
- http://www.cs.cornell.edu/courses/cs1114/2009sp/lectures/CS1114-lec14.pdf
- http://eeweb.poly.edu/~yao/EL5123/lecture12_ImageWarping.pdf

2
Sampling, Fourier Transform, and Convolution

In this chapter, we'll discuss 2D signals in the time and frequency domains. We'll first talk about spatial sampling, an important concept that is used in resizing an image, and about the challenges in sampling. We'll try solving these problems using the functions in the Python library. We'll also introduce intensity quantization in an image; intensity quantizing means how many bits will be used to store a pixel in an image and what impact it will have on the quality of the image. You will surely want to know about the **Discrete Fourier Transform (DFT)** that can be used to transform an image from the spatial (time) domain into the frequency domain. You'll learn to implement DFT with the **Fast Fourier Transform (FFT)** algorithm using `numpy` and `scipy` functions and will be able to apply this implementation on an image!

You will also be interested in knowing about 2D convolutions that increase the speed of convolution. We'll also understand the basic concepts of the convolution theorem. We'll try and clear up the age-old confusion between correlation and convolution using an example. Moreover, we'll describe an example from SciPy that will show you how to find the location of specific patterns in an image using a template by applying cross-correlation.

We'll also be covering a few filtering techniques and will understand how to implement them with Python libraries. You'll be interested to see the results that we'll obtain after denoising an image using these filters.

The topics that we'll be covering in this chapter are as follows:

- Image formation – Sampling and quantization
- Discrete Fourier Transform
- Understanding convolution

Image formation – sampling and quantization

In this section, we'll describe two important concepts for image formation, namely, sampling and quantization, and see how we can resize an image with sampling and colors quantized with `PIL` and `scikit-image` libraries. We'll use a hands-on approach here and we'll define the concepts while seeing them in action. Ready?

Let's start by importing all of the required packages:

```
% matplotlib inline # for inline image display inside notebook
from PIL import Image
from skimage.io import imread, imshow, show
import scipy.fftpack as fp
from scipy import ndimage, misc, signal
from scipy.stats import signaltonoise
from skimage import data, img_as_float
from skimage.color import rgb2gray
from skimage.transform import rescale
import matplotlib.pylab as pylab
import numpy as np
import numpy.fft
import timeit
```

Sampling

Sampling refers to the selection/rejection of image pixels, which means that it is a spatial operation. We can use sampling to increase or reduce the size of an image, with up-sampling and down-sampling, respectively. In the next few sections, we'll discuss different sampling techniques with examples.

Up-sampling

As discussed briefly in Chapter 1, *Getting Started with Image Processing*, in order to increase the size of an image we need to up-sample the image. The challenge is that the new larger images will have some pixels that have no corresponding pixel in the original smaller image, and we need to guess those unknown pixel values. We can guess the value of an unknown pixel using the following:

- An aggregate, for example, the mean value of its nearest known one or more pixel-neighbors values
- An interpolated value using pixel-neighbors with bi-linear or cubic interpolation

Nearest neighbor-based up-sampling may result in a poor quality output image. Let's code to verify this:

```
im = Image.open("../new images/clock.jpg") # the original small clock image
pylab.imshow(im), pylab.show()
```

You'll see this, the original small clock image:

Let's now increase the width and height of the original image to a factor of five (thereby increasing the image size 25 times):

```
im1 = im.resize((im.width*5, im.height*5), Image.NEAREST) # nearest neighbor interpolation
pylab.figure(figsize=(10,10)), pylab.imshow(im1), pylab.show()
```

Here's the output of the nearest neighbor up-sampling, which does not work well; we obtain a larger pixelated image:

As we can see, the output image, created with the nearest-neighbor method, is 25 times larger than the input image, using the PIL library's resize() function. But clearly the output image is pixelated (with the blocking artifacts and jagged edges) and is of poor quality.

Up-sampling and interpolation

In order to improve the up-sampled output image quality, we can use some interpolation method such as bi-linear or bi-cubic interpolation. Let's see how.

Bi-linear interpolation

Let's consider a grayscale image, which is basically a 2D matrix of pixel values at integer grid locations. To interpolate the pixel value at any point *P* on the grid, the 2D analogue of linear interpolation: bilinear interpolation can be used. In this case, for each possible point *P* (that we would like to interpolate), four neighbors (namely, Q_{11}, Q_{12}, Q_{22}, and Q_{21}) are going to be there and the intensity values of these four neighbors are to be combined to compute the interpolated intensity at the point P, as shown in the following figure:

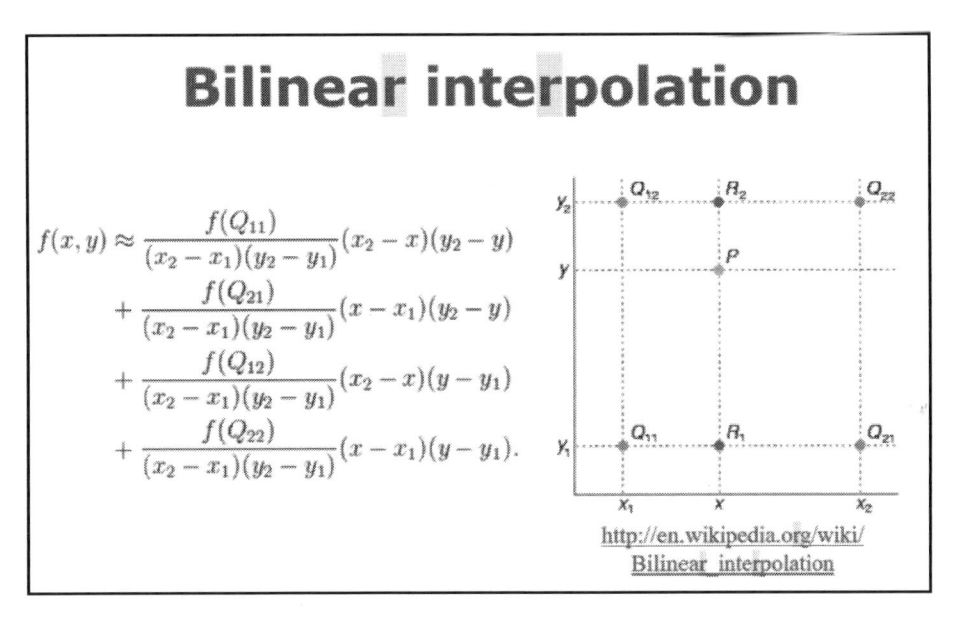

Bilinear interpolation

$$f(x,y) \approx \frac{f(Q_{11})}{(x_2 - x_1)(y_2 - y_1)}(x_2 - x)(y_2 - y)$$
$$+ \frac{f(Q_{21})}{(x_2 - x_1)(y_2 - y_1)}(x - x_1)(y_2 - y)$$
$$+ \frac{f(Q_{12})}{(x_2 - x_1)(y_2 - y_1)}(x_2 - x)(y - y_1)$$
$$+ \frac{f(Q_{22})}{(x_2 - x_1)(y_2 - y_1)}(x - x_1)(y - y_1).$$

http://en.wikipedia.org/wiki/Bilinear_interpolation

Let's use the PIL `resize()` function for bi-linear interpolation:

```
im1 = im.resize((im.width*5, im.height*5), Image.BILINEAR) # up-sample with
bi-linear interpolation
pylab.figure(figsize=(10,10)), pylab.imshow(im1), pylab.show()
```

Here's the resized image. Notice how the quality improves when bi-linear interpolation is used with up-sampling:

Bi-cubic interpolation

It is an extension of cubic interpolation for interpolating data points on a 2D regular grid. The interpolated surface is smoother than corresponding surfaces obtained by bi-linear interpolation or nearest-neighbor interpolation.

Bi-cubic interpolation can be accomplished using either Lagrange polynomials, cubic splines, or the cubic convolution algorithm. PIL uses cubic spline interpolation in a 4 x 4 environment.

Let's use the PIL `resize()` function for bi-cubic interpolation:

```
im.resize((im.width*10, im.height*10), Image.BICUBIC).show()   # bi-cubic interpolation
pylab.figure(figsize=(10,10)), pylab.imshow(im1), pylab.show()
```

Look at how the quality of the resized image improves when we use bi-cubic interpolation:

Down-sampling

In order to decrease the size of an image, we need to down-sample the image. For each pixel in the new smaller image, there will be multiple pixels in the original larger image. We can compute the value of a pixel in the new image by doing the following:

- Dropping some pixels (for example, dropping every other row and column if we want an image a fourth of the size of the original image) from the larger image in a systematic way
- Computing the new pixel value as an aggregate value of the corresponding multiple pixels in the original image

Sampling, Fourier Transform, and Convolution

Let's use the `tajmahal.jpg` image and resize it to an output image of a size 25 times smaller than the input image using the `resize()` function, again from the PIL library:

```
im = Image.open("../images/tajmahal.jpg")
im.show()
```

Reduce the width and height of the input image by a factor of five (that is, reduce the size of the image 25 times) simply by choosing every row in five rows and every column in five columns from the input image:

```
im = im.resize((im.width//5, im.height//5))
pylab.figure(figsize=(15,10)), pylab.imshow(im), pylab.show()
```

Here's the output:

As you can see, it contains some black patches/artifacts and patterns that were not present in the original image—this effect is called **aliasing**.

Aliasing happens typically because the sampling rate is lower (we had too few pixels!) than the Nyquist rate (so one way to avoid aliasing is to increase the sampling rate above the Nyquist rate, but what if we want an output image of a smaller size?).

Down-sampling and anti-aliasing

As we have seen, down-sampling is not very good for shrinking images as it creates an aliasing effect. For instance, if we try to resize (down-sample) the original image by reducing the width and height a factor of 5, we shall get such patchy and bad output.

Anti-aliasing

The problem here is that a single pixel in the output image corresponds to 25 pixels in the input image, but we are sampling the value of a single pixel instead. We should be averaging over a small area in the input image. This can be done using ANTIALIAS (a high-quality down-sampling filter); this is how you can do it:

```
im = im.resize((im.width//5, im.height//5), Image.ANTIALIAS)
pylab.figure(figsize=(15,10)), pylab.imshow(im), pylab.show()
```

An image, the same as the previous one but with much nicer quality (almost without any artifact/aliasing effect), is created using PIL with anti-aliasing:

Sampling, Fourier Transform, and Convolution

Anti-aliasing is generally done by smoothing an image (via convolution of the image with a low-pass filter such as a Gaussian filter) before down-sampling.

Let's now use the scikit-image `transform` module's `rescale()` function with anti-aliasing to overcome the aliasing problem for another image, namely the `umbc.png` image:

```
im = imread('../images/umbc.png')
im1 = im.copy()
pylab.figure(figsize=(10,8))
for i in range(4):
  pylab.subplot(2,2,i+1), pylab.imshow(im1, cmap='gray'), pylab.axis('off')
  pylab.title('image size = ' + str(im1.shape[1]) + 'x' + str(im1.shape[0]))
  im1 = rescale(im1, scale = 0.5, multichannel=True, anti_aliasing=False)
pylab.subplots_adjust(wspace=0.1, hspace=0.1)
pylab.show()
```

The next screenshot shows the output of the previous code. As can be seen, the image is down-sampled to create smaller and smaller output—the aliasing effect becomes more prominent when no anti-aliasing technique is used:

Let's change the line of code to use anti-aliasing:

```
im1 = rescale(im1, scale = 0.5, multichannel=True, anti_aliasing=True)
```

This yields an image of better quality:

> To learn more about interpolation and anti-aliasing, please visit my blog: `https://sandipanweb.wordpress.com/2018/01/21/recursive-graphics-bilinear-interpolation-and-image-transformation-in-Python/`.

Quantization

Quantization is related to the intensity of an image and can be defined by the number of bits used per pixel. Digital images typically are quantized to 256 gray levels. Here, we will see that, as the number of bits for pixel storage decreases, the quantization error increases, leading to artificial boundaries or contours and pixelating and resulting in the poor quality of an image.

Quantizing with PIL

Let's use the PIL `Image` module's `convert()` function for color quantization, with the `P` mode and the color argument as the maximum number of possible colors. We'll also use the SciPy `stats` module's `signaltonoise()` function to find the **Signal-to-Noise Ratio (SNR)** of an image (`parrot.jpg`), which is defined as the mean divided by the standard deviation of the image array:

```
im = Image.open('../images/parrot.jpg')
pylab.figure(figsize=(20,30))
num_colors_list = [1 << n for n in range(7,-1,-1)]
snr_list = []
i = 1
for num_colors in num_colors_list:
  im1 = im.convert('P', palette=Image.ADAPTIVE, colors=num_colors)
  pylab.subplot(4,2,i), pylab.imshow(im1), pylab.axis('off')
  snr_list.append(signaltonoise(im1, axis=None))
  pylab.title('Image with # colors = ' + str(num_colors) + ' SNR = ' + str(np.round(snr_list[i-1],3)), size=20)
  i += 1
pylab.subplots_adjust(wspace=0.2, hspace=0)
pylab.show()
```

This shows how the image quality decreases with color-quantization, as the number of bits to store a pixel reduces:

Frame two is as follows:

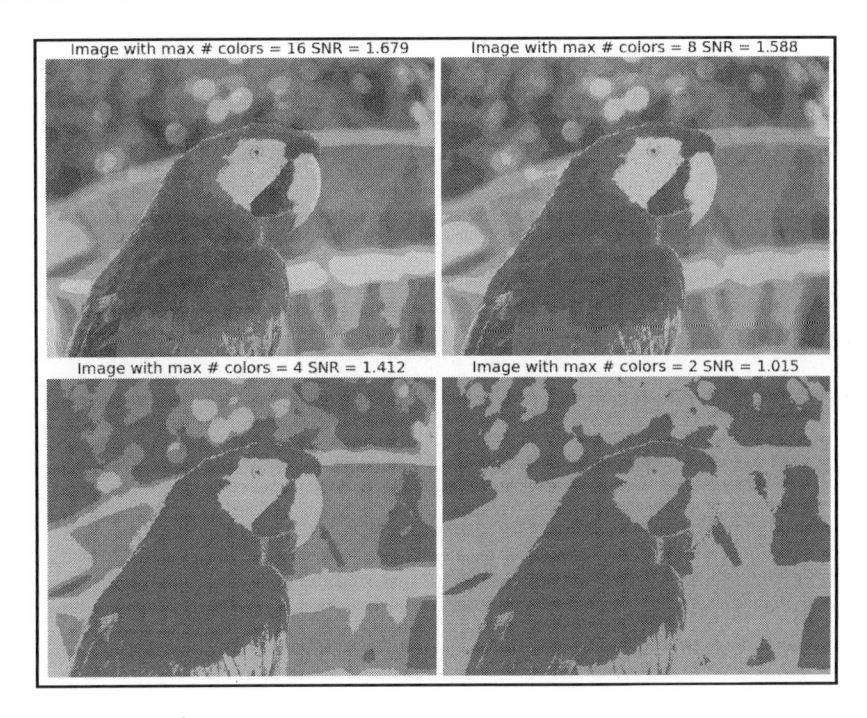

We'll now plot the impact of color-quantization on the SNR of the image, which is typically a measure for image quality—the higher the SNR, the better the quality:

```
pylab.plot(num_colors_list, snr_list, 'r.-')
pylab.xlabel('# colors in the image')
pylab.ylabel('SNR')
pylab.title('Change in SNR w.r.t. # colors')
pylab.xscale('log', basex=2)
pylab.gca().invert_xaxis()
pylab.show()
```

As can be seen, although the color-quantization reduces image size (since the number of bits/pixel gets reduced), it also makes the quality of the image poorer, measured by the SNR:

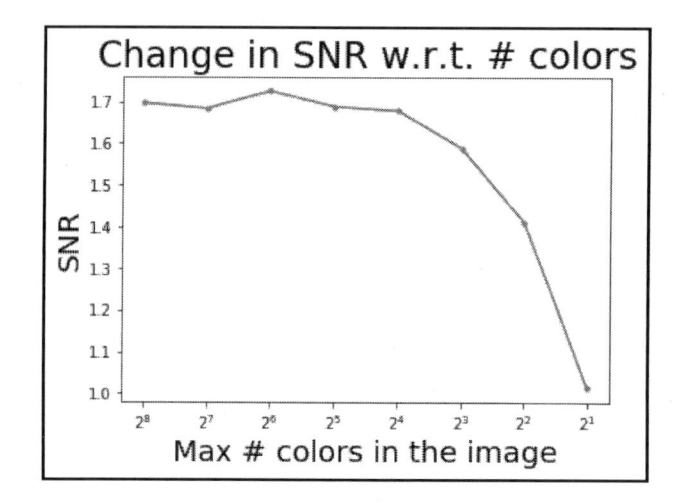

Discrete Fourier Transform

The Fourier transform method has a long mathematical history and we are not going to discuss it here (it can be found in any digital signal processing or digital image processing theory book). As far as image processing is concerned, we shall focus only on 2D **Discrete Fourier Transform** (**DFT**). The basic idea behind the Fourier transform method is that an image can be thought of as a 2D function, f, that can be expressed as a weighted sum of sines and cosines (Fourier basic functions) along two dimensions.

We can transition from a set of grayscale pixel values in the image (spatial/time domain) to a set of Fourier coefficients (frequency domain) using the DFT, and it is discrete since the spatial and the transform variables to be used can only take a set of discrete consecutive integer values (typically the locations of a 2D array representing the image).

In a similar way, the frequency domain 2D array of Fourier coefficients can be converted back into the spatial domain using the **Inverse Discrete Fourier Transform (IDFT)**, which is also known as reconstruction of the image using the Fourier coefficients. The DFT and IDFT are mathematically defined as follows:

2D Discrete Fourier Transform (DFT)

$$F[u, v] = \frac{1}{MN} \sum_{x=0}^{M-1} \sum_{y=0}^{N-1} f[x, y] e^{-2\pi i \left(\frac{ux}{M} + \frac{vy}{N}\right)}$$

frequencies(frequeny domain) *image (time domain)*

$u = 0, 1, .., M-1$
$v = 0, 1, .., N-1$

2D Inverse Discrete Fourier Transform (IDFT)

$$f[x, y] = \sum_{u=0}^{M-1} \sum_{v=0}^{N-1} F[u, v] e^{2\pi i \left(\frac{ux}{M} + \frac{vy}{N}\right)}$$

image (time domain) *frequencies(frequeny domain)*

$x = 0, 1, .., M-1$
$y = 0, 1, .., N-1$

Why do we need the DFT?

First of all, transformation to the frequency domain leads to a better understanding of an image. As we'll see in the next few sections, the low frequencies in the frequency domain correspond to the average gross level of information in an image, whereas the higher frequencies correspond to edges, noise, and more detailed information.

Typically, images by nature are smooth and that is why most images can be represented using a handful of DFT coefficients and all of the remaining higher coefficients tend to be almost negligible/zeros.

This is is very useful in image compression, particularly for Fourier-sparse images, where only a handful of Fourier coefficients are required to reconstruct an image, hence only those frequencies can be stored and others can be discarded, leading to high compression (for example, in the JPEG image compression algorithm a similar transformation, **Discrete Cosine Transform (DCT)** is used. Also, as we shall see later in this chapter, filtering with the DFT in the frequency domain can be much faster than filtering in the spatial domain.

The Fast Fourier Transform algorithm to compute the DFT

The **Fast Fourier Transform (FFT)** is a divide and conquer
algorithm to recursively compute the DFT much quicker (with O ($N.\log_2 N$) time complexity) than the much slower O ($N2$) naive computation for an *n x n* image. In Python, both the `numpy` and `scipy` libraries provide functions to compute 2D DFT/IDFT using the FFT algorithm. Let's see a few examples.

The FFT with the scipy.fftpack module

We'll use the `scipy.fftpack` module's `fft2()/ifft2()` function to
compute the DFT/IDFT with the FFT algorithm using a grayscale image, `rhino.jpg`:

```
im = np.array(Image.open('../images/rhino.jpg').convert('L')) # we shall
work with grayscale image
snr = signaltonoise(im, axis=None)
print('SNR for the original image = ' + str(snr))
# SNR for the original image = 2.023722773801701
# now call FFT and IFFT
freq = fp.fft2(im)
im1 = fp.ifft2(freq).real
snr = signaltonoise(im1, axis=None)
print('SNR for the image obtained after reconstruction = ' + str(snr))
# SNR for the image obtained after reconstruction = 2.0237227738013224
assert(np.allclose(im, im1)) # make sure the forward and inverse FFT are
close to each other
pylab.figure(figsize=(20,10))
pylab.subplot(121), pylab.imshow(im, cmap='gray'), pylab.axis('off')
pylab.title('Original Image', size=20)
pylab.subplot(122), pylab.imshow(im1, cmap='gray'), pylab.axis('off')
pylab.title('Image obtained after reconstruction', size=20)
pylab.show()
```

Here's the output:

As can be seen from the SNR values from the inline output and from the visual difference in the input and the reconstructed image, the reconstructed image loses some information. The difference is negligible if we use all of the coefficients obtained for reconstruction

Plotting the frequency spectrum

As Fourier coefficients are complex numbers, we can view magnitudes directly. Displaying magnitudes of Fourier transforms is called the **spectrum of the transform**. The value F [0,0] of the DFT is called the **DC coefficient.**

The DC coefficient is too large for the other coefficient values to be seen, which is why we need to stretch the transform values by displaying the logarithm of the transform. Also, for display convenience, the transform coefficients are shifted (with `fftshift()`) so that the DC component is in the center. Excited to create a Fourier spectrum of the rhino image? Code this:

```
# the quadrants are needed to be shifted around in order that the low
spatial frequencies are in the center of the 2D fourier-transformed image.
freq2 = fp.fftshift(freq)
pylab.figure(figsize=(10,10)), pylab.imshow( (20*np.log10( 0.1 +
freq2)).astype(int)), pylab.show()
```

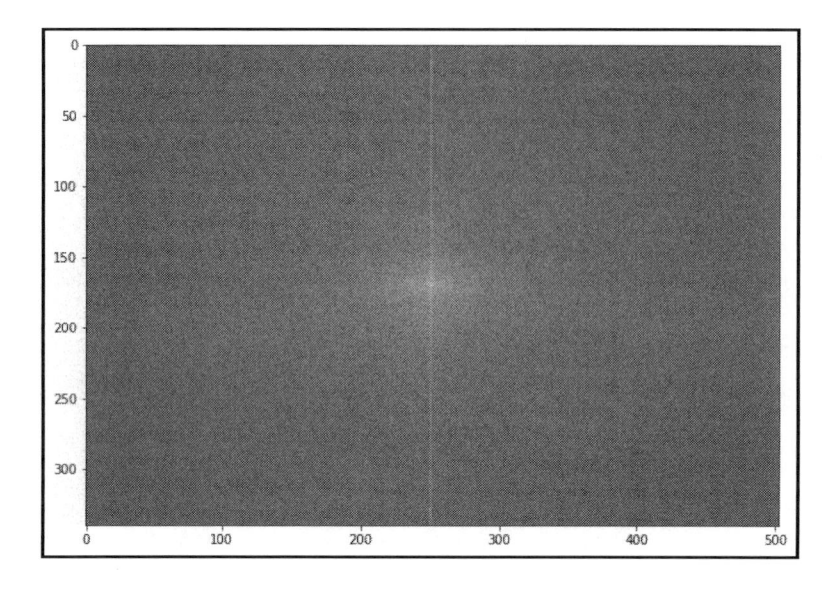

Are you surprised? This is what the rhino image looks like, in its Fourier spectrum form:

The FFT with the numpy.fft module

The DFT of an image can be computed with the `numpy.fft` module's similar set of functions. We'll see some examples.

Computing the magnitude and phase of a DFT

We'll use the `house.png` image as input and thus `fft2()` to get the real and imaginary components of the Fourier coefficients; after that, we'll compute the magnitude/spectrum and the phase and, finally, use `ifft2()` to reconstruct the image:

```
import numpy.fft as fp
im1 = rgb2gray(imread('../images/house.png'))
pylab.figure(figsize=(12,10))
freq1 = fp.fft2(im1)
im1_ = fp.ifft2(freq1).real
pylab.subplot(2,2,1), pylab.imshow(im1, cmap='gray'), pylab.title('Original Image', size=20)
pylab.subplot(2,2,2), pylab.imshow(20*np.log10( 0.01 + np.abs(fp.fftshift(freq1))), cmap='gray')
pylab.title('FFT Spectrum Magnitude', size=20)
pylab.subplot(2,2,3), pylab.imshow(np.angle(fp.fftshift(freq1)),
```

```
cmap='gray')
pylab.title('FFT Phase', size=20)
pylab.subplot(2,2,4), pylab.imshow(np.clip(im1_,0,255), cmap='gray')
pylab.title('Reconstructed Image', size=20)
pylab.show()
```

You'll get this output:

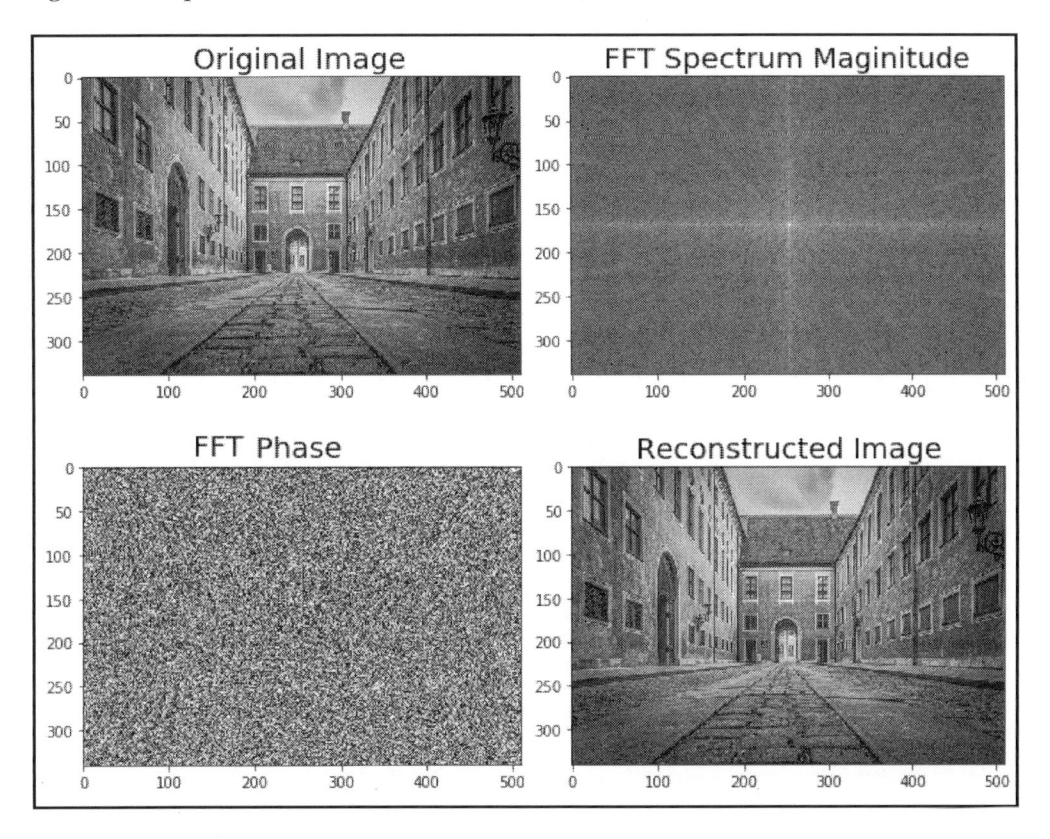

As can be seen, the magnitude $|F(u,v)|$ generally decreases with higher spatial frequencies and the FFT phase appears to be less informative.

Let's now compute the spectrum/magnitude, phase, and reconstructed image with another input image, `house2.png`:

```
im2 = rgb2gray(imread('../images/house2.png'))
pylab.figure(figsize=(12,10))
freq2 = fp.fft2(im2)
im2_ = fp.ifft2(freq2).real
pylab.subplot(2,2,1), pylab.imshow(im2, cmap='gray'), pylab.title('Original Image', size=20)
pylab.subplot(2,2,2), pylab.imshow(20*np.log10( 0.01 + np.abs(fp.fftshift(freq2))), cmap='gray')
pylab.title('FFT Spectrum Magnitude', size=20)
pylab.subplot(2,2,3), pylab.imshow(np.angle(fp.fftshift(freq2)), cmap='gray')
pylab.title('FFT Phase', size=20)
pylab.subplot(2,2,4), pylab.imshow(np.clip(im2_,0,255), cmap='gray')
pylab.title('Reconstructed Image', size=20)
pylab.show()
```

The output that you should get is as follows:

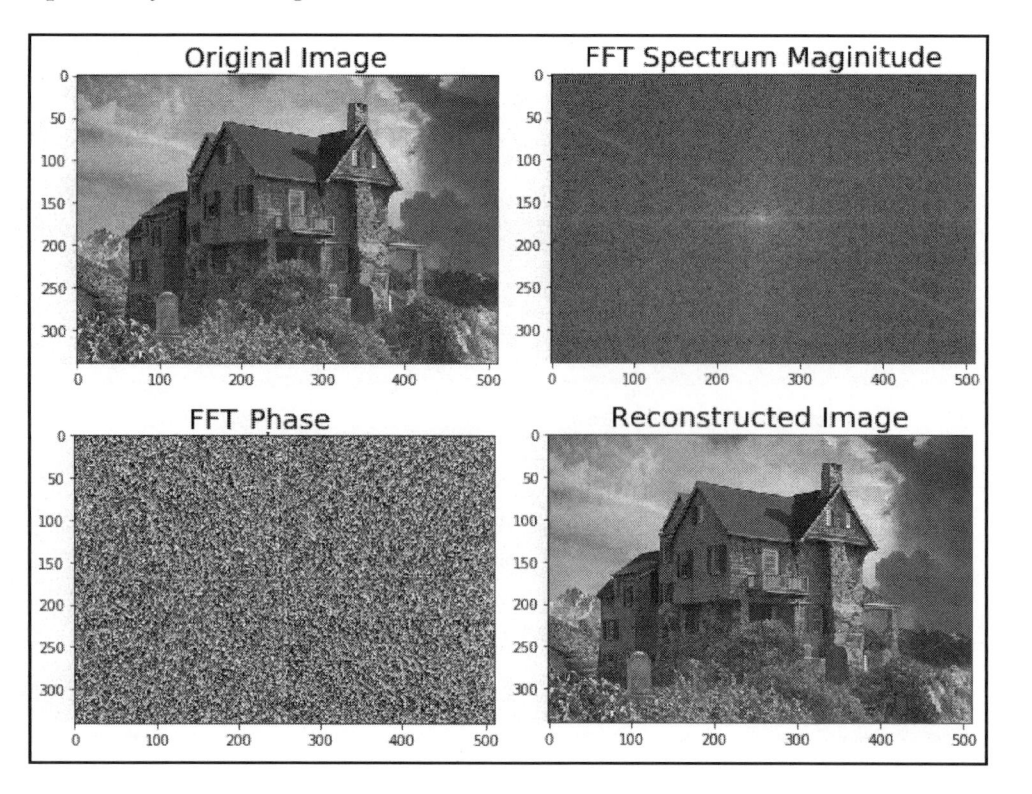

Although it's not as informative as the magnitude, the DFT phase is also important information and an image can't be reconstructed properly if the phase is not available or if we use a different phase array.

To witness this, let's see how a reconstructed output image gets distorted if we use the real components of the frequency spectrum from one image and imaginary components from another one:

```
pylab.figure(figsize=(20,15))
im1_ = fp.ifft2(np.vectorize(complex)(freq1.real, freq2.imag)).real
im2_ = fp.ifft2(np.vectorize(complex)(freq2.real, freq1.imag)).real
pylab.subplot(211), pylab.imshow(np.clip(im1_,0,255), cmap='gray')
pylab.title('Reconstructed Image (Re(F1) + Im(F2))', size=20)
pylab.subplot(212), pylab.imshow(np.clip(im2_,0,255), cmap='gray')
pylab.title('Reconstructed Image (Re(F2) + Im(F1))', size=20)
pylab.show()
```

Here are the reconstructed images with real and imaginary frequency components mixed with each other:

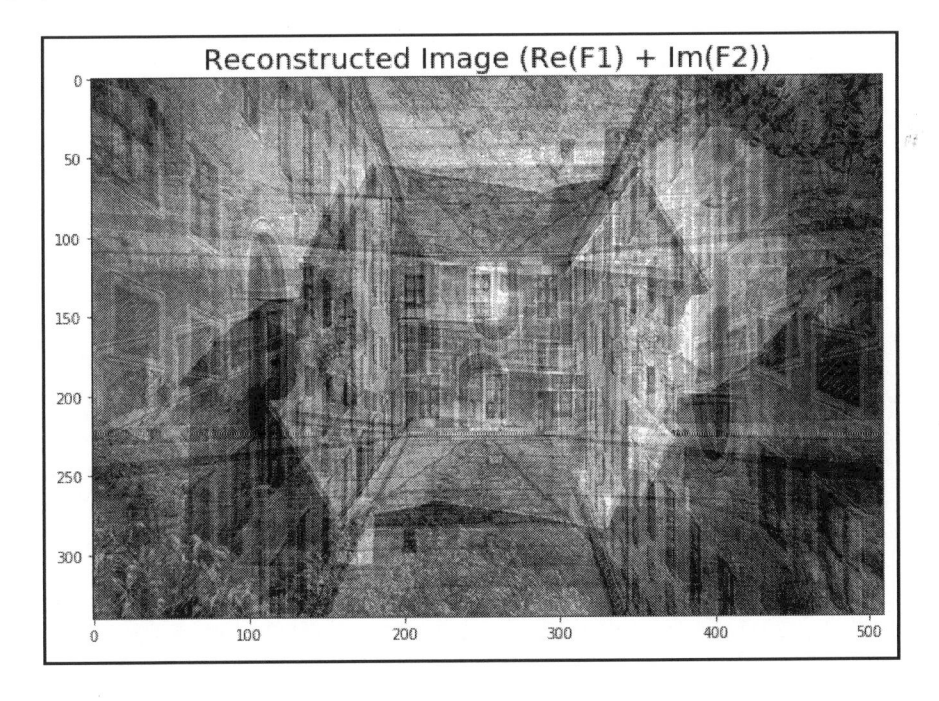

Frame two is as follows:

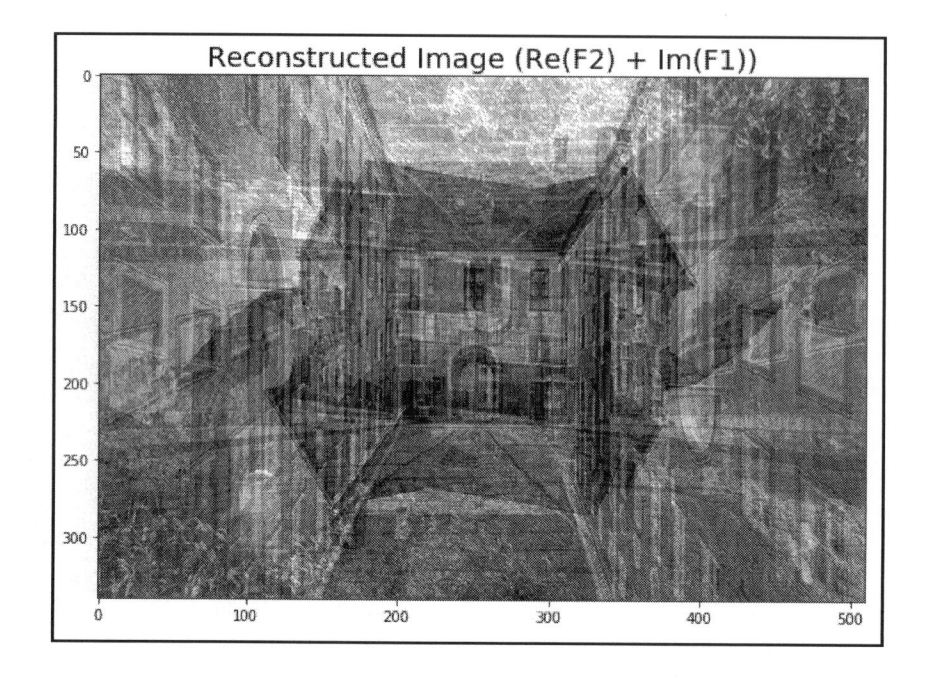

Reconstructed Image (Re(F2) + Im(F1))

Understanding convolution

Convolution is an operation that operates on two images, one being an input image and the other one being a mask (also called the **kernel**) as a filter on the input image, producing an output image.

Convolution filtering is used to modify the spatial frequency characteristics of an image. It works by determining the value of a central pixel by adding the weighted values of all of its neighbors together to compute the new value of the pixel in the output image. The pixel values in the output image are computed by traversing the kernel window through the input image, as shown in the next screenshot (for convolution with the valid mode; we'll see convolution modes later in this chapter):

3x3 Nbd of I[1,1] | Convolution with *'valid'* mode

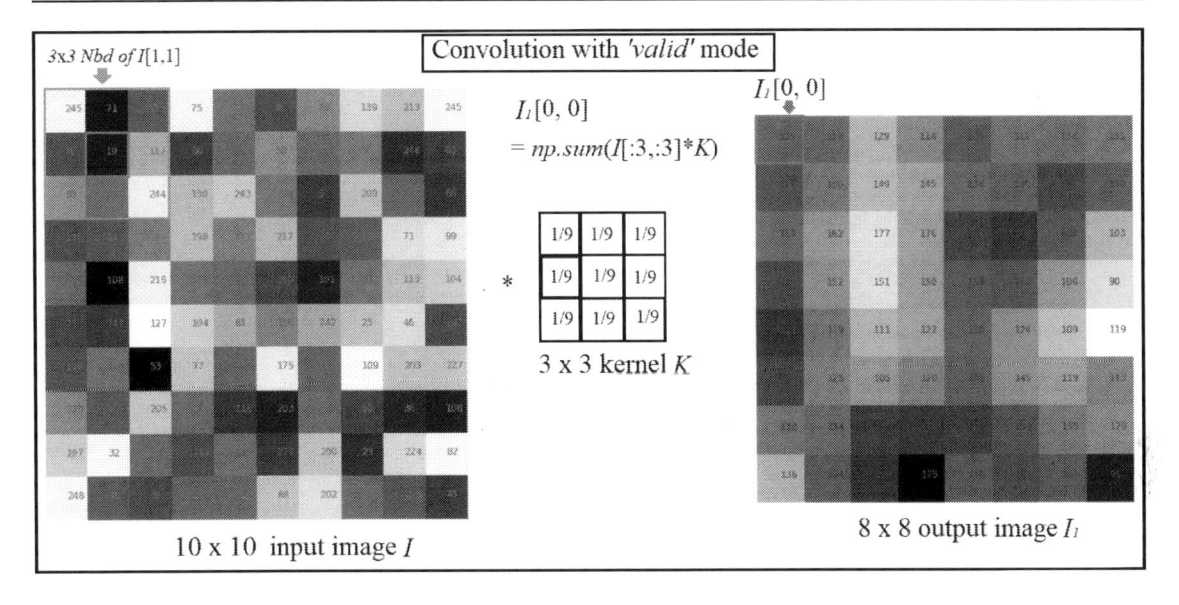

$I_1[0, 0]$
$= np.sum(I[:3,:3]*K)$

3 x 3 kernel K

10 x 10 input image I

8 x 8 output image I_1

As you can see, the kernel window, marked by an arrow in the input image, traverses through the image and obtains values that are mapped on the output image after convolving.

Why convolve an image?

Convolution applies a general-purpose filter effect on the input image. This is done in order to achieve various effects with appropriate kernels on an image, such as smoothing, sharpening, and embossing, and in operations such as edge detection.

Convolution with SciPy signal's convolve2d

The SciPy signal module's `convolve2d()` function can be used for correlation. We are going to apply convolution on an image with a kernel using this function.

Applying convolution to a grayscale image

Let's first detect edges from a grayscale `cameraman.jpg` image using convolution with the Laplace kernel and also blur an image using the `box` kernel:

```
im = rgb2gray(imread('../image s/cameraman.jpg')).astype(float)
print(np.max(im))
# 1.0
print(im.shape)
# (225, 225)
blur_box_kernel = np.ones((3,3)) / 9
edge_laplace_kernel = np.array([[0,1,0],[1,-4,1],[0,1,0]])
im_blurred = signal.convolve2d(im, blur_box_kernel)
im_edges = np.clip(signal.convolve2d(im, edge_laplace_kernel), 0, 1)
fig, axes = pylab.subplots(ncols=3, sharex=True, sharey=True, figsize=(18, 6))
axes[0].imshow(im, cmap=pylab.cm.gray)
axes[0].set_title('Original Image', size=20)
axes[1].imshow(im_blurred, cmap=pylab.cm.gray)
axes[1].set_title('Box Blur', size=20)
axes[2].imshow(im_edges, cmap=pylab.cm.gray)
axes[2].set_title('Laplace Edge Detection', size=20)
for ax in axes:
  ax.axis('off')
pylab.show()
```

Here is the output—the original `cameraman` image along with the ones created after convolving with the `box` blur and Laplace kernel, which we obtained using the `scipy.signal` module's `convolve2d()` function:

Convolution modes, pad values, and boundary conditions

Depending on what you want to do with the edge pixels, there are three arguments: mode, boundary, and fillvalue, which can be passed to the SciPy convolve2d() function. Here, we'll briefly discuss the mode argument:

- mode='full': This is the default mode, in which the output is the full discrete linear convolution of the input.
- mode='valid': This ignores edge pixels and only computes for those pixels with all neighbors (pixels that do not need zero-padding). The output image size is less than the input image size for all kernels (except 1 x 1).
- mode='same': The output image has the same size as the input image; it is centered with regards to the 'full' output.

Applying convolution to a color (RGB) image

With scipy.convolve2d(), we can sharpen an RGB image as well. We have to apply the convolution separately for each image channel.

Let's use the tajmahal.jpg image, with the emboss kernel and the schar edge detection complex kernel:

```
im = misc.imread('../images/tajmahal.jpg')/255 # scale each pixel value in
[0,1]
print(np.max(im))
# 1.0
print(im.shape)
# (1018, 1645, 3)
emboss_kernel = np.array([[-2,-1,0],[-1,1,1],[0,1,2]])
edge_schar_kernel = np.array([[ -3-3j, 0-10j, +3 -3j], [-10+0j, 0+ 0j, +10
+0j], [ -3+3j, 0+10j, +3 +3j]])
im_embossed = np.ones(im.shape)
im_sharpened = np.ones(im.shape)
for i in range(3):
  im_embossed[...,i] = np.clip(signal.convolve2d(im[...,i], emboss_kernel,
mode='same', boundary="symm"),0,1)
for i in range(3):
  im_edges[:,:,i] = np.clip(signal.convolve2d(im[...,i], edge_schar_kernel,
mode='same', boundary="symm"),0,1)
fig, axes = pylab.subplots(nrows=3, figsize=(20, 36))
axes[0].imshow(im)
axes[0].set_title('Original Image', size=20)
axes[1].imshow(im_embossed)
axes[1].set_title('Embossed Image', size=20)
```

```
axes[2].imshow(im_edges)
axes[2].set_title('Schar Edge Detection', size=20)
for ax in axes:
 ax.axis('off')
pylab.show()
```

You'll get your original image along with the convolved images with a couple of different kernels:

The embossed image is as follows:

The image with schar edge detection is as follows:

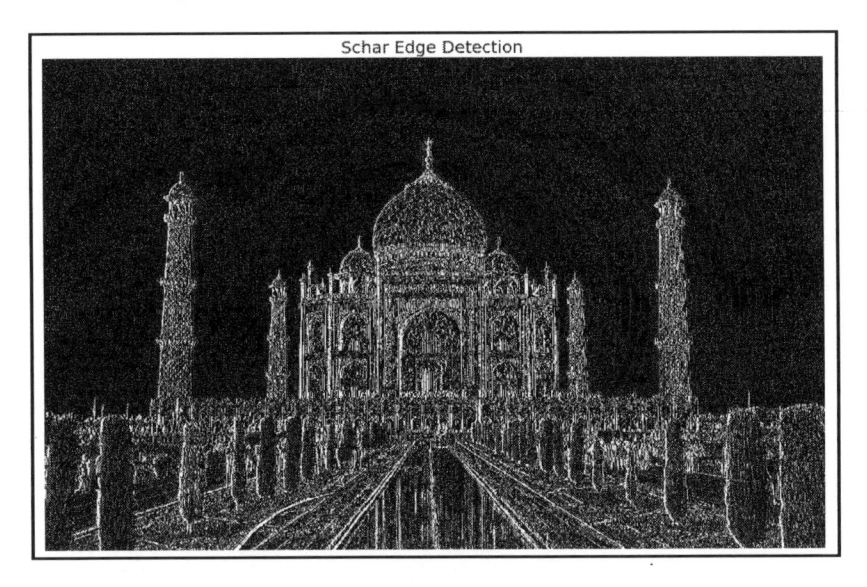

Schar Edge Detection

Convolution with SciPy ndimage.convolve

With `scipy.ndimage.convolve()`, we can sharpen an RGB image directly (we do not have to apply the convolution separately for each image channel).

Use the `victoria_memorial.png` image with the `sharpen` kernel and the `emboss` kernel:

```
im = misc.imread('../images/victoria_memorial.png').astype(np.float) # read as float
print(np.max(im))
# 255.0
sharpen_kernel = np.array([0, -1, 0, -1, 5, -1, 0, -1, 0]).reshape((3, 3, 1))
emboss_kernel = np.array(np.array([[-2,-1,0],[-1,1,1],[0,1,2]])).reshape((3, 3, 1))
im_sharp = ndimage.convolve(im, sharpen_kernel, mode='nearest')
im_sharp = np.clip(im_sharp, 0, 255).astype(np.uint8) # clip (0 to 255) and convert to unsigned int
im_emboss = ndimage.convolve(im, emboss_kernel, mode='nearest')
im_emboss = np.clip(im_emboss, 0, 255).astype(np.uint8)
pylab.figure(figsize=(20,40))
pylab.subplot(311), pylab.imshow(im.astype(np.uint8)), pylab.axis('off')
pylab.title('Original Image', size=25)
pylab.subplot(312), pylab.imshow(im_sharp), pylab.axis('off')
```

```
pylab.title('Sharpened Image', size=25)
pylab.subplot(313), pylab.imshow(im_emboss), pylab.axis('off')
pylab.title('Embossed Image', size=25)
pylab.tight_layout()
pylab.show()
```

You'll get these convolved images:

The sharpened image is as follows:

The embossed image is as follows:

Embossed Image

Correlation versus convolution

Correlation is very similar to the convolution operation in the sense that it also takes an input image and another kernel and traverses the kernel window through the input by computing a weighted combination of pixel neighborhood values with the kernel values and producing the output image.

The only difference is that, unlike correlation, convolution flips the kernel twice (with regards to the horizontal and vertical axis) before computing the weighted combination.

Sampling, Fourier Transform, and Convolution

The next diagram mathematically describes the difference between correlation and convolution on an image:

Correlation

$$g(x, y) = f \star K = \sum_{u=-h}^{h} \sum_{v=-h}^{h} f(x+u, y+v) K(u, v)$$

⇩

Convolution $h \times h$ kernel K

⇧

$$g(x, y) = f * K = \sum_{u=-h}^{h} \sum_{v=-h}^{h} f(x-u, y-v) K(u, v)$$

The SciPy signal module's `correlated2d()` function can be used for correlation. Correlation is similar to convolution if the kernel is symmetric.

But if the kernel is not symmetric, in order to get the same results as with `convolution2d()`, before placing the kernel onto the image, one must flip it upside-down and left-to-right.

This is illustrated in the following screenshot; you can go ahead and write code for this in order to get this output now that you know the logic! Use the lena_g image as input and apply an asymmetric 3 x 3 ripple kernel ([[0,-1,√2],[1,0,-1],[-√2,1,0]]) onto it separately with `correlation2d()` and `convolution2d()`:

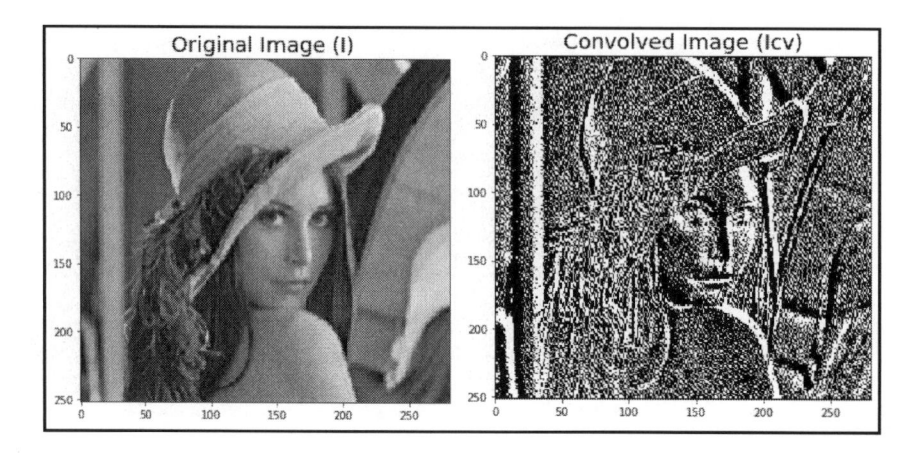

Frame two is as follows:

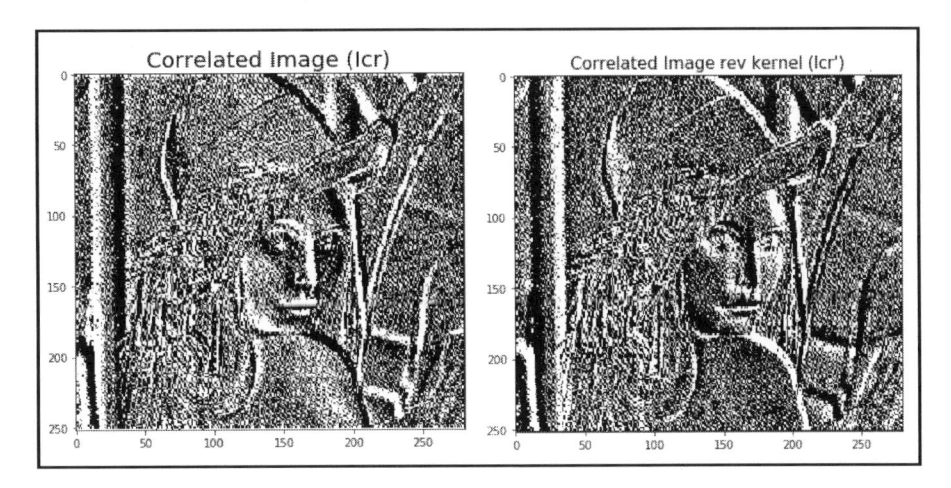

Frame three is as follows:

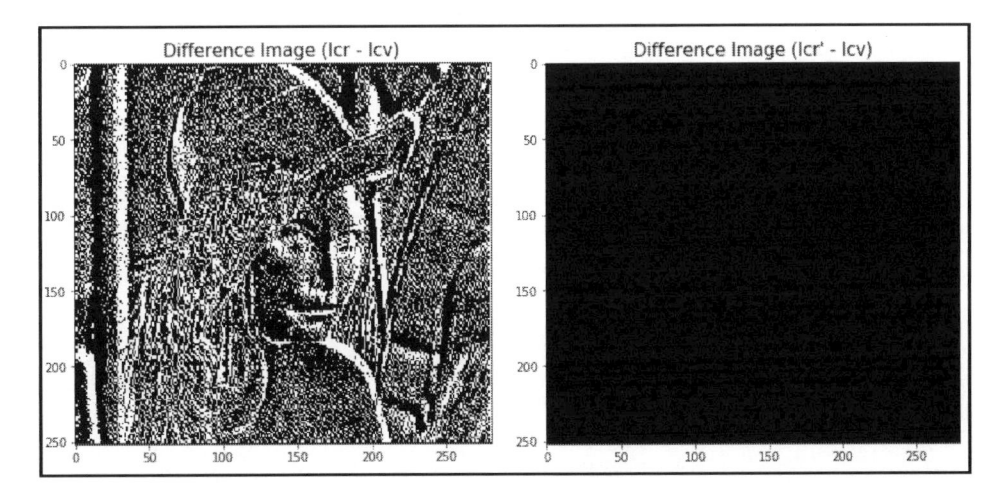

It can be seen that the difference between the output images obtained with correlation and convolution is blank if the asymmetric kernel is flipped before applying `correlation2d()`.

Let's move on to see an interesting application of correlation.

Template matching with cross-correlation between the image and template

In this example, we'll use cross-correlation with the eye template image (using a kernel with the image for cross-correlation) and the location of the eye in the raccoon-face image can be found as follows:

```
face_image = misc.face(gray=True) - misc.face(gray=True).mean()
template_image = np.copy(face_image[300:365, 670:750]) # right eye
template_image -= template_image.mean()
face_image = face_image + np.random.randn(*face_image.shape) * 50 # add random noise
correlation = signal.correlate2d(face_image, template_image, boundary='symm', mode='same')
y, x = np.unravel_index(np.argmax(correlation), correlation.shape) # find the match
fig, (ax_original, ax_template, ax_correlation) = pylab.subplots(3, 1, figsize=(6, 15))
ax_original.imshow(face_image, cmap='gray')
ax_original.set_title('Original', size=20)
ax_original.set_axis_off()
ax_template.imshow(template_image, cmap='gray')
ax_template.set_title('Template', size=20)
ax_template.set_axis_off()
ax_correlation.imshow(correlation, cmap='afmhot')
ax_correlation.set_title('Cross-correlation', size=20)
ax_correlation.set_axis_off()
ax_original.plot(x, y, 'ro')
fig.show()
```

You have marked the location with the largest cross-correlation value (the best match with the template) with a red dot:

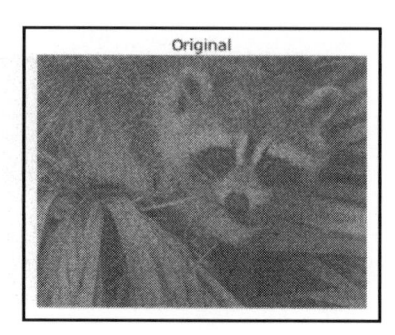

Here's the template:

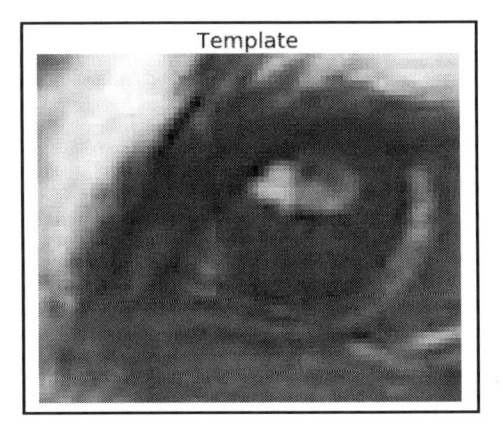

Applying cross-correlation gives the following output:

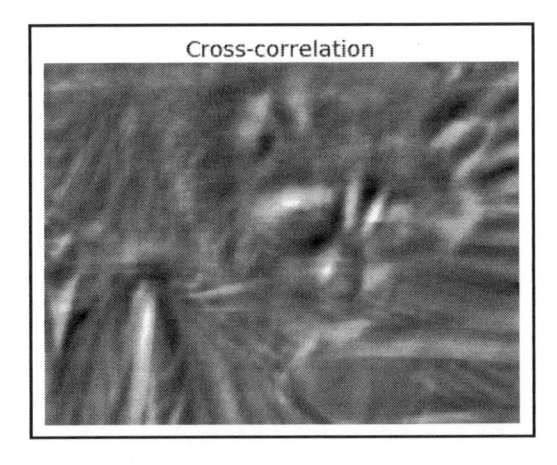

As can be seen from the previous image, one of the eyes of the raccoon in the input image has got the highest cross-correlation with the eye-template image.

Summary

We discussed a few important concepts primarily related to 2D DFT and its related applications in image processing, such as filtering in the frequency domain, and we worked on quite a few examples using scikit-image `numpy.fft`, `scipy.fftpack`, `signal`, and `ndimage` modules.

Hopefully, you are now clear on sampling and quantization, the two important image formation techniques. We have seen 2D DFT, Python implementations of FFT algorithms, and applications such as image denoising and restoration, correlation and convolution of the DFT in image processing, and application of convolution with an appropriate kernel in filter design and the application of correlation in template matching.

You should now be able to write Python code to do sampling and quantization using PIL/SciPy/sckit-image libraries and to perform 2D FT/IFT in Python using the FFT algorithm. We saw how easy it was to do basic 2D convolutions on images with some kernels.

In the next chapter, we'll discuss more on convolution and explore its wide range of applications. We'll also learn about frequency domain filtering, along with various frequency domain filters.

Questions

The following are the questions:

1. Implement down-sampling with anti-aliasing using the Gaussian LPF (hint: reduce the house grayscale image four times, first by applying a Gaussian filter and then by filtering every other row and column. Compare the output images with and without pre-processing with LPF before down-sampling).
2. Use the FFT to up-sample an image: first double the size of the `lena` grayscale image by padding zero rows/columns at every alternate positions, then use the FFT followed by an LPF and then by the IFFT to get the output image. Why does it work?
3. Try to apply the Fourier transform and image reconstruction with a color (RGB) image. (Hint: apply the FFT for each channel separately).
4. Show (mathematically and with a 2D kernel example) that the Fourier transform of a Gaussian kernel is another Gaussian kernel.

5. Use the `lena` image and the asymmetric ripple kernel to generate images with correlation and convolution. Show that output images are different. Now, flip the kernel twice (upside-down and left-right) and apply the correlation with the flipped kernel—is the output image the same as the one obtained using the original kernel with convolution?

Further reading

The following are the various references from various sources:

- Lecture notes from `http://fy.chalmers.se/~romeo/RRY025/notes/E1.pdf` and `http://web.pdx.edu/~jduh/courses/Archive/geog481w07/Students/Ludwig_ImageConvolution.pdf`
- These slides (`https://web.cs.wpi.edu/~emmanuel/courses/cs545/S14/slides/lecture10.pdf`) by Prof. Emmanuel Agu
- This lecture from Oxford university: `http://www.robots.ox.ac.uk/~az/lectures/ia/lect2.pdf`

3
Convolution and Frequency Domain Filtering

In this chapter, we will continue with 2D convolution and understand how convolution can be done faster in the frequency domain (with basic concepts of the convolution theorem). We will see the basic differences between correlation and convolution with an example on an image. We will also describe an example from SciPy that will show how to find the location of specific patterns in an image with a template image using cross-correlation. Finally, we will describe a few filtering techniques (that can be implemented with convolution using kernels, such as box-kernel or Gaussian kernel) in the frequency domain, such as high-pass, low-pass, band-pass, and band-stop filters, and how to implement them with Python libraries by using examples. We shall demonstrate with examples how some filters can be used for image denoising (for example, the `band-reject` or `notch` filters to remove periodic noise from an image, or the inverse or Wiener filters to deblur an image that's blurred with a Gaussian / motion-blur kernel).

The topics to be covered in this chapter are as follows:

- Convolution theorem and frequency domain Gaussian blur
- Filtering in the frequency domain (with the SciPy `ndimage` module and `scikit-image`)

Convolution theorem and frequency domain Gaussian blur

In this section, we will see more applications of convolution on images using Python modules such as `scipy signal` and `ndimage`. Let's start with convolution theorem and see how the convolution operation becomes easier in the frequency domain.

Application of the convolution theorem

The convolution theorem says that **convolution** in an image domain is equivalent to a simple multiplication in the frequency domain:

$$\text{Convolution theorem}$$
$$f(x,y) * h(x,y) \Leftrightarrow F(u,v)H(u,v)$$
$$\text{Space convolution = frequency multiplication}$$

Following diagram shows the application of fourier transforms:

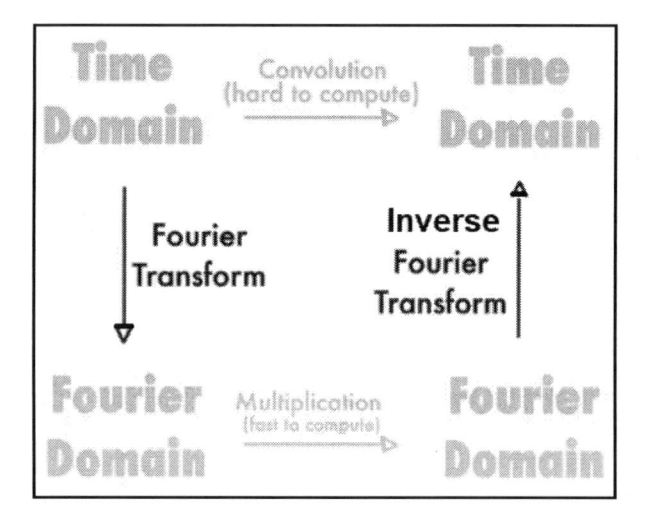

The next diagram shows the basic steps in frequency domain filtering. We have the original image, **F**, and a **kernel** (a mask or a degradation/enhancement function) as input. First, both input items need to be converted into the frequency domain with **DFT**, and then the convolution needs to be applied, which by convolution theorem is just an (element-wise) multiplication. This outputs the convolved image in the frequency domain, on which we need to apply **IDFT** to obtain the reconstructed image (with some degradation or enhancement on the original image):

Convolution in the Frequency Domain

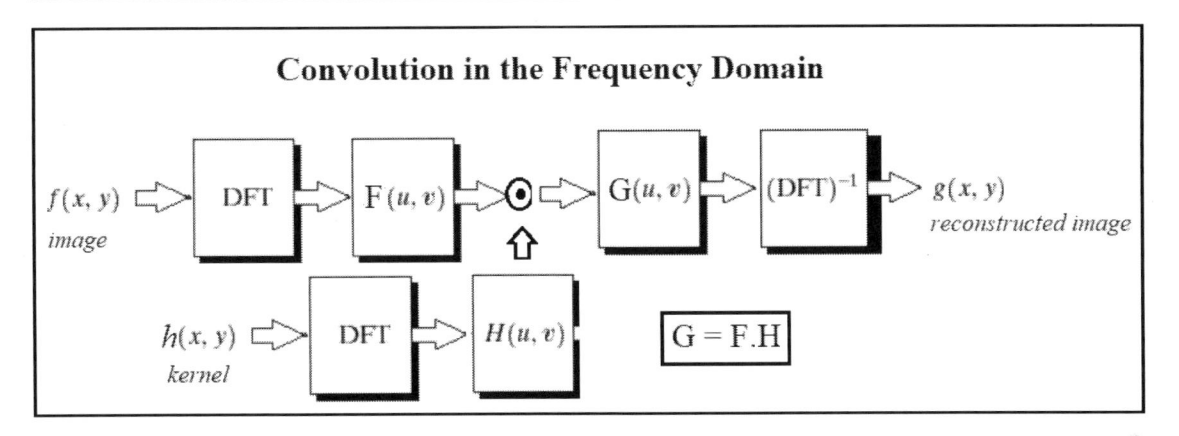

$f(x, y)$ image → DFT → $F(u, v)$ → ⊙ → $G(u, v)$ → $(DFT)^{-1}$ → $g(x, y)$ reconstructed image

$h(x, y)$ kernel → DFT → $H(u, v)$

$G = F.H$

Let's now see the demonstration of the theorem on a few images and with a few Python library functions. We need to import all of the required libraries just as we did in the last chapter.

Frequency domain Gaussian blur filter with numpy fft

The following code block shows how to apply a Gaussian filter in the frequency domain using the convolution theorem and `numpy fft` (since in the frequency domain it is simply multiplication):

```
import numpy.fft as fp
pylab.screenshot(figsize=(20,15))
pylab.gray() # show the filtered result in grayscale
im = np.mean(imread('../images/lena.jpg'), axis=2)
gauss_kernel = np.outer(signal.gaussian(im.shape[0], 5),
signal.gaussian(im.shape[1], 5))
freq = fp.fft2(im)
assert(freq.shape == gauss_kernel.shape)
freq_kernel = fp.fft2(fp.ifftshift(gauss_kernel))
convolved = freq*freq_kernel # by the convolution theorem, simply multiply
in the frequency domain
im1 = fp.ifft2(convolved).real
pylab.subplot(2,3,1), pylab.imshow(im), pylab.title('Original Image',
size=20), pylab.axis('off')
pylab.subplot(2,3,2), pylab.imshow(gauss_kernel), pylab.title('Gaussian
Kernel', size=20)
pylab.subplot(2,3,3), pylab.imshow(im1) # the imaginary part is an artifact
pylab.title('Output Image', size=20), pylab.axis('off')
pylab.subplot(2,3,4), pylab.imshow( (20*np.log10( 0.1 +
fp.fftshift(freq))).astype(int))
pylab.title('Original Image Spectrum', size=20), pylab.axis('off')
```

```
pylab.subplot(2,3,5), pylab.imshow( (20*np.log10( 0.1 +
fp.fftshift(freq_kernel))).astype(int))
pylab.title('Gaussian Kernel Spectrum', size=20), pylab.subplot(2,3,6)
pylab.imshow( (20*np.log10( 0.1 + fp.fftshift(convolved))).astype(int))
pylab.title('Output Image Spectrum', size=20), pylab.axis('off')
pylab.subplots_adjust(wspace=0.2, hspace=0)
pylab.show()
```

The following screenshot shows the output of the preceding code, the original `lena` image, the kernel, and the output image obtained after convolution, both in the spatial and frequency domains:

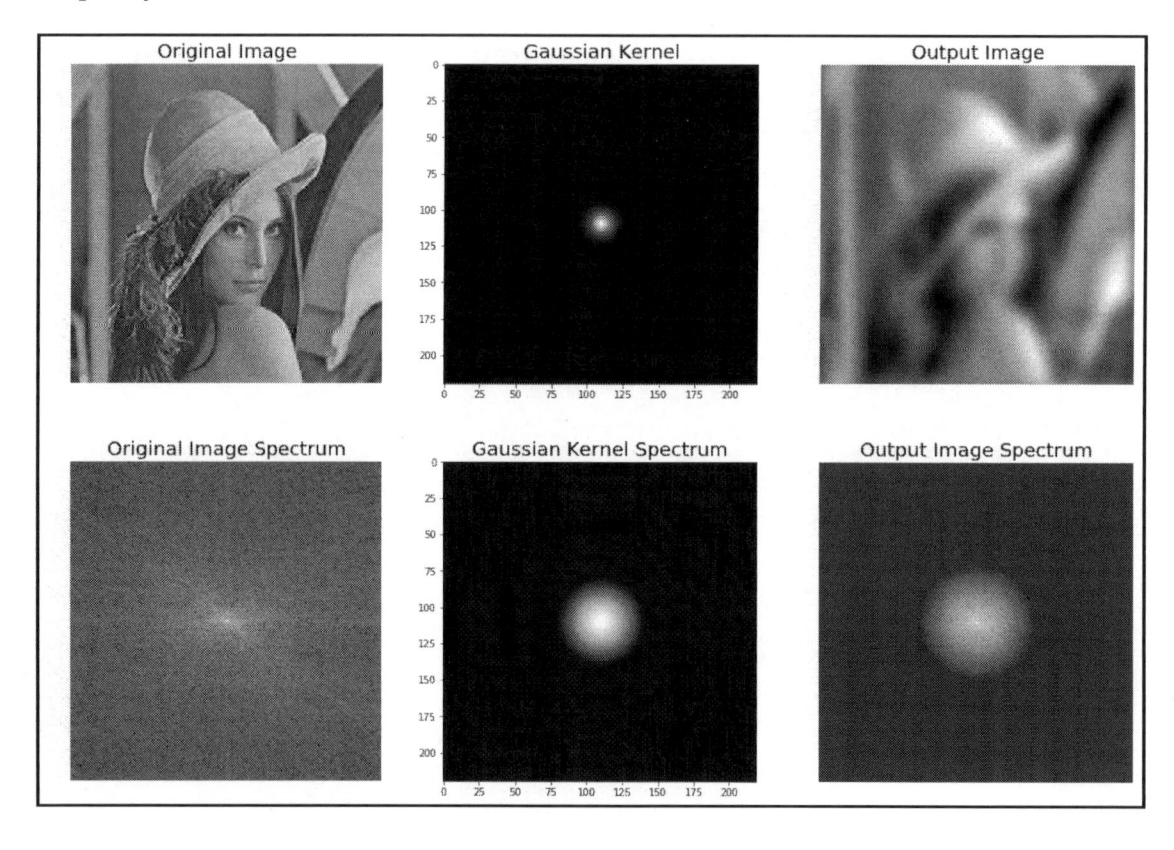

Gaussian kernel in the frequency domain

In this section, we will see how the Gaussian kernel looks like in the frequency domain in 2D and 3D plot.

The Gaussian LPF kernel spectrum in 2D

The next code block shows how to plot the spectrum of a Gaussian kernel in 2D with the `log` transform:

```
im = rgb2gray(imread('../images/lena.jpg'))
gauss_kernel = np.outer(signal.gaussian(im.shape[0], 1),
signal.gaussian(im.shape[1], 1))
freq = fp.fft2(im)
freq_kernel = fp.fft2(fp.ifftshift(gauss_kernel))
pylab.imshow( (20*np.log10( 0.01 +
fp.fftshift(freq_kernel))).real.astype(int), cmap='coolwarm') # 0.01 is
added to keep the argument to log function always positive
pylab.colorbar()
pylab.show()
```

The following screenshot shows the output of the preceding code with a color bar. Since the Gaussian kernel is a low-pass filter, its frequency spectrum has higher values for the frequencies in the center (it allows more low-frequency values), and gradually decreases as one moves away from the center to the higher frequency values:

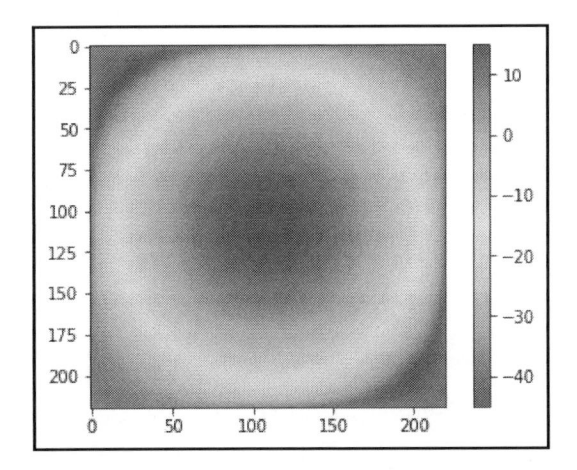

The next screenshot shows the frequency spectrum of the Gaussian kernel in 3-D, with and without the logarithm scale, along the response axis. As can be seen, the DFT of a Gaussian kernel is yet another Gaussian kernel. The Python code for the 3-D plots are left as an exercise (Question 3, with hints) for the reader.

The Gaussian LPF kernel spectrum in 3D

The horizontal plane represents the frequency plane and the vertical axis the response of the Gaussian kernel in the frequency domain, without and with the logarithm axis, respectively:

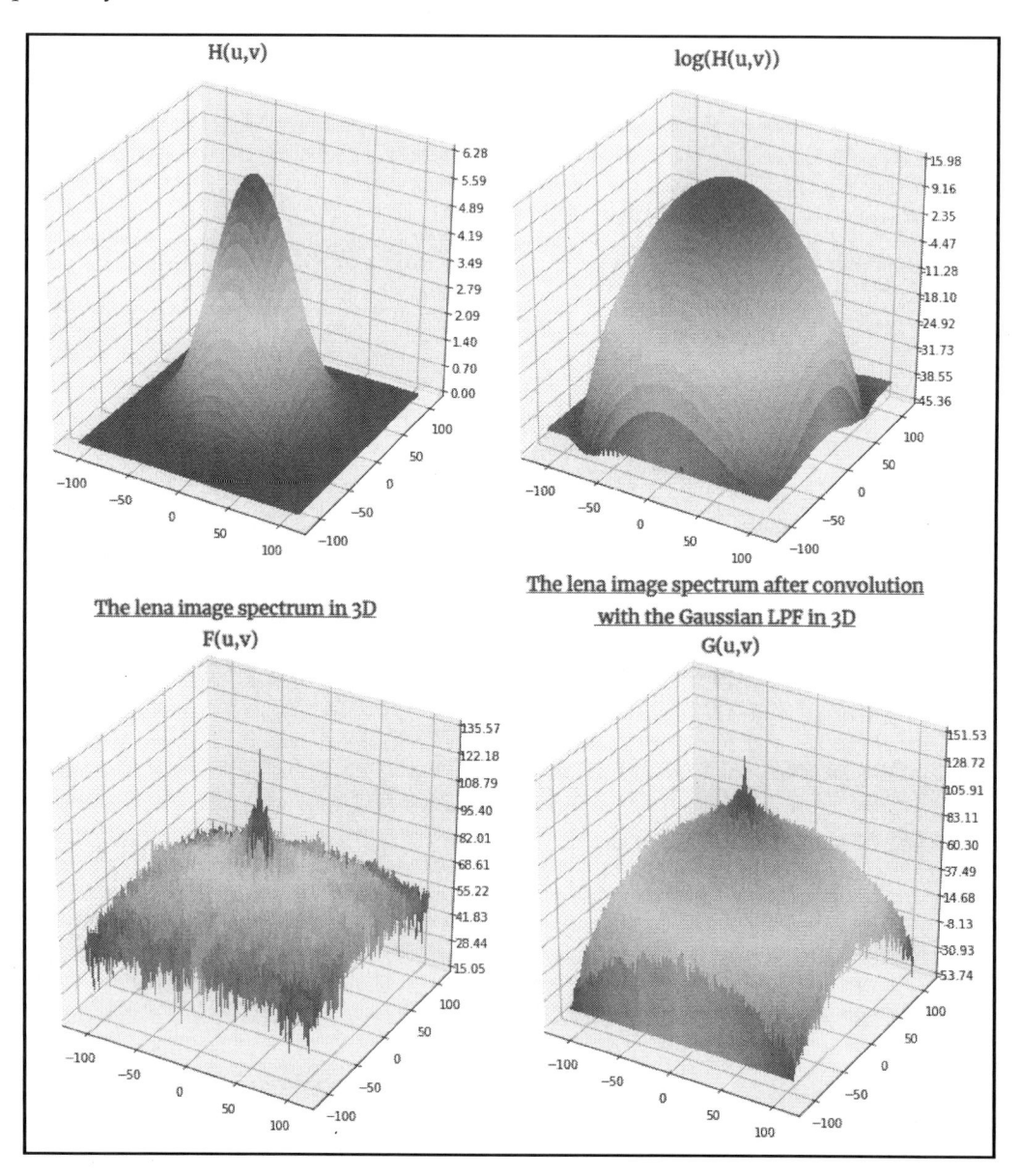

Frequency domain Gaussian blur filter with scipy signal.fftconvolve()

The following code block shows how the SciPy signal module's `fftconvolve()` function can be used to run the convolution in the frequency domain (internally by just a multiplication and the convolution theorem):

```
im = np.mean(misc.imread('../images/mandrill.jpg'), axis=2)
print(im.shape)
# (224, 225)
gauss_kernel = np.outer(signal.gaussian(11, 3), signal.gaussian(11, 3)) # 2D Gaussian kernel of size 11x11 with σ = 3
im_blurred = signal.fftconvolve(im, gauss_kernel, mode='same')
fig, (ax_original, ax_kernel, ax_blurred) = pylab.subplots(1, 3, figsize=(20,8))
ax_original.imshow(im, cmap='gray')
ax_original.set_title('Original', size=20)
ax_original.set_axis_off()
ax_kernel.imshow(gauss_kernel)
ax_kernel.set_title('Gaussian kernel', size=15)
ax_kernel.set_axis_off()
ax_blurred.imshow(im_blurred, cmap='gray')
ax_blurred.set_title('Blurred', size=20)
ax_blurred.set_axis_off()
fig.show()
```

The following screenshot shows the output of the preceding code block in the spatial domain:

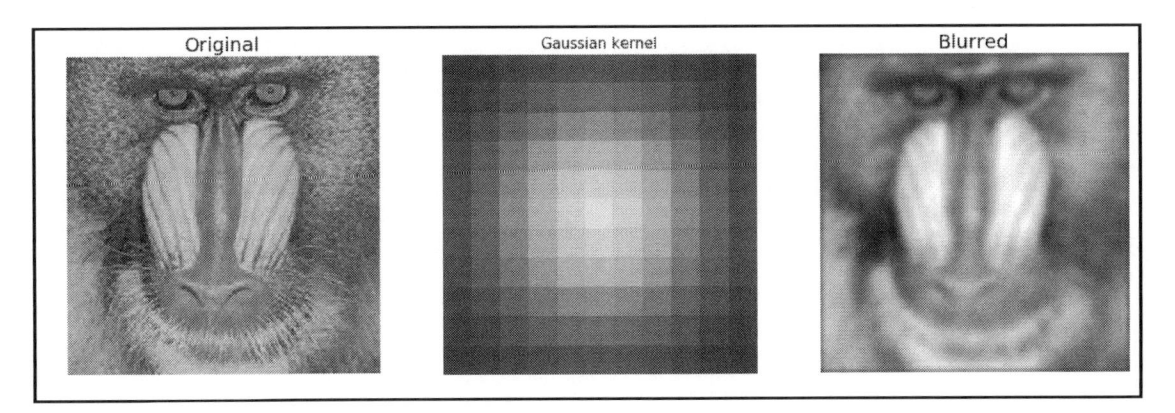

The following code block shows how to plot the original and the blurred image spectrum after convolution:

```
F1 = fftpack.fft2((im).astype(float))
F2 = fftpack.fftshift( F1 )
pylab.screenshot(figsize=(15,8))
pylab.subplot(1,2,1), pylab.imshow( (20*np.log10( 0.1 + F2)).astype(int), cmap=pylab.cm.gray)
pylab.title('Original Image Spectrum', size=20)
F1 = fftpack.fft2((im_blurred).astype(float))
F2 = fftpack.fftshift( F1 )
pylab.subplot(1,2,2), pylab.imshow( (20*np.log10( 0.1 + F2)).astype(int), cmap=pylab.cm.gray)
pylab.title('Blurred Image Spectrum', size=20)
pylab.show()
```

The following screenshot shows the output of the preceding code block in the frequency domain:

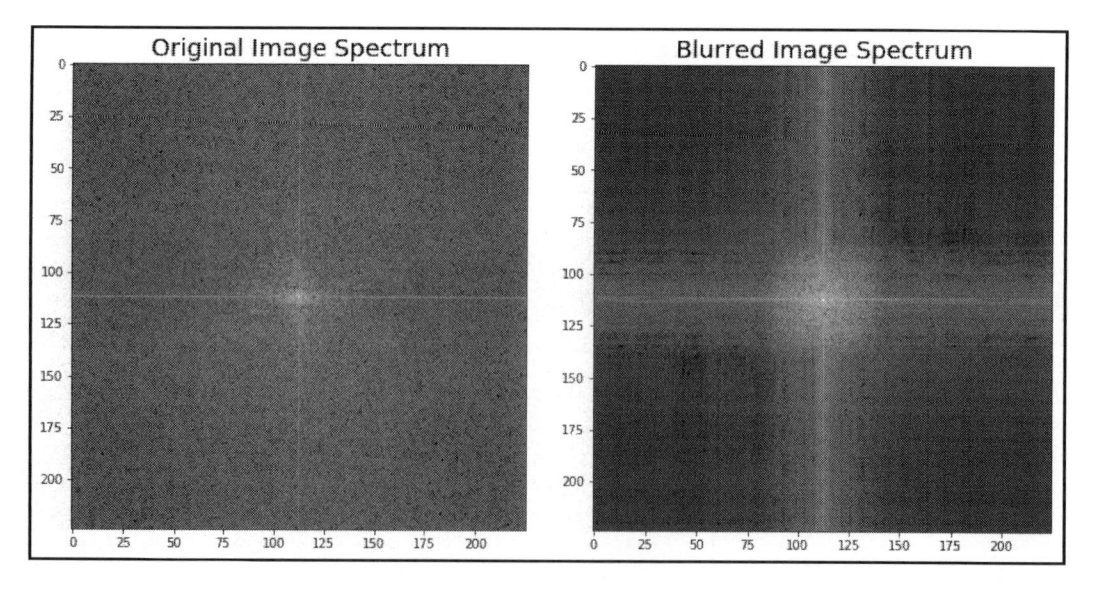

The same code block as the previous one is used to compute a blurred version of the Victoria Memorial Hall image, but this time the `fftconvolve()` function is invoked with a larger (50 x 50) Gaussian kernel with σ=10. The following screenshot shows the output of the same code with the new image and the modified kernel:

Comparing the runtimes of SciPy convolve() and fftconvolve() with the Gaussian blur kernel

We can use the Python `timeit` module to compare the runtimes of the image domain and the frequency domain convolution functions. Since the frequency domain convolution involves a single matrix multiplication instead of a series of sliding window arithmetic computations, it is expected to be much faster. The following code compares the runtimes:

```
im = np.mean(misc.imread('../images/mandrill.jpg'), axis=2)
print(im.shape)
# (224, 225)
gauss_kernel = np.outer(signal.gaussian(11, 3), signal.gaussian(11, 3)) #
2D Gaussian kernel of size 11x11 with σ = 3
im_blurred1 = signal.convolve(im, gauss_kernel, mode="same")
im_blurred2 = signal.fftconvolve(im, gauss_kernel, mode='same')
def wrapper_convolve(func):
 def wrapped_convolve():
  return func(im, gauss_kernel, mode="same")
 return wrapped_convolve
wrapped_convolve = wrapper_convolve(signal.convolve)
wrapped_fftconvolve = wrapper_convolve(signal.fftconvolve)
times1 = timeit.repeat(wrapped_convolve, number=1, repeat=100)
times2 = timeit.repeat(wrapped_fftconvolve, number=1, repeat=100)
```

Convolution and Frequency Domain Filtering

The following code block displays the original Mandrill image, as well as the blurred images, using both functions:

```
pylab.screenshot(figsize=(15,5))
pylab.gray()
pylab.subplot(131), pylab.imshow(im), pylab.title('Original Image',
size=15), pylab.axis('off')
pylab.subplot(132), pylab.imshow(im_blurred1), pylab.title('convolve
Output', size=15), pylab.axis('off')
pylab.subplot(133), pylab.imshow(im_blurred2), pylab.title('ffconvolve
Output', size=15),pylab.axis('off')
```

The output of the preceding code is shown in the following screenshot. As expected, both the `convolve()` and `fftconvolve()` functions result in the same blurred output image:

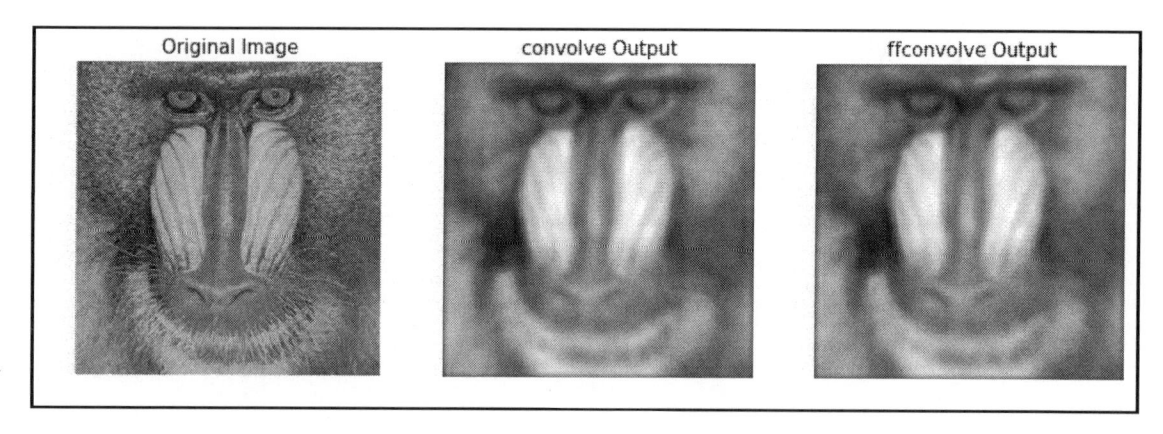

The following code visualizes the difference in between runtimes. Each of the functions has been run on the same input image with the same Gaussian kernel 100 times and then the boxplot of the times taken for each function is plotted:

```
data = [times1, times2]
pylab.screenshot(figsize=(8,6))
box = pylab.boxplot(data, patch_artist=True) #notch=True,
colors = ['cyan', 'pink']
for patch, color in zip(box['boxes'], colors):
 patch.set_facecolor(color)
pylab.xticks(np.arange(3), ('', 'convolve', 'fftconvolve'), size=15)
pylab.yticks(fontsize=15)
pylab.xlabel('scipy.signal convolution methods', size=15)
pylab.ylabel('time taken to run', size = 15)
pylab.show()
```

[104]

The following screenshot shows the output of the preceding code. As can be seen, `fftconvolve()` runs faster on average:

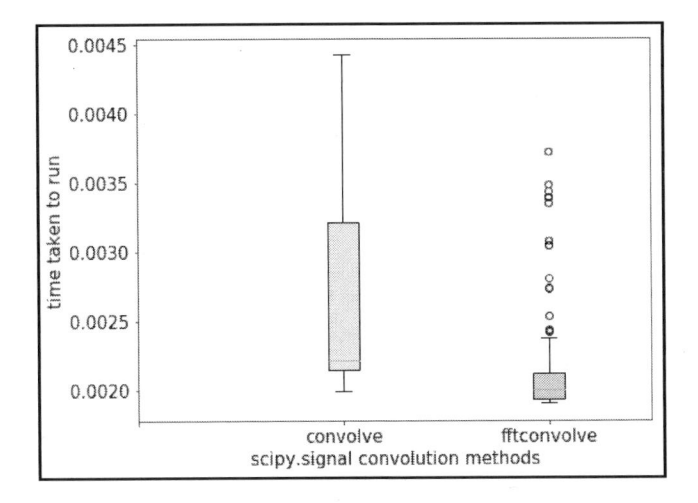

Filtering in the frequency domain (HPF, LPF, BPF, and notch filters)

If we remember from the image processing pipeline described in Chapter 1, *Getting Started with Image Processing*, the immediate next step after image acquisition is image preprocessing. Images are often corrupted by random variations in intensity and illumination or have poor contrast, and therefore can't be used directly and need to be enhanced. This is where the filters are used.

What is a filter?

Filtering refers to transforming pixel intensity values to reveal certain image characteristics such as:

- **Enhancement**: This image characteristic improves contrast
- **Smoothing**: This image characteristic removes noise
- **Template matching**: This image characteristic detects known patterns

The filtered image is described by a discrete convolution and the filter is described by a *n* x *n* discrete convolution mask.

High-Pass Filter (HPF)

This filter allows only high frequencies from the frequency domain representation of the image (obtained with DFT) and blocks all low frequencies beyond a **cut-off** value. The image is reconstructed with inverse DFT, and since the high-frequency components correspond to edges, details, noise, and so on, HPFs tend to extract or enhance them. The next few sections demonstrate how to use different functions from the `numpy`, `scipy`, and `scikit-image` libraries to implement an HPF and the impact of an HPF on an image.

We can implement a HPF on an image with the following steps:

1. Perform a 2D FFT with `scipy.fftpack fft2` and obtain the frequency domain representation of the image
2. Keep only the high frequency components (get rid of the low frequency components)
3. Perform an inverse FFT to reconstruct the image

The Python code to implement an HPF is shown in the following code. As can be seen, the high frequency components correspond more to the edges of an image, and the average (flat) image information is lost as we get rid of more and more low frequency components:

```
im = np.array(Image.open('../images/rhino.jpg').convert('L'))
pylab.screenshot(figsize=(10,10)), pylab.imshow(im, cmap=pylab.cm.gray),
pylab.axis('off'), pylab.show()
```

The following screenshot shows the original rhino image, the output of the preceding code:

The following code block shows how to plot the original rhino image spectrum in the logarithm domain:

```
freq = fp.fft2(im)
(w, h) = freq.shape
half_w, half_h = int(w/2), int(h/2)
freq1 = np.copy(freq)
freq2 = fp.fftshift(freq1)
pylab.screenshot(figsize=(10,10)), pylab.imshow( (20*np.log10( 0.1 + freq2)).astype(int)), pylab.show()
```

The following screenshot shows the original rhino image spectrum, the output of the preceding code:

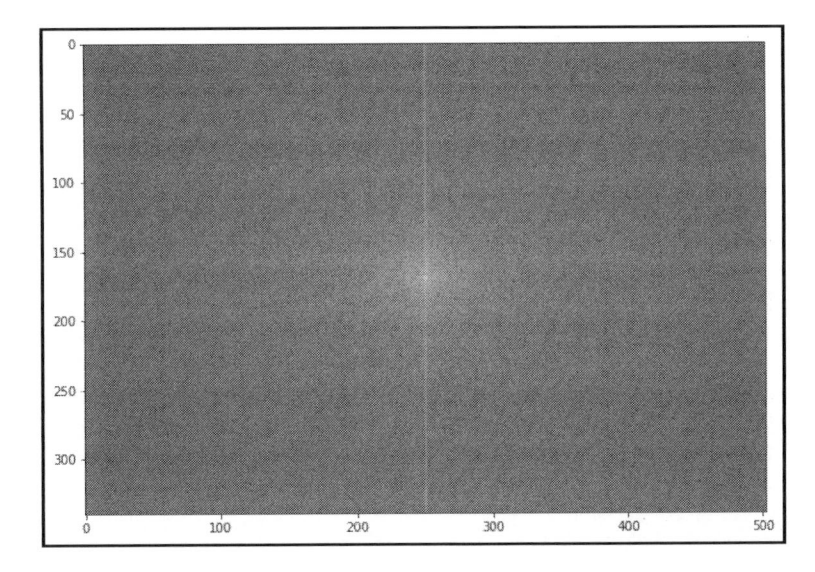

The following code block shows how to apply the HPF by blocking the low frequencies in the NumPy 2D array:

```
# apply HPF
freq2[half_w-10:half_w+11,half_h-10:half_h+11] = 0 # select all but the first 20x20 (low) frequencies
pylab.screenshot(figsize=(10,10))
pylab.imshow( (20*np.log10( 0.1 + freq2)).astype(int))
pylab.show()
```

[107]

The following screenshot shows the spectrum of the rhino image after applying the HPF, the output of the previous code:

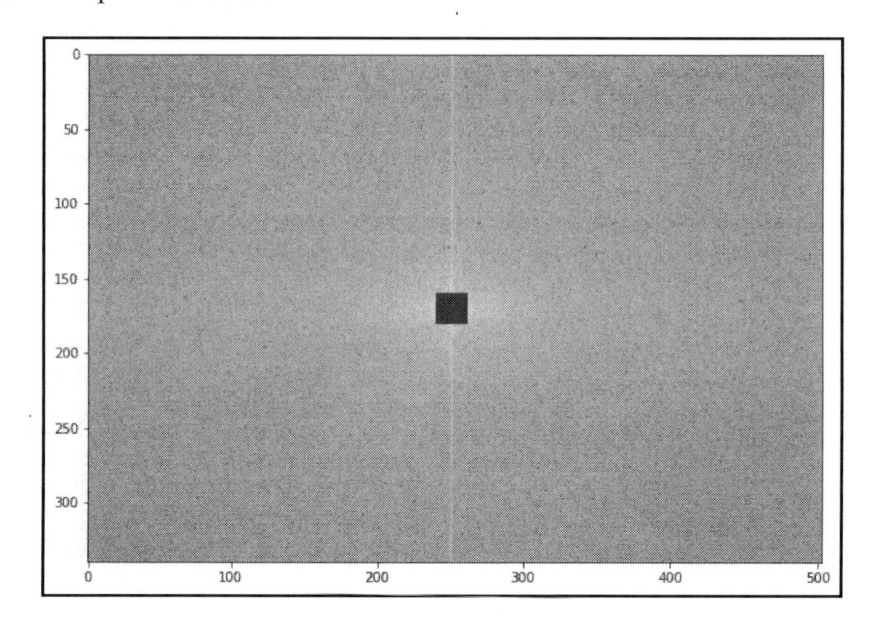

The following code block shows how to obtain the image back from the previous spectrum by applying `ifft2()`:

```
im1 = np.clip(fp.ifft2(fftpack.ifftshift(freq2)).real,0,255) # clip pixel
values after IFFT
print(signaltonoise(im1, axis=None))
# 0.5901647786775175
pylab.imshow(im1, cmap='gray'), pylab.axis('off'), pylab.show()
```

The following screenshot shows the output of the preceding code: the rhino image after the HPF is applied. As can be seen, the edges in the image become more prominent—HPF finds the edges (which correspond to higher frequencies) in the image:

Now let's see how the frequency cutoff value for an HPF changes the output image. We start from the grayscale cameraman image, apply FFT to it, and reconstruct the output image by blocking the low frequencies below the cut-of value F, which is also varied to see the impact on the output obtained:

The following code block shows the application of the HPF on the cameraman grayscale image, with different frequency cut-off values, F:

```
from scipy import fftpack
im = np.array(Image.open('../images/cameraman.jpg').convert('L'))
freq = fp.fft2(im)
(w, h) = freq.shape
half_w, half_h = int(w/2), int(h/2)
snrs_hp = []
lbs = list(range(1,25))
```

Convolution and Frequency Domain Filtering

```
pylab.screenshot(figsize=(20,20))
for l in lbs:
 freq1 = np.copy(freq)
 freq2 = fftpack.fftshift(freq1)
 freq2[half_w-l:half_w+l+1,half_h-l:half_h+l+1] = 0 # select all but the
first lxl (low) frequencies
 im1 = np.clip(fp.ifft2(fftpack.ifftshift(freq2)).real,0,255) # clip pixel
values after IFFT
 snrs_hp.append(signaltonoise(im1, axis=None))
 pylab.subplot(6,4,1), pylab.imshow(im1, cmap='gray'), pylab.axis('off')
 pylab.title('F = ' + str(l+1), size=20)
pylab.subplots_adjust(wspace=0.1, hspace=0)
pylab.show()
```

The following screenshot shows how the HPF detects edges more and discards the gross level information in the image as the cutoff frequency (**F**) increases:

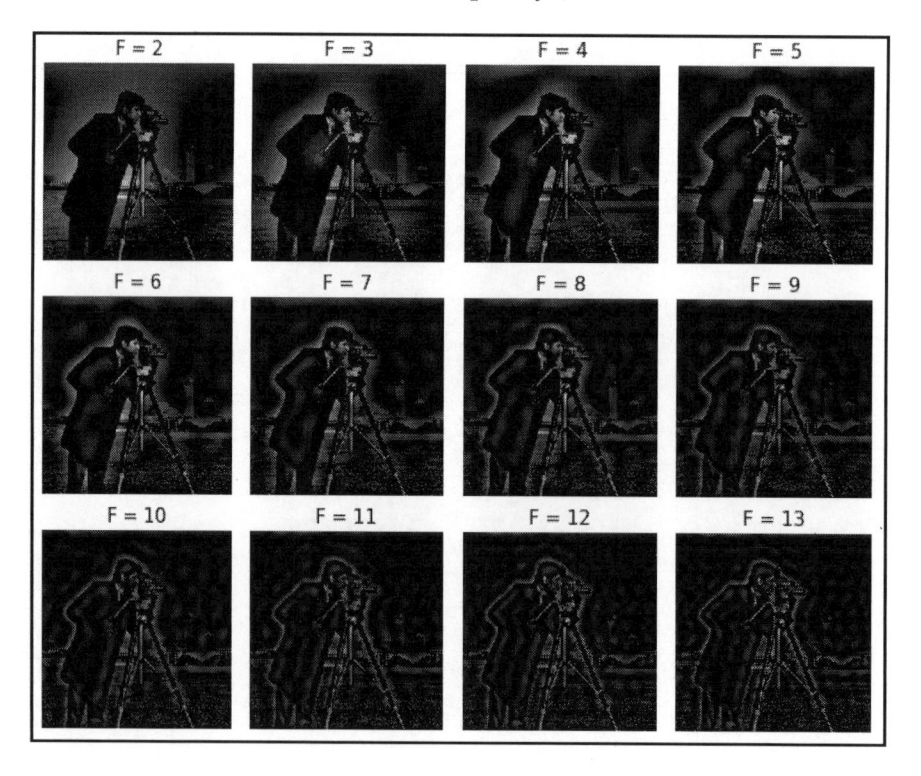

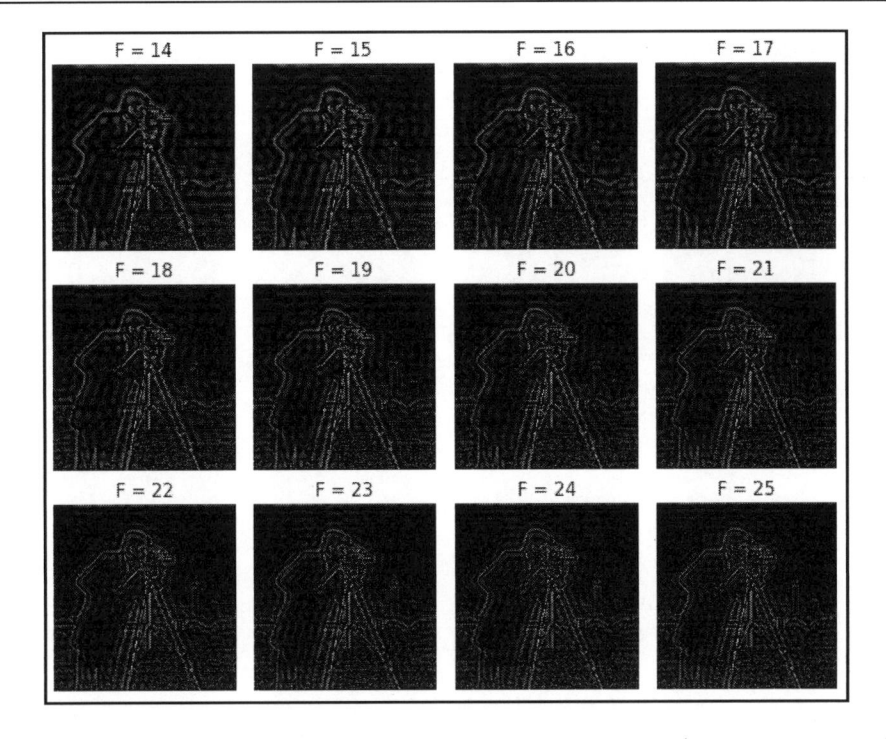

How SNR changes with frequency cut-off

The following code block shows how to plot the change in the **signal to noise ratio** (**SNR**) with the cutoff frequency (F) for the HPF:

```
pylab.plot(lbs, snrs_hp, 'b.-')
pylab.xlabel('Cutoff Freqeuncy for HPF', size=20)
pylab.ylabel('SNR', size=20)
pylab.show()
```

The following screenshot shows how the SNR of the output image decreases with the increase in the cutoff frequency of the HPF:

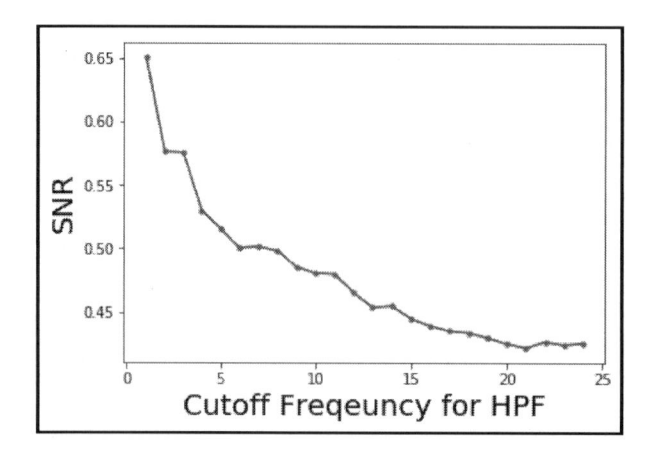

Low-pass filter (LPF)

This filter allows only the low frequencies from the frequency domain representation of the image (obtained with DFT), and blocks all high frequencies beyond a cut-off value. The image is reconstructed with inverse DFT, and since the high-frequency components correspond to edges, details, noise, and so on, LPF tends to remove these. The next few sections demonstrate how to use different functions from the numpy, scipy, and scikit-image libraries to implement an LPF and the impact of an LPF on an image.

LPF with scipy ndimage and numpy fft

The numpy fft module's fft2() function can also be used to run FFT on an image. The scipy ndimage module provides a bunch of functions to apply LPF on image in the frequency domain. The next section demonstrates one of these filters (namely fourier_gaussian()) with an example.

LPF with fourier_gaussian

This function from the scipy ndimage module implements a multi-dimensional Gaussian Fourier filter. The frequency array is multiplied with the Fourier transform of a Gaussian kernel of a given size.

The next code block demonstrates how to use the LPF (**weighted average** filter) to blur the `lena` grayscale image:

```
import numpy.fft as fp
fig, (axes1, axes2) = pylab.subplots(1, 2, figsize=(20,10))
pylab.gray() # show the result in grayscale
im = np.mean(imread('../images/lena.jpg'), axis=2)
freq = fp.fft2(im)
freq_gaussian = ndimage.fourier_gaussian(freq, sigma=4)
im1 = fp.ifft2(freq_gaussian)
axes1.imshow(im), axes1.axis('off'), axes2.imshow(im1.real) # the imaginary part is an artifact
axes2.axis('off')
pylab.show()
```

The following screenshot shows the output of the preceding code block:

The preceding code block displays the frequency spectrum of the image after the box kernel is applied:

```
pylab.screenshot(figsize=(10,10))
pylab.imshow( (20*np.log10( 0.1 +
numpy.fft.fftshift(freq_gaussian))).astype(int))
pylab.show()
```

The following screenshot shows the output of the preceding code block and displays the frequency spectrum of the image after the Gaussian kernel is applied:

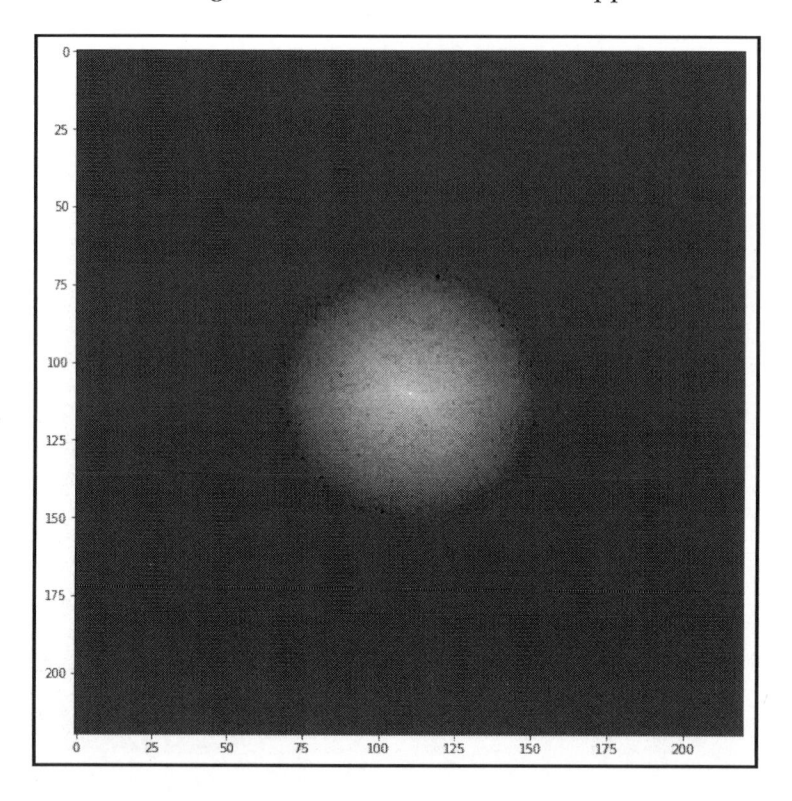

LPF with scipy fftpack

We can implement a LPF on an image with the following steps:

1. Perform a 2D FFT with `scipy.fftpack fft2` and obtain the frequency domain representation of the image
2. Keep only the low frequency components (get rid of the high frequency components)
3. Perform an inverse FFT to reconstruct the image

The Python code to implement an LPF is shown in the following code. As can be seen from the next screenshots, the high frequency components correspond more to the average (flat) image information and the detailed information (for example, the edges) of an image is lost as we get rid of more and more high-frequency components. For example, if we keep only the first-frequency component and discard all others, in the resulting image obtained after inverse FFT we can hardly see the rhinos, but as we keep more and more higher frequencies, they become prominent in the final image:

```
from scipy import fftpack
im = np.array(Image.open('../images/rhino.jpg').convert('L'))
# low pass filter
freq1 = np.copy(freq)
freq2 = fftpack.fftshift(freq1)
freq2_low = np.copy(freq2)
freq2_low[half_w-10:half_w+11,half_h-10:half_h+11] = 0 # block the low-
frequencies
freq2 -= freq2_low # select only the first 20x20 (low) frequencies, block
the high frequencies
im1 = fp.ifft2(fftpack.ifftshift(freq2)).real
print(signaltonoise(im1, axis=None))
# 2.389151856495427
pylab.imshow(im1, cmap='gray'), pylab.axis('off')
pylab.show()
```

The following screenshot shows the output of the preceding code, the gross output image obtained without the finer details by applying LPF on the input rhino image:

The following code block shows how to plot the spectrum of the image in the logarithm domain after blocking the high frequencies; in other words, only allowing the low frequencies:

```
pylab.screenshot(figsize=(10,10))
pylab.imshow( (20*np.log10( 0.1 + freq2)).astype(int))
pylab.show()
```

The following screenshot shows the output of the preceding code, the spectrum obtained after applying LPF on the image:

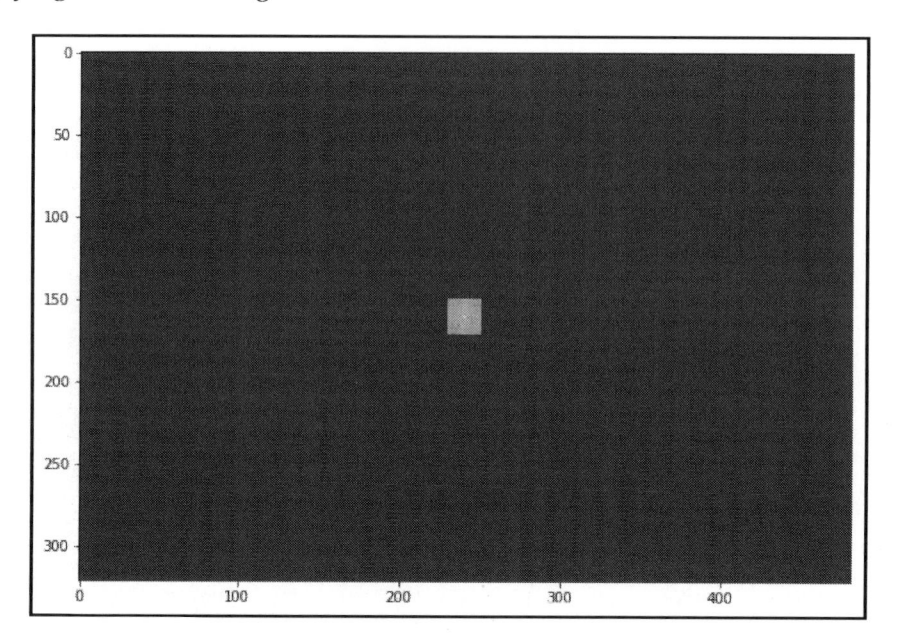

The following code block shows the application of LPF on the cameraman grayscale image, with different frequency cutoff values, F:

```
im = np.array(Image.open('../images/cameraman.jpg').convert('L'))
freq = fp.fft2(im)
(w, h) = freq.shape
half_w, half_h = int(w/2), int(h/2)
snrs_lp = []
ubs = list(range(1,25))
pylab.screenshot(figsize=(20,20))
for u in ubs:
  freq1 = np.copy(freq)
  freq2 = fftpack.fftshift(freq1)
  freq2_low = np.copy(freq2)
  freq2_low[half_w-u:half_w+u+1,half_h-u:half_h+u+1] = 0
  freq2 -= freq2_low # select only the first 20x20 (low) frequencies
  im1 = fp.ifft2(fftpack.ifftshift(freq2)).real
  snrs_lp.append(signaltonoise(im1, axis=None))
  pylab.subplot(6,4,u), pylab.imshow(im1, cmap='gray'), pylab.axis('off')
  pylab.title('F = ' + str(u), size=20)
pylab.subplots_adjust(wspace=0.1, hspace=0)
pylab.show()
```

Chapter 3

The following screenshot shows how LPF detects more and more details in the image as the cutoff frequency, **F**, increases:

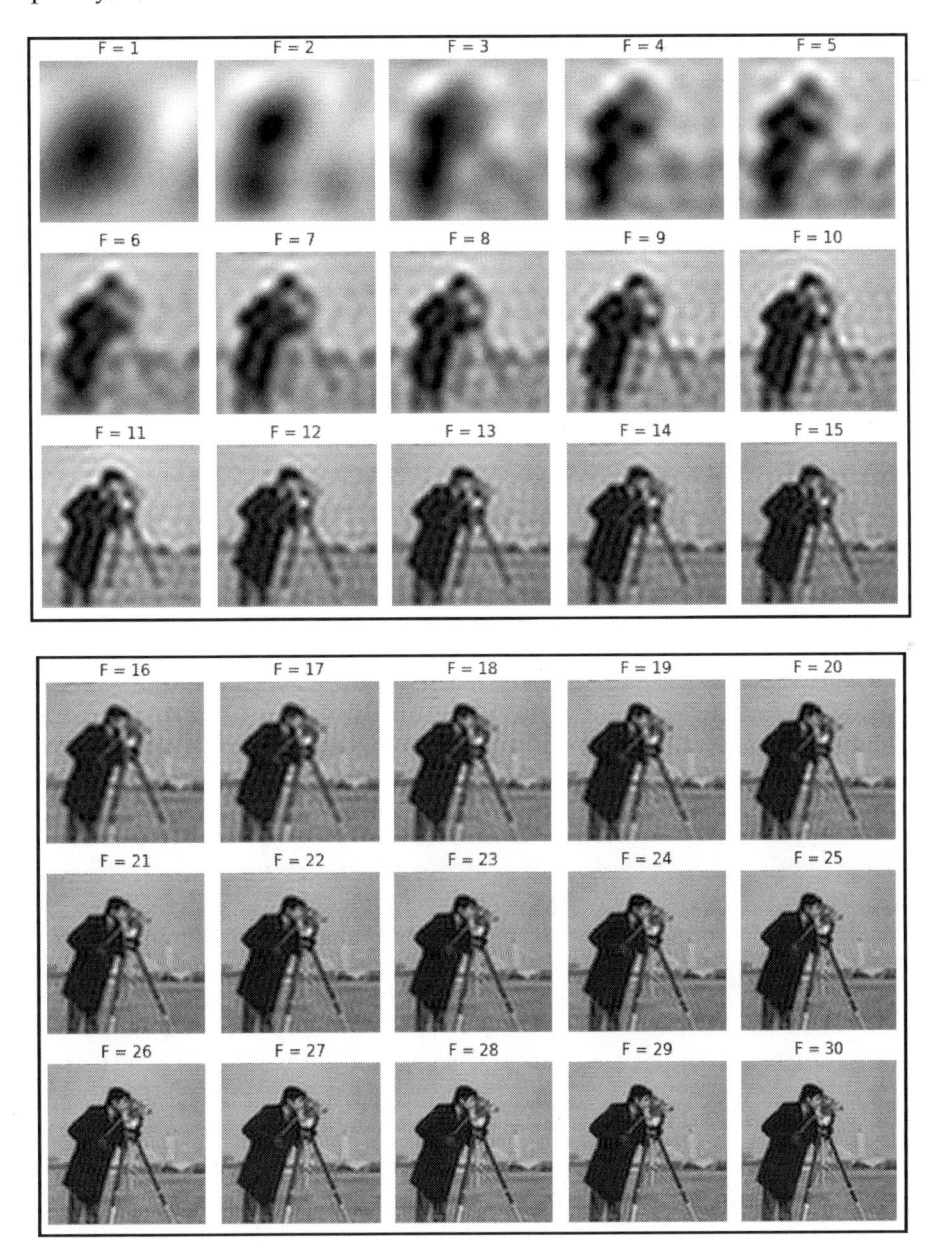

How SNR changes with frequency cutoff

The following code block shows how to plot the change in **signal to noise ratio** (SNR) with cutoff frequency (F) for LPF:

```
pylab.plot(ubs, snrs_lp, 'b.-')
pylab.plot(range(25), [snr]*25, 'r-')
pylab.xlabel('Cutoff Freqeuncy for LPF', size=20)
pylab.ylabel('SNR', size=20)
pylab.show()
```

The following screenshot shows how SNR of the output image decreases with the increase in the cut-off frequency of LPF. The red horizontal line indicates the original image's SNR, plotted for comparison:

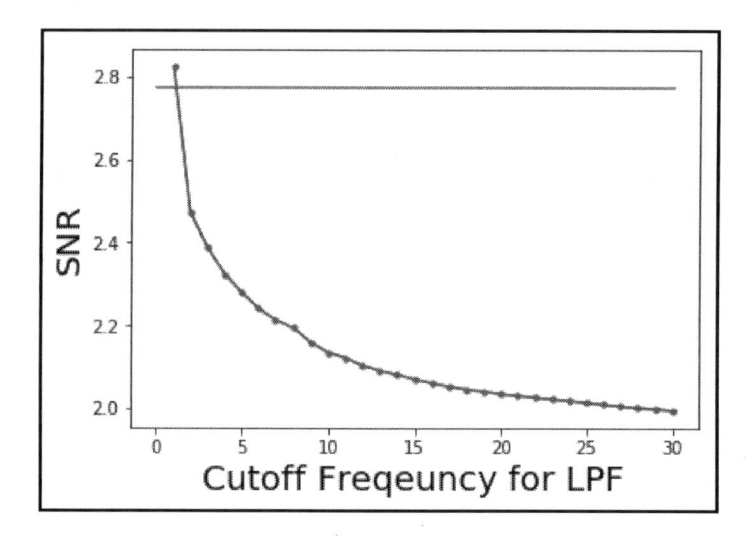

Band-pass filter (BPF) with DoG

The **Difference of Gaussian (DoG)** kernel can be used as a BPF to allow the frequencies in a certain band and discard all other frequencies. The following code block shows how the DoG kernel can be used with `fftconvolve()` to implement a BPF:

```
from skimage import img_as_float
im = img_as_float(pylab.imread('../images/tigers.jpeg'))
pylab.screenshot(), pylab.imshow(im), pylab.axis('off'), pylab.show()
x = np.linspace(-10, 10, 15)
kernel_1d = np.exp(-0.005*x**2)
kernel_1d /= np.trapz(kernel_1d) # normalize the sum to 1
```

```
gauss_kernel1 = kernel_1d[:, np.newaxis] * kernel_1d[np.newaxis, :]
kernel_1d = np.exp(-5*x**2)
kernel_1d /= np.trapz(kernel_1d) # normalize the sum to 1
gauss_kernel2 = kernel_1d[:, np.newaxis] * kernel_1d[np.newaxis, :]
DoGKernel = gauss_kernel1[:, :, np.newaxis] - gauss_kernel2[:, :,
np.newaxis]
im = signal.fftconvolve(im, DoGKernel, mode='same')
pylab.screenshot(), pylab.imshow(np.clip(im, 0, 1)), print(np.max(im)),
pylab.show()
```

The following screenshot shows the output of the preceding code block, the output image obtained with the BPF:

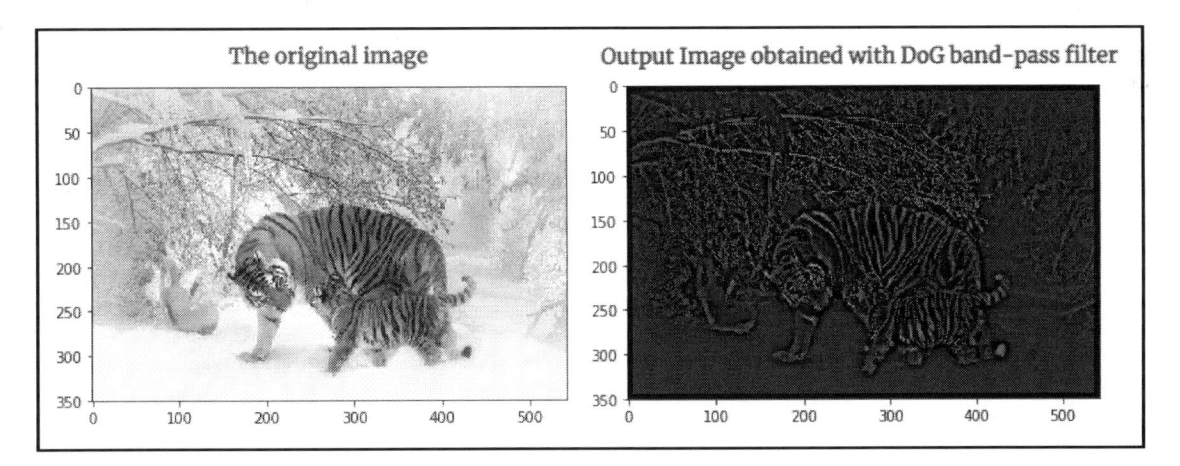

Band-stop (notch) filter

This filter blocks/rejects a few chosen frequencies from the frequency domain representation of the image (obtained with DFT), and hence the name. It is useful for removing **periodic noise** from images, as discussed in the next section.

Using a notch filter to remove periodic noise from images

In this example, we will first add some periodic (sinusoidal) noise to the parrot image to create a noisy parrot image (this can happen because of **interference** with some electrical signal) and then observe the effect of the noise in the frequency domain of the image using the following code block:

```
from scipy import fftpack
pylab.screenshot(figsize=(20,10))
im = img_as_float(np.mean(imread("../images/parrot.png"), axis=2))
pylab.subplot(2,2,1), pylab.imshow(im, cmap='gray'), pylab.axis('off')
pylab.title('Original Image')
F1 = fftpack.fft2((im).astype(float))
F2 = fftpack.fftshift( F1 )
pylab.subplot(2,2,2), pylab.imshow( (20*np.log10( 0.1 + F2)).astype(int), cmap=pylab.cm.gray)
pylab.xticks(np.arange(0, im.shape[1], 25))
pylab.yticks(np.arange(0, im.shape[0], 25))
pylab.title('Original Image Spectrum')
# add periodic noise to the image
for n in range(im.shape[1]):
  im[:, n] += np.cos(0.1*np.pi*n)
pylab.subplot(2,2,3), pylab.imshow(im, cmap='gray'), pylab.axis('off')
pylab.title('Image after adding Sinusoidal Noise')
F1 = fftpack.fft2((im).astype(float)) # noisy spectrum
F2 = fftpack.fftshift( F1 )
pylab.subplot(2,2,4), pylab.imshow( (20*np.log10( 0.1 + F2)).astype(int), cmap=pylab.cm.gray)
pylab.xticks(np.arange(0, im.shape[1], 25))
pylab.yticks(np.arange(0, im.shape[0], 25))
pylab.title('Noisy Image Spectrum')
pylab.tight_layout()
pylab.show()
```

The following screenshot shows the output of the preceding code block. As can be seen, the periodic noise there on the horizontal line became more prominent in the frequency spectrum around u = 175:

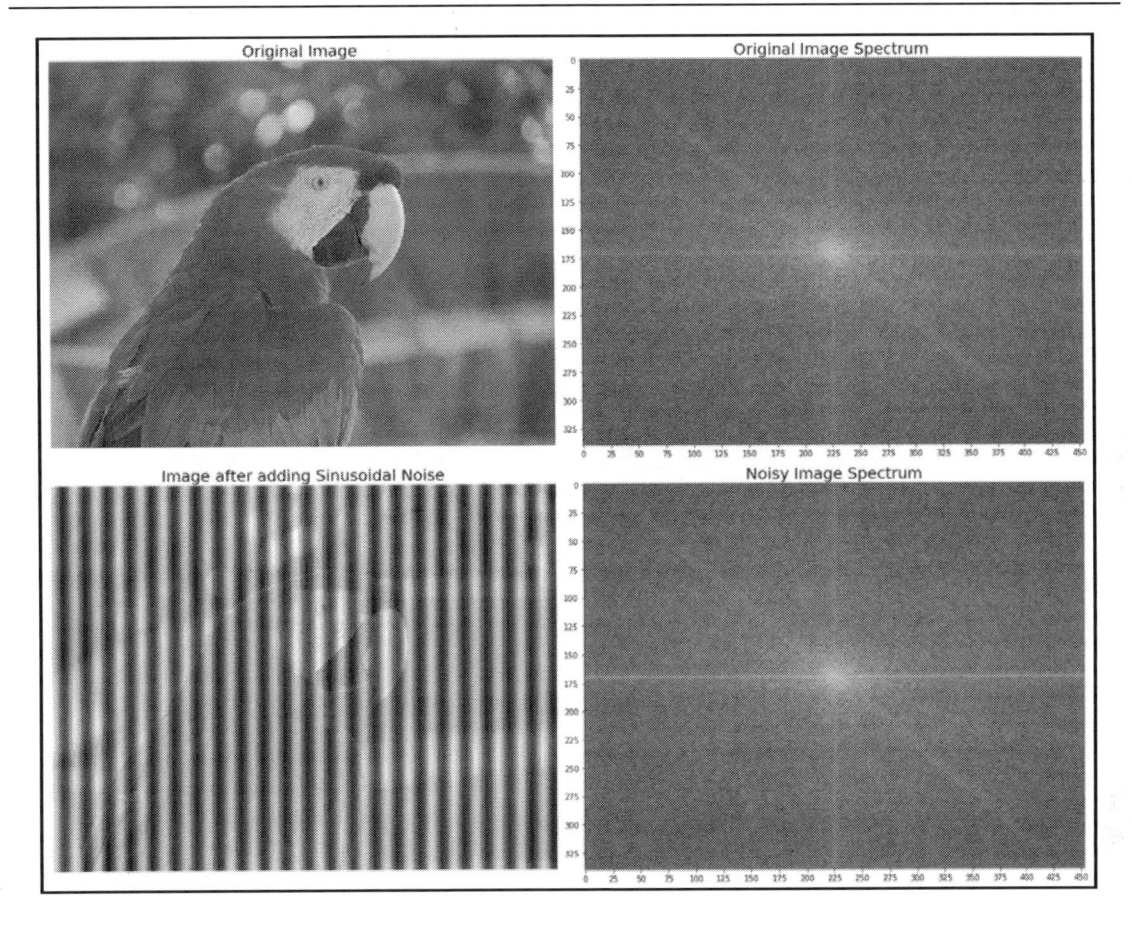

Now let's design a band-stop/band-reject (notch) filter to eliminate the frequencies that are responsible for noise by setting the corresponding frequency components to zero in the next code block:

```
F2[170:176,:220] = F2[170:176,230:] = 0 # eliminate the frequencies most
likely responsible for noise (keep some low frequency components)
im1 = fftpack.ifft2(fftpack.ifftshift( F2 )).real
pylab.axis('off'), pylab.imshow(im1, cmap='gray'), pylab.show()
```

The following screenshot shows the output of the preceding code block, the restored image by applying the notch filter. As can be seen, the original image looks sharper than the restored one, since some true frequencies from the original image are also rejected by the band-reject filter along with the noise:

Image restoration

In image restoration, the **degradation** is modeled. This enables the effects of the degradation to be (largely) removed. The challenge is the loss of information and noise. The following diagram shows the basic image degradation model:

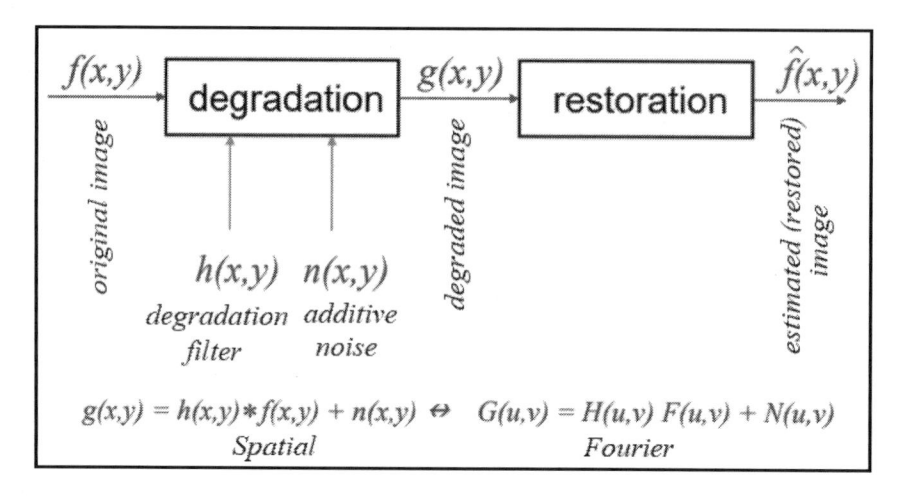

$$g(x,y) = h(x,y) * f(x,y) + n(x,y) \leftrightarrow G(u,v) = H(u,v) F(u,v) + N(u,v)$$

Spatial Fourier

Deconvolution and inverse filtering with FFT

Given a blurred image with a known (assumed) blur kernel, a typical image processing task is to get back (at least an approximation of) the original image. This particular task is known as **deconvolution**. One of the naive filters that can be applied in the frequency domain to achieve this is the inverse filter that we are going to discuss in this section. Let's first start by blurring the grayscale `lena` image with Gaussian blur using the following code:

```
im = rgb2gray(imread('../images/lena.jpg'))
gauss_kernel = np.outer(signal.gaussian(im.shape[0], 3),
signal.gaussian(im.shape[1], 3))
freq = fp.fft2(im)
freq_kernel = fp.fft2(fp.ifftshift(gauss_kernel)) # this is our H
convolved = freq*freq_kernel # by convolution theorem
im_blur = fp.ifft2(convolved).real
im_blur = 255 * im_blur / np.max(im_blur) # normalize
```

Now we can use the inverse filter on the blurred image (using the same H) to get back the original image. The following code block demonstrates how to do it:

```
epsilon = 10**-6
freq = fp.fft2(im_blur)
freq_kernel = 1 / (epsilon + freq_kernel) # avoid division by zero
convolved = freq*freq_kernel
im_restored = fp.ifft2(convolved).real
im_restored = 255 * im_restored / np.max(im_restored)
pylab.screenshot(figsize=(10,10))
pylab.subplot(221), pylab.imshow(im), pylab.title('Original image'),
pylab.axis('off')
pylab.subplot(222), pylab.imshow(im_blur), pylab.title('Blurred image'),
pylab.axis('off')
pylab.subplot(223), pylab.imshow(im_restored), pylab.title('Restored image
with inverse filter'), pylab.axis('off')
pylab.subplot(224), pylab.imshow(im_restored - im), pylab.title('Diff
restored & original image')
pylab.axis('off')
pylab.show()
```

The following screenshot shows the output. As can be seen, although the inverse filter deblurs the blurred image, there is some loss of information:

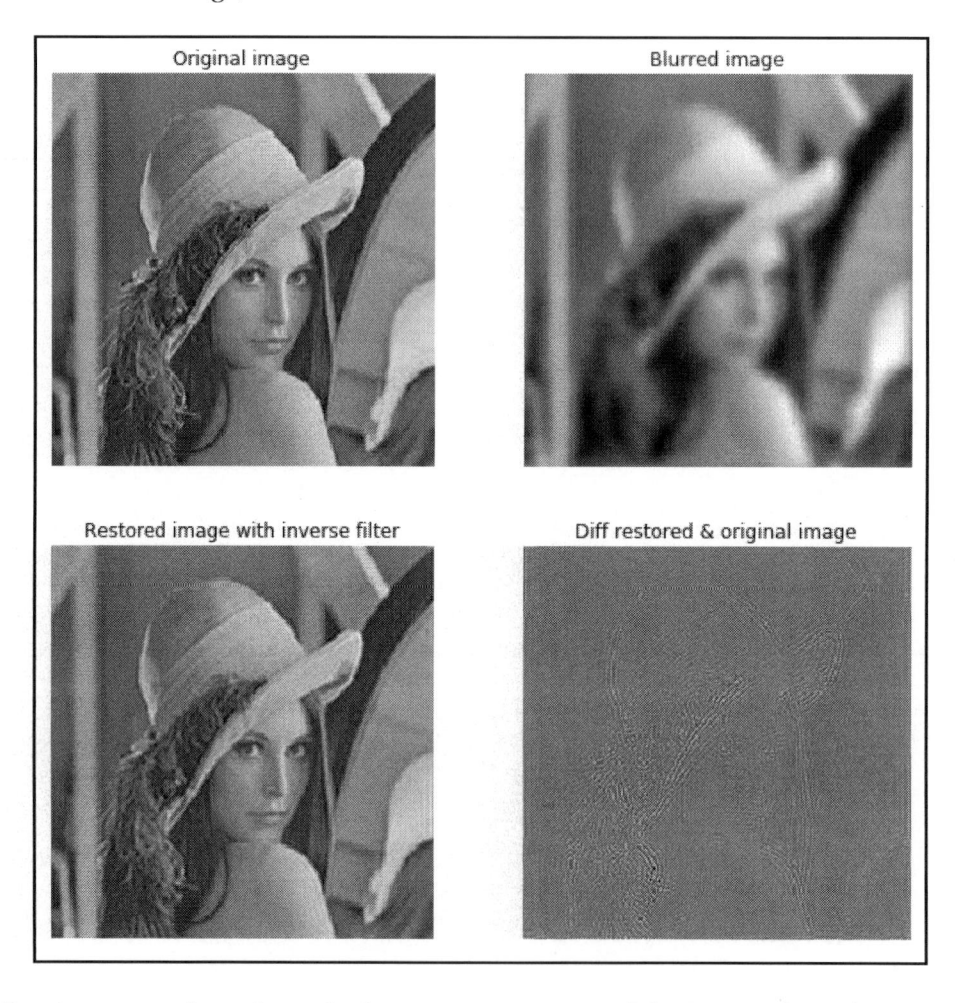

The following screenshots show the frequency spectrum of the inverse kernel (HPF), the original `lena` image, the blurred `lena` image with Gaussian LPF, and that of the restored image, respectively, in the logarithm scale. The Python code is left for you as an exercise (3):

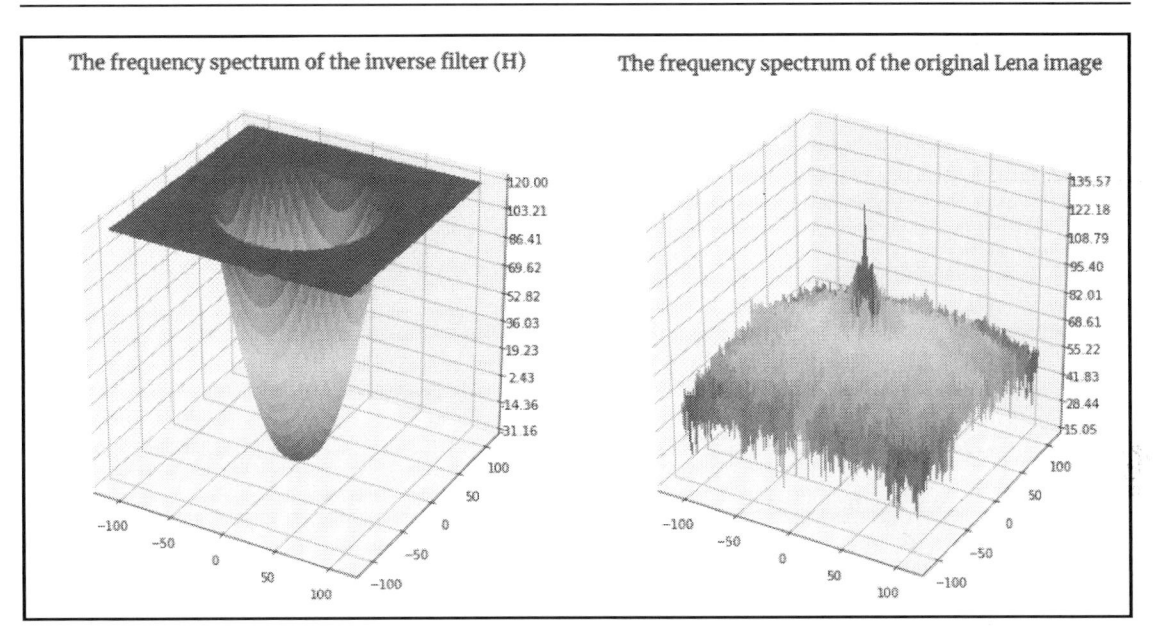

Chapter 3

The frequency spectrum of the inverse filter (H)

The frequency spectrum of the original Lena image

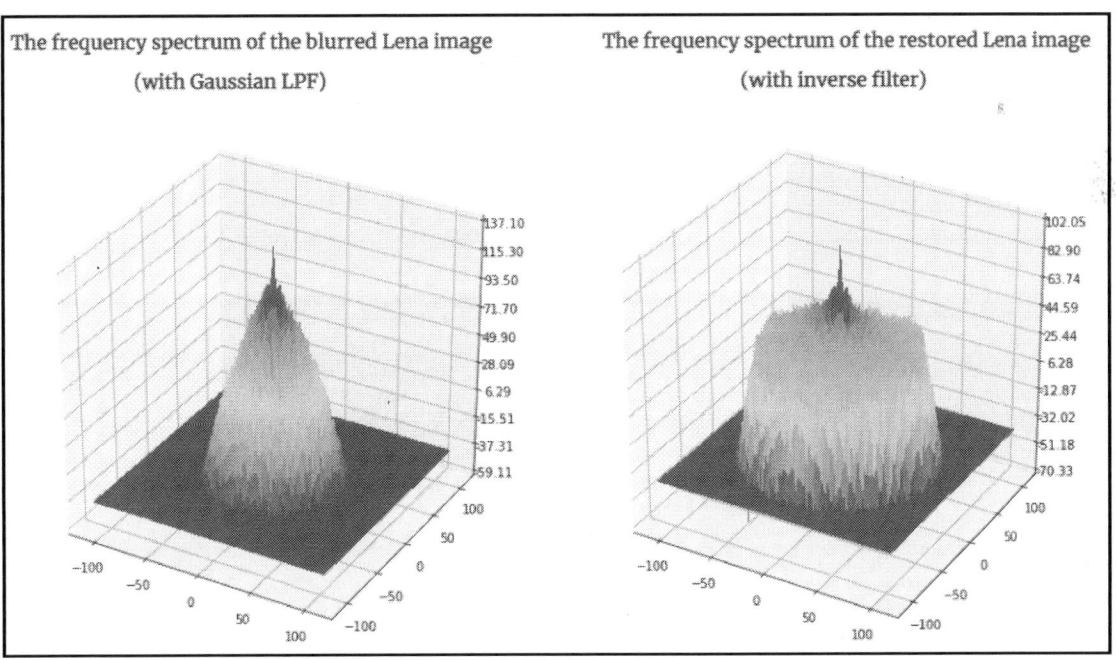

The frequency spectrum of the blurred Lena image
(with Gaussian LPF)

The frequency spectrum of the restored Lena image
(with inverse filter)

Convolution and Frequency Domain Filtering

If the input image is noisy, the inverse filter (which is an HPF) performs poorly, since the noise also gets enhanced in the output image (see question 4 in the *Questions* section).

Similarly, we can deblur an image blurred with a known motion blur kernel using the inverse filter. The code remains the same; only the kernel changes, as shown in the following code. Note that we need to create a **zero-padded kernel** of a size equal to the size of the original image before we can apply the convolution in the frequency domain (using `np.pad()`; the details are left as an exercise for you):

```
kernel_size = 21 # a 21 x 21 motion blurred kernel
mblur_kernel = np.zeros((kernel_size, kernel_size))
mblur_kernel[int((kernel_size-1)/2), :] = np.ones(kernel_size)
mblur_kernel = mblur_kernel / kernel_size
# expand the kernel by padding zeros
```

The following screenshot shows the frequency spectrum of the motion blur kernel defined previously:

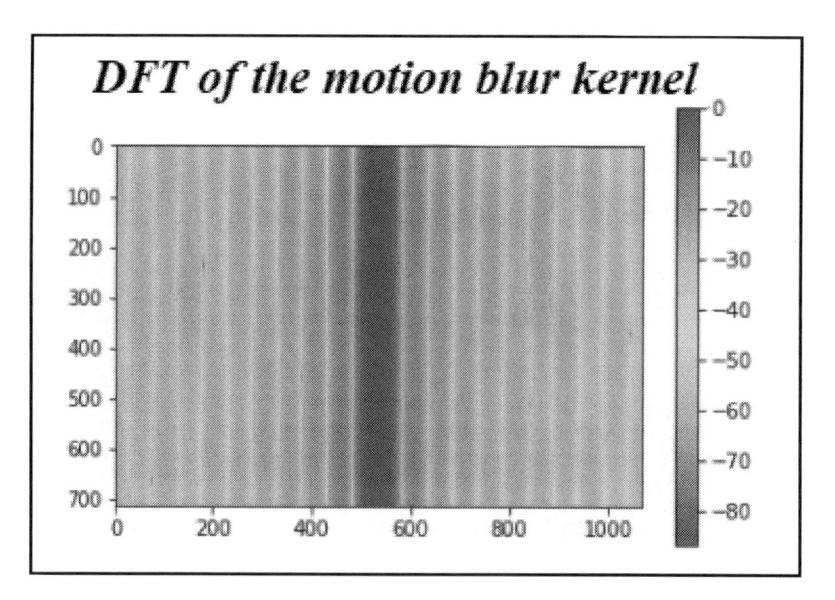

The following screenshot shows the output of the inverse filter with a motion-blurred image:

Image deconvolution with the Wiener filter

We already saw how to to obtain the (approximate) original image from the blurred image (with a known blur kernel) using the inverse filter in the last section. Another important task in image processing is the removal of noise from a **corrupted** signal. This is also known as **image restoration**. The following code block shows how the `scikit-image` `restoration` module's **unsupervised Wiener filter** can be used for image denoising with deconvolution:

```
from skimage import color, data, restoration
im = color.rgb2gray(imread('../images/elephant_g.jpg'))
from scipy.signal import convolve2d as conv2
```

```
n = 7
psf = np.ones((n, n)) / n**2
im1 = conv2(im, psf, 'same')
im1 += 0.1 * astro.std() * np.random.standard_normal(im.shape)
im2, _ = restoration.unsupervised_wiener(im1, psf)
fig, axes = pylab.subplots(nrows=1, ncols=3, figsize=(20, 4), sharex=True,
sharey=True)
pylab.gray()
axes[0].imshow(im), axes[0].axis('off'), axes[0].set_title('Original
image', size=20)
axes[1].imshow(im1), axes[1].axis('off'), axes[1].set_title('Noisy blurred
image', size=20)
axes[2].imshow(im2), axes[2].axis('off'), axes[2].set_title('Self tuned
restoration', size=20)
fig.tight_layout()
pylab.show()
```

The following screenshot shows the output of the previous code—the original, blurred-noisy, and restored image using the unsupervised Wiener filter:

Image denoising with FFT

The next example is taken from http://www.scipy-lectures.org/intro/scipy/auto_examples/solutions/plot_fft_image_denoise.html. This example demonstrates how to denoise an image first by blocking Fourier elements with high frequencies using a LPF with FFT. Let's first display the noisy grayscale image with the following code block:

```
im = pylab.imread('../images/moonlanding.png').astype(float)
pylab.screenshot(figsize=(10,10))
pylab.imshow(im, pylab.cm.gray), pylab.axis('off'), pylab.title('Original
image'), pylab.show()
```

The following screenshot shows the output of the preceding code block, the original noisy image:

The following code block displays the frequency spectrum of the noisy image:

```
from scipy import fftpack
from matplotlib.colors import LogNorm
im_fft = fftpack.fft2(im)
def plot_spectrum(im_fft):
 pylab.screenshot(figsize=(10,10))
 pylab.imshow(np.abs(im_fft), norm=LogNorm(vmin=5), cmap=pylab.cm.afmhot),
pylab.colorbar()
pylab.screenshot(), plot_spectrum(fftpack.fftshift(im_fft))
pylab.title('Spectrum with Fourier transform', size=20)
```

The following screenshot shows the output of the preceding code, the Fourier spectrum of the original noisy image:

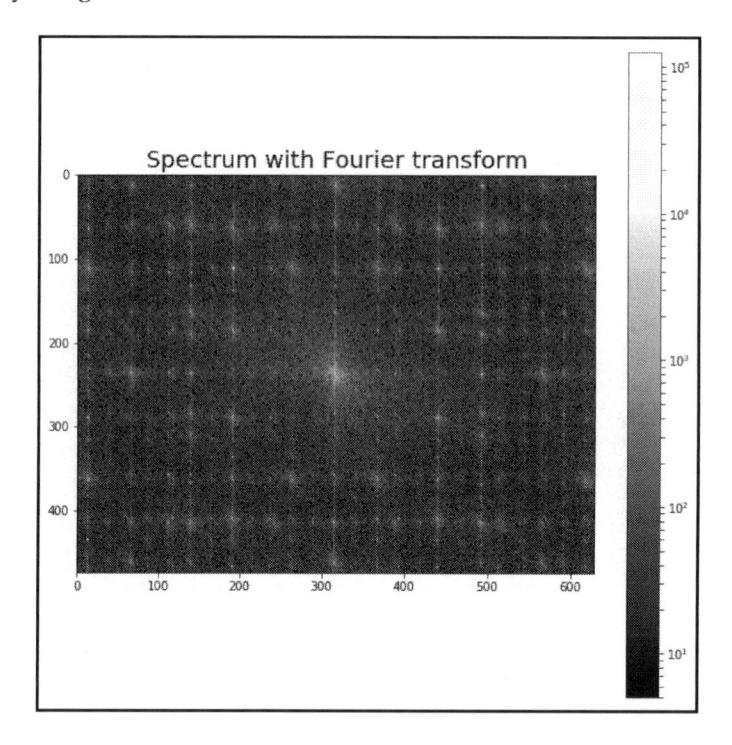

Filter in FFT

The following code block shows how to reject a bunch of high frequencies and implement an LPF to attenuate noise (which corresponds to high-frequency components) from the image:

```
# Copy the original spectrum and truncate coefficients.
# Define the fraction of coefficients (in each direction) to keep as
keep_fraction = 0.1
im_fft2 = im_fft.copy()
# Set r and c to the number of rows and columns of the array.
r, c = im_fft2.shape
# Set all rows to zero with indices between r*keep_fraction and r*(1-
keep_fraction)
im_fft2[int(r*keep_fraction):int(r*(1-keep_fraction))] = 0
# Similarly with the columns
im_fft2[:, int(c*keep_fraction):int(c*(1-keep_fraction))] = 0
pylab.screenshot(), plot_spectrum(fftpack.fftshift(im_fft2)),
pylab.title('Filtered Spectrum')
```

The following screenshot shows the output of the preceding code, the filtered spectrum with the LPF:

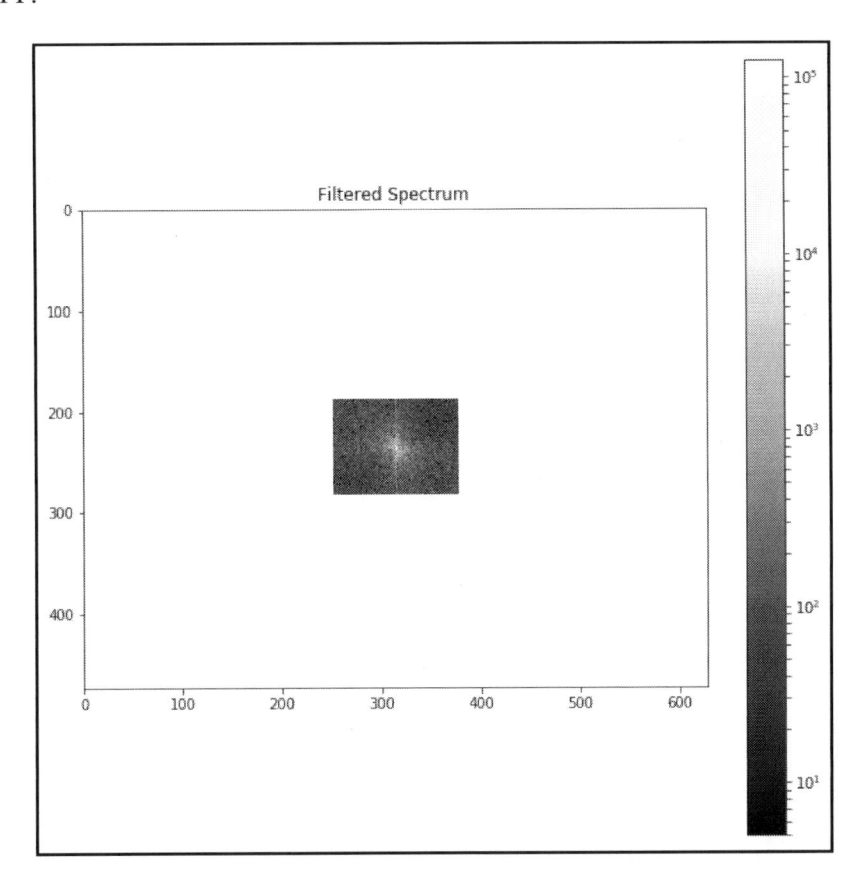

Reconstructing the final image

The following code block shows how to reconstruct the image with IFFT from the filtered Fourier coefficients:

```
# Reconstruct the denoised image from the filtered spectrum, keep only the
real part for display.
im_new = fp.ifft2(im_fft2).real
pylab.screenshot(figsize=(10,10)), pylab.imshow(im_new, pylab.cm.gray),
pylab.axis('off')
pylab.title('Reconstructed Image', size=20)
```

The following screenshot shows the output of the preceding code—a much cleaner output image obtained from the original noisy image with filtering in the frequency domain:

Summary

In this chapter, we discussed a few important concepts primarily related to 2D convolution and its related applications in image processing, such as filtering in the spatial domain. We also discussed a few different frequency domain filtering techniques and illustrated them with quite a few examples with the `scikit-image numpy fft`, `scipy`, `fftpack`, `signal`, and `ndimage` modules. We started with the convolution theorem and its application in frequency domain filtering, various frequency domain filters such as LPF, HPF, and notch filters, and finally deconvolution and its application in designing filters for image restoration, such as inverse and Wiener filters.

On completion of this chapter, the reader should be able to write Python code to do 2D convolution/filtering, and should also be able to write Python code to implement time/frequency domain filters with/without convolution.

In the next chapter, we will start on different image enhancement techniques based on the concepts introduced in the last two chapters.

Questions

1. Plot the frequency spectrum of an image, a Gaussian kernel, and the image obtained after convolution in the frequency domain, in 3D (the output should be like the surfaces shown in the sections) using the `mpl_toolkits.mplot3d` module. (Hint: the `np.meshgrid()` function will come in handy for the `surface` plot). Repeat the exercise for the inverse filter too.
2. Add some random noise to the `lena` image, blur the image with a Gaussian kernel, and then try to restore the image using an inverse filter, as shown in the corresponding example. What happens and why?
3. Use SciPy signal's `fftconvolve()` function to apply a Gaussian blur on a color image in the frequency domain.
4. Use the `fourier_uniform()` and `fourier_ellipsoid()` functions of the `ndimage` module of SciPy to apply LPFs with box and ellipsoid kernels, respectively, on an image in the frequency domain.

Further reading

- https://www.cs.cornell.edu/courses/cs1114/2013sp/sections/S06_convolution.pdf
- http://www.aip.de/groups/soe/local/numres/bookcpdf/c13-3.pdf
- http://www.cse.usf.edu/~r1k/MachineVisionBook/MachineVision.files/MachineVision_Chapter4.pdf
- https://web.stanford.edu/class/ee367/slides/lecture6.pdf
- https://pdfs.semanticscholar.org/presentation/50e8/fb095faf6ed51e03c85a2fcb7eb1ae1b1009.pdf
- http://www.robots.ox.ac.uk/~az/lectures/ia/lect2.pdf

4
Image Enhancement

In this chapter, we will discuss some of the most basic tools in image processing, such as mean/median filtering and histogram equalization, which are still among the most powerful tools. The objective of image enhancement is to improve the quality of an image or make particular features appear more prominent. These techniques are more general purpose techniques, and a strong model of the degradation process is not assumed (unlike image restoration). Some examples of image enhancement techniques are contrast stretching, smoothing, and sharpening. We will describe the basic concepts and implementation of these techniques using Python library functions and using `PIL`, `scikit-image`, and `scipy ndimage` libraries. We will become familiar with simple and still-popular approaches.

We will start with point-wise intensity transformation, and then discuss contrast stretching, thresholding, half-toning, and dithering algorithms, and the corresponding Python library functions. Then we will discuss different histogram processing techniques such as histogram equalization (both its global and adaptive version) and histogram matching. Then, a few techniques to denoise an image will be described. First, a few linear smoothing techniques such as the average filter and Gaussian filter will be described, followed by relatively more recent non-linear noise smoothing techniques such as median filtering, bilateral filtering, and non-local means filtering, along with how to implement them in Python. Finally, different image operations with mathematical morphology and their applications, along with implementations, will be described.

The topics to be covered in this chapter are as follows:

- Point-wise intensity transformations – pixel transformation
- Histogram processing, histogram equalization, histogram matching
- Linear noise smoothing (mean filter)
- Non-linear noise smoothing (median filter)

Point-wise intensity transformations – pixel transformation

As discussed in the Chapter 1, *Getting Started with Image Processing*, the point-wise intensity transformation operation applies a transfer function, *T*, to each pixel, *f(x,y)*, of the input image to generate a corresponding pixel in the output image. The transformation can be expressed as *g(x,y) = T(f(x,y))* or, equivalently, *s = T(r)*, where *r* is the gray-level of a pixel in the input image and *s* is the transformed gray-level of the same pixel in the output image. It's a memory-less operation, and the output intensity at the location,(*x*, *y*), depends only on the input intensity at the same point. Pixels of the same intensity get the same transformation. This does not bring in new information and may cause loss of information, but can improve the visual appearance or make features easier to detect—that is why these transformations are often applied at the pre-processing step in the image processing pipeline. The following screenshot shows the point processing, as well as the mask/kernel processing (for spatial filters that consider neighborhood pixels also for transformation, as we have already seen):

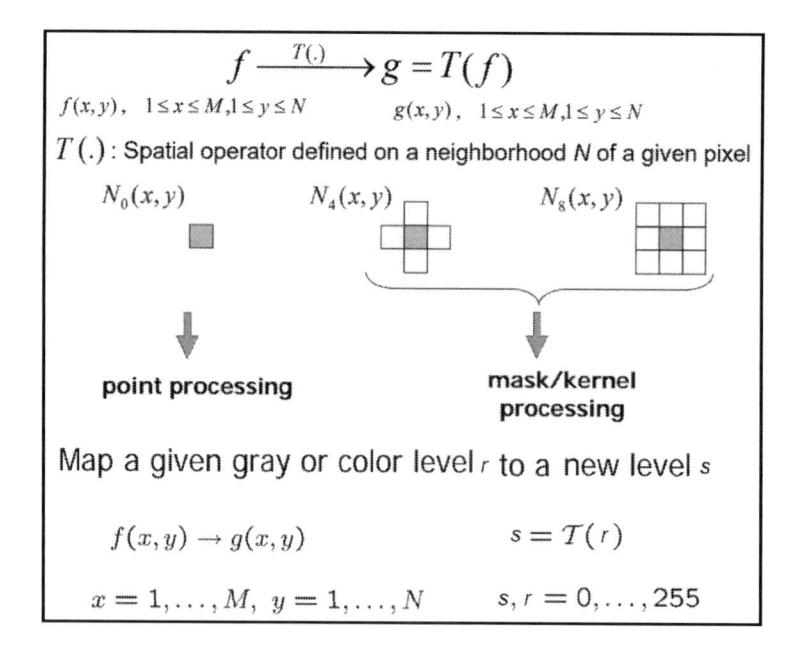

$$f \xrightarrow{T(.)} g = T(f)$$

$f(x,y), \ 1 \le x \le M, 1 \le y \le N \qquad g(x,y), \ 1 \le x \le M, 1 \le y \le N$

$T(.)$: Spatial operator defined on a neighborhood *N* of a given pixel

$N_0(x,y) \qquad N_4(x,y) \qquad N_8(x,y)$

↓   ↓

point processing   **mask/kernel processing**

Map a given gray or color level *r* to a new level *s*

$f(x,y) \rightarrow g(x,y) \qquad\qquad s = T(r)$

$x = 1, \ldots, M, \ y = 1, \ldots, N \qquad s, r = 0, \ldots, 255$

Some popular intensity transformations are the following:

- Image negatives
- Color space transformation
- Log transform
- Power-law transformation
- Contrast stretching
- Scalar quantization
- Thresholding

We already discussed a few of them in the Chapter 1, *Getting Started with Image Processing*. Here, we will start with log transformation on a colored RGB image using PIL, and then discuss a few transformations that we have not yet covered.

As usual, we will start by importing all the required modules from the relevant Python libraries:

```
import numpy as np
from skimage import data, img_as_float, img_as_ubyte, exposure, io, color
from skimage.io import imread
from skimage.exposure import cumulative_distribution
from skimage.restoration import denoise_bilateral, denoise_nl_means, estimate_sigma
from skimage.measure import compare_psnr
from skimage.util import random_noise
from skimage.color import rgb2gray
from PIL import Image, ImageEnhance, ImageFilter
from scipy import ndimage, misc
import matplotlib.pylab as pylab
```

Log transform

The log transformation is very useful when we need to compress or stretch a certain range of gray-levels in an image; for example, in order to display the Fourier spectrum (where the DC component value is much higher than the others, so that without the log transform the other frequency components almost always cannot even be seen). The point transformation function for a log transform is of the general form, $s = T(r) = c.log(1+r)$, where c is a constant.

Let's implement the histogram for the color channels of the input image:

```
def plot_image(image, title=''):
    pylab.title(title, size=20), pylab.imshow(image)
    pylab.axis('off') # comment this line if you want axis ticks

def plot_hist(r, g, b, title=''):
    r, g, b = img_as_ubyte(r), img_as_ubyte(g), img_as_ubyte(b)
    pylab.hist(np.array(r).ravel(), bins=256, range=(0, 256), color='r', alpha=0.5)
    pylab.hist(np.array(g).ravel(), bins=256, range=(0, 256), color='g', alpha=0.5)
    pylab.hist(np.array(b).ravel(), bins=256, range=(0, 256), color='b', alpha=0.5)
    pylab.xlabel('pixel value', size=20), pylab.ylabel('frequency', size=20)
    pylab.title(title, size=20)

im = Image.open("../images/parrot.png")
im_r, im_g, im_b = im.split()
pylab.style.use('ggplot')
pylab.screenshot(figsize=(15,5))
pylab.subplot(121), plot_image(im, 'original image')
pylab.subplot(122), plot_hist(im_r, im_g, im_b,'histogram for RGB channels')
pylab.show()
```

The following screenshot shows the output—the histograms for the color channels for the original image before applying the log transformation:

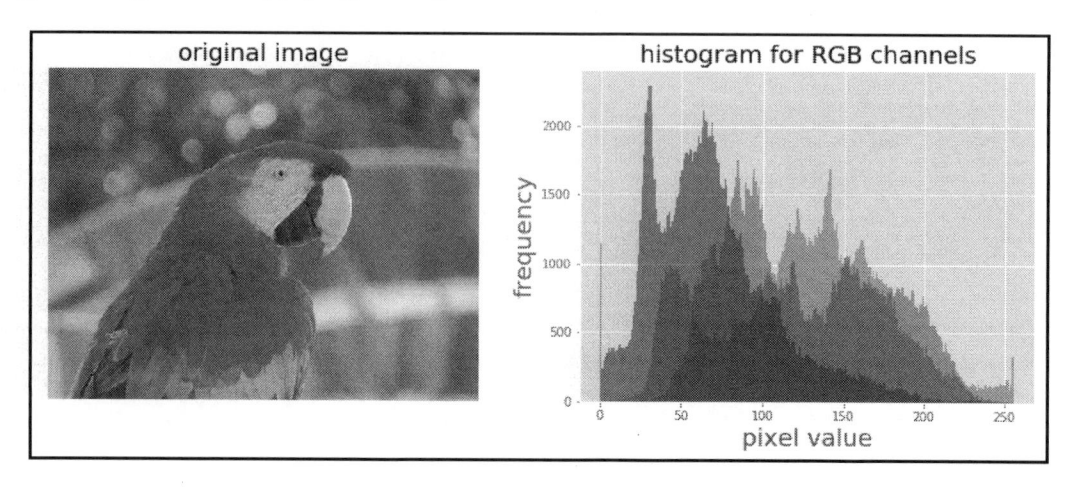

Let's now apply a log transform using the PIL image module's `point()` function and impact on the transformation on the histograms of different color channels for an RGB image:

```
im = im.point(lambda i: 255*np.log(1+i/255))
im_r, im_g, im_b = im.split()
pylab.style.use('ggplot')
pylab.screenshot(figsize=(15,5))
pylab.subplot(121), plot_image(im, 'image after log transform')
pylab.subplot(122), plot_hist(im_r, im_g, im_b, 'histogram of RGB channels log transform')
pylab.show()
```

The output shows how the histograms are squeezed for different color channels:

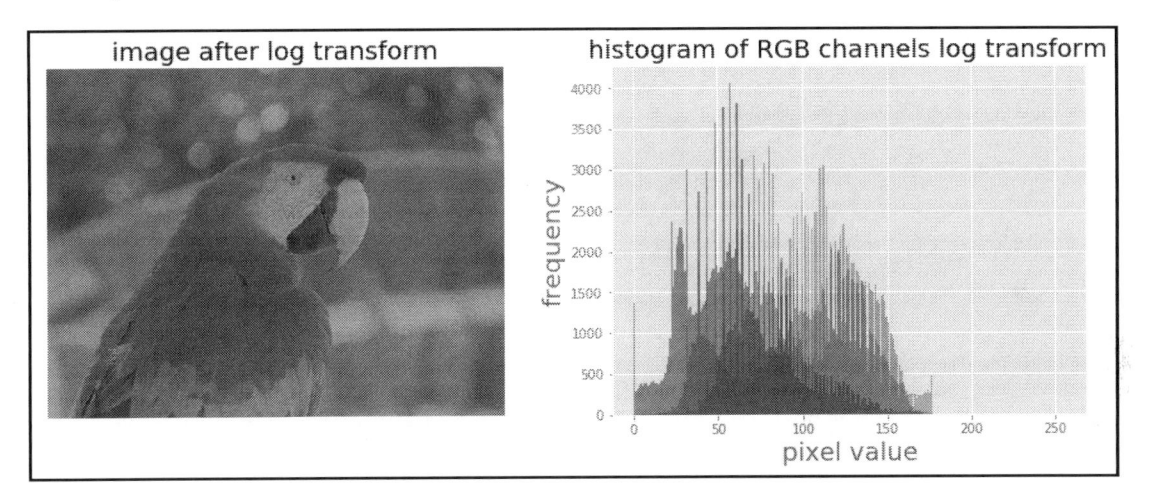

Power-law transform

As we have already seen, this point transform (the transfer function is of the general form, $s=T(r) = c.r^{\gamma}$, where c is a constant) on a grayscale image using the PIL `point()` function in the Chapter 1, *Getting Started with Image Processing*, let's apply power-law transform on a RGB color image with `scikit-image` this time, and then visualize the impact of the transform on the color channel histograms:

```
im = img_as_float(imread('../images/earthfromsky.jpg'))
gamma = 5
im1 = im**gamma
pylab.style.use('ggplot')
pylab.screenshot(figsize=(15,5))
```

Image Enhancement

```
pylab.subplot(121), plot_hist(im[...,0]), im[...,1]), im[...,2], 'histogram
for RGB channels (input)')
pylab.subplot(122), plot_hist(im1[...,0]), im1[...,1]), im1[...,2],
'histogram for RGB channels (output)')
pylab.show()
```

Here is the output:

The input image (the Earth from the sky):

The output image (γ = 5):

[140]

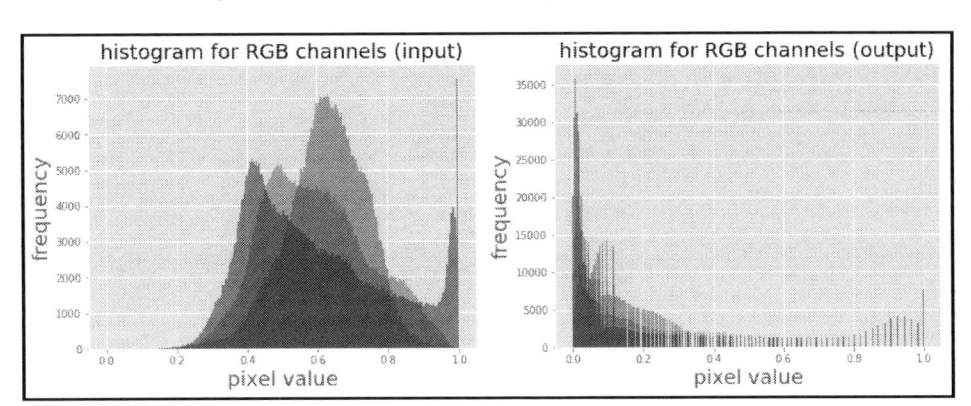

The color channel histograms before and after the power-law transform:

Contrast stretching

The contrast stretching operation takes a low-contrast image as input and stretches the narrower range of the intensity values to span a desired wider range of values in order to output a high-contrast output image, thereby enhancing the image's contrast. It is just a linear scaling function that is applied to image pixel values, and hence the image enhancement is less drastic (than its more sophisticated counterpart histogram equalization, to be described shortly). The following screenshot shows the point transformation function for contrast stretching:

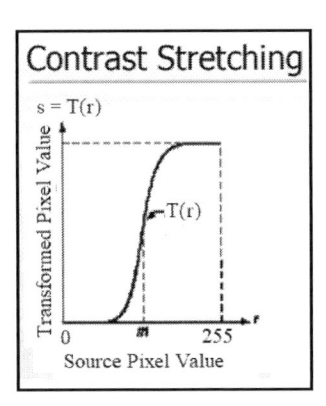

Image Enhancement

As can be seen from the previous screenshot, the upper and lower pixel value limits (over which the image is to be normalized), need to be specified before the stretching can be performed (for example, for a gray-level image, the limits are often set to 0 and 255, in order for the output image to span the entire range of available pixel values). All we need to find is a suitable value of m from the CDF of the original image. The contrast stretching transform produces higher contrast than the original by darkening the levels below the value m (in other words, stretching the values toward the lower limit) in the original image and brightening the levels previous to value m (stretching the values toward the upper limit) in the original image. The following sections describe how to implement contrast-stretching using the PIL library.

Using PIL as a point operation

Let us first load a colored RGB image and split it across the color channels to visualize the histograms of pixel values for different color channels:

```
im = Image.open('../images/cheetah.png')
im_r, im_g, im_b, _ = im.split()
pylab.style.use('ggplot')
pylab.screenshot(figsize=(15,5))
pylab.subplot(121)
plot_image(im)
pylab.subplot(122)
plot_hist(im_r, im_g, im_b)
pylab.show()
```

The following screenshot shows the output of the previous code block. As can be seen, the input cheetah image is a low-contrast image since the color channel histograms are concentrated at a certain range of values (right-skewed), not spread over all possible pixel values:

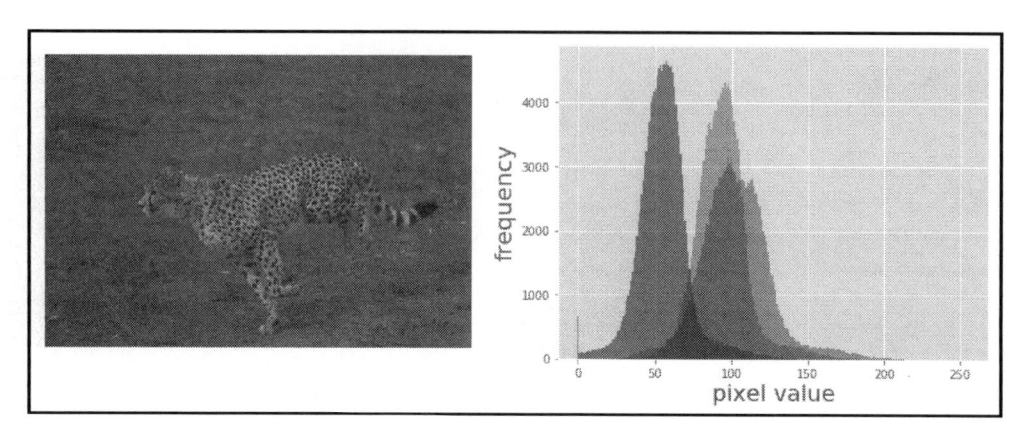

The contrast stretching operation stretches the over-concentrated gray-levels. The transfer function can be thought of as a piece-wise linear function, where the slope in the stretching region is greater than one. This can be seen from the following screenshot:

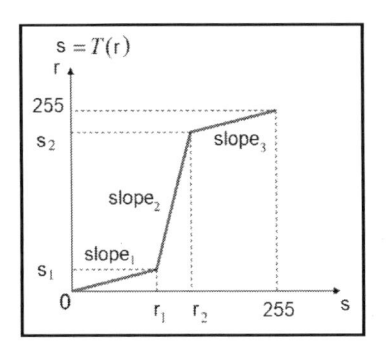

The following code block shows how the PIL `point()` function can be used to implement contrast stretching. The transfer function is defined by the `contrast()` function as a piece wise linear function:

```
def contrast(c):
    return 0 if c < 70 else (255 if c > 150 else (255*c - 22950) / 48) # piece-wise linear function

im1 = im.point(contrast)
im_r, im_g, im_b, _ = im1.split()
pylab.style.use('ggplot')
pylab.screenshot(figsize=(15,5))
pylab.subplot(121)
plot_image(im1)
pylab.subplot(122)
plot_hist(im_r, im_g, im_b)
pylab.yscale('log',basey=10)
pylab.show()
```

Image Enhancement

The following screenshot shows the output. As can be seen, the histogram of each channel has been stretched to the endpoints of the pixel values with the point operation:

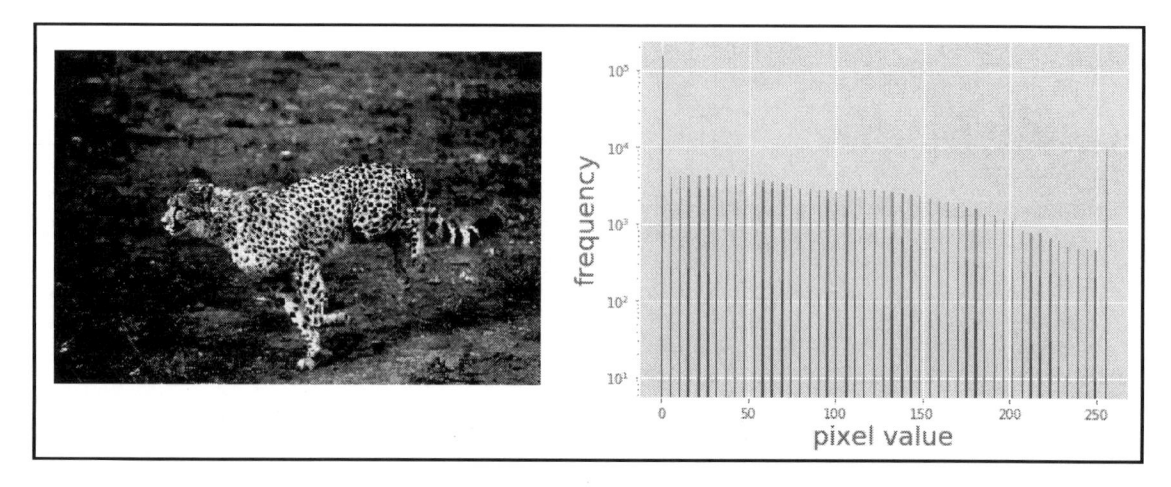

Using the PIL ImageEnhance module

The `ImageEnhance` module can also be used for contrast stretching. The following code block shows how to use the `enhance()` method from the contrast object to enhance the contrast of the same input image:

```
contrast = ImageEnhance.Contrast(im)
im1 = np.reshape(np.array(contrast.enhance(2).getdata()).astype(np.uint8),
 (im.height, im.width, 4)) pylab.style.use('ggplot')
pylab.screenshot(figsize=(15,5))
pylab.subplot(121), plot_image(im1)
pylab.subplot(122), plot_hist(im1[...,0], im1[...,1], im1[...,2])),
pylab.yscale('log',basey=10)
pylab.show()
```

The following shows the output of the code. As can be seen, the contrast of the input image has been enhanced and the color channel histograms are stretched towards the endpoints:

Thresholding

This is a point operation that creates binary images from gray-level ones by turning all pixels below some threshold to zero and all pixels above that threshold to one, as shown in the following screenshot:

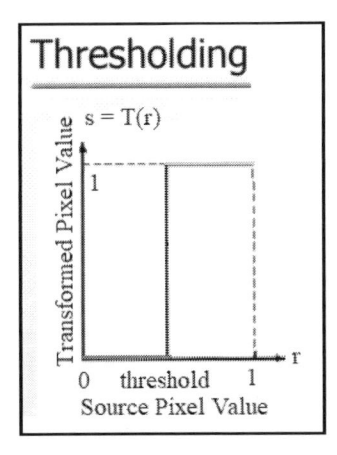

If $g(x, y)$ is a thresholded version of $f(x, y)$ at some global threshold T, then the following can be applied:

$$g(x,y) = \begin{cases} 1, & f(x,y) > T \\ 0, & otherwise \end{cases}$$

Image Enhancement

Why do we need a binary image? A few reasons are, for example, that we may be interested in separating an image into foreground and background; that the image is to be printed with a black and white printer (and all the shades of gray need to be represented using black and white dots only); or that we want to pre-process the image with morphological operations, as we shall discuss later in this chapter.

With a fixed threshold

The following code block shows how to to use the PIL point() function for thresholding with a fixed threshold:

```
im = Image.open('../images/swans.jpg').convert('L')
pylab.hist(np.array(im).ravel(), bins=256, range=(0, 256), color='g')
pylab.xlabel('Pixel values'), pylab.ylabel('Frequency'),
pylab.title('Histogram of pixel values')
pylab.show()
pylab.screenshot(figsize=(12,18))
pylab.subplot(221), plot_image(im, 'original image'), pylab.axis('off')
th = [0, 50, 100, 150, 200]
for i in range(2, 5):
  im1 = im.point(lambda x: x > th[i])
  pylab.subplot(2,2,i), plot_image(im1, 'binary image with threshold=' + str(th[i]))
pylab.show()
```

The following screenshots show the output of the previous code. First, we can see the distribution of the pixel values in the input image from the following:

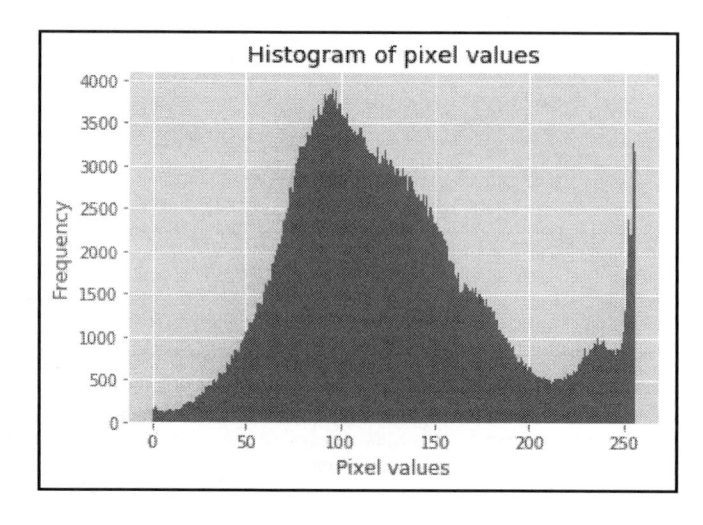

Also, as can be seen from the following, the binary images obtained with different gray-level thresholds are not shaded properly—resulting in an artefact known as *false contours*:

We shall discuss a few different thresholding algorithms in more details in Chapter 6, *Morphological Image Processing*, when we discuss image segmentation.

Image Enhancement

Half-toning

One way to reduce the false contour artefacts in thresholding (binary quantization) is to add uniformly distributed white noise to the input image prior to quantization. Specifically, to each input pixel of the grayscale image, *f(x, y)*, we add an independent uniform [-128,128] random number, and then the thresholding is done. This technique is called half-toning. The following code block shows an implementation:

```
im = Image.open('../images/swans.jpg').convert('L')
im = Image.fromarray(np.clip(im + np.random.randint(-128, 128, (im.height, im.width)), 0, 255).astype(np.uint8))
pylab.screenshot(figsize=(12,18))
pylab.subplot(221), plot_image(im, 'original image (with noise)')
th = [0, 50, 100, 150, 200]
for i in range(2, 5):
  im1 = im.point(lambda x: x > th[i])
  pylab.subplot(2,2,i), plot_image(im1, 'binary image with threshold=' + str(th[i]))
pylab.show()
```

Notice that even though the resulting binary images are somewhat noisy, the false contouring has been dramatically reduced, and with enough blurring (for example, when looking at them from a distance), they give us the impression of having several gray-levels:

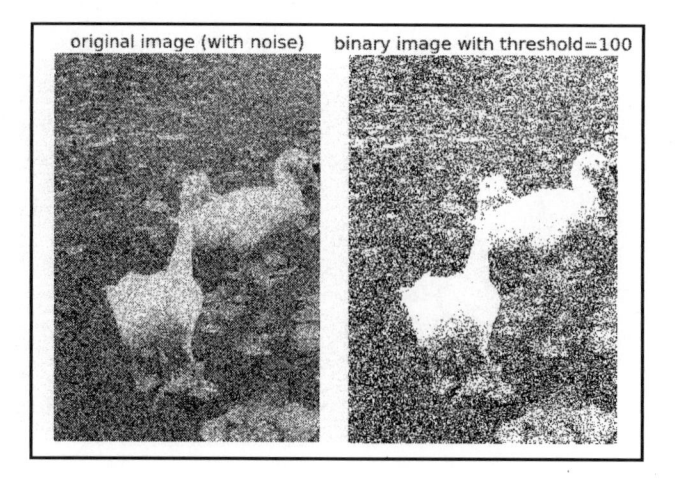

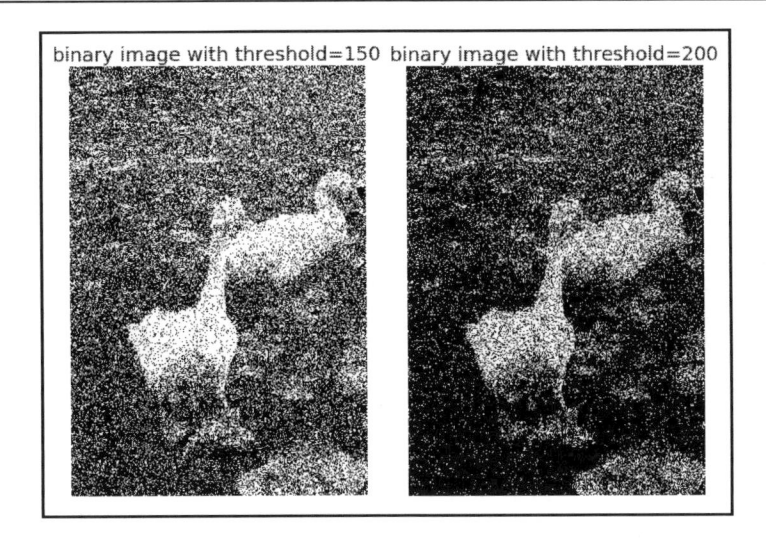

Floyd-Steinberg dithering with error diffusion

Again, in order to prevent large-scale patterns (such as false contours), an intentionally applied form of noise is used to randomize the quantization error. This process is known as **dithering**. The Floyd-Steinberg algorithm implements dithering using the error diffusion technique—in other words, it pushes (adds) the residual quantization error of a pixel onto its neighboring pixels, to be dealt with later. It spreads the quantization error out according to the distribution shown in the following screenshot, as a map of the neighboring pixels:

$$\begin{bmatrix} & & * & \frac{7}{16} & \cdots \\ \cdots & \frac{3}{16} & \frac{5}{16} & \frac{1}{16} & \cdots \end{bmatrix}$$

In the previous screenshot, the current pixel is represented with a star (*) and the blank pixels represent the previously-scanned pixels. The algorithm scans the image from left to right and top to bottom. It sequentially quantizes the pixel values one by one, each time the quantization error is distributed among the neighboring pixels (yet to be scanned), while not affecting the pixels that already got quantized. Hence, if a number of pixels have been rounded downward, it becomes more likely that the following pixel will be rounded upward by the algorithm so that the average quantization error is close to zero.

The following screenshot shows the algorithm pseudocode:

```
for each y from top to bottom
    for each x from left to right
        oldpixel   := pixel[x][y]
        newpixel   := find_closest_palette_color(oldpixel)
        pixel[x][y] := newpixel
        quant_error := oldpixel - newpixel
        pixel[x + 1][y    ] := pixel[x + 1][y    ] + quant_error * 7 / 16
        pixel[x - 1][y + 1] := pixel[x - 1][y + 1] + quant_error * 3 / 16
        pixel[x    ][y + 1] := pixel[x    ][y + 1] + quant_error * 5 / 16
        pixel[x + 1][y + 1] := pixel[x + 1][y + 1] + quant_error * 1 / 16
```

The following screenshot shows the output binary image obtained with a Python implementation of the previous pseudocode; it shows a drastic improvement over the previous half-toning method in the quality of the binary image obtained:

The code is left as an exercise.

Histogram processing – histogram equalization and matching

Histogram processing techniques provide a better method for altering the dynamic range of pixel values in an image so that its intensity histogram has a desired shape. As we have seen, image enhancement by the contrast stretching operation is limited in the sense that it can apply only linear scaling functions.

Histogram processing techniques can be more powerful by employing non-linear (and non-monotonic) transfer functions to map the input pixel intensities to the output pixel intensities. In this section, we shall demonstrate the implementation of a couple of such techniques, namely histogram equalization and histogram matching, using the `scikit-image` library's exposure module.

Contrast stretching and histogram equalization with scikit-image

Histogram equalization uses a monotonic and a non-linear mapping which reassigns the pixel intensity values in the input image in such a way that the output image has a uniform distribution of intensities (a flat histogram), and thereby enhances the contrast of the image. The following screenshot describes the transformation function for histogram equalization:

$$s_k = T(r_k) = \sum_{j=0}^{k} P_r(r_j) = \sum_{j=0}^{k} n_j / N$$

$$0 \leq r_k \leq 1, \quad k = 0,1,2,....,255$$

N: total number of pixels
n_j: frequency of pixel with gray-level j

The following code block shows how to use the exposure module's `equalize_hist()` function to do histogram equalization with scikit-image. The histogram equalization implementation has two different flavors: one is a global operation over the entire image, while the second is local (adaptive) and done by dividing the image into blocks and running histogram equalization on each of them:

```
img = rgb2gray(imread('../images/earthfromsky.jpg'))
# histogram equalization
img_eq = exposure.equalize_hist(img)
# adaptive histogram equalization
img_adapteq = exposure.equalize_adapthist(img, clip_limit=0.03)
pylab.gray()
images = [img, img_eq, img_adapteq]
titles = ['original input (earth from sky)', 'after histogram equalization', 'after adaptive histogram equalization']
for i in range(3):
  pylab.screenshot(figsize=(20,10)), plot_image(images[i], titles[i])
```

Image Enhancement

```
pylab.screenshot(figsize=(15,5))
for i in range(3):
    pylab.subplot(1,3,i+1), pylab.hist(images[i].ravel(), color='g'),
pylab.title(titles[i], size=15)
pylab.show()
```

The following screenshots show the output of the previous code block. As can be seen, after histogram equalization, the output image histogram becomes almost uniform (the *x* axis represents pixel values and the *y* axis corresponding frequencies), although adaptive histogram equalization reveals the details of the image more clearly than the global histogram equalization:

Chapter 4

after adaptive histogram equalization

The following screenshot shows how the distribution of pixels change for local(near-uniform)versus adaptive (stretched and piece-wise uniform) histogram equalization:

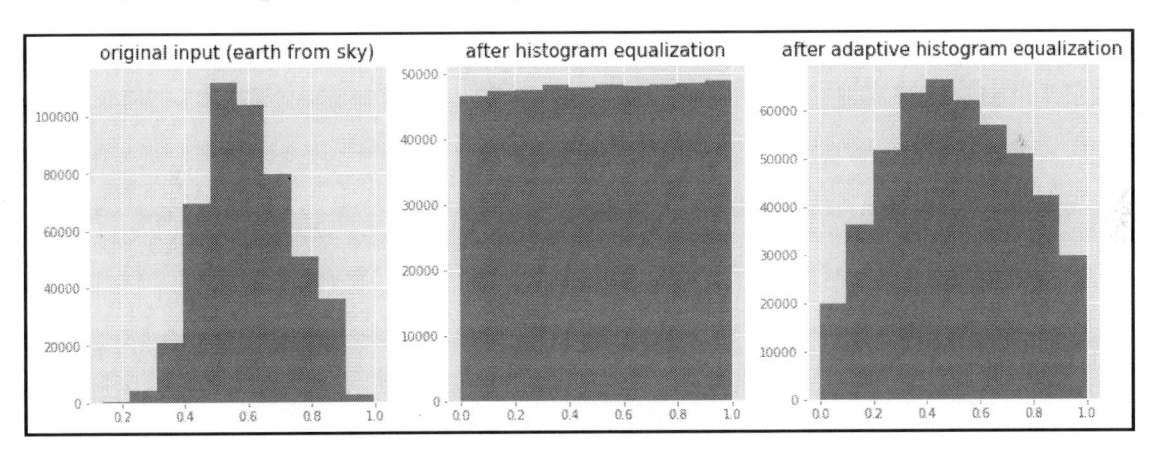

The following code block compares the image enhancements obtained using two different histogram processing techniques, namely contrast stretching and histogram equalization, with `scikit-image`:

```
matplotlib.rcParams['font.size'] = 8

def plot_image_and_hist(image, axes, bins=256):
  image = img_as_float(image)
  axes_image, axes_hist = axes
  axes_cdf = axes_hist.twinx()
  axes_image.imshow(image, cmap=pylab.cm.gray)
```

Image Enhancement

```
    axes_image.set_axis_off()
    axes_hist.hist(image.ravel(), bins=bins, histtype='step', color='black')
    axes_hist.set_xlim(0, 1)
    axes_hist.set_xlabel('Pixel intensity', size=15)
    axes_hist.ticklabel_format(axis='y', style='scientific', scilimits=(0, 0))
    axes_hist.set_yticks([])
    image_cdf, bins = exposure.cumulative_distribution(image, bins)
    axes_cdf.plot(bins, image_cdf, 'r')
    axes_cdf.set_yticks([])
    return axes_image, axes_hist, axes_cdf

im = io.imread('../images/beans_g.png')
p2, p98 = np.percentile(img, (2, 98)) # contrast stretching
im_rescale = exposure.rescale_intensity(im, in_range=(p2, p98))
im_eq = exposure.equalize_hist(im) # histogram equalization
im_adapteq = exposure.equalize_adapthist(im, clip_limit=0.03) # adaptive
histogram equalization

fig = pylab.screenshot(figsize=(15, 7))
axes = np.zeros((2, 4), dtype = np.object)
axes[0, 0] = fig.add_subplot(2, 4, 1)
for i in range(1, 4):
   axes[0, i] = fig.add_subplot(2, 4, 1+i, sharex=axes[0,0], sharey=axes[0,0])
for i in range(0, 4):
   axes[1, i] = fig.add_subplot(2, 4, 5+i)
axes_image, axes_hist, axes_cdf = plot_image_and_hist(im, axes[:, 0])
axes_image.set_title('Low contrast image', size=20)
y_min, y_max = axes_hist.get_ylim()
axes_hist.set_ylabel('Number of pixels', size=20)
axes_hist.set_yticks(np.linspace(0, y_max, 5))
axes_image, axes_hist, axes_cdf = plot_image_and_hist(im_rescale, axes[:, 1])
axes_image.set_title('Contrast stretching', size=20)
axes_image, axes_hist, axes_cdf = plot_image_and_hist(im_eq, axes[:, 2])
axes_image.set_title('Histogram equalization', size=20)
axes_image, axes_hist, axes_cdf = plot_image_and_hist(im_adapteq, axes[:, 3])
axes_image.set_title('Adaptive equalization', size=20)
axes_cdf.set_ylabel('Fraction of total intensity', size=20)
axes_cdf.set_yticks(np.linspace(0, 1, 5))
fig.tight_layout()
pylab.show()
```

Chapter 4

The following screenshot shows the output of the previous code. As can be seen, adaptive histogram equalization provides better results than histogram equalization in terms of making the details of the output image clearer:

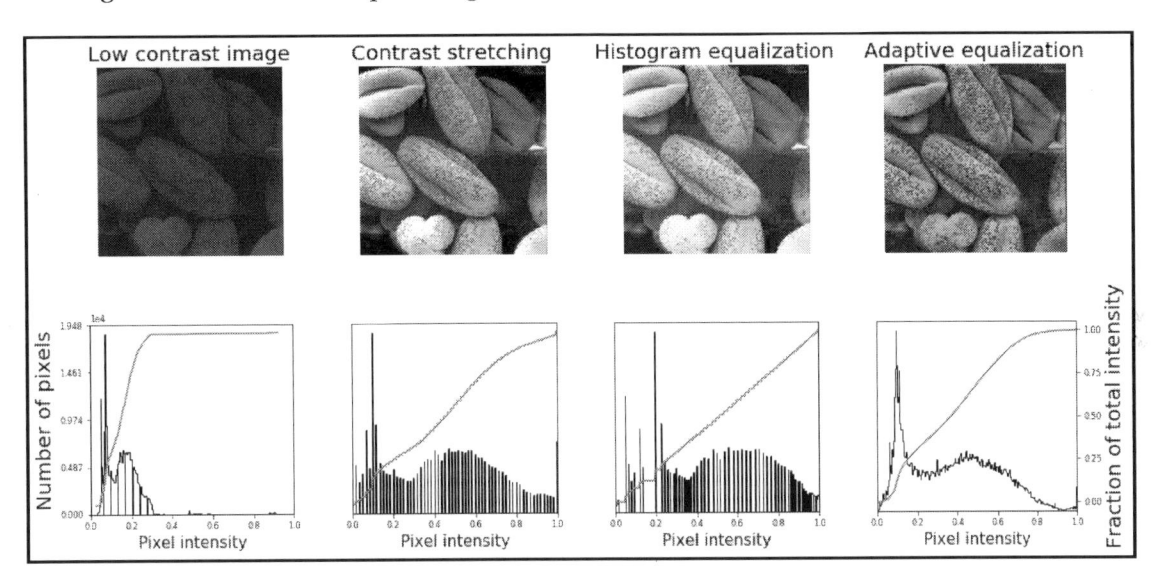

Using the low-contrast colored cheetah input image instead, the previous code produces the following output:

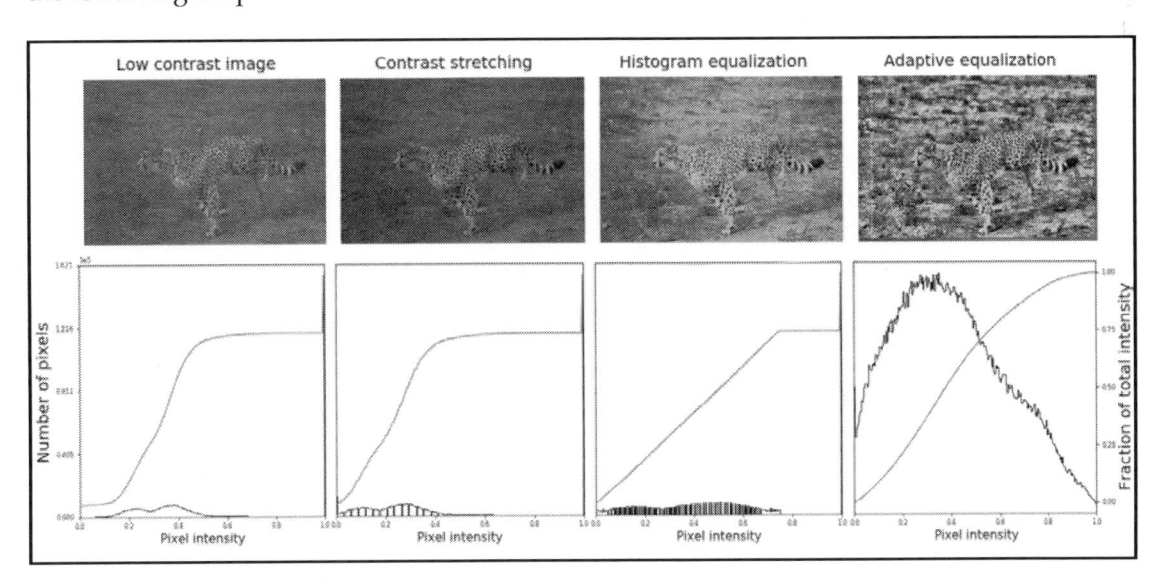

[155]

Histogram matching

Histogram matching is a process where an image is altered in such a way that its histogram matches that of another reference (template) image's histogram. The algorithm is as follows:

1. The cumulative histogram is computed for each image, as shown in the following screenshot.
2. For any given pixel value, x_i, in the input image (to be adjusted), we need to find the corresponding pixel value, x_j, in the output image by matching the input image's histogram with the template image's histogram.
3. The x_i pixel value has a cumulative histogram value given by $G(x_i)$. Find a pixel value, x_j, so that the cumulative distribution value in the reference image, namely $H(x_j)$, is equal to $G(x_i)$.
4. The input data value x_i is replaced by x_j:

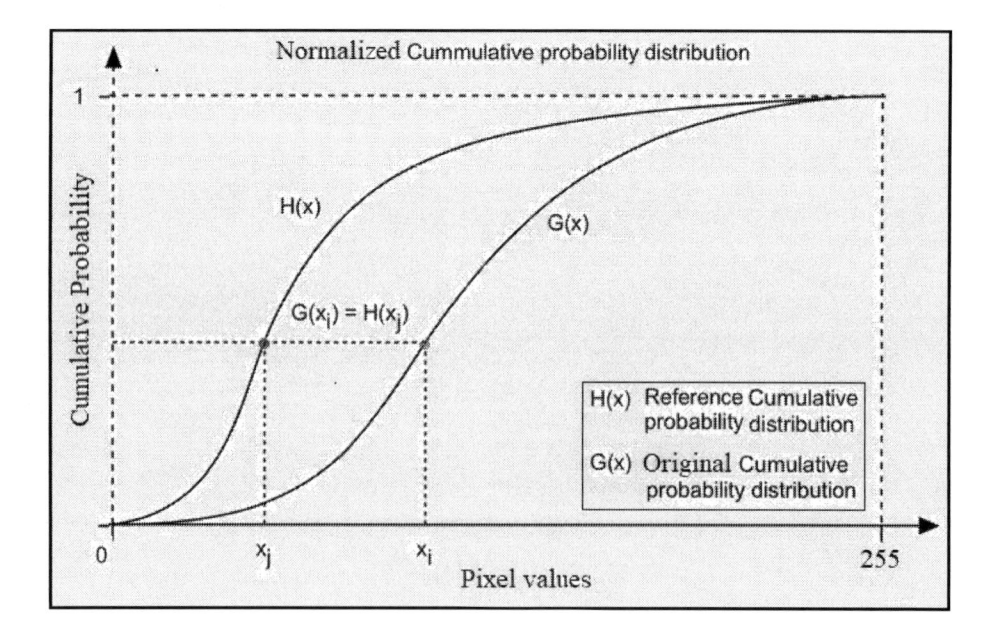

The following code block shows how histogram matching can be implemented using Python:

```
def cdf(im):
    '''
    computes the CDF of an image im as 2D numpy ndarray
    '''
    c, b = cumulative_distribution(im)
    # pad the beginning and ending pixels and their CDF values
    c = np.insert(c, 0, [0]*b[0])
    c = np.append(c, [1]*(255-b[-1]))
    return c

def hist_matching(c, c_t, im):
    '''
    c: CDF of input image computed with the function cdf()
    c_t: CDF of template image computed with the function cdf()
    im: input image as 2D numpy ndarray
    returns the modified pixel values for the input image
    '''
    pixels = np.arange(256)
    # find closest pixel-matches corresponding to the CDF of the input image, given the value of the CDF H of
    # the template image at the corresponding pixels, s.t. c_t = H(pixels) <=> pixels = H-1(c_t)
    new_pixels = np.interp(c, c_t, pixels)
    im = (np.reshape(new_pixels[im.ravel()], im.shape)).astype(np.uint8)
    return im

pylab.gray()
im = (rgb2gray(imread('../images/beans_g.png'))*255).astype(np.uint8)
im_t = (rgb2gray(imread('../images/lena_g.png'))*255).astype(np.uint8)
pylab.screenshot(figsize=(20,12))
pylab.subplot(2,3,1), plot_image(im, 'Input image')
pylab.subplot(2,3,2), plot_image(im_t, 'Template image')
c = cdf(im)
c_t = cdf(im_t)
pylab.subplot(2,3,3)
p = np.arange(256)
pylab.plot(p, c, 'r.-', label='input')
pylab.plot(p, c_t, 'b.-', label='template')
pylab.legend(prop={'size': 15})
pylab.title('CDF', size=20)
im = hist_matching(c, c_t, im)
pylab.subplot(2,3,4), plot_image(im, 'Output image with Hist. Matching')
c1 = cdf(im)
pylab.subplot(2,3,5)
pylab.plot(np.arange(256), c, 'r.-', label='input')
```

Image Enhancement

```
pylab.plot(np.arange(256), c_t, 'b.-', label='template')
pylab.plot(np.arange(256), c1, 'g.-', label='output')
pylab.legend(prop={'size': 15})
pylab.title('CDF', size=20)
pylab.show()
```

The following screenshot shows the output of the previous code. As can be seen, the output bean image's CDF coincides with the input Lena image's CDF after histogram matching, and this enhances the contrast of the low-contrast input bean image:

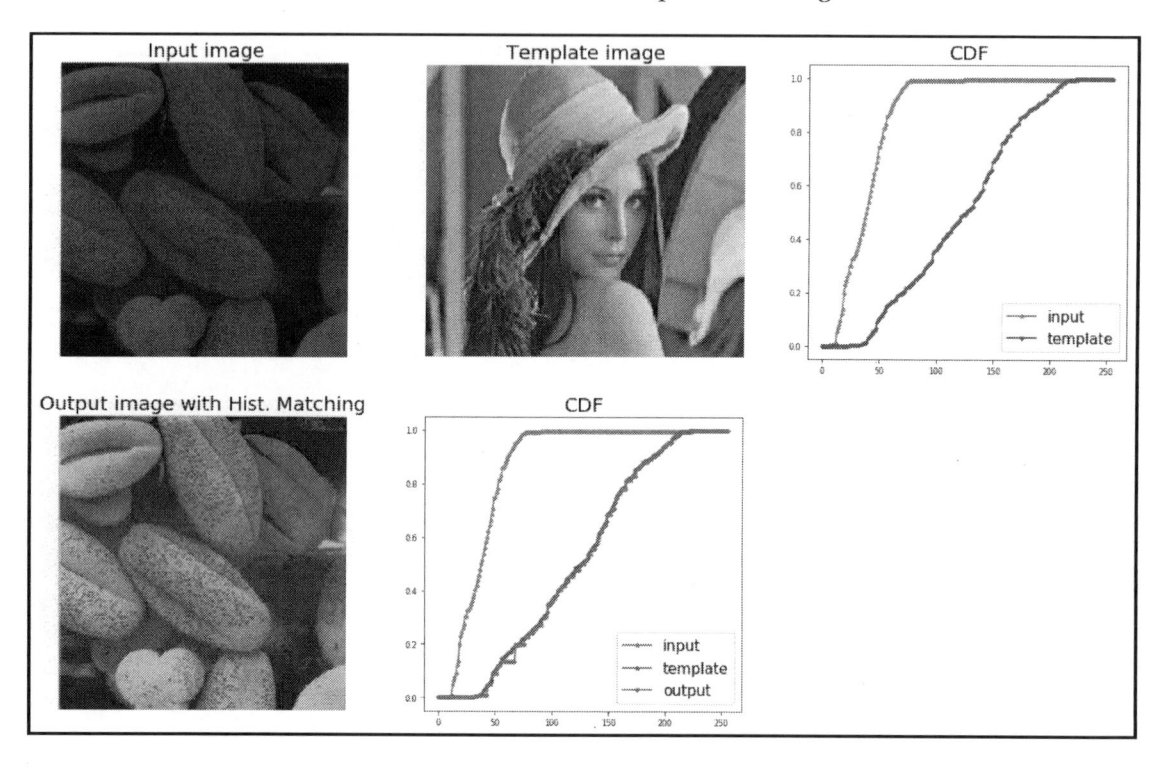

Histogram matching for an RGB image

For each of the color channels, the matching can be done independently to obtain output as in the following:

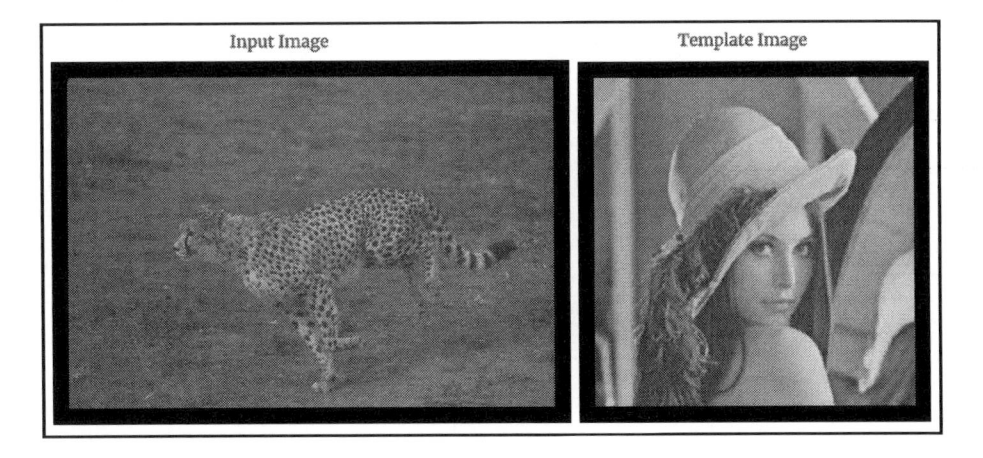

Output image

The Python code to implement this is left to the reader as an exercise (question 1 in the "Questions" section).

Linear noise smoothing

Linear (spatial) filtering is a function with a weighted sum of pixel values (in a neighborhood). It is a linear operation on an image that can be used for blurring/noise reduction. Blurring is used in pre-processing steps; for example, in the removal of small (irrelevant) details. A few popular linear filters are the box filter and the Gaussian filter. The filter is implemented with a small (for example, 3 x 3) kernel (mask), and the pixel values are recomputed by sliding the mask over the input image and applying the filter function to every possible pixel in the input image (the input image's center pixel value corresponding to the mask is replaced by the weighted sum of pixel values, with the weights from the mask). The box filter (also called the averaging filter), for example, replaces each pixel with an average of its neighborhood and achieves a smoothing effect(by removing sharp features; for example, it blurs edges, whereas spatial averaging removes noise).

The following sections illustrate how to apply linear noise smoothing on images first using the PIL `ImageFilter` module and then using the SciPy `ndimage` module's `filter` functions.

Smoothing with PIL

The following sections demonstrate how the functions from the PIL `ImageFilter` module can be used for linear noise smoothing; in other words, noise smoothing with linear filters.

Smoothing with ImageFilter.BLUR

The following shows how the PIL `ImageFilter` module's filter function can be used to apply a blur to denoise a noisy image. The noise level on the input image is varied to see its impact on the blur filter. The popular mandrill (baboon) image is used as the input image for this example; the image is protected by a Creative Commons license (https://creativecommons.org/licenses/by-sa/2.0/) and can be found at https://www.flickr.com/photos/uhuru1701/2249220078 and in the SIPI image database: http://sipi.usc.edu/database/database.php?volume=miscimage=10#top:

```
i = 1
pylab.screenshot(figsize=(10,25))
for prop_noise in np.linspace(0.05,0.3,3):
 im = Image.open('../images/mandrill.jpg')
 # choose 5000 random locations inside image
 n = int(im.width * im.height * prop_noise)
 x, y = np.random.randint(0, im.width, n), np.random.randint(0, im.height,
```

```
n)
    for (x,y) in zip(x,y):
       im.putpixel((x, y), ((0,0,0) if np.random.rand() < 0.5 else
(255,255,255))) # generate salt-and-pepper noise
    im.save('../images/mandrill_spnoise_' + str(prop_noise) + '.jpg')
    pylab.subplot(6,2,i), plot_image(im, 'Original Image with ' +
str(int(100*prop_noise)) + '% added noise')
    i += 1
    im1 = im.filter(ImageFilter.BLUR)
    pylab.subplot(6,2,i), plot_image(im1, 'Blurred Image')
    i += 1

pylab.show()
```

The following screenshot shows the output. The smoothed image quality gets poorer as the input image gets noisier, as expected:

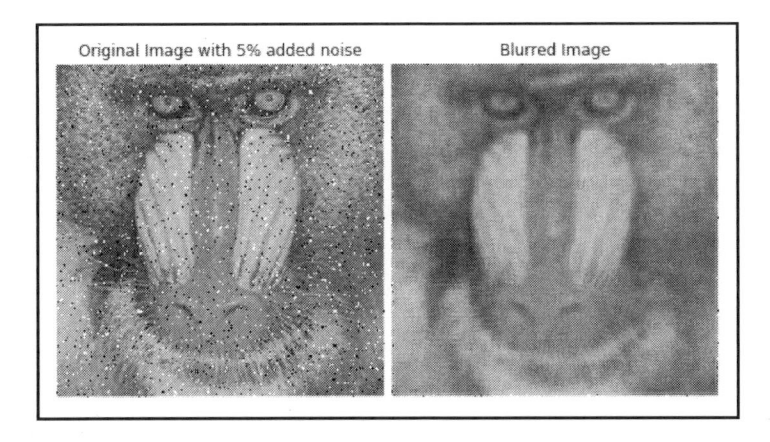

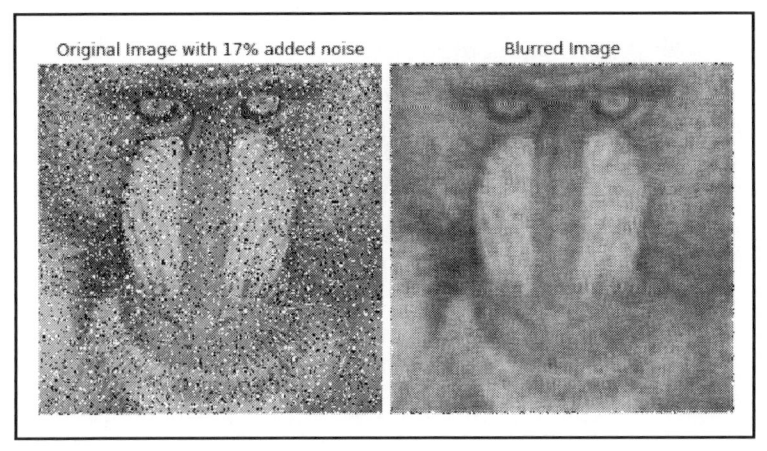

Image Enhancement

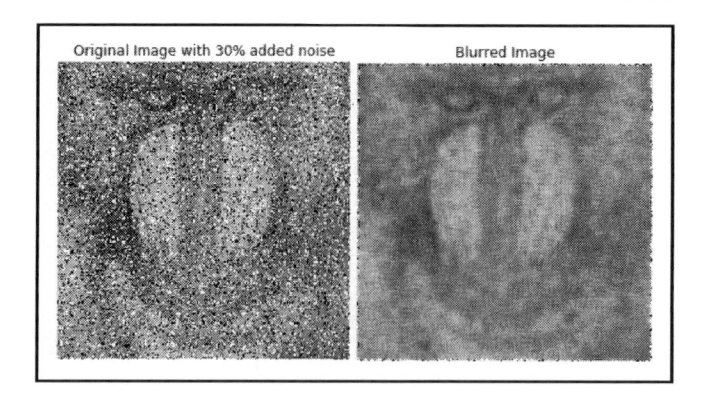

Smoothing by averaging with the box blur kernel

The following code block shows how to use the PIL `ImageFilter.Kernel()` function and box blur kernels (mean filters) of a size of 3 x 3 and 5 x 5 to smooth a noisy image:

```
im = Image.open('../images/mandrill_spnoise_0.1.jpg')
pylab.screenshot(figsize=(20,7))
pylab.subplot(1,3,1), pylab.imshow(im), pylab.title('Original Image',
size=30), pylab.axis('off')
for n in [3,5]:
  box_blur_kernel = np.reshape(np.ones(n*n),(n,n)) / (n*n)
  im1 = im.filter(ImageFilter.Kernel((n,n), box_blur_kernel.flatten()))
  pylab.subplot(1,3,(2 if n==3 else 3))
  plot_image(im1, 'Blurred with kernel size = ' + str(n) + 'x' + str(n))
pylab.suptitle('PIL Mean Filter (Box Blur) with different Kernel size',
size=30)
pylab.show()
```

The following screenshot shows the output of the previous code. As can be seen, the output image is obtained by convolving the larger size box-blur kernel with the noisy image smoothed:

PIL Mean Filter (Box Blur) with different Kernel size
Original Image | Blurred with kernel size = 3x3 | Blurred with kernel size = 5x5

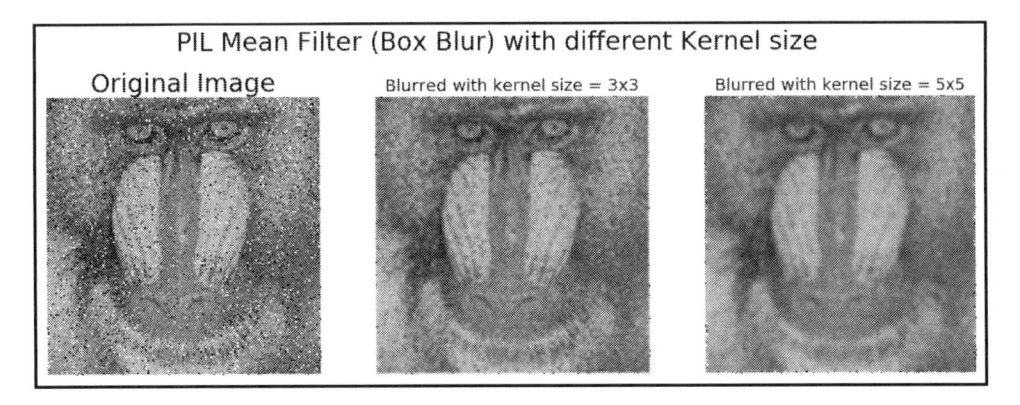

Smoothing with the Gaussian blur filter

The Gaussian blur filter is also a linear filter but, unlike the simple mean filter, it takes the weighted average of the pixels inside the kernel window to smooth a pixel (the weight corresponding to a neighbor pixel decreases exponentially with the distance of the neighbor from the pixel). The following code shows how the PIL `ImageFilter.GaussianBlur()` can be used to smooth a noisier image with different radius parameter values for the kernel:

```
im = Image.open('../images/mandrill_spnoise_0.2.jpg')
pylab.screenshot(figsize=(20,6))
i = 1
for radius in range(1, 4):
    im1 = im.filter(ImageFilter.GaussianBlur(radius))
    pylab.subplot(1,3,i), plot_image(im1, 'radius = ' +
str(round(radius,2)))
    i += 1
pylab.suptitle('PIL Gaussian Blur with different Radius', size=20)
pylab.show()
```

Image Enhancement

The following screenshot shows the output. As can be seen, with a higher radius with the Gaussian filter, the image becomes smoother with the removal of more and more noise, while at the same time blurring the image more:

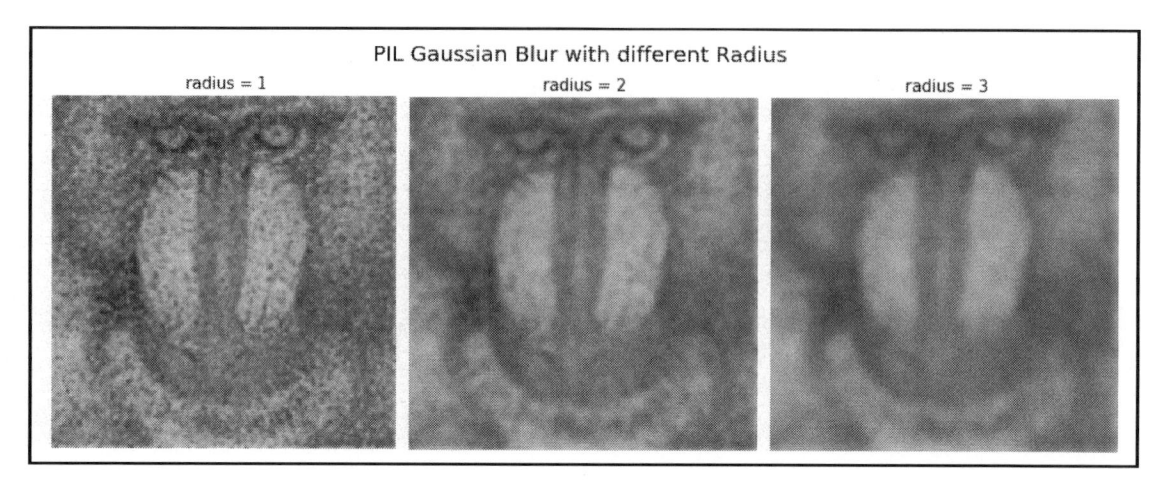

Comparing smoothing with box and Gaussian kernels using SciPy ndimage

We can apply a linear filter to smooth images using SciPy's `ndimage` module functions too. The following code snippet shows a demonstration of the results of applying the linear filters on the mandrill image degraded with impulse (salt-and-pepper) noise:

```
from scipy import misc, ndimage
import matplotlib.pylab as pylab
im = misc.imread('../images/mandrill_spnoise_0.1.jpg')
k = 7 # 7x7 kernel
im_box = ndimage.uniform_filter(im, size=(k,k,1))
s = 2 # sigma value
t = (((k - 1)/2)-0.5)/s # truncate parameter value for a kxk gaussian kernel with sigma s
im_gaussian = ndimage.gaussian_filter(im, sigma=(s,s,0), truncate=t)
fig = pylab.screenshot(figsize=(30,10))
pylab.subplot(131), plot_image(im, 'original image')
pylab.subplot(132), plot_image(im_box, 'with the box filter')
pylab.subplot(133), plot_image(im_gaussian, 'with the gaussian filter')
pylab.show()
```

The following screenshot shows the output of the previous code. As can be seen, the box filter of the same kernel size blurs the output image more than the Gaussian filter of same size with σ=2:

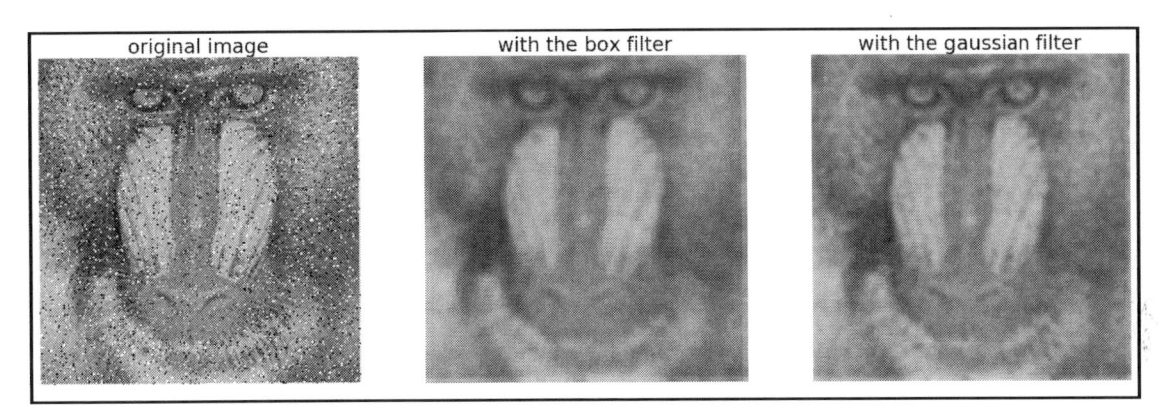

Nonlinear noise smoothing

Nonlinear (spatial) filters also operate on neighborhoods and are implemented by sliding a kernel (mask) over an image like a linear filter. However, the filtering operation is based conditionally on the values of the pixels in the neighborhood, and they do not explicitly use coefficients in the sum-of-products manner in general. For example, noise reduction can be effectively done with a non-linear filter whose basic function is to compute the median gray-level value in the neighborhood where the filter is located. This filter is a nonlinear filter, since the median computation is a non-linear operation. Median filters are quite popular since, for certain types of random noise (for example, impulse noise), they provide excellent noise-reduction capabilities, with considerably less blurring than linear smoothing filters of similar size. Non-linear filters are more powerful than linear filters; for example, in terms of suppression of non-Gaussian noise such as spikes and for edge/texture preserving properties. Some examples of non-linear filters are median, bilateral, non-local means, and morphological filters. The following sections demonstrate the implementation of a few non-linear filters with `PIL`, `scikit-image`, and `scipy ndimage` library functions.

Smoothing with PIL

The PIL `ImageFilter` module provides a set of functions for non-linear denoising of an image. In this section, we shall demonstrate some of them with examples.

Using the median filter

The median filter replaces each pixel with the median of the values of its neighbor pixels. This filter is great for removing of salt-and-pepper noise, although it removes small details from the image. We need to give first rank to the neighborhood intensities and then select the middle value. Median filtering is resilient to statistical outliers, incurs less blurring, and is simple to implement. The following code block shows how the PIL `ImageFilter` module's `MedianFilter()` function can be used to remove salt-and-pepper noise from the noisy mandrill image, with different levels of noise added and a different size of the kernel window used for the median filter:

```
i = 1
pylab.screenshot(figsize=(20,35))
for prop_noise in np.linspace(0.05,0.3,3):
  im = Image.open('../images/mandrill.jpg')
  # choose 5000 random locations inside image
  n = int(im.width * im.height * prop_noise)
  x, y = np.random.randint(0, im.width, n), np.random.randint(0, im.height, n)
  for (x,y) in zip(x,y):
     im.putpixel((x, y), ((0,0,0) if np.random.rand() < 0.5 else (255,255,255))) # geenrate salt-and-pepper noise
  im.save('../images/mandrill_spnoise_' + str(prop_noise) + '.jpg')
  pylab.subplot(6,4,i)
  plot_image(im, 'Original Image with ' + str(int(100*prop_noise)) + '% added noise')
  i += 1
  for sz in [3,7,11]:
     im1 = im.filter(ImageFilter.MedianFilter(size=sz))
     pylab.subplot(6,4,i),   plot_image(im1, 'Output (Median Filter size=' + str(sz) + ')')
     i += 1
pylab.show()
```

The following screenshot shows the output of the previous code, the output images after applying the median filter on the noisy images with different levels of added noise with a different kernel size. As can be seen, the results show that the non-linear median filter works much better for impulse (salt-and-pepper) noise than the linear mean and weighted mean (Gaussian) filters, although with some patchy effects and the loss of some details:

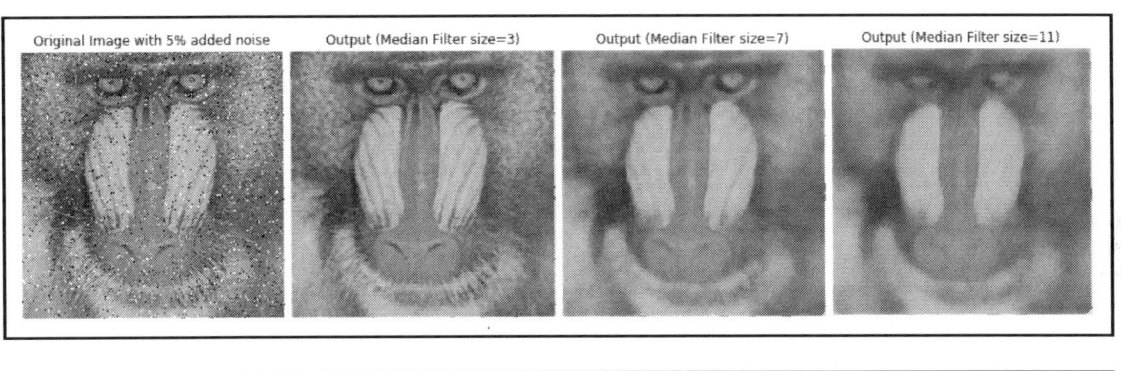

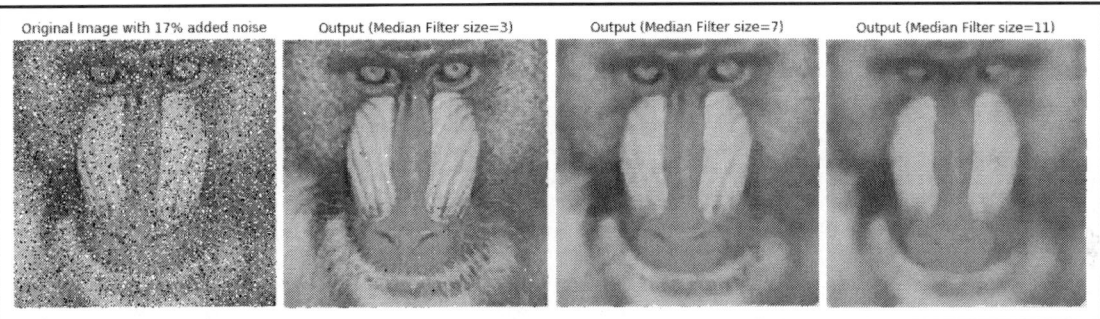

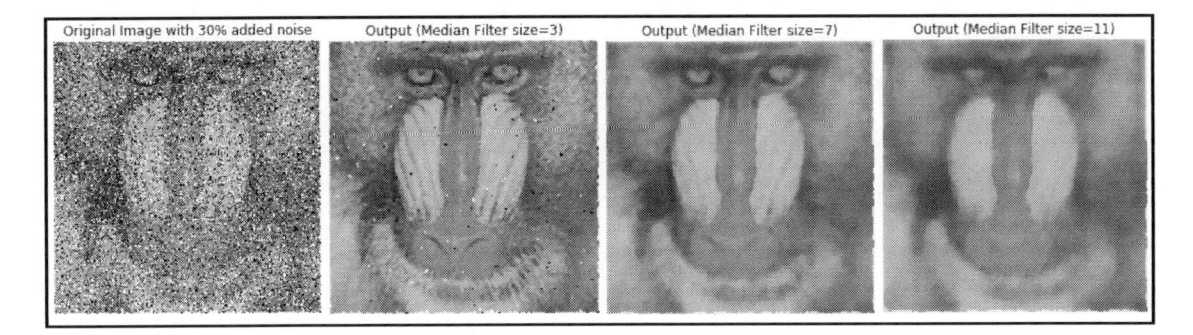

Using max and min filter

The following code shows how to use the `MaxFilter()` to remove the pepper noise followed by a `MinFilter()` to remove the salt noise from an image:

```
im = Image.open('../images/mandrill_spnoise_0.1.jpg')
pylab.subplot(1,3,1)
plot_image(im, 'Original Image with 10% added noise')
im1 = im.filter(ImageFilter.MaxFilter(size=sz))
pylab.subplot(1,3,2), plot_image(im1, 'Output (Max Filter size=' + str(sz) + ')')
im1 = im1.filter(ImageFilter.MinFilter(size=sz))
pylab.subplot(1,3,3), plot_image(im1, 'Output (Min Filter size=' + str(sz) + ')', size=15)
pylab.show()
```

The following screenshot shows the output of the previous code block. It can be seen that the maximum and minimum filters are somewhat effective in removing the salt-and-pepper noise from the noisy image, respectively:

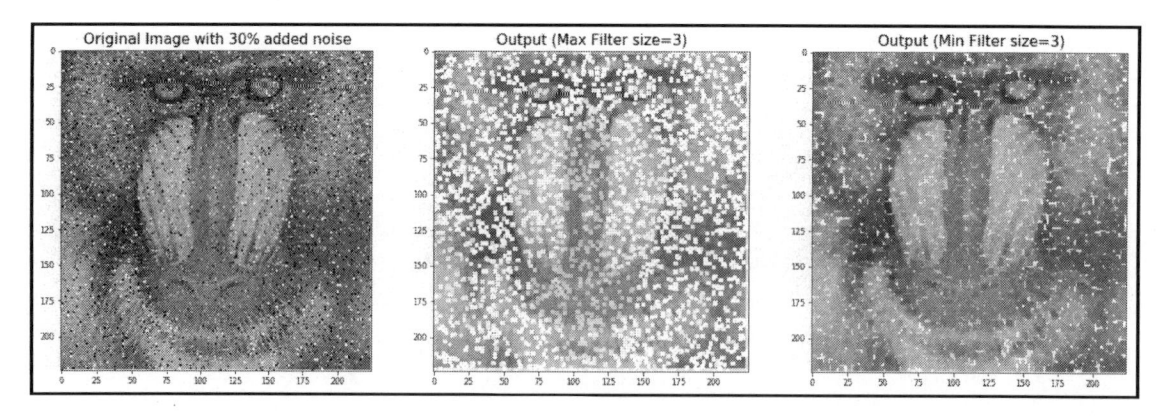

Smoothing (denoising) with scikit-image

The `scikit-image` library also provides a set of non-linear filters in the restoration module. In the following sections, we will discuss about a couple of such very useful filters, namely bilateral and non-local means filters.

Using the bilateral filter

The bilateral filter is an edge-preserving smoothing filter. For this filter, the center pixel is set to the weighted average of the pixel values of some of its neighbors only the ones with roughly similar brightness as the center pixel. In this section, we shall see how we can use `scikit-image` package's bilateral filter implementation to denoise an image. Let us first start by creating a noisy image from the following gray scale mountain image:

The following code block demonstrates how to use the numpy `random_noise()` function:

```
im = color.rgb2gray(img_as_float(io.imread('../images/mountain.png')))
sigma = 0.155
noisy = random_noise(im, var=sigma**2)
pylab.imshow(noisy)
```

Image Enhancement

The following screenshot shows the noisy image created by adding random noise with the original image using the previous code:

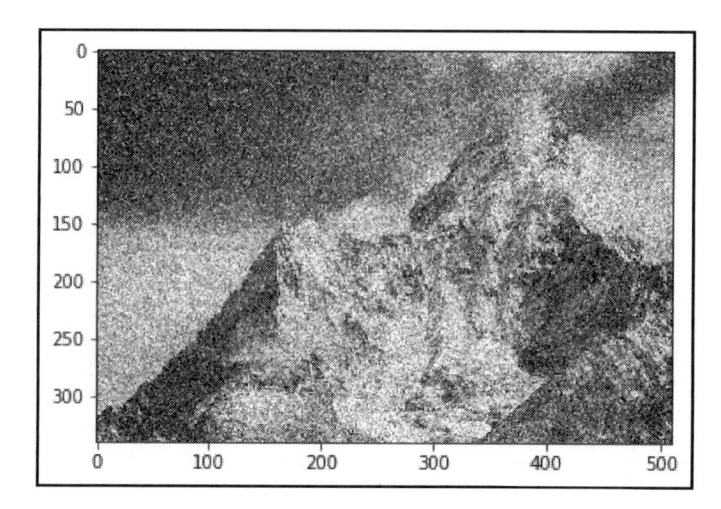

The following code block demonstrates how to use the bilateral filter to denoise the previous noisy image, with different values for the parameters, σ_{color} and $\sigma_{spatial}$:

```
pylab.screenshot(figsize=(20,15))
i = 1
for sigma_sp in [5, 10, 20]:
  for sigma_col in [0.1, 0.25, 5]:
    pylab.subplot(3,3,i)
    pylab.imshow(denoise_bilateral(noisy, sigma_color=sigma_col,
sigma_spatial=sigma_sp,   multichannel=False))
    pylab.title(r'$\sigma_r=$' + str(sigma_col) + r', $\sigma_s=$' +
str(sigma_sp), size=20)
    i += 1
pylab.show()
```

The following screenshot shows the output of the previous code. As can be seen, if the standard deviation is higher, the image gets less noisy but more blurred. It takes a few minutes to execute the previous code block, as the implementation is even slower on RGB images:

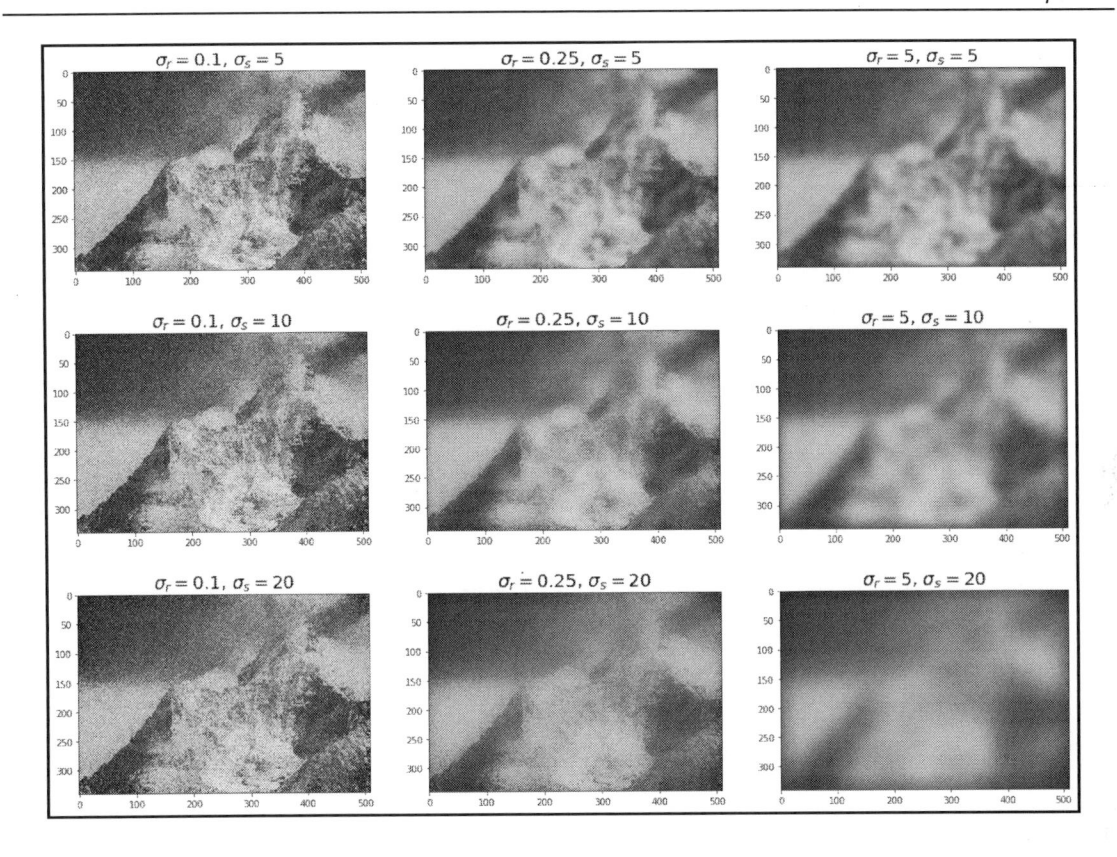

[Grid of 9 images showing denoising results with varying parameters: $\sigma_r = 0.1, 0.25, 5$ across columns and $\sigma_s = 5, 10, 20$ across rows]

Using non-local means

Non-local means is a non-linear denoising algorithm that preserves textures. In this algorithm, for any given pixel, a weighted average of values of only those nearby pixels that have similar local neighbors as the pixel of interest are used to set the value of the given pixel. In other words, small patches centered on the other pixels are compared to the patch centered on the pixel of interest. In this section, we demonstrate the algorithm by denoising a noisy parrot image using the non-local means filter. The h parameter to the function controls the decay in patch weights as a function of the distance between patches. If h is large, it allows more smoothing between dissimilar patches. The following code block shows how to denoise with non-local means:

```
def plot_image_axes(image, axes, title):
    axes.imshow(image)
    axes.axis('off')
    axes.set_title(title, size=20)
```

Image Enhancement

```python
parrot = img_as_float(imread('../images/parrot.png'))
sigma = 0.25
noisy = parrot + sigma * np.random.standard_normal(parrot.shape)
noisy = np.clip(noisy, 0, 1)
# estimate the noise standard deviation from the noisy image
sigma_est = np.mean(estimate_sigma(noisy, multichannel=True))
print("estimated noise standard deviation = {}".format(sigma_est))
# estimated noise standard deviation = 0.22048519002358943
patch_kw = dict(patch_size=5, # 5x5 patches
 patch_distance=6, # 13x13 search area
 multichannel=True)
# slow algorithm
denoise = denoise_nl_means(noisy, h=1.15 * sigma_est, fast_mode=False,
**patch_kw)
# fast algorithm
denoise_fast = denoise_nl_means(noisy, h=0.8 * sigma_est, fast_mode=True,
**patch_kw)
fig, axes = pylab.subplots(nrows=2, ncols=2, figsize=(15, 12), sharex=True,
sharey=True)
plot_image_axes(noisy, axes[0, 0], 'noisy')
plot_image_axes(denoise, axes[0, 1], 'non-local means\n(slow)')
plot_image_axes(parrot, axes[1, 0], 'original\n(noise free)')
plot_image_axes(denoise_fast, axes[1, 1], 'non-local means\n(fast)')
fig.tight_layout()
# PSNR metric values
psnr_noisy = compare_psnr(parrot, noisy)
psnr = compare_psnr(parrot, denoise.astype(np.float64))
psnr_fast = compare_psnr(parrot, denoise_fast.astype(np.float64))
print("PSNR (noisy) = {:0.2f}".format(psnr_noisy))
print("PSNR (slow) = {:0.2f}".format(psnr))
print("PSNR (fast) = {:0.2f}".format(psnr_fast))
# PSNR (noisy) = 13.04 # PSNR (slow) = 26.25 # PSNR (fast) = 25.84
pylab.show()
```

The following screenshot shows the output. As can be seen, the slow version of the algorithm achieves better PSNR than the faster version, representing a trade-off. Both of the algorithm output images have much higher PSNR than the noisy image:

Smoothing with scipy ndimage

The scipy `ndimage` module provides a function named `percentile_filter()`, which is a generic version of the median filter. The following code block demonstrates how to use this filter:

```
lena = misc.imread('../images/lena.jpg')
# add salt-and-pepper noise to the input image
noise = np.random.random(lena.shape)
lena[noise > 0.9] = 255
lena[noise < 0.1] = 0
plot_image(lena, 'noisy image')
pylab.show()
fig = pylab.screenshot(figsize=(20,15))
i = 1
for p in range(25, 100, 25):
 for k in range(5, 25, 5):
    pylab.subplot(3,4,i), filtered = ndimage.percentile_filter(lena, percentile=p, size=(k,k,1))
    plot_images(filtered, str(p) + ' percentile, ' + str(k) + 'x' + str(k) + ' kernel')
    i += 1
pylab.show()
```

[173]

Image Enhancement

The following screenshot shows the output of the previous code. As can be seen, out of all of the percentile filters, the median filter (corresponding to the 50th percentile) with a small kernel size does the best to remove salt-and-pepper noise, while at the same time losing the fewest possible details in the image:

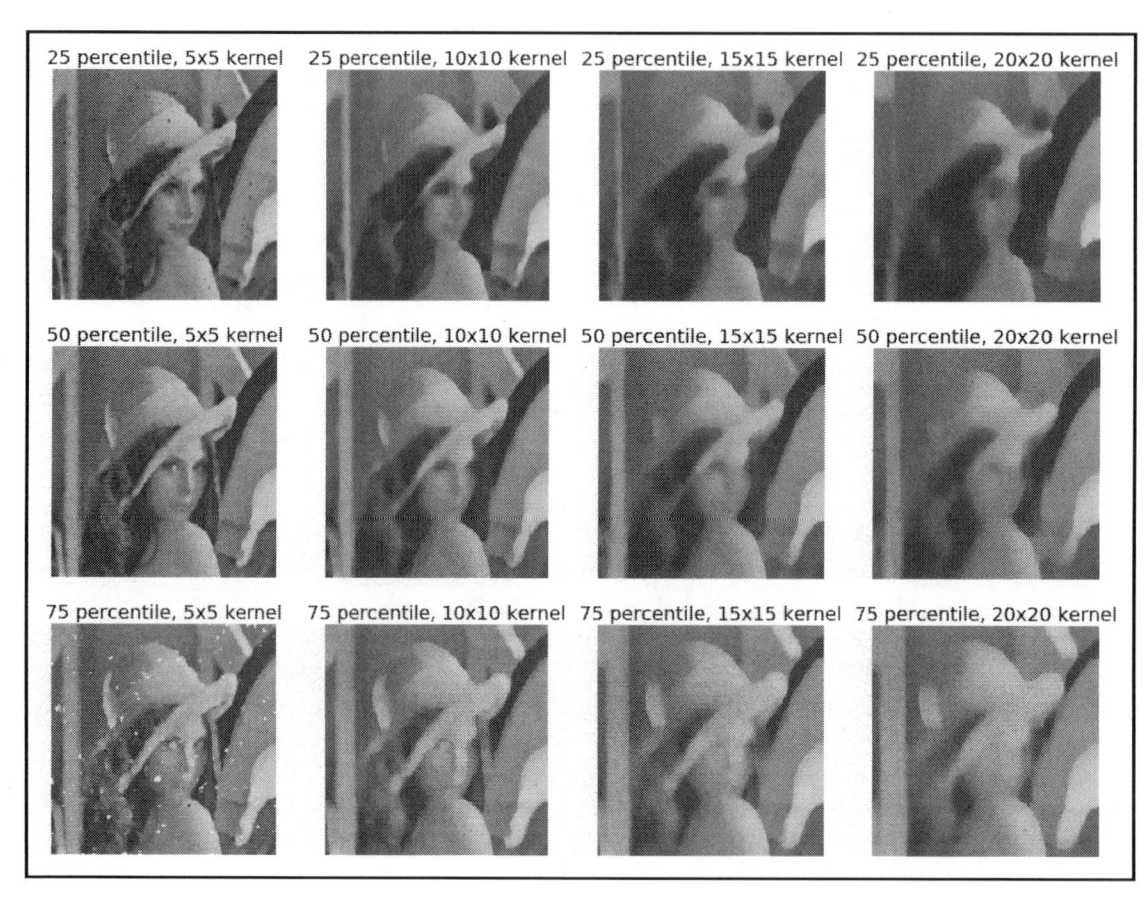

Summary

In this chapter, we discussed different image enhancement methods, starting from point transformations (for example, contrast stretching and thresholding), then techniques based on histogram processing (for example, histogram equalization and histogram matching), followed by image denoising techniques with linear (for example, mean and Gaussian) and non-linear (for example, median, bilateral, and non-local means) filters.

By the end of this chapter, the reader should be able to write Python codes for point transformations (for example, negative, power-law transform, and contrast stretching), histogram-based image enhancements (for example, histogram equalization/matching), and image denoising (for example, mean/median filters).

In the following chapter, we shall continue discussing more image enhancement techniques based on image derivatives and gradients.

Questions

1. Implement histogram matching for colored RGB images.
2. Use the `equalize()` function from `skimage.filters.rank` to implement local histogram equalization and compare it with the global histogram equalization from `skimage.exposure` with a grayscale image.
3. Implement Floyd-Steinberg error-diffusion dithering using the algorithm described here https://en.wikipedia.org/wiki/Floyd%E2%80%93Steinberg_dithering and convert a grayscale image into a binary image.
4. Use `ModeFilter()` from PIL for linear smoothing with an image. When is it useful?
5. Show an image that can be recovered from a few noisy images obtained by adding random Gaussian noise to the original image by simply taking the average of the noisy images. Does taking the median also work?

Further reading

- http://paulbourke.net/miscellaneous/equalisation/
- https://pdfs.semanticscholar.org/presentation/3fb7/fa0fca1bab83d523d882e98efa0f5769ec64.pdf
- https://www.comp.nus.edu.sg/~cs4243/doc/SciPy%20reference.pdf
- https://en.wikipedia.org/wiki/Floyd%E2%80%93Steinberg_dithering
- https://en.wikipedia.org/wiki/Floyd%E2%80%93Steinberg_dithering

5
Image Enhancement Using Derivatives

In this chapter, we shall continue our discussion on image enhancement, which is the problem of improving the appearance or usefulness of an image. We shall concentrate mainly on spatial filtering techniques to compute image gradients/derivatives, and how these techniques can be used for edge detection in an image. First, we shall start with the basic concepts of image gradients using the first order (partial) derivatives, how to compute the discrete derivatives, and then discuss the second order Derivative/Laplacian. We shall see how they can be used to find edges in an image. Next, we shall discuss a few ways to sharpen/unsharp mask an image using the Python image processing libraries PIL, the filter module of `scikit-image`, and the `ndimage` module of SciPy. Next, we shall see how to use different filters (`sobel`, `canny`, `LoG`, and so on) and convolve them with the image to detect edges in an image. Finally, we shall discuss how to compute Gaussian/Laplacian image pyramids (with `scikit-image`) and use the image pyramids to blend two images smoothly. The topics to be covered in this chapter are as follows:

- Image Derivatives—Gradient, Laplacian
- Sharpening and unsharp masking (with PIL, `scikit-image`, SciPy `ndimage`)
- Edge detection using derivatives and filters (Sobel, Canny, LOG, DOG, and so on with PIL, `scikit-image`)
- Image pyramids (Gaussian and Laplacian)—Blending images (with `scikit-image`)

Image derivatives – Gradient and Laplacian

We can compute the (partial) derivatives of a digital image using finite differences. In this section, let us discuss how to compute the image derivatives, Gradient and Laplacian, and why they are useful. As usual, let us start by importing the required libraries, as shown in the following code block:

```
import numpy as np
from scipy import signal, misc, ndimage
from skimage import filters, feature, img_as_float
from skimage.io import imread
from skimage.color import import rgb2gray
from PIL import Image, ImageFilter
import matplotlib.pylab as pylab
```

Derivatives and gradients

The following diagram shows how to compute the **partial derivatives** of an image I (which is a function $f(x, y)$), using **finite differences** (with **forward** and **central** differences, the latter one being more accurate), which can be implemented using convolution with the kernels shown. The diagram also defines the gradient vector, its magnitude (which corresponds to the strength of an edge), and direction (perpendicular to an edge). Locations where the intensity (gray level value) changes sharply in an input image correspond to the locations where there are peaks/spikes (or valleys) in the intensity of the first-order derivative(s) of the image. In other words, the peaks in gradient magnitude mark the edge locations, and we need to threshold the gradient magnitude to find edges in an image:

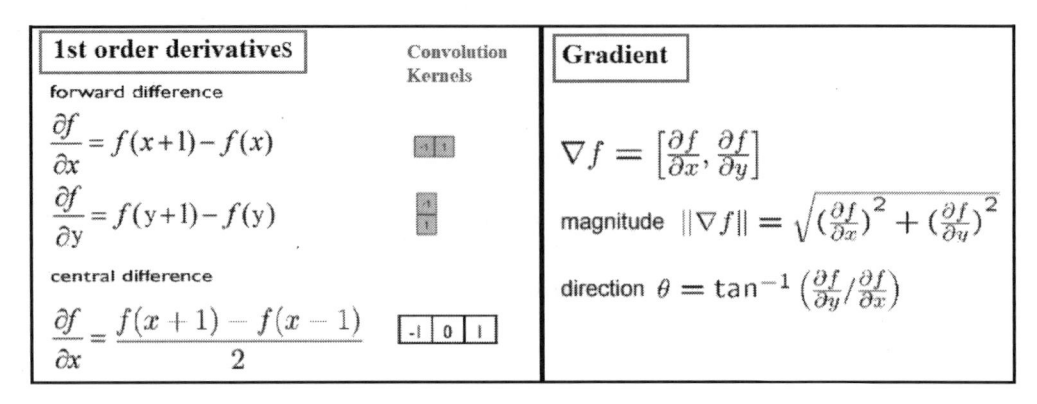

1st order derivatives	Convolution Kernels	Gradient
forward difference $\frac{\partial f}{\partial x} = f(x+1) - f(x)$ $\frac{\partial f}{\partial y} = f(y+1) - f(y)$ central difference $\frac{\partial f}{\partial x} = \frac{f(x+1) - f(x-1)}{2}$		$\nabla f = \left[\frac{\partial f}{\partial x}, \frac{\partial f}{\partial y}\right]$ magnitude $\|\nabla f\| = \sqrt{\left(\frac{\partial f}{\partial x}\right)^2 + \left(\frac{\partial f}{\partial y}\right)^2}$ direction $\theta = \tan^{-1}\left(\frac{\partial f}{\partial y} / \frac{\partial f}{\partial x}\right)$

The following code block shows how to compute the gradient (along with the magnitude and the direction) with the convolution kernels shown previously, with the gray-scale chess image as input. It also plots how the image pixel values and the x-component of the gradient vector changes with the y coordinates for the very first row in the image (x=0):

```
def plot_image(image, title):
    pylab.imshow(image), pylab.title(title, size=20), pylab.axis('off')

ker_x = [[-1, 1]]
ker_y = [[-1], [1]]
im = rgb2gray(imread('../images/chess.png'))
im_x = signal.convolve2d(im, ker_x, mode='same')
im_y = signal.convolve2d(im, ker_y, mode='same')
im_mag = np.sqrt(im_x**2 + im_y**2)
im_dir = np.arctan(im_y/im_x)
pylab.gray()
pylab.figure(figsize=(30,20))
pylab.subplot(231), plot_image(im, 'original'), pylab.subplot(232),
plot_image(im_x, 'grad_x')
pylab.subplot(233), plot_image(im_y, 'grad_y'), pylab.subplot(234),
plot_image(im_mag, '||grad||')
pylab.subplot(235), plot_image(im_dir, r'$\theta$'), pylab.subplot(236)
pylab.plot(range(im.shape[1]), im[0,:], 'b-', label=r'$f(x,y)|_{x=0}$',
linewidth=5)
pylab.plot(range(im.shape[1]), im_x[0,:], 'r-', label=r'$grad_x
(f(x,y))|_{x=0}$')
pylab.title(r'$grad_x (f(x,y))|_{x=0}$', size=30)
pylab.legend(prop={'size': 20})
pylab.show()
```

Image Enhancement Using Derivatives

The following diagram shows the output of the preceding code block. As can be seen from the following diagram, the partial derivatives in the x and y directions detect the vertical and horizontal edges in the image, respectively. The gradient magnitude shows the strength of the edges at different locations in the image. Also, if we pick all the pixels from the original image corresponding to a single row (row 0, for instance), we can see a square wave (corresponding to alternating white and black intensity patterns), whereas the gradient magnitude for the same set of pixels have spikes (a sudden increase/decrease) in intensity, and these correspond to the (vertical) edges:

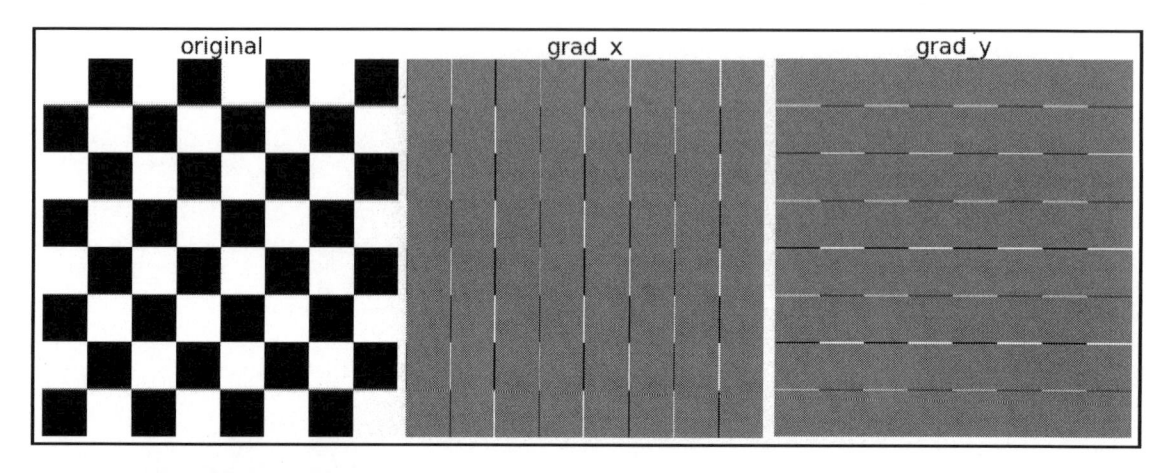

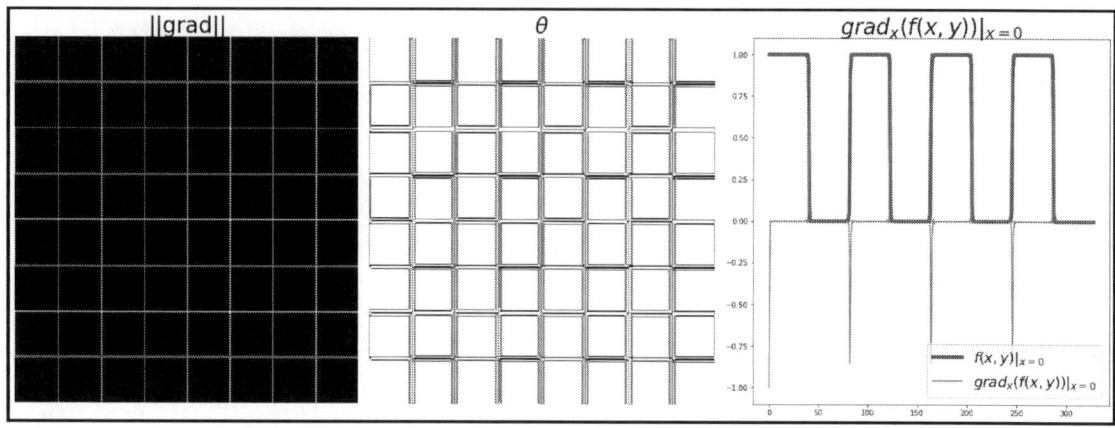

Displaying the magnitude and the gradient on the same image

In the earlier example, the magnitude and direction of the edges were shown in different images. We can create an RGB image and set the *R*, *G*, and *B* values as follows to display both magnitude and direction in the same image:

$$\begin{cases} g(x,y,R) = |\nabla I(x,y)|.\sin(\theta) \\ g(x,y,G) = |\nabla I(x,y)|.\cos(\theta) \\ g(x,y,B) = 0 \end{cases}$$

With the same code as in the last example, we only replace the right bottom subplot code with the following code:

```
im = np.zeros((im.shape[0],im.shape[1],3))
im[...,0] = im_mag*np.sin(im_ang)
im[...,1] = im_mag*np.cos(im_ang)
pylab.title(r'||grad||+$\theta$', size=30), pylab.imshow(im),
pylab.axis('off')
```

And then, using a tiger image instead, we get the output shown in the following screenshot. The last subplot shows both the magnitude and the direction of edges with colors:

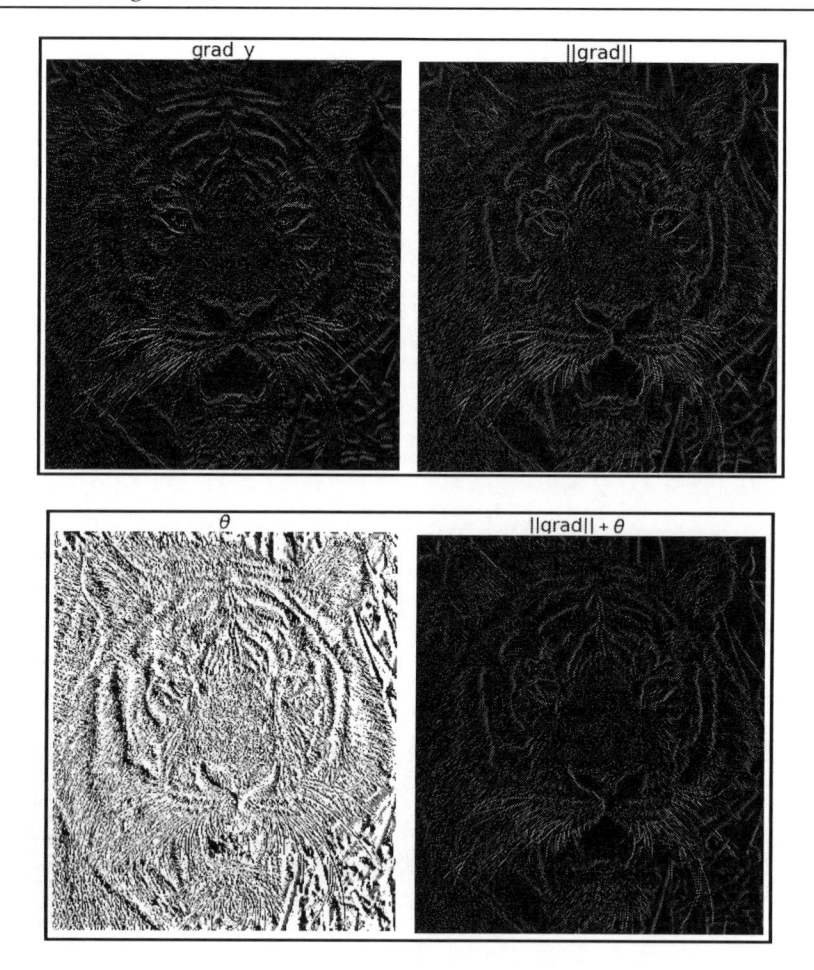

Laplacian

It has been shown by Rosenfeld and Kak that the simplest **isotropic** derivative operator is the Laplacian, which is defined as shown in the following diagram. The Laplacian approximates the second derivative of an image and detects edges. It is an isotropic (rotationally invariant) operator and the zero-crossings mark edge location; we shall discuss more about that later in the chapter. In other words, in locations where we have spikes/peaks (or valleys) in the first-order derivative(s) of an input image, we have **zero-crossings** in the corresponding locations of the second-order derivative(s) of the input image:

2nd order derivative

$$\frac{\partial^2 f}{\partial x^2} = f(x+1) + f(x-1) - 2f(x)$$

$$\frac{\partial^2 f}{\partial y^2} = f(y+1) + f(y-1) - 2f(y)$$

Convolution Kernel

	1	
1	-4	1
	1	

Laplacian

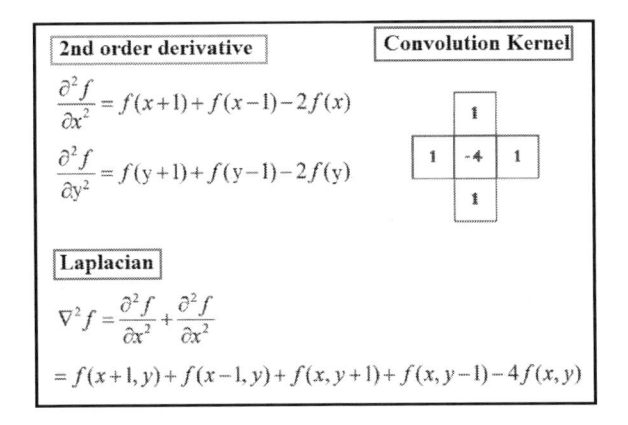

$$\nabla^2 f = \frac{\partial^2 f}{\partial x^2} + \frac{\partial^2 f}{\partial x^2}$$

$$= f(x+1,y) + f(x-1,y) + f(x,y+1) + f(x,y-1) - 4f(x,y)$$

Some notes about the Laplacian

Let's take a look at the following notes:

- $\nabla^2 f(x,y)$ is a scalar (unlike the gradient, which is a vector)
- A single kernel (mask) is used to compute the Laplacian (unlike the gradient where we usually have two kernels, the partial derivatives in the *x* and *y* directions, respectively)
- Being a scalar, it does not have any direction and hence we lose the orientation information
- $\nabla^2 f(x,y)$ is the sum of the **second-order partial derivatives** (the gradient represents a vector consisting of the first-order partial derivatives), but the higher the order of the derivative, the more is the increase in noise
- Laplacian is very sensitive to noise
- Hence, the Laplacian is always preceded by a smoothing operation (for example, with a Gaussian filter), otherwise the noise can be greatly aggravated

The following code snippet shows how to compute the Laplacian of an image using convolution with the kernel shown previously:

```
ker_laplacian = [[0,-1,0],[-1, 4, -1],[0,-1,0]]
im = rgb2gray(imread('../images/chess.png'))
im1 = np.clip(signal.convolve2d(im, ker_laplacian, mode='same'),0,1)
pylab.gray()
pylab.figure(figsize=(20,10))
pylab.subplot(121), plot_image(im, 'original')
pylab.subplot(122), plot_image(im1, 'laplacian convolved')
pylab.show()
```

Image Enhancement Using Derivatives

The following screenshot shows the output of the preceding code snippet. As can be seen, the Laplacian output also finds the edges in the image:

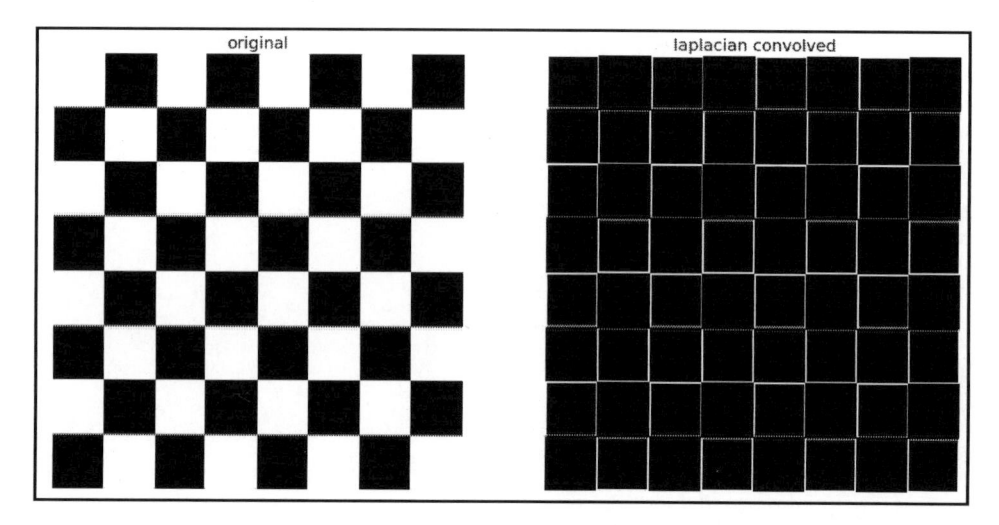

Effects of noise on gradient computation

Derivative filters computed using finite difference are quite sensitive to noise. As we saw in the last chapter, the pixels in an image that have very different intensity values from their neighbors are generally the noise pixels. In general, the more the noise the larger the change in intensity, and the stronger is the response obtained with the filters. The next code block adds some Gaussian noise to the image to see the effects on the gradient. Let us again consider a single row (row 0, precisely) of the image, and let us plot the intensity as a function of the *x* location:

```
from skimage.util import random_noise
sigma = 1 # sd of noise to be added
im = im + random_noise(im, var=sigma**2)
```

The following diagram shows the output of the previous code block after adding some random noise to the chess image. As we can see, adding random noise to the input image has a high impact on the (partial) derivatives and the gradient magnitude; the peaks corresponding to the edges become almost indistinguishable from the noise and the pattern gets destroyed:

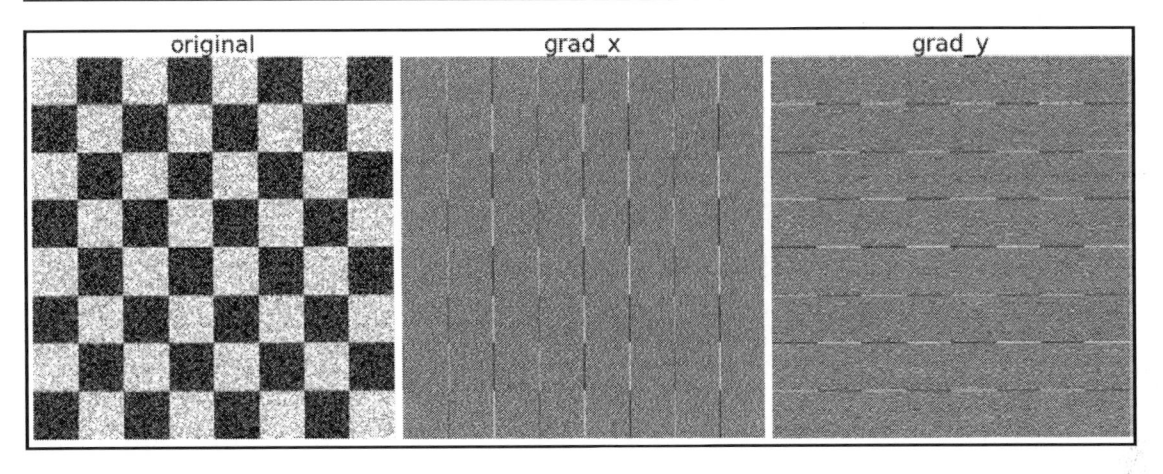

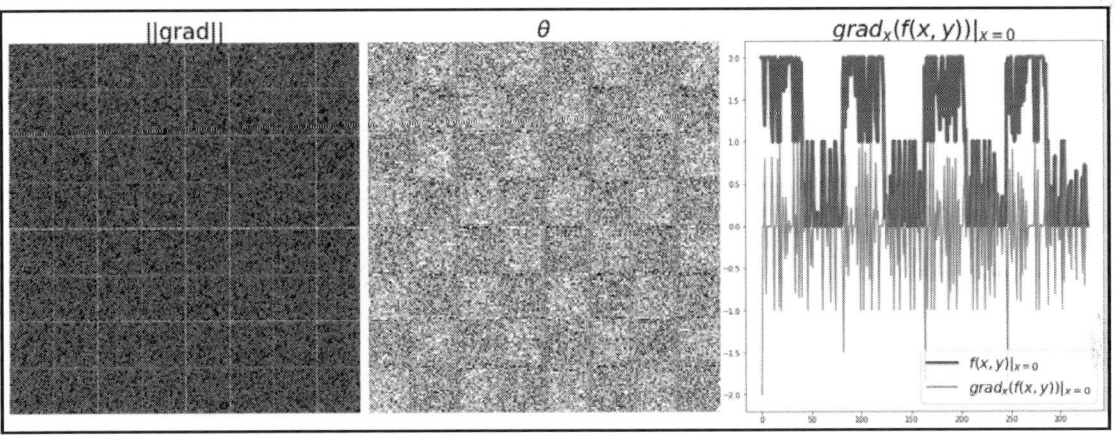

Smoothing the image before applying the derivative filter should be helpful, as it removes the high frequency components likely to be noise and forces the (noisy) pixels (that are different from their neighbors) to look more like their neighbors. Hence, the solution is to first smooth the input image with an LPF (such as the Gaussian filter) and then find peaks (using a threshold) in the smoothed image. This gives rise to the LoG filter (if we use the second-order derivative filter) that we shall explore later in this chapter.

Sharpening and unsharp masking

The objective of sharpening is to highlight detail in an image or to enhance detail that has been blurred. In this section, we discuss a few techniques along with a few examples demonstrating a couple of different ways to sharpen an image.

Sharpening with Laplacian

An image can be sharpened using the Laplacian filter with the following couple of steps:

1. Apply the Laplacian filter to the original input image.
2. Add the output image obtained from *step 1* and the original input image (to obtain the sharpened image). The following code block demonstrates how to implement the preceding algorithm using `scikit-image filters` module's `laplace()` function:

```
from skimage.filters import laplace
im = rgb2gray(imread('../images/me8.jpg'))
im1 = np.clip(laplace(im) + im, 0, 1)
pylab.figure(figsize=(20,30))
pylab.subplot(211), plot_image(im, 'original image')
pylab.subplot(212), plot_image(im1, 'sharpened image')
pylab.tight_layout()
pylab.show()
```

The following is the output of the preceding code block, the original image, and the sharpened image using the previous algorithm:

sharpened image

Unsharp masking

Unsharp masking is a technique to sharpen images, where a **blurred** version of an image is subtracted from the image itself. The typical blending formula used for **unsharp masking** is as follows: *sharpened = original + (original − blurred) × amount*.

Here, *amount* is a parameter. The next few sections demonstrate how to implement this with the `ndimage` module of SciPy functions in Python.

With the SciPy ndimage module

As discussed, we can first blur an image and then compute the detail image as the difference between the original and the blurred image to implement unsharp masking. The sharpened image can be computed as a linear combination of the original image and the detail image. The following diagram illustrates the concept again:

```
Original Image  -  Smoothed Image     =  Detail Image
                   (with Gaussian Filter)

Original Image  +  α.(Detail Image)   =  Sharpened Image
```

Image Enhancement Using Derivatives

The following code block shows how the unsharp mask operation can be implemented with the SciPy `ndimage` module for a gray-scale image (the same can be done with a color image, which is left as an exercise for the reader), using the preceding concept:

```python
def rgb2gray(im):
    '''
    the input image is an RGB image
    with pixel values for each channel in [0,1]
    '''
    return np.clip(0.2989 * im[...,0] + 0.5870 * im[...,1] + 0.1140 * im[...,2], 0, 1)

im = rgb2gray(img_as_float(misc.imread('../images/me4.jpg')))
im_blurred = ndimage.gaussian_filter(im, 5)
im_detail = np.clip(im - im_blurred, 0, 1)
pylab.gray()
fig, axes = pylab.subplots(nrows=2, ncols=3, sharex=True, sharey=True, figsize=(15, 15))
axes = axes.ravel()
axes[0].set_title('Original image', size=15), axes[0].imshow(im)
axes[1].set_title('Blurred image, sigma=5', size=15),
axes[1].imshow(im_blurred)
axes[2].set_title('Detail image', size=15), axes[2].imshow(im_detail)
alpha = [1, 5, 10]
for i in range(3):
  im_sharp = np.clip(im + alpha[i]*im_detail, 0, 1)
  axes[3+i].imshow(im_sharp),  axes[3+i].set_title('Sharpened image, alpha=' + str(alpha[i]), size=15)
for ax in axes:
  ax.axis('off')
fig.tight_layout()
pylab.show()
```

The following screenshot shows the output of the preceding code block. As can be seen, the output gets sharper as the value of α is increased:

Edge detection using derivatives and filters (Sobel, Canny, and so on)

As discussed earlier, the pixels that construct the edges in an image are the ones where there are sudden rapid changes (discontinuities) in the image intensity function, and the goal of edge detection is to identify these changes. Hence, edge detection is a preprocessing technique where the input is a 2D (gray-scale) image and the output is a set of curves (that are called the **edges**). The salient features of an image are extracted in the edges detection process; an image representation using edges is more compact than one using pixels. The edge detectors output the magnitude of the gradients (as a gray-scale image), and now, to get the edge pixels (as a binary image), we need to threshold the gradient image. Here, a very simple fixed gray-level thresholding is used (assigning all negative-valued pixels to zero with the `numpy's clip()` function); to obtain the binary images, we can use more sophisticated methods (such as thresholding using ostu's segmentation), as we shall see later in Chapter 8, *Image Segmentation*. Let's start on the edge detectors with gradient magnitude computed using finite-difference approximations of the partial derivatives, and then proceed on to the Sobel filter.

With gradient magnitude computed using the partial derivatives

Gradient magnitude (which can be thought of as the strength of edges) computed using (forward) finite-difference approximations of the partial derivatives can be used for edge detection, as we saw earlier. The following screenshot shows the output obtained by using the same code as the previous time to compute the gradient magnitude, and then clip the pixel values in a [0, 1] interval, with the zebra's input gray-scale image:

The following screenshot shows the gradient magnitude image. As can be seen, the edges appear to be thicker and multipixel wide:

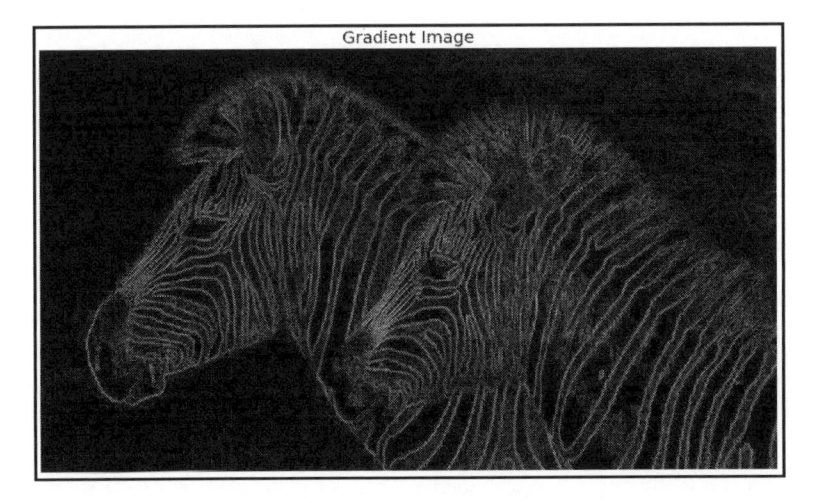

Image Enhancement Using Derivatives

In order to obtain a binary image with each edge one-pixel wide, we need to apply the **non-maximum suppression** algorithm, which removes a pixel if it is not a local maximum along the gradient direction in the pixel's neighborhood. The implementation of the algorithm is left as an exercise for the reader. The following screenshot shows the output with **non-max suppression**:

After Non-Maximum suppression

The non-maximum suppression algorithm

1. The algorithm starts by inspecting the angles (directions) of the edges (output by the edge detector).
2. If a pixel value is non-maximum in a line tangential to its edge angle, it is a candidate to be removed from the edge map.
3. This is implemented by splitting the edge direction (360) into eight equal intervals with an angle of 22.50 degrees. The following table shows different cases and the actions to take:

edge direction	pixels to compare
horizontal	top and bottom
vertical	left and right
north west or south east	top right and bottom left
north east or south west	bottom right and top left

4. We may do this by looking in a π/8 range and setting the tangential comparison accordingly with a series of if conditions.
5. The effect of edge thinning is clearly observed (from the previous image) when comparing the gradient image with and without the non-maximum suppression.

Sobel edge detector with scikit-image

The (first order) derivatives can be approximated better than using the finite difference. The Sobel operators shown in the following diagram are used quite frequently:

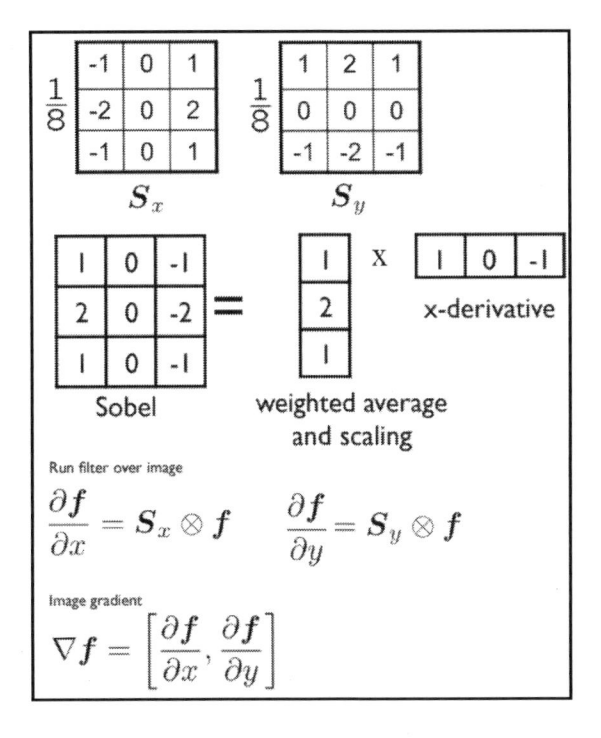

$$\frac{\partial f}{\partial x} = S_x \otimes f \qquad \frac{\partial f}{\partial y} = S_y \otimes f$$

$$\nabla f = \left[\frac{\partial f}{\partial x}, \frac{\partial f}{\partial y} \right]$$

Image Enhancement Using Derivatives

The 1/8 term is not included in the standard definition of the Sobel operator as for edge detection purposes, it does not make a difference, although the normalization term is needed to get the gradient value correctly. The next Python code snippet shows how to use the `sobel_h()`, `sobel_y()`, and `sobel()` functions of the `filters` module of `scikit-image` to find the horizontal/vertical edges and compute the gradient magnitude using the Sobel operators, respectively:

```python
im = rgb2gray(imread('../images/tajmahal.jpg')) # RGB image to gray scale
pylab.gray()
pylab.figure(figsize=(20,18))
pylab.subplot(2,2,1)
plot_image(im, 'original')
pylab.subplot(2,2,2)
edges_x = filters.sobel_h(im)
plot_image(edges_x, 'sobel_x')
pylab.subplot(2,2,3)
edges_y = filters.sobel_v(im)
plot_image(edges_y, 'sobel_y')
pylab.subplot(2,2,4)
edges = filters.sobel(im)
plot_image(edges, 'sobel')
pylab.subplots_adjust(wspace=0.1, hspace=0.1)
pylab.show()
```

The following screenshot shows the output of the preceding code block. As can be seen, the horizontal and vertical edges of the image are detected by the horizontal and vertical Sobel filters, whereas the gradient magnitude image computed using the Sobel filter detects the edges in both directions:

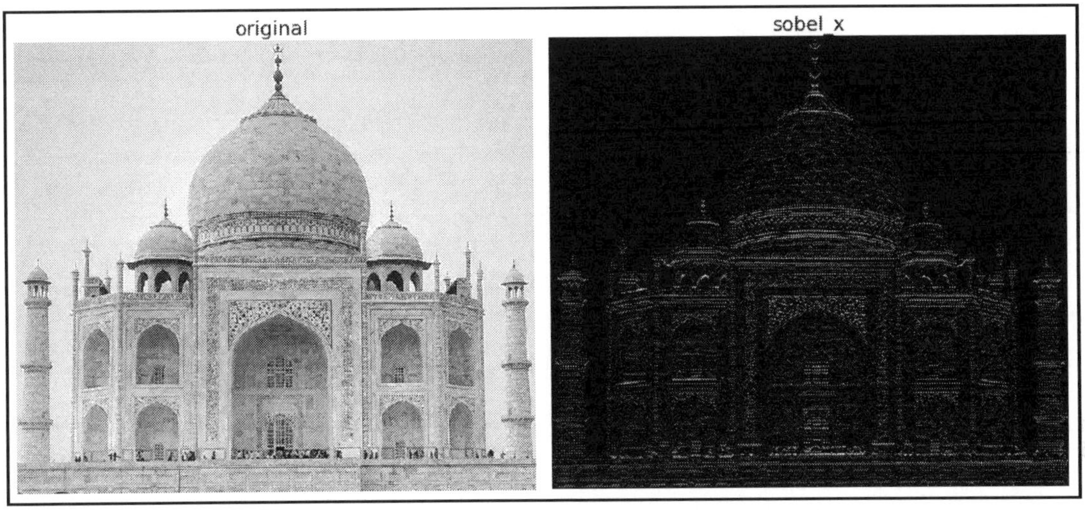
original
sobel_x

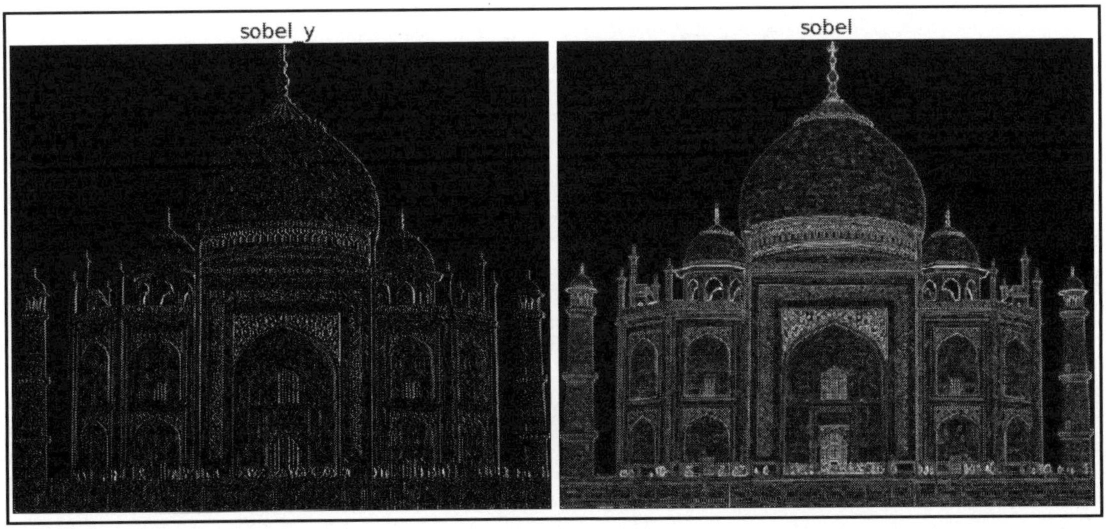
sobel_y
sobel

Different edge detectors with scikit-image – Prewitt, Roberts, Sobel, Scharr, and Laplace

There are quite a few different edge detection operators used in image processing algorithms; all of them are discrete (first or second order) differentiation operators and they try to approximate the gradient of the image intensity function (for instance, the Sobel operator, which we discussed previously). The kernels shown in the following diagram are a few popular ones used for edge detection. For example, popular derivative filters approximating the **1st Order** image derivatives are Sobel, Prewitt, Sharr, and Roberts filters, whereas a derivative filter approximating the **2nd Order** derivatives is the Laplacian:

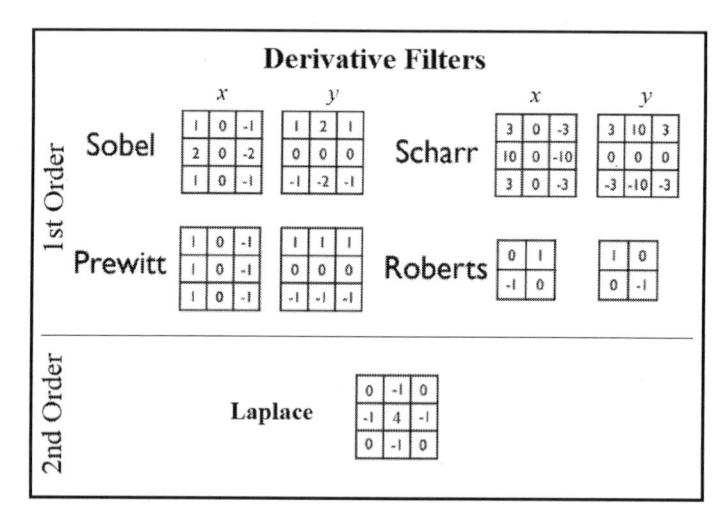

Derivative Filters

	x	y
Sobel	1 0 -1 / 2 0 -2 / 1 0 -1	1 2 1 / 0 0 0 / -1 -2 -1
Prewitt	1 0 -1 / 1 0 -1 / 1 0 -1	1 1 1 / 0 0 0 / -1 -1 -1

	x	y
Scharr	3 0 -3 / 10 0 -10 / 3 0 -3	3 10 3 / 0 0 0 / -3 -10 -3
Roberts	0 1 / -1 0	1 0 / 0 -1

Laplace: 0 -1 0 / -1 4 -1 / 0 -1 0

(1st Order: Sobel, Prewitt, Scharr, Roberts; 2nd Order: Laplace)

As discussed in the `scikit-image` documentation, the finite-difference approximations of the gradient computed by different operators are different. For example, the Sobel filter in general performs better than the Prewitt filter, whereas the Scharr filter results in a less rotational variance than the Sobel filter. The following code block applies different edge detector filters on the golden gate gray-scale image, and shows the gradient magnitudes obtained:

```
im = rgb2gray(imread('../new images/goldengate.jpg')) # RGB image to gray
scale
pylab.gray()
pylab.figure(figsize=(20,24))
pylab.subplot(3,2,1), plot_image(im, 'original')
edges = filters.roberts(im)
pylab.subplot(3,2,2), plot_image(edges, 'roberts')
edges = filters.scharr(im)
pylab.subplot(3,2,3), plot_image(edges, 'scharr')
```

```
edges = filters.sobel(im)
pylab.subplot(3,2,4), plot_image(edges, 'sobel')
edges = filters.prewitt(im)
pylab.subplot(3,2,5), plot_image(edges, 'prewitt')
edges = np.clip(filters.laplace(im), 0, 1)
pylab.subplot(3,2,6), plot_image(edges, 'laplace')
pylab.subplots_adjust(wspace=0.1, hspace=0.1)
pylab.show()
```

The following screenshot shows the output of the preceding code block:

prewitt | laplace

Again, a post-processing step for edge detection is non-maximum suppression that thins the (thick) edges obtained using the first order derivatives; we have not previously done this operation. In the next section, as we shall see, a more advanced state-of-the-art edge detector, Canny, does it automatically.

The Canny edge detector with scikit-image

The Canny edge detector is a popular edge detection algorithm, developed by John F. Canny. This algorithm has the following multiple steps:

1. **Smoothing/noise reduction**: The edge detection operation is sensitive to noise. Hence, at the very outset, a 5 x 5 Gaussian filter is used to remove noise from the image.
2. **Computing magnitude and orientation of the gradient**: The Sobel horizontal and vertical filters are then applied to the image to compute the edge gradient **magnitude** and **direction** for each pixel, as discussed previously. The gradient angle (direction) computed is then rounded to one of four angles representing horizontal, vertical, and two diagonal directions for each pixel.
3. **Non-maximum suppression**: In this step, the edges are thinned – any unwanted pixels which may not constitute an edge are removed. To do this, every pixel is checked if it is a local maximum in its neighborhood in the direction of gradient. As a result, a binary image is obtained with thin edges.

4. **Linking and hysteresis thresholding**: In this step, whether all the edges detected are strong edges or not is decided. For this, a couple of (hysteresis) threshold values, min_val and max_val, are used. Sure edges are the ones that have an intensity gradient value higher than max_val. Sure non-edges are the ones that have an intensity gradient value below min_val, and they are discarded. The edges that lie between these two thresholds are classified as edges or non-edges, based on their connectivity. If they are connected to sure-edge pixels, they are considered to be part of edges. Otherwise, they are also discarded. This step also removes small pixel noise (assuming that the edges are long lines).

So finally, the algorithm outputs the strong edges of the image. The following code block shows how the Canny edge detector can be implemented with scikit-image:

```
im = rgb2gray(imread('../images/tiger3.jpg'))
im = ndimage.gaussian_filter(im, 4)
im += 0.05 * np.random.random(im.shape)
edges1 = feature.canny(im)
edges2 = feature.canny(im, sigma=3)
fig, (axes1, axes2, axes3) = pylab.subplots(nrows=1, ncols=3, figsize=(30, 12), sharex=True, sharey=True)
axes1.imshow(im, cmap=pylab.cm.gray), axes1.axis('off'),
axes1.set_title('noisy image', fontsize=50)
axes2.imshow(edges1, cmap=pylab.cm.gray), axes2.axis('off')
axes2.set_title('Canny filter, $\sigma=1$', fontsize=50)
axes3.imshow(edges2, cmap=pylab.cm.gray), axes3.axis('off')
axes3.set_title('Canny filter, $\sigma=3$', fontsize=50)
fig.tight_layout()
pylab.show()
```

The following screenshot shows the output of the previous code; the edges are detected with the Canny filter with different sigma values for the initial Gaussian LPF. As can be seen, with a lower value of sigma, the original image gets less blurred to start with and hence more edges (finer details) can be found:

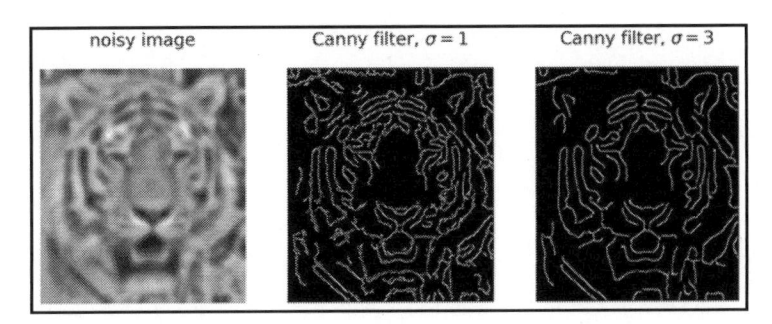

The LoG and DoG filters

Laplacian of a Gaussian (LoG) is just another linear filter which is a combination of Gaussian followed by the Laplacian filter on an image. Since the 2nd derivative is very sensitive to noise, it is always a good idea to remove noise by smoothing the image before applying the Laplacian to ensure that noise is not aggravated. Because of the associative property of convolution, it can be thought of as taking the 2nd derivative (Laplacian) of the Gaussian filter and then applying the resulting (combined) filter onto the image, hence the name LoG. It can be efficiently approximated using the difference of two Gaussians (DoG) with different scales (variances), as shown in the following diagram:

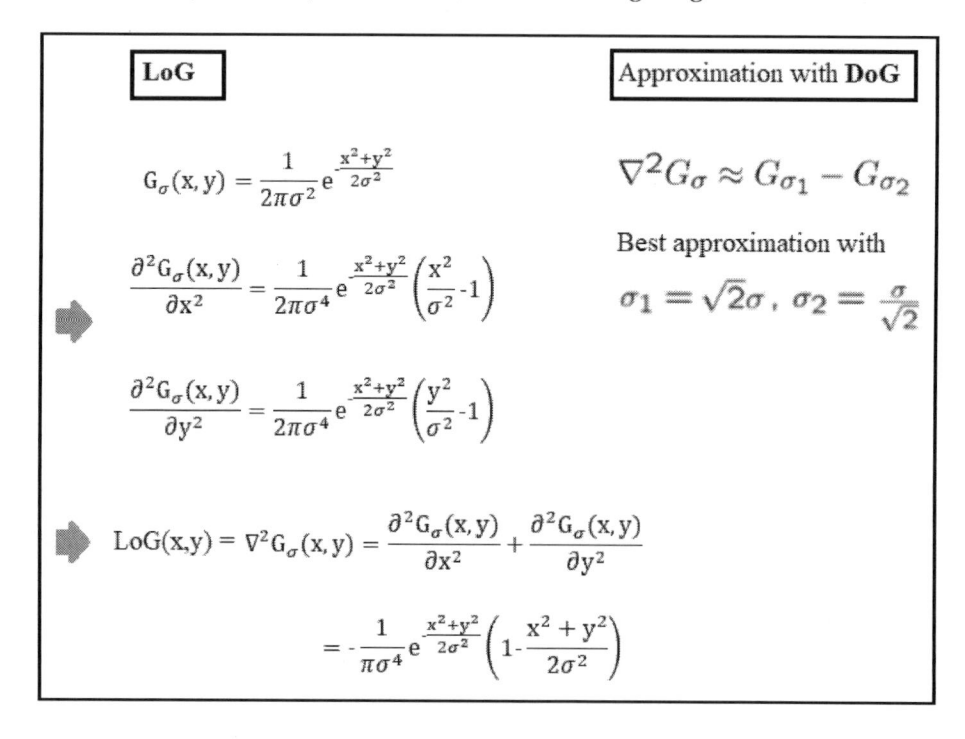

LoG	Approximation with DoG
$G_\sigma(x,y) = \dfrac{1}{2\pi\sigma^2} e^{-\frac{x^2+y^2}{2\sigma^2}}$	$\nabla^2 G_\sigma \approx G_{\sigma_1} - G_{\sigma_2}$
$\dfrac{\partial^2 G_\sigma(x,y)}{\partial x^2} = \dfrac{1}{2\pi\sigma^4} e^{-\frac{x^2+y^2}{2\sigma^2}} \left(\dfrac{x^2}{\sigma^2} - 1\right)$	Best approximation with $\sigma_1 = \sqrt{2}\sigma,\ \sigma_2 = \dfrac{\sigma}{\sqrt{2}}$
$\dfrac{\partial^2 G_\sigma(x,y)}{\partial y^2} = \dfrac{1}{2\pi\sigma^4} e^{-\frac{x^2+y^2}{2\sigma^2}} \left(\dfrac{y^2}{\sigma^2} - 1\right)$	
$\text{LoG}(x,y) = \nabla^2 G_\sigma(x,y) = \dfrac{\partial^2 G_\sigma(x,y)}{\partial x^2} + \dfrac{\partial^2 G_\sigma(x,y)}{\partial y^2}$	
$= -\dfrac{1}{\pi\sigma^4} e^{-\frac{x^2+y^2}{2\sigma^2}} \left(1 - \dfrac{x^2+y^2}{2\sigma^2}\right)$	

The following code block shows how to compute the `LOG` filter and the corresponding best DoG approximation (with a given value of σ) and apply them on the same input image, using SciPy `signal` module's `convolve2d()` function:

```
from scipy.signal import convolve2d
from scipy.misc import imread
from scipy.ndimage import gaussian_filter

def plot_kernel(kernel, s, name):
    pylab.imshow(kernel, cmap='YlOrRd') #cmap='jet') #'gray_r')
```

```python
    ax = pylab.gca()
    ax.set_xticks(np.arange(-0.5, kernel.shape[0], 2.5))
    ax.set_yticks(np.arange(-0.5, kernel.shape[1], 2.5))
    pylab.colorbar()

def LOG(k=12, s=3):
    n = 2*k+1 # size of the kernel
    kernel = np.zeros((n,n))
    for i in range(n):
        for j in range(n):
            kernel[i,j] = -(1-((i-k)**2+(j-k)**2)/(2.*s**2))*np.exp(-((i-k)**2+(j-k)**2)/(2.*s**2))/(pi*s**4)
    kernel = np.round(kernel / np.sqrt((kernel**2).sum()),3)
    return kernel

def DOG(k=12, s=3):
    n = 2*k+1 # size of the kernel
    s1, s2 = s * np.sqrt(2), s / np.sqrt(2)
    kernel = np.zeros((n,n))
    for i in range(n):
        for j in range(n):
            kernel[i,j] = np.exp(-((i-k)**2+(j-k)**2)/(2.*s1**2))/(2*pi*s1**2) - np.exp(-((i-k)**2+(j-k)**2)/(2.*s2**2))/(2*pi*s2**2)
    kernel = np.round(kernel / np.sqrt((kernel**2).sum()),3)
    return kernel

s = 3 # sigma value for LoG
img = rgb2gray(imread('../images/me.jpg'))
kernel = LOG()
outimg = convolve2d(img, kernel)
pylab.figure(figsize=(20,20))
pylab.subplot(221), pylab.title('LOG kernel', size=20), plot_kernel(kernel, s, 'DOG')
pylab.subplot(222), pylab.title('output image with LOG', size=20)
pylab.imshow(np.clip(outimg,0,1), cmap='gray') # clip the pixel values in between 0 and 1
kernel = DOG()
outimg = convolve2d(img, DOG())
pylab.subplot(223), pylab.title('DOG kernel', size=20), plot_kernel(kernel, s, 'DOG')
pylab.subplot(224), pylab.title('output image with DOG', size=20)
pylab.imshow(np.clip(outimg,0,1), cmap='gray')
pylab.show()
```

Image Enhancement Using Derivatives

The following images show the input image and the output images obtained with the LoG and DoG filters (with σ=3), along with the visualization of the corresponding kernels. From the kernel visualizations, it can be seen that LoG is going to act as a BPF on the input image (since it blocks both low and high frequencies). The band-pass nature of LoG can also be explained by the DoG approximation (the Gaussian filter being a LPF). Also, we can see that the output images obtained with LoG/DoG filters are quite similar:

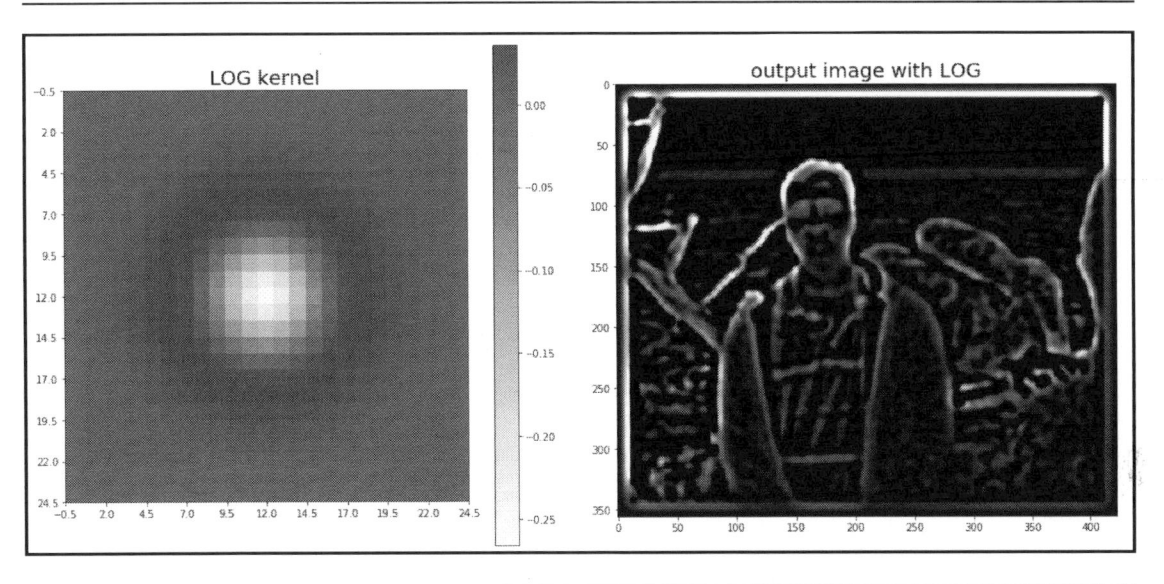

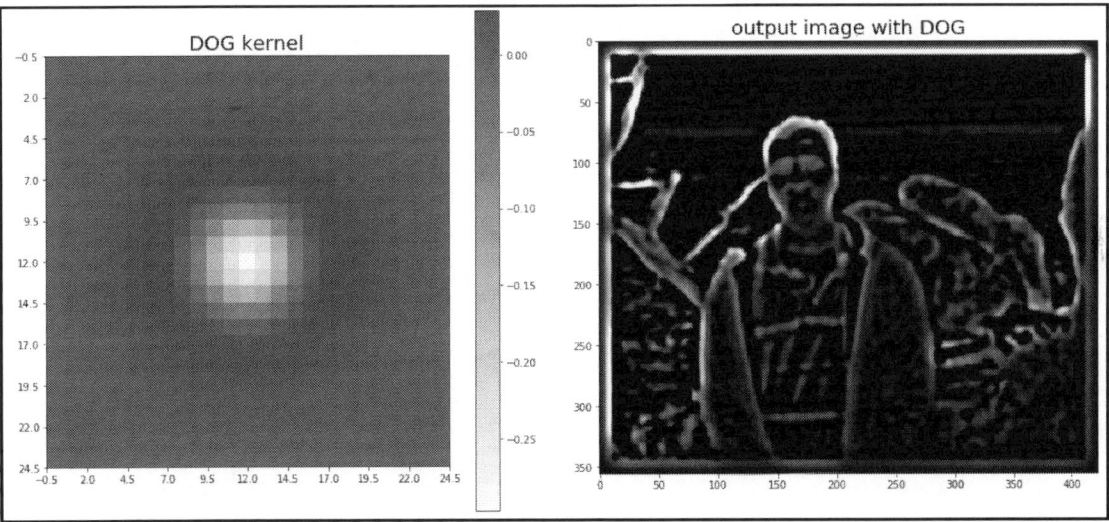

We can see from these images that the LoG filter is quite useful for edge detection. As we shall see shortly, LoG is also useful for finding **blobs** in an image.

The LoG filter with the SciPy ndimage module

The SciPy `ndimage` module's `gaussian_laplace()` function can also be used to implement LoG, as shown in the following code block:

```
img = rgb2gray(imread('../images/zebras.jpg'))
fig = pylab.figure(figsize=(25,15))
pylab.gray() # show the filtered result in grayscale
for sigma in range(1,10):
 pylab.subplot(3,3,sigma)
 img_log = ndimage.gaussian_laplace(img, sigma=sigma)
 pylab.imshow(np.clip(img_log,0,1)), pylab.axis('off')
 pylab.title('LoG with sigma=' + str(sigma), size=20)
pylab.show()
```

The following images show the input image and the output images obtained with the LoG filter with different values of the smoothing parameter σ (standard deviation of the Gaussian filter):

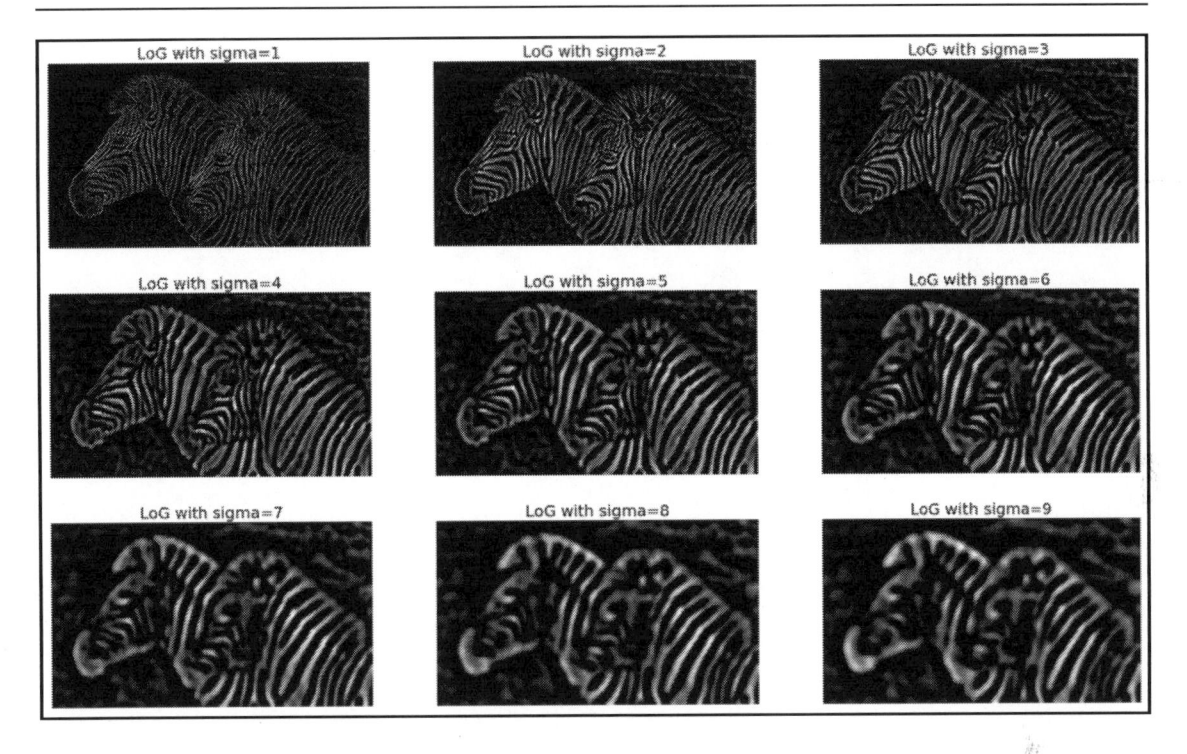

Edge detection with the LoG filter

The following describes the steps in edge detection with an `LOG` filter:

- First, the input image needs to be smoothed (by convolution with the Gaussian filter).
- Then, the smoothed image needs to be convolved with the Laplacian filter to obtain the output image as $\nabla^2 (I(x,y) * G(x,y))$.

- Finally the zero-crossings from the image obtained in the last step need to be computed, as shown in the following diagram:

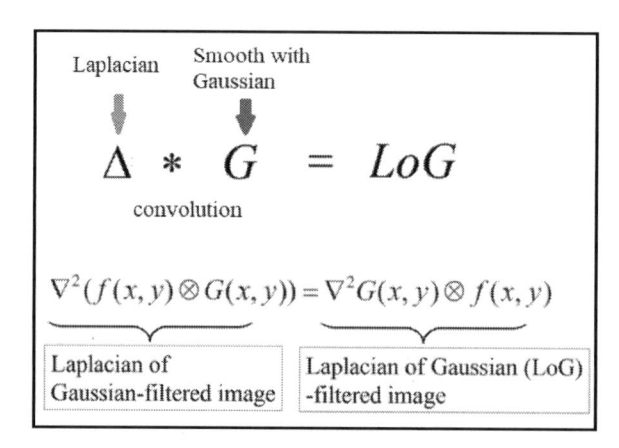

$$\underset{\text{Laplacian}}{\Delta} \underset{\text{convolution}}{*} \underset{\text{Smooth with Gaussian}}{G} = LoG$$

$$\underbrace{\nabla^2(f(x,y) \otimes G(x,y))}_{\text{Laplacian of Gaussian-filtered image}} = \underbrace{\nabla^2 G(x,y) \otimes f(x,y)}_{\text{Laplacian of Gaussian (LoG)-filtered image}}$$

Edge detection with the Marr and Hildreth's algorithm using the zero-crossing computation

Computing the zero-crossings in the **LoG-convolved** image (to detect edges as a binary image) was proposed by Marr and Hildreth. Identification of the edge pixels can be done by viewing the sign of the **LoG-smoothed** image by defining it as a binary image. The algorithm to compute the zero-crossing is as follows:

1. First, convert the LoG-convolved image to a binary image by replacing the pixel values by 1 for positive values and 0 for negative values
2. In order to compute the zero-crossing pixels, we need to simply look at the boundaries of the non-zero regions in this binary image
3. Boundaries can be found by finding any non-zero pixel that has an immediate neighbor that is zero
4. Hence, for each pixel, if it is non-zero, consider its eight neighbors; if any of the neighboring pixels is zero, the pixel can be identified as an edge

The implementation of this function is left as an exercise. The following code block depicts the edges of the same zebra image detected with zero-crossings:

```
fig = pylab.figure(figsize=(25,15))
pylab.gray() # show the filtered result in grayscale
for sigma in range(2,10, 2):
 pylab.subplot(2,2,sigma/2)
 result = ndimage.gaussian_laplace(img, sigma=sigma)
 pylab.imshow(zero_crossing(result)) # implement the function
```

```
zero_crossing() using the above algorithm
 pylab.axis('off')
 pylab.title('LoG with zero-crossing, sigma=' + str(sigma), size=20)
pylab.show()
```

The following screenshot shows the output of the preceding code block, with edges identified by zero-crossing alone at different σ scales:

The previous images show zero-crossings with LoG/DoG as an edge detector. It should be noticed that the zero-crossings form **closed contours**.

Finding and enhancing edges with PIL

PIL's `ImageFilter` module's `filter` function can also be used to find and **enhance** edges in an image. The following code block shows an example with the UMBC library image as input:

```
from PIL.ImageFilter import (FIND_EDGES, EDGE_ENHANCE, EDGE_ENHANCE_MORE)
im = Image.open('../images/umbc_lib.jpg')
pylab.figure(figsize=(18,25))
```

Image Enhancement Using Derivatives

```
pylab.subplot(2,2,1)
plot_image(im, 'original (UMBC library)')
i = 2
for f in (FIND_EDGES, EDGE_ENHANCE, EDGE_ENHANCE_MORE):
 pylab.subplot(2,2,i)
 im1 = im.filter(f)
 plot_image(im1, str(f))
 i += 1
pylab.show()
```

The following screenshot shows the output of the preceding code with different edge finding/enhancing filters:

Image pyramids (Gaussian and Laplacian) – blending images

We can construct the Gaussian pyramid of an image by starting with the original image and creating smaller images iteratively, first by smoothing (with a Gaussian filter to avoid **anti-aliasing**), and then by subsampling (collectively called **reducing**) from the previous level's image at each iteration until a minimum resolution is reached. The image pyramid created in this way is called a **Gaussian pyramid**. These are good for searching over scale (for instance, template-matching), precomputation, and image processing tasks by editing frequency bands separately (for instance, image blending). Similarly, a **Laplacian pyramid** for the image can be constructed by starting from the smallest sized image in the Gaussian pyramid and then by expanding (up-sampling plus smoothing) the image from that level and subtracting it from the image from the next level of the Gaussian pyramid, and repeating this process iteratively until the original image size is reached. In this section, we shall see how to write python code to compute the image pyramids, and then look at an application of the image pyramids for blending two images.

A Gaussian pyramid with scikit-image transform pyramid module

The Gaussian pyramid from an input image can be computed using the `scikit-image.transform.pyramid` module's `pyramid_gaussian()` function. Starting with the original image, the function calls the `pyramid_reduce()` function to obtain the smoothed and down-sampled images recursively. The following code block demonstrates how to compute and display such a Gaussian pyramid with the `lena` RGB input image:

```
from skimage.transform import pyramid_gaussian
image = imread('../images/lena.jpg')
nrows, ncols = image.shape[:2]
pyramid = tuple(pyramid_gaussian(image, downscale=2))
pylab.figure(figsize=(20,5))
i, n = 1, len(pyramid)
for p in pyramid:
 pylab.subplot(1,n,i), pylab.imshow(p)
 pylab.title(str(p.shape[0]) + 'x' + str(p.shape[1])), pylab.axis('off')
 i += 1
pylab.suptitle('Gaussian Pyramid', size=30)
pylab.show()
compos_image = np.zeros((nrows, ncols + ncols // 2, 3), dtype=np.double)
compos_image[:nrows, :ncols, :] = pyramid[0]
i_row = 0
for p in pyramid[1:]:
 nrows, ncols = p.shape[:2]
 compos_image[i_row:i_row + nrows, cols:cols + ncols] = p
 i_row += nrows
fig, axes = pylab.subplots(figsize=(20,20))
axes.imshow(compos_image)
pylab.show()
```

The following images show the output of the preceding code block: the images from the Gaussian pyramid. As we can see, there are nine levels in the pyramid, the top level being the original image of resolution 220 x 220, and the last image being the smallest image consisting of a single pixel; at each consecutive level down the pyramid, the image height and width get reduced by a factor of two:

Image Enhancement Using Derivatives

A Laplacian pyramid with scikit-image transform's pyramid module

The Laplacian pyramid from an input image can be computed using the `scikit-image.transform.pyramid` module's `pyramid_laplacian()` function. Starting with the difference image of original image and its smoothed version, the function computes the down-sampled and the smoothed image, and takes the difference of these two images to compute the image corresponding to each layer recursively. Motivation for creating a Laplacian pyramid is to achieve compression, since the compression rates are higher for predictable values around 0.

The code to compute the Laplacian pyramid is similar to that of the previous code for computing the Gaussian pyramid; it is left as an exercise for the reader. The following screenshot shows the Laplacian pyramid for the `lena` gray-scale image:

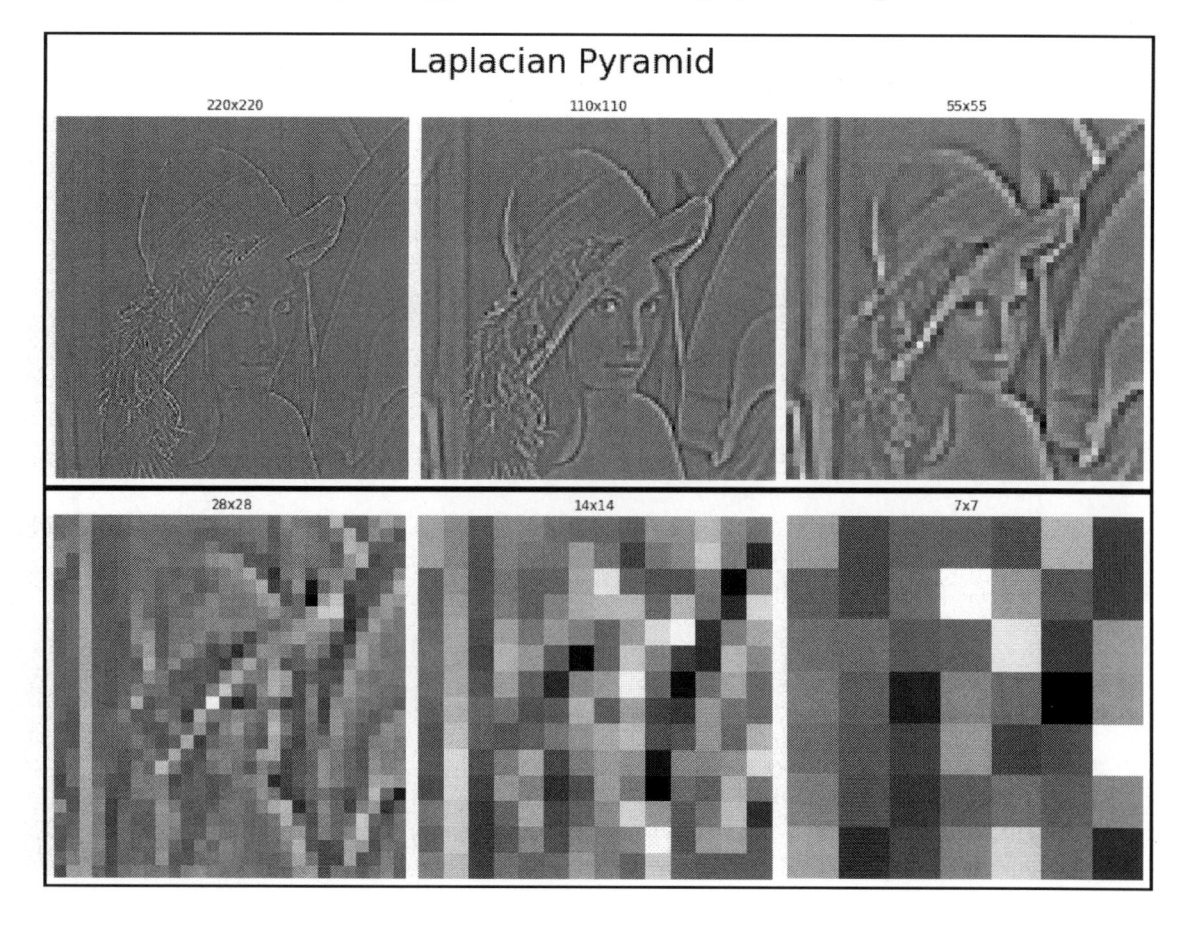

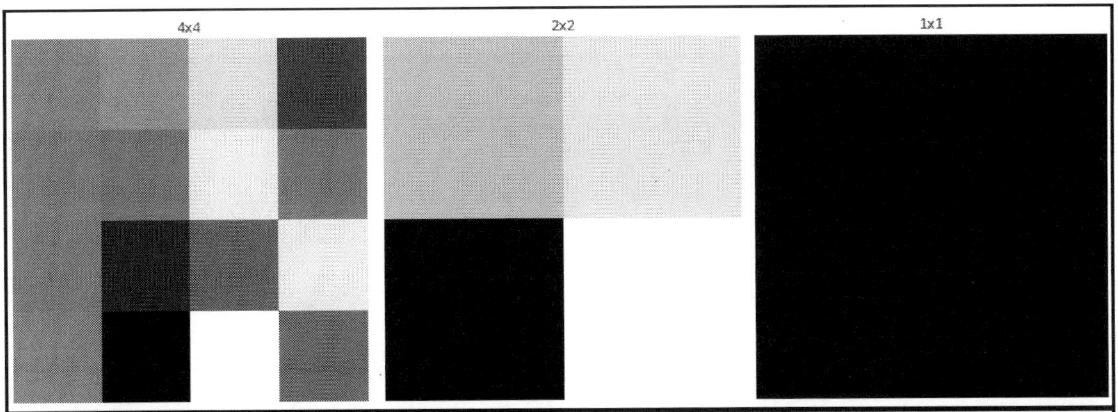
4x4
2x2
1x1

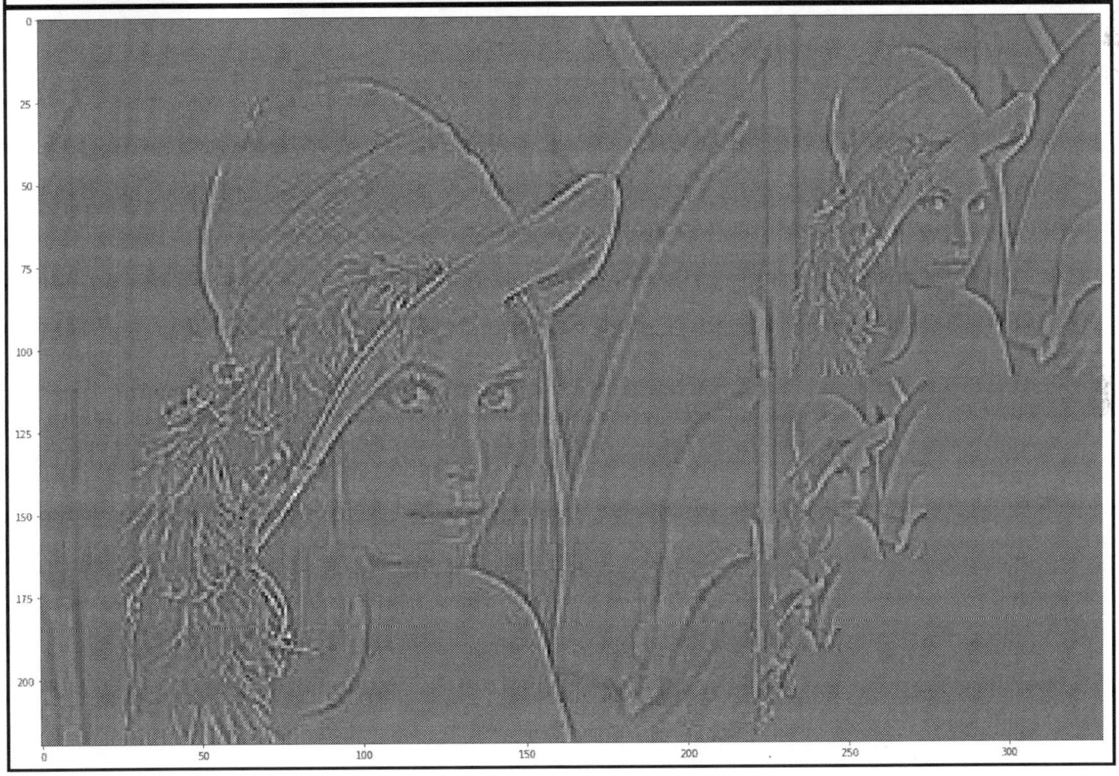
0
25
50
75
100
125
150
175
200
0
50
100
150
200
250
300

Notice that the lowest resolution image in the Laplacian pyramid and the lowest resolution image in the Gaussian pyramid are going to be different images if we use the `pyramid_gaussian()` and `pyramid_laplacian()` functions of `scikit-image`, which is something that we do not want. We want to build a Laplacian pyramid where the smallest resolution image is exactly the same as that of the Gaussian pyramid, as this will enable us to construct an image only from its Laplacian pyramid. In the next couple of sections, we shall discuss the algorithms to construct our own pyramids by using the `expand()` and `reduce()` functions of `scikit-image`.

Constructing the Gaussian Pyramid

The Gaussian pyramid can be computed with the following steps:

1. Start with the original image.
2. Iteratively compute the image at each level of the pyramid, first by smoothing the image (with the Gaussian filter) and then down-sampling it.
3. Stop at a level where the image size becomes sufficiently small (for example, 1 x 1).
4. The function to implement the previous algorithm is left as an exercise for the reader; we just need to add a few lines in the following function to complete the implementation:

```
from skimage.transform import pyramid_reduce

def get_gaussian_pyramid(image):
    '''
    input: an RGB image
    output: the Gaussian Pyramid of the image as a list
    '''
    gaussian_pyramid = []
    # add code here
    # iteratively compute the image at each level of the pyramid
with the reduce() function and append
    return gaussian_pyramid
```

The Laplacian pyramid can be computed with the following algorithm:

1. Start with the Gaussian pyramid and with the smallest image.
2. Iteratively compute the difference image in-between the image at the current level and the image obtained by first up-sampling and then smoothing the image (with Gaussian filter) from the previous level of the Gaussian pyramid.
3. Stop at a level where the image size becomes equal to the original image size.
4. The function to implement the previous algorithm is left as an exercise to the reader as well; we just need to add a few lines in the following function to complete the implementation:

```
from skimage.transform import pyramid_expand, resize

def get_laplacian_pyramid(gaussian_pyramid):
    '''
    input: the Gaussian Pyramid of an image as a list
    output: the Laplacian Pyramid of the image as a list
    '''
    laplacian_pyramid = []
    # add code here
    # iteratively compute the image at each level of the pyramid with the expand() function and append
    return laplacian_pyramid
```

The following code block with the input antelope's image should produce the outputs if the functions are implemented correctly:

```
image = imread('../images/antelops.jpeg')
gaussian_pyramid = get_gaussian_pyramid(image)
laplacian_pyramid = get_laplacian_pyramid(gaussian_pyramid)

w, h = 20, 12
for i in range(3):
 pylab.figure(figsize=(w,h))
 p = gaussian_pyramid[i]
 pylab.imshow(p), pylab.title(str(p.shape[0]) + 'x' + str(p.shape[1]), size=20), pylab.axis('off')
 w, h = w / 2, h / 2
pylab.show()

w, h = 10, 6
for i in range(1,4):
 pylab.figure(figsize=(w,h))
 p = laplacian_pyramid[i]
 pylab.imshow(rgb2gray(p), cmap='gray'),
 pylab.title(str(p.shape[0]) + 'x' + str(p.shape[1]), size=20)
```

Image Enhancement Using Derivatives

```
pylab.axis('off')
w, h = w / 2, h / 2
pylab.show()
```

Some images from the Gaussian pyramid:

350x523

175x262

Some images from the Laplacian pyramid:

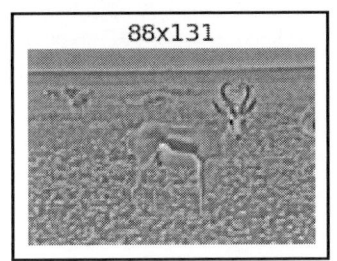

44x66

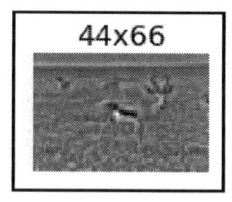

Reconstructing an image only from its Laplacian pyramid

The following diagram shows how to reconstruct an image from only its Laplacian pyramid, if we construct one by following the algorithms described in the previous section:

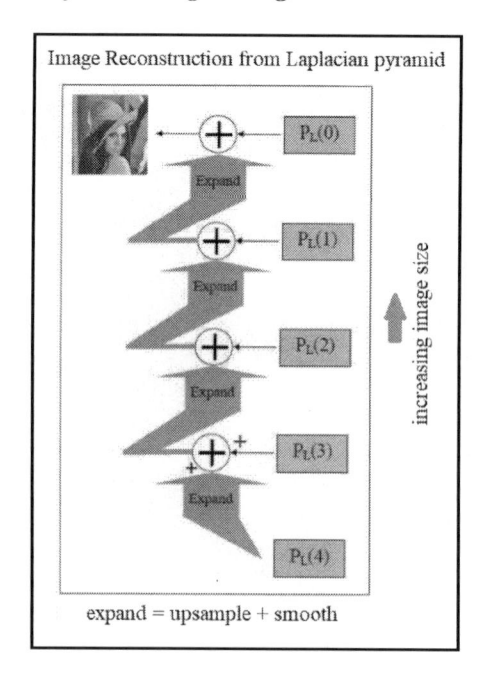

Image Reconstruction from Laplacian pyramid

$P_L(0)$
$P_L(1)$
$P_L(2)$
$P_L(3)$
$P_L(4)$

expand = upsample + smooth

Take a look at the following code block:

```
def reconstruct_image_from_laplacian_pyramid(pyramid):
    i = len(pyramid) - 2
    prev = pyramid[i+1]
    pylab.figure(figsize=(20,20))
    j = 1
    while i >= 0:
```

```
        prev = resize(pyramid_expand(prev, upscale=2), pyramid[i].shape)
        im = np.clip(pyramid[i] + prev,0,1)
        pylab.subplot(3,3,j), pylab.imshow(im)
        pylab.title('Level=' + str(j) + ' ' + str(im.shape[0]) + 'x' +
str(im.shape[1]), size=20)
        prev = im
        i -= 1
        j += 1
    pylab.subplot(3,3,j), pylab.imshow(image)
    pylab.title('Original image' + ' ' + str(image.shape[0]) + 'x' +
str(image.shape[1]), size=20)
    pylab.show()
    return im

image = img_as_float(imread('../images/apple.png')[...,:3]) # only use the
color channels and discard the alpha
pyramid = get_laplacian_pyramid(get_gaussian_pyramid(image))
im = reconstruct_image_from_laplacian_pyramid(pyramid)
```

The following screenshot shows the output of the preceding code, how the original image is finally constructed from its Laplacian pyramid only using the `expand()` operation on each level's image, and adding it to the next level's image iteratively:

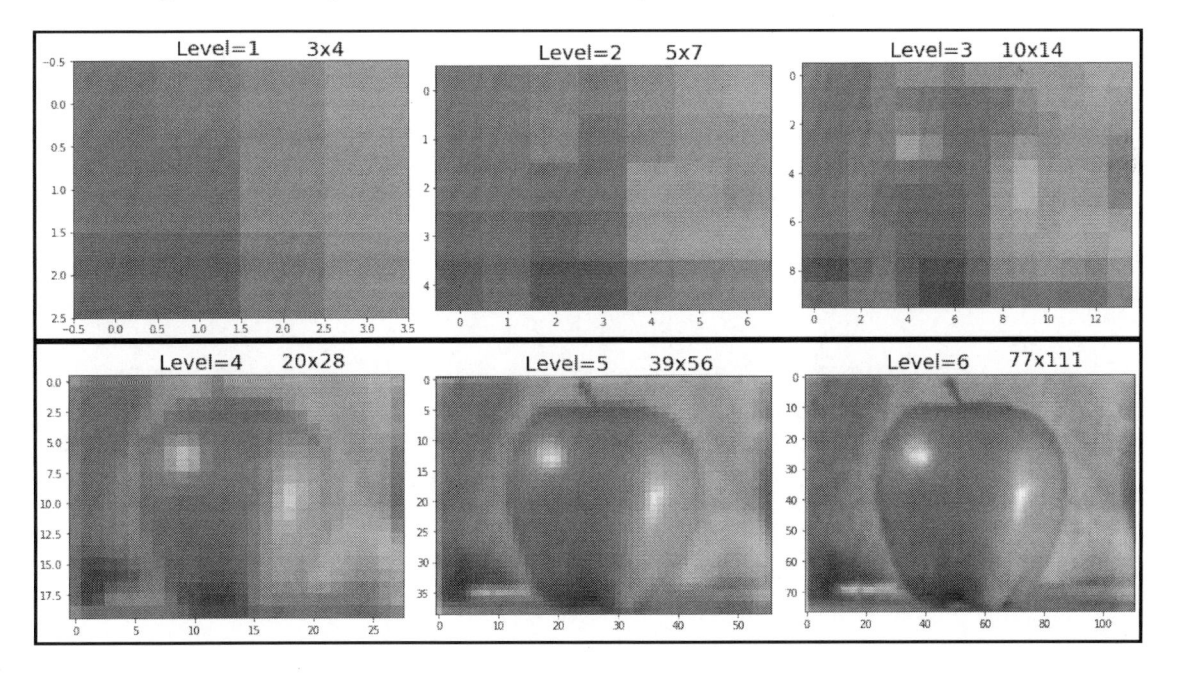

Blending images with pyramids

Let's say we have a couple of RGB color input images, **A** (apple) and **B** (orange), and a third binary mask image, **M**; all three images are of the same size. The objective is to blend image **A** with **B**, guided by the mask, **M** (if a pixel in the mask image M has a value of 1, it implies that this pixel is be taken from the image **A**, otherwise from image **B**). The following algorithm can be used to blend two images using the Laplacian pyramids of images **A** and **B** (by computing the blended pyramid using the linear combination of the images at the same levels of the Laplacian pyramids from **A** and **B**, with the weights from the same level of the Gaussian pyramid of the mask image **M**), followed by reconstructing the output image from the Laplacian pyramid:

Laplacian Pyramid: Blending

General Approach:

1. Build Laplacian pyramids *LA* and *LB* from images *A* and *B*
2. Build a Gaussian pyramid *GR* from selected mask region *M*
3. Form a combined pyramid *LS* from *LA* and *LB* using nodes of *GR* as weights:
   - $LS(i,j) = G_M(i,j)*LA(i,j) + (1-G_M(i,j))*LB(i,j)$
4. Collapse the *LS* pyramid to get the final blended image

http://graphics.cs.cmu.edu/courses/15-463/2005_fall/www/Lectures/Pyramids.pdf

The following code block shows how to implement the algorithm in Python using the functions we already implemented:

```
A = img_as_float(imread('../images/apple.png')[...,:3])    # dropping the 4th channel, the alpha level
B = img_as_float(imread('../images/orange.png')[...,:3])   # using only the RGB channels
M = img_as_float(imread('../images/mask.png')[...,:3])     # scale pixel values in between [0,1]

pyramidA = get_laplacian_pyramid(get_gaussian_pyramid(A))
pyramidB = get_laplacian_pyramid(get_gaussian_pyramid(B))
pyramidM = get_gaussian_pyramid(M)

# construct the blended pyramid
pyramidC = []
for i in range(len(pyramidM)):
  im = pyramidM[i]*pyramidA[i] + (1-pyramidM[i])*pyramidB[i]
  pyramidC.append(im)

I = reconstruct_image_from_laplacian_pyramid(pyramidC)
```

The following screenshot show the input images and the output images generated with the preceding code block:

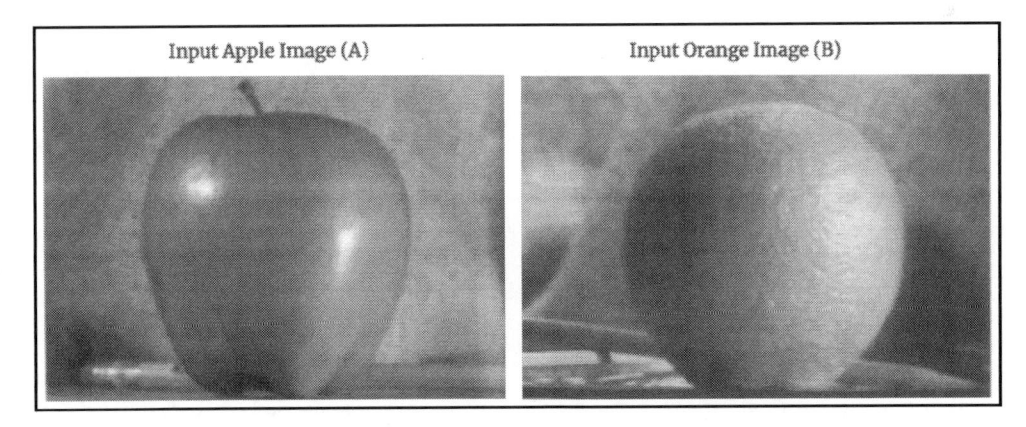

Image Enhancement Using Derivatives

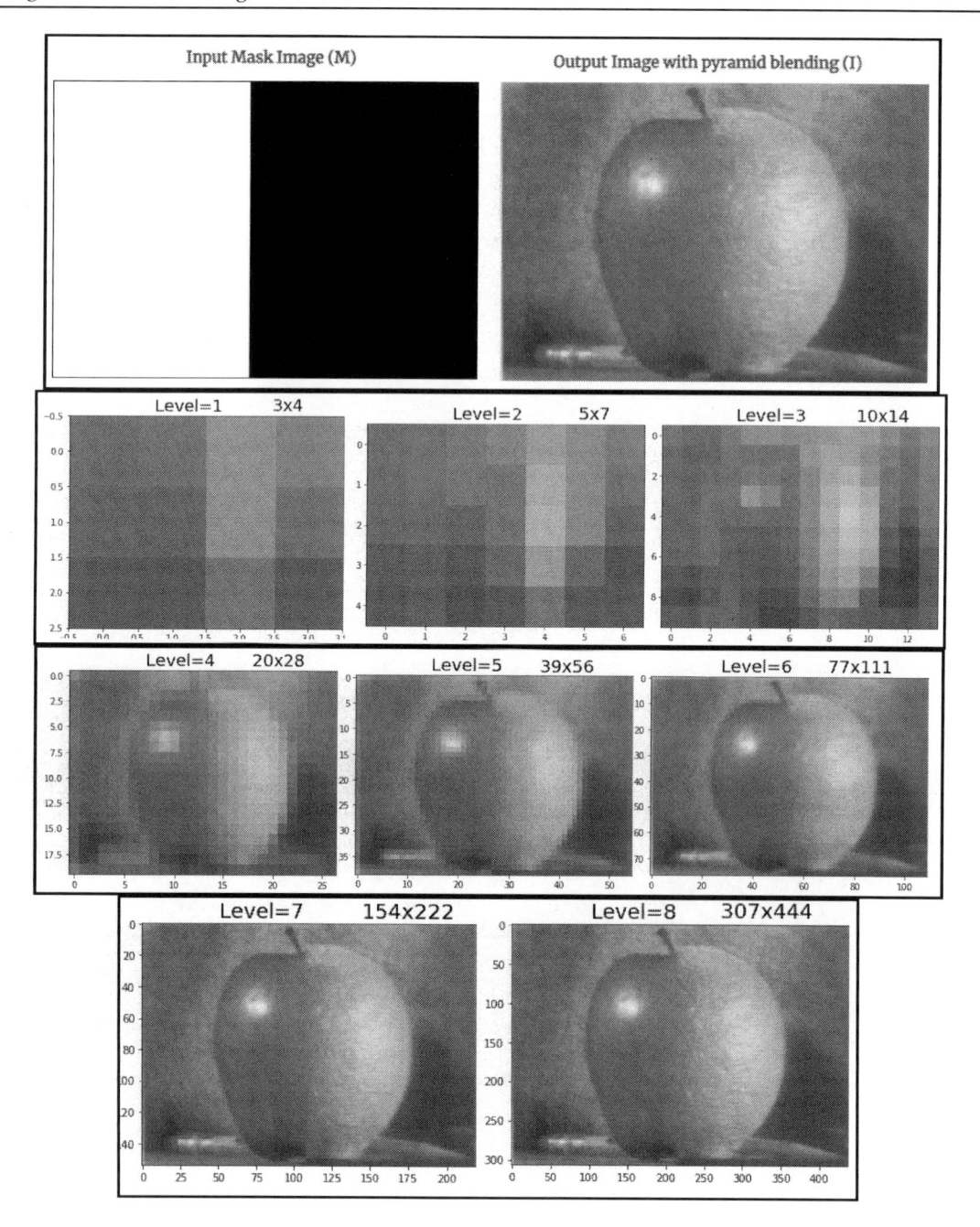

[222]

Summary

In this chapter, we first discussed edge detection of images using several filters (Sobel, Prewitt, Canny, and so on) and by computing the gradient and Laplacian of an image. Then, we discussed LoG/DoG operators and how to implement them and detect edges with zero-crossing. Next, we discussed how to compute image pyramids and use Laplacian pyramids to blend two images smoothly. Finally, we discussed how to detect blobs with `scikit-image`. On completion of this chapter, the reader should be able to implement edge detectors (Sobel, Canny, and so forth) in an image with Python using different filters. Also, the reader should be able to implement filters to sharpen an image, and find edges at different scales using LoG/DoG. Finally, they should be able to blend images with Laplacian/Gaussian pyramids and implement blob detection in an image at different scale-spaces. In the next chapter, we shall discuss feature detection and extraction techniques from images.

Questions

1. Use the `skimage.filters` module's `unsharp_mask()` function with different values of the `radius` and `amount` parameters to sharpen an image.
2. Use the PIL `ImageFilter` module's `UnsharpMask()` function with different values of the `radius` and `percent` parameters to sharpen an image.
3. Sharpen a color (RGB) image using the sharpen kernel [[0, -1, 0], [-1, 5, -1], [0, -1, 0]]. (Hint: use SciPy `signal` module's `convolve2d()` function for each of the color channels one by one.)
4. With the SciPy `ndimage` module, sharpen a color image directly (without sharpening individual color channels one by one).
5. Compute and display a Gaussian pyramid with the `lena` gray-scale input image using the `skimage.transform` module's `pyramid_laplacian()` function.

6. Construct the Gaussian pyramid with the `reduce()` function of the `transform` module of `scikit-image` and Laplacian pyramid from the Gaussian pyramid and `expand()` function, with the algorithm discussed.
7. Compute the Laplacian pyramid for an image and construct the original image from it.
8. Show that the LoG and DoG kernels look like a Mexican hat in a 3D surface plot.
9. Implement Marr and Hildreth's zero-crossing algorithm for edge detection with LoG.
10. Implement the non-max suppression algorithm to thin the edges in a gradient magnitude image.

Further reading

- https://web.stanford.edu/class/cs448f/lectures/5.2/Gradient%20Domain.pdf
- https://web.stanford.edu/class/ee368/Handouts/Lectures/2014_Spring/Combined_Slides/11-Edge-Detection-Combined.pdf
- https://www.cs.cornell.edu/courses/cs6670/2011sp/lectures/lec02_filter.pdf
- http://www.cs.toronto.edu/~mangas/teaching/320/slides/CSC320L05.pdf
- http://www.cse.psu.edu/~rtc12/CSE486/lecture11.pdf
- http://graphics.cs.cmu.edu/courses/15-463/2005_fall/www/Lectures/Pyramids.pdf
- http://www.eng.tau.ac.il/~ipapps/Slides/lecture05.pdf
- https://sandipanweb.wordpress.com/2017/05/16/some-more-computational-photography-merging-and-blending-images-using-gaussian-and-laplacian-pyramids-in-python/
- http://www.me.umn.edu/courses/me5286/vision/VisionNotes/2017/ME5286-Lecture7-2017-EdgeDetection2.pdf
- https://www.cs.rutgers.edu/~elgammal/classes/cs334/EdgesandContours.pdf
- https://web.fe.up.pt/~campilho/PDI/NOTES/EdgeDetection.pdf

- http://www.cs.cornell.edu/courses/cs664/2008sp/handouts/edges.pdf
- http://www.cs.cmu.edu/~16385/s17/Slides/4.0_Image_Gradients_and_Gradient_Filtering.pdf
- http://www.hms.harvard.edu/bss/neuro/bornlab/qmbc/beta/day4/marr-hildreth-edge-prsl1980.pdf
- http://citeseerx.ist.psu.edu/viewdoc/download?doi=10.1.1.420.3300rep=rep1type=pdf
- http://persci.mit.edu/pub_pdfs/pyramid83.pdf
- http://persci.mit.edu/pub_pdfs/spline83.pdf
- http://ftp.nada.kth.se/CVAP/reports/cvap198.pdf
- https://www.cs.toronto.edu/~mangas/teaching/320/assignments/a3/tcomm83.pdf
- https://www.cs.toronto.edu/~mangas/teaching/320/assignments/a3/spline83.pdf
- http://6.869.csail.mit.edu/fa16/lecture/lecture6.pdf
- https://docs.opencv.org/3.1.0/dc/dff/tutorial_py_pyramids.html

6
Morphological Image Processing

In this chapter, we will discuss mathematical morphology and morphological image processing. Morphological image processing is a collection of non-linear operations related to the shape or morphology of features in an image. These operations are particularly suited to the processing of binary images (where pixels are represented as 0 or 1 and, by convention, the foreground of the object = 1 or white and the background = 0 or black), although it can be extended to grayscale images.

In morphological operations, a structuring element (a small template image) is used to probe the input image. The algorithms work by positioning the structuring element at all possible locations in the input image and comparing it with the corresponding neighborhood of the pixels with a set operator. Some operations test whether the element fits within the neighborhood, while others test whether it hits or intersects the neighborhood. A few popular morphological operators or filters are binary dilation and erosion, opening and closing, thinning, skeletonizing, morphological edge detectors, hit or miss filters, rank filters, median filters, and majority filters.

This chapter will demonstrate how to use morphological operators or filters on binary and grayscale images along with their applications, using functions from the scikit-image and SciPy `ndimage.morphology` module.

The topics to be covered in this chapter are as follows:

- Morphological image processing with the scikit-image morphology module
- Morphological image processing with the scikit-image filter.rank module
- Morphological image processing with the scipy.ndimage.morphology module

The scikit-image morphology module

In this section, we shall demonstrate how to use the functions from scikit-image's morphology module to implement a few morphological operations, first on binary images and then on grayscale images.

Binary operations

Let's start with morphological operations on binary images. We need to create a binary input image (for example, with simple thresholding which has a fixed threshold) before invoking the functions.

Erosion

Erosion is a basic morphological operation that shrinks the size of the foreground objects, smooths the object boundaries, and removes peninsulas, fingers, and small objects. The following code block shows how to use the binary_erosion() function that computes fast binary morphological erosion of a binary image:

```
from skimage.morphology import binary_erosion, rectangle
im = rgb2gray(imread('../images/clock2.jpg'))
im[im <= 0.5] = 0 # create binary image with fixed threshold 0.5
im[im > 0.5] = 1
pylab.gray()
pylab.screenshot(figsize=(20,10))
pylab.subplot(1,3,1), plot_image(im, 'original')
im1 = binary_erosion(im, rectangle(1,5))
pylab.subplot(1,3,2), plot_image(im1, 'erosion with rectangle size (1,5)')
im1 = binary_erosion(im, rectangle(1,15))
pylab.subplot(1,3,3), plot_image(im1, 'erosion with rectangle size (1,15)')
pylab.show()
```

The following screenshot shows the output of the previous code. As can be seen, using erosion with the structuring element as a thin, small, vertical rectangle, the small ticks from the binary clock image are removed first. Next, a taller vertical rectangle is used to erode the clock hands too:

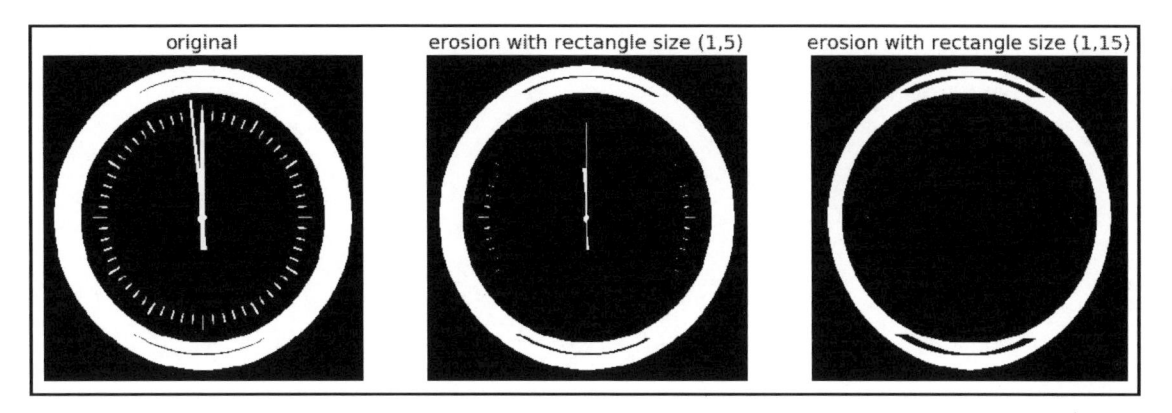

Dilation

Dilation is another basic morphological operation that expands the size of the foreground objects, smooths object boundaries, and closes holes and gaps in a binary image. This is a dual operation of erosion. The following code snippet shows how to use the `binary_dilation()` function on Tagore's binary image with a disk structuring elements of different sizes:

```
from skimage.morphology import binary_dilation
im = img_to_float(imread('../images/tagore.png')) # for this binary png image the pixel values are stored in the 4th channel
im[im <= 0.5] = 0 # binarize the image with a fixed threshold
im[im > 0.5] = 1
pylab.gray()
pylab.screenshot(figsize=(18,9))
pylab.subplot(131), plot_image(im, 'original')
for d in range(1,3):
  im1 = binary_dilation(im, disk(2*d))
  pylab.subplot(1,3,d+1), plot_image(im1, 'dilation with disk size ' + str(2*d))
pylab.show()
```

The following screenshot shows the output of the previous code block. As can be seen, with a smaller size structuring element, a few details (that are treated as background or gaps) from the face got removed and, with the larger size disk, all of the small gaps were filled:

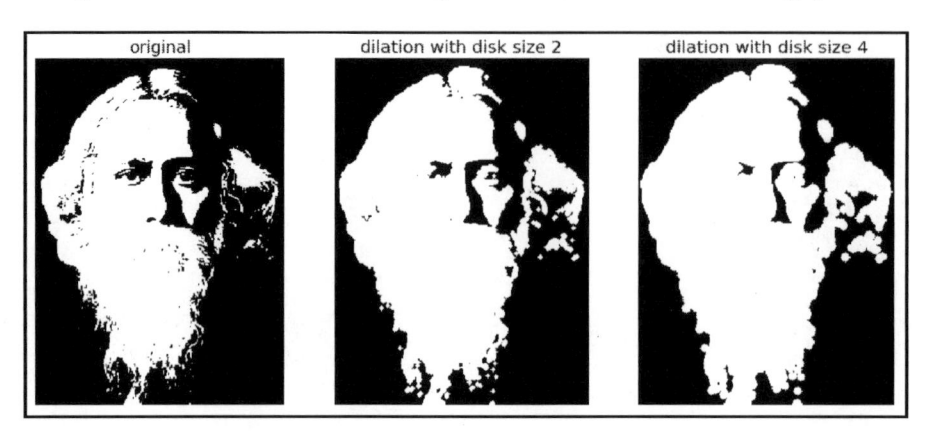

Opening and closing

Opening is a morphological operation that can be expressed as a combination of first erosion and then dilation operations; it removes small objects from a binary image. **Closing**, to the contrary, is another morphological operation that can be expressed as a combination of first dilation and then erosion operations; it removes small holes from a binary image. These two are dual operations. The following code snippet shows how to use the scikit-image `morphology` module's corresponding functions to remove small objects and small holes, respectively, from a binary image:

```
from skimage.morphology import binary_opening, binary_closing,
binary_erosion, binary_dilation, disk
im = rgb2gray(imread('../images/circles.jpg'))
im[im <= 0.5] = 0
im[im > 0.5] = 1
pylab.gray()
pylab.screenshot(figsize=(20,10))
pylab.subplot(1,3,1), plot_image(im, 'original')
im1 = binary_opening(im, disk(12))
pylab.subplot(1,3,2), plot_image(im1, 'opening with disk size ' + str(12))
im1 = binary_closing(im, disk(6))
pylab.subplot(1,3,3), plot_image(im1, 'closing with disk size ' + str(6),
size=20)
pylab.show()
```

The following screenshot shows the output of the previous code block—the patterns generated with binary opening and closing operations with disk structuring element of different sizes. As expected, the opening operation only retains the larger circles:

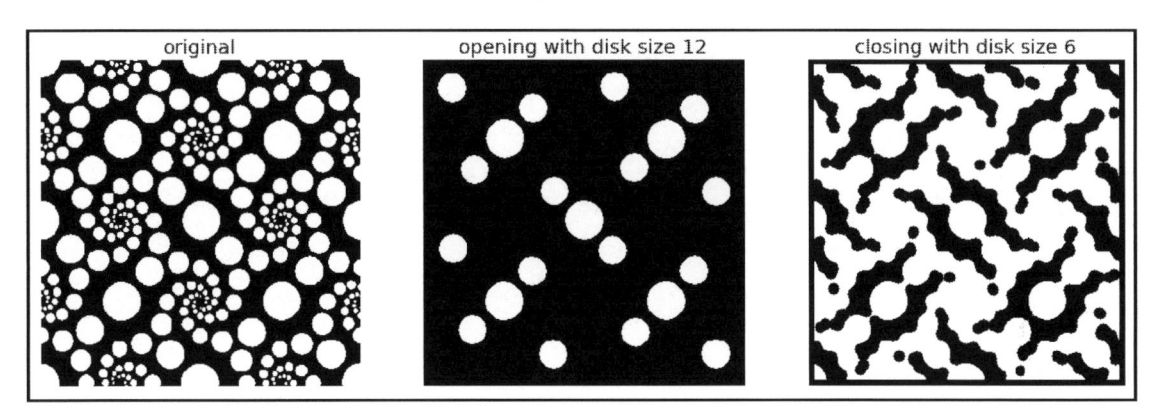

Now let's compare opening with erosion and closing with dilation (by replacing `binary_opening()` with `binary_erosion()` and `binary_closing()` with `binary_dilation()`, respectively, with the same structuring element as in the last code block. The following screenshot shows the output images obtained with erosion and dilation instead:

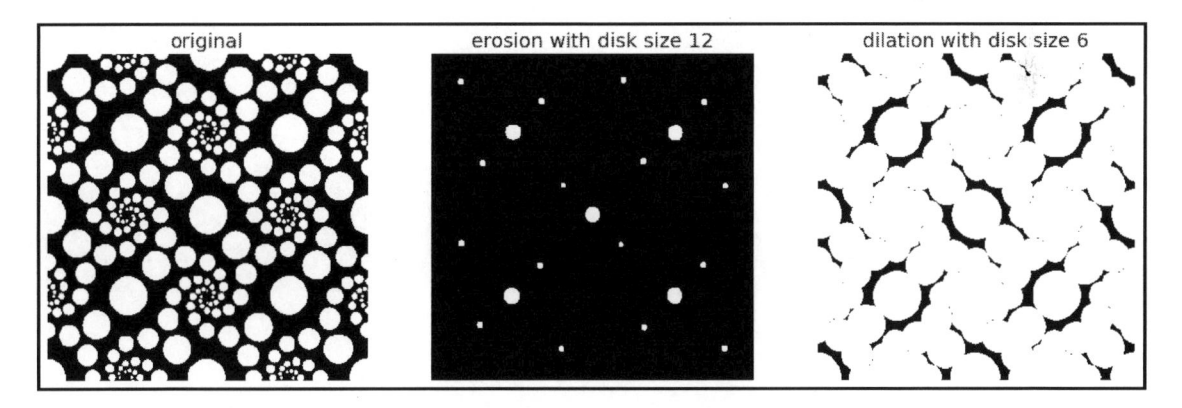

Skeletonizing

In this operation, each connected component in a binary image is reduced to a single pixel-wide skeleton using a morphological thinning operation. The following code block shows how to skeletonize a binary image of a dinosaur:

```
def plot_images_horizontally(original, filtered, filter_name, sz=(18,7)):
 pylab.gray()
 pylab.screenshot(figsize = sz)
 pylab.subplot(1,2,1), plot_image(original, 'original')
 pylab.subplot(1,2,2), plot_images(filtered, filter_name)
 pylab.show()

from skimage.morphology import skeletonize
im = img_as_float(imread('../images/dynasaur.png')[...,3])
threshold = 0.5
im[im <= threshold] = 0
im[im > threshold] = 1
skeleton = skeletonize(im)
plot_images_horizontally(im, skeleton, 'skeleton',sz=(18,9))
```

The following screenshot shows the output of the previous code:

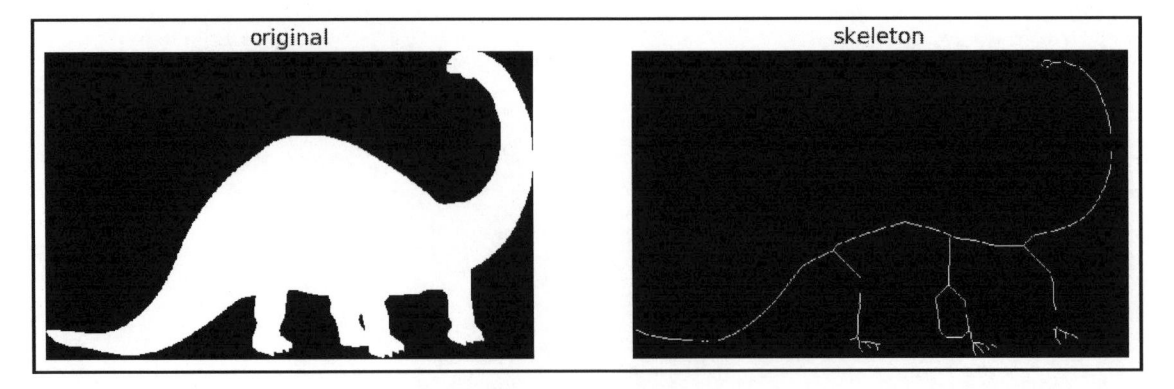

Computing the convex hull

The **convex hull** is defined by the smallest convex polygon that surrounds all foreground (white pixels) in the input image. The following code block demonstrates how to compute the `convex hull` for a binary image:

```
from skimage.morphology import convex_hull_image
im = rgb2gray(imread('../images/horse-dog.jpg'))
threshold = 0.5
```

```
im[im < threshold] = 0 # convert to binary image
im[im >= threshold] = 1
chull = convex_hull_image(im)
plot_images_horizontally(im, chull, 'convex hull', sz=(18,9))
```

The following screenshot shows the output:

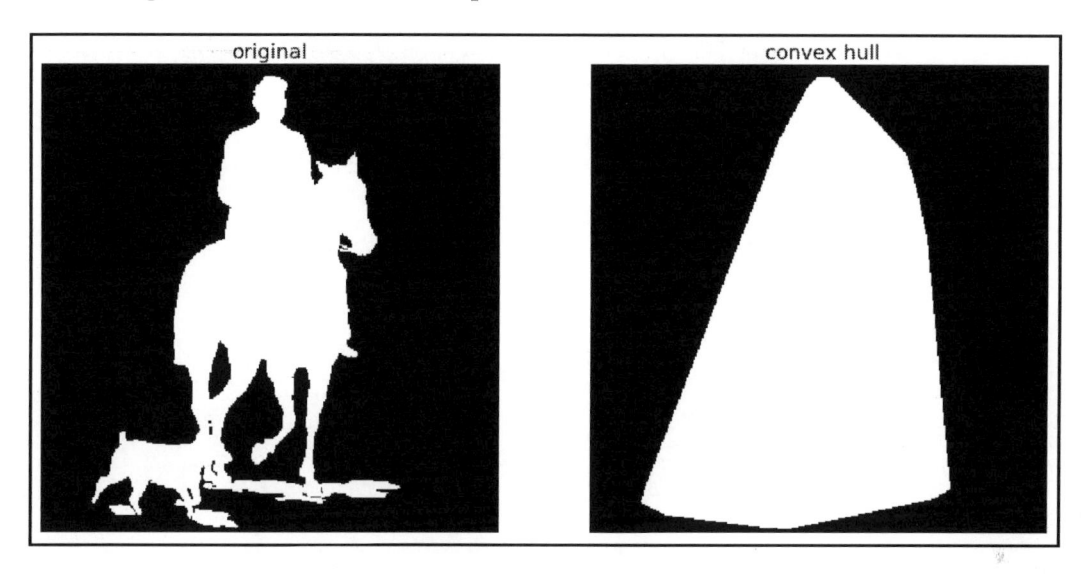

The following code block plots the difference image of the original binary image and the computed convex hull image:

```
im = im.astype(np.bool)
chull_diff = img_as_float(chull.copy())
chull_diff[im] = 2
pylab.screenshot(figsize=(20,10))
pylab.imshow(chull_diff, cmap=pylab.cm.gray, interpolation='nearest')
pylab.title('Difference Image', size=20)
pylab.show()
```

The following screenshot shows the output of the previous code:

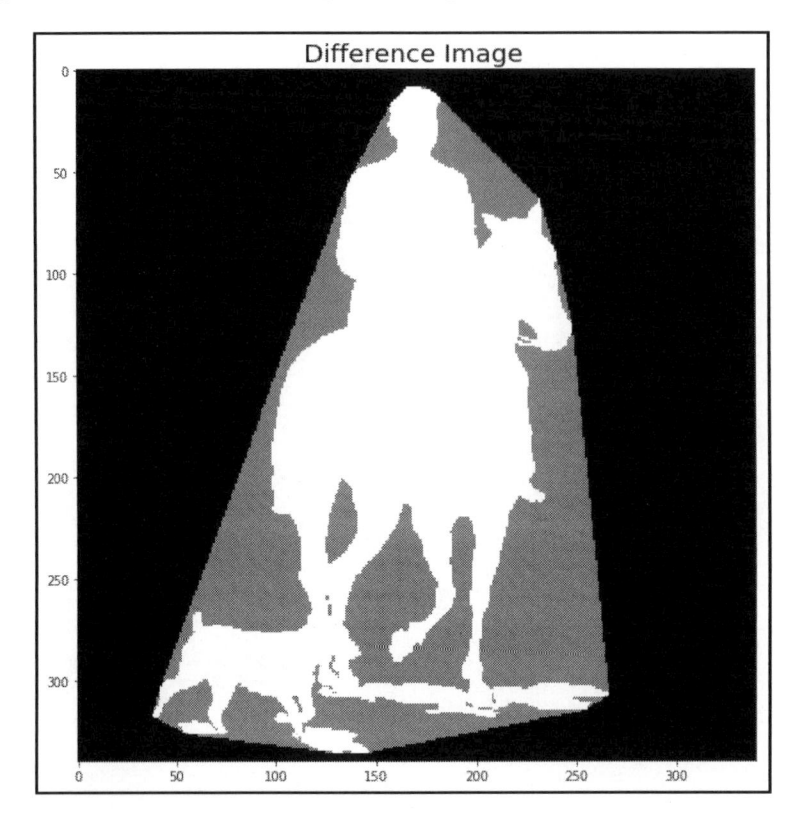

Removing small objects

The following code block shows how the `remove_small_objects()` function can be used to remove objects smaller than a specified minimum size threshold—the higher the specified threshold, the more objects get removed:

```
from skimage.morphology import remove_small_objects
im = rgb2gray(imread('../images/circles.jpg'))
im[im > 0.5] = 1 # create binary image by thresholding with fixed threshold
0.5
im[im <= 0.5] = 0
im = im.astype(np.bool)
pylab.screenshot(figsize=(20,20))
pylab.subplot(2,2,1), plot_image(im, 'original')
i = 2
for osz in [50, 200, 500]:
```

```
    im1 = remove_small_objects(im, osz, connectivity=1)
    pylab.subplot(2,2,i), plot_image(im1, 'removing small objects below size '
+ str(osz))
    i += 1
pylab.show()
```

The following screenshot shows the output of the previous code block. As expected, the higher the minimum size threshold specified, the more objects are removed:

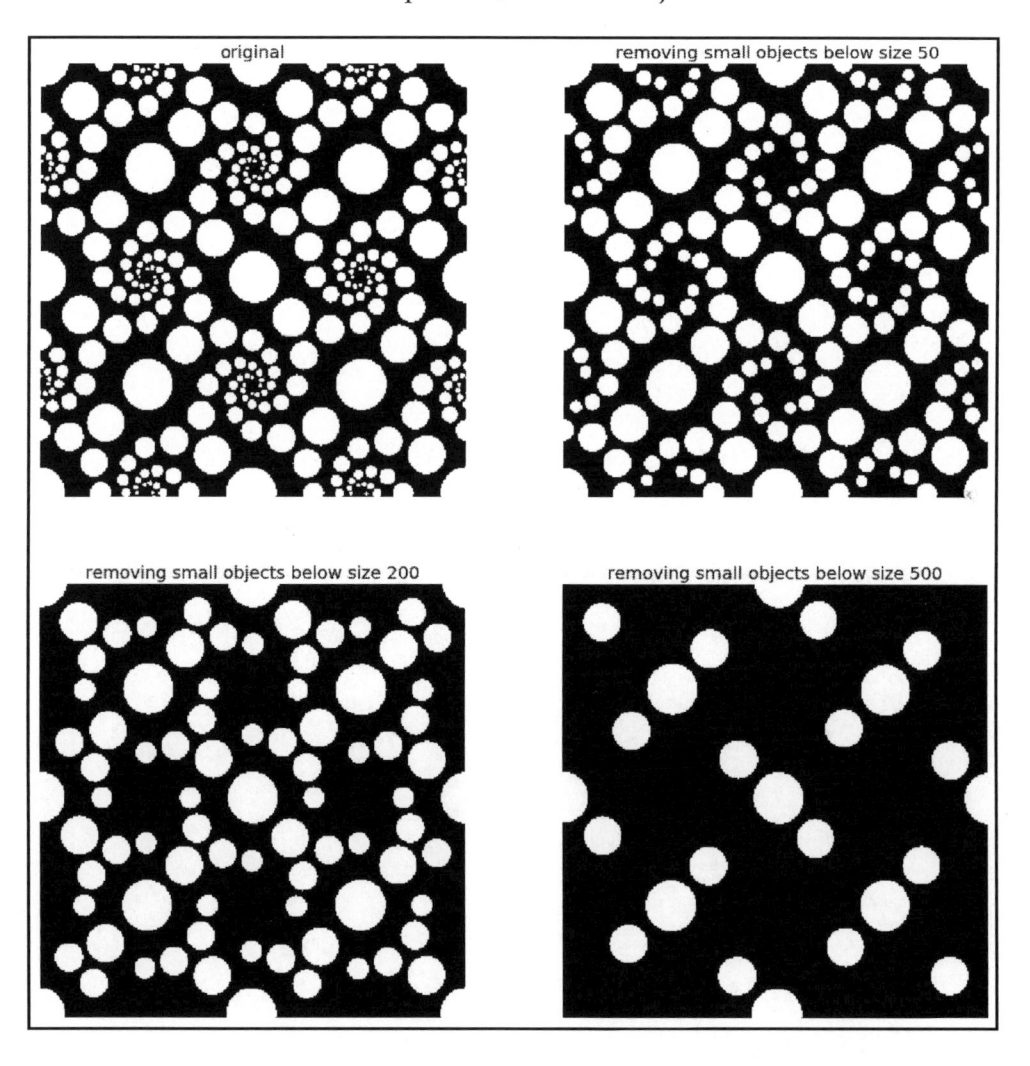

White and black top-hats

The **white top-hat** of an image computes the bright spots smaller than the structuring element. It is defined as the difference image of the original image and its morphological opening. Similarly, the **black top-hat** of an image computes the dark spots smaller than the structuring element. It is defined as the difference image of the morphological closing image of original image. The dark spots in the original image become bright spots after the black top-hat operation. The following code block demonstrates how to use these two morphological operations using the scikit-image `morphology` module functions on the input binary image of Tagore:

```
from scipy.ndimage.morphology import binary_fill_holes
im = imread('../images/tagore.png')[...,3]
im[im <= 0.5] = 0
im[im > 0.5] = 1
im1 = white_tophat(im, square(5))
im2 = black_tophat(im, square(5))
pylab.screenshot(figsize=(20,15))
pylab.subplot(1,2,1), plot_image(im1, 'white tophat')
pylab.subplot(1,2,2), plot_image(im2, 'black tophat')
pylab.show()
```

The following screenshot shows the output for the white and black top-hats:

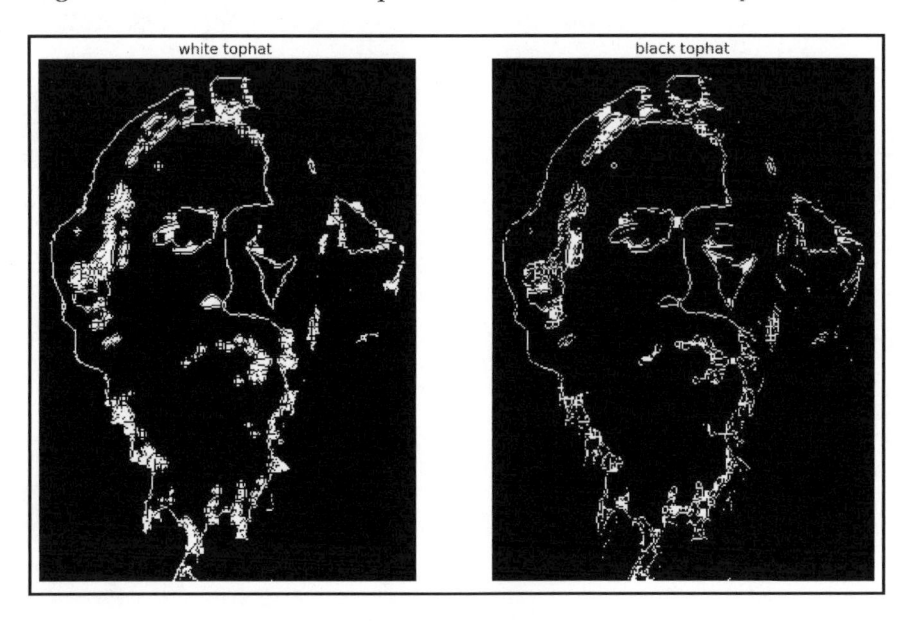

Extracting the boundary

The erosion operation can be used to extract the boundary of a binary image—we just need to subtract the eroded image from the input binary image to extract the boundary. The following code block implements this:

```
from skimage.morphology import binary_erosion
im = rgb2gray(imread('../images/horse-dog.jpg'))
threshold = 0.5
im[im < threshold] = 0
im[im >= threshold] = 1
boundary = im - binary_erosion(im)
plot_images_horizontally(im, boundary, 'boundary',sz=(18,9))
```

The following screenshot shows the output of the previous code block:

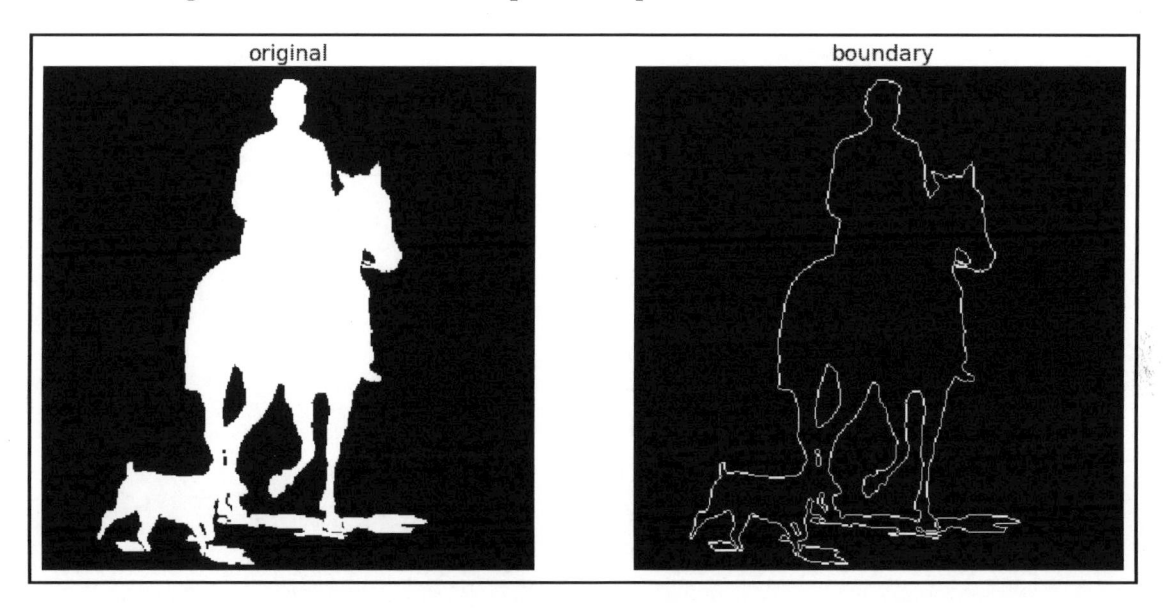

Fingerprint cleaning with opening and closing

Opening and closing can be sequentially used to remove noise (small foreground objects) from a binary image. This can be used in cleaning a fingerprint image as a preprocessing step. The following code block demonstrates how to implement it:

```
im = rgb2gray(imread('../images/fingerprint.jpg'))
im[im <= 0.5] = 0 # binarize
im[im > 0.5] = 1
```

Morphological Image Processing

```
im_o = binary_opening(im, square(2))
im_c = binary_closing(im, square(2))
im_oc = binary_closing(binary_opening(im, square(2)), square(2))
pylab.screenshot(figsize=(20,20))
pylab.subplot(221), plot_image(im, 'original')
pylab.subplot(222), plot_image(im_o, 'opening')
pylab.subplot(223), plot_image(im_c, 'closing')
pylab.subplot(224), plot_image(im_oc, 'opening + closing')
pylab.show()
```

The following screenshot shows the output of the previous code. As can be seen, the successive application of opening and closing cleans the noisy binary fingerprint image:

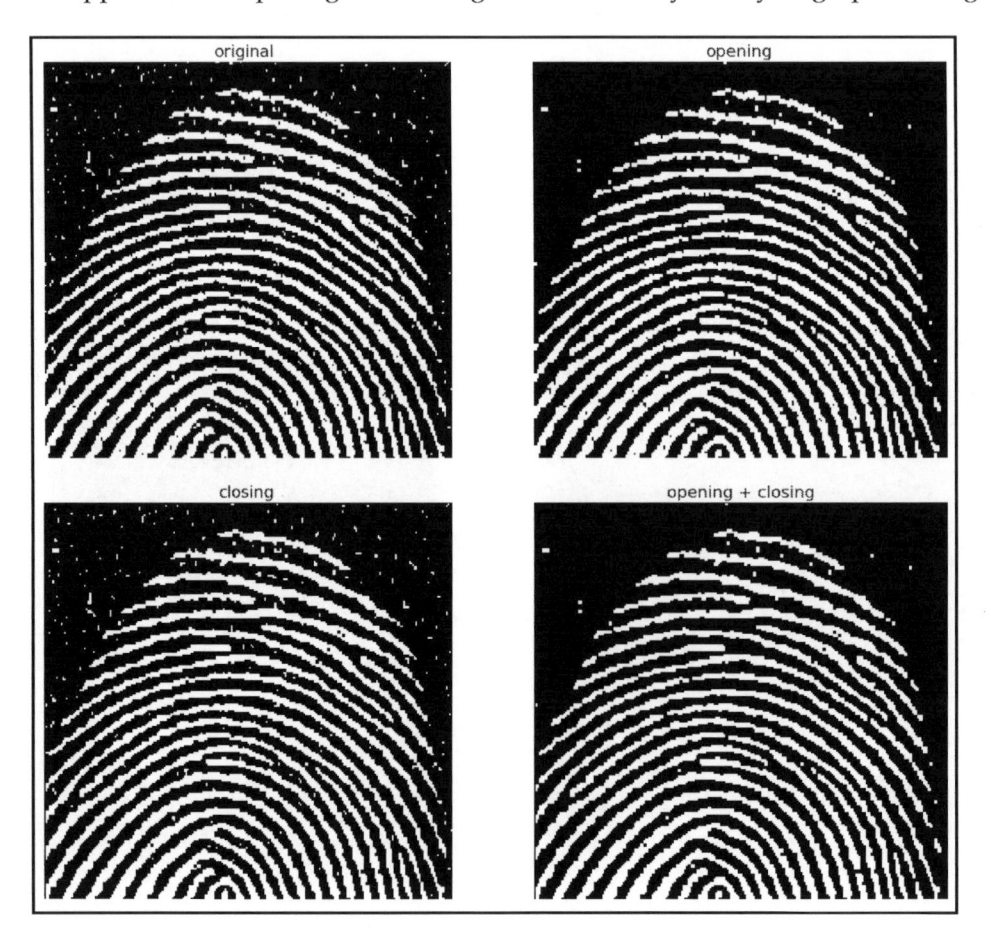

Grayscale operations

The following few code blocks show how to apply the morphological operations on grayscale images. First, let's start with gray-level erosion:

```
from skimage.morphology import dilation, erosion, closing, opening, square
im = imread('../images/zebras.jpg')
im = rgb2gray(im)
struct_elem = square(5)
eroded = erosion(im, struct_elem)
plot_images_horizontally(im, eroded, 'erosion')
```

The following screenshot shows the output of the previous code block. As can be seen, the black stripes are widened with erosion:

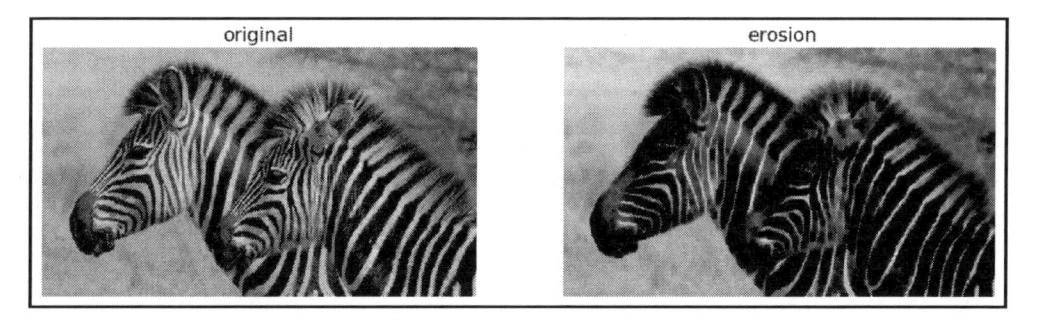

The following code block shows how to apply `dilation` on the same input grayscale image:

```
dilated = dilation(im, struct_elem)
plot_images_horizontally(im, dilated, 'dilation')
```

The following screenshot shows the output of the previous code block. As can be seen, the black stripes are narrowed down with dilation:

Morphological Image Processing

The following code block shows how to apply the morphological gray-level `opening` operation on the same input grayscale image:

```
opened = opening(im, struct_elem)
plot_images_horizontally(im, opened, 'opening')
```

The following screenshot shows the output. As can be seen, the width of the black stripes did not change with opening, although some thin white stripes were removed:

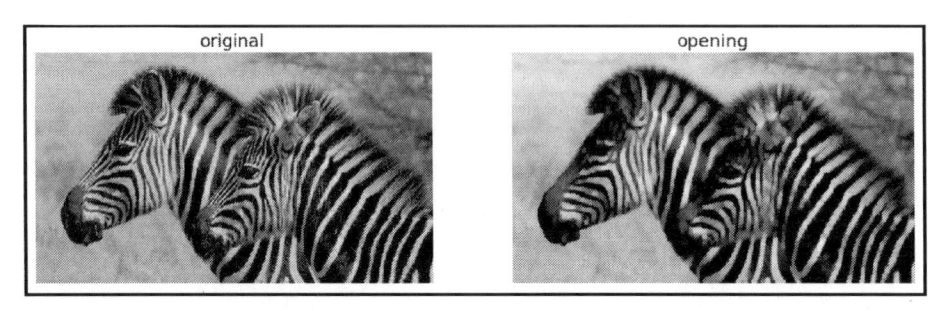

The following code block shows how to apply the morphological gray-level `closing` operation on the same input grayscale image:

```
closed = closing(im, struct_elem)
plot_images_horizontally(im, closed, 'closing')
```

The following screenshot shows the output. As can be seen, the width of the white stripes did not change with closing, although some thin black stripes were removed:

The scikit-image filter.rank module

The scikit-image's `filter.rank` module provides functions to implement morphological filters; for example, the morphological median filter and morphological contrast enhancement filter. The following sections demonstrate a couple of these filters.

Morphological contrast enhancement

The morphological contrast enhancement filter operates on each pixel by considering only the pixels in a neighborhood defined by a structuring element. It replaces the central pixel either by the local minimum or the local maximum pixel in the neighborhood, depending on which one the original pixel is closest to. The following code block shows a comparison of the output obtained using the morphological contrast enhancement filter and the exposure module's adaptive histogram equalization, with both the filters being local:

```
from skimage.filters.rank import enhance_contrast

def plot_gray_image(ax, image, title):
    ax.imshow(image, vmin=0, vmax=255, cmap=pylab.cm.gray),
ax.set_title(title), ax.axis('off')
    ax.set_adjustable('box-forced')

image = rgb2gray(imread('../images/squirrel.jpg'))
sigma = 0.05
noisy_image = np.clip(image + sigma *
np.random.standard_normal(image.shape), 0, 1)
enhanced_image = enhance_contrast(noisy_image, disk(5))
equalized_image = exposure.equalize_adapthist(noisy_image)
fig, axes = pylab.subplots(1, 3, figsize=[18, 7], sharex='row',
sharey='row')
axes1, axes2, axes3 = axes.ravel()
plot_gray_image(axes1, noisy_image, 'Original')
plot_gray_image(axes2, enhanced_image, 'Local morphological contrast
enhancement')
plot_gray_image(axes3, equalized_image, 'Adaptive Histogram equalization')
```

The following screenshot shows the output, comparing the input image with the output images obtained using morphological contrast enhancement and adaptive histogram equalization:

Noise removal with the median filter

The following code block shows how to use scikit-image `filters.rank` module's morphological `median` filter. Some impulse noise is added to the input grayscale `Lena` image by randomly setting 10% of the pixels to `255` (salt) and another 10% to `0` (pepper). The structuring elements used are disks with different sizes in order to remove the noise with the `median` filter:

```
from skimage.filters.rank import median
from skimage.morphology import disk
noisy_image = (rgb2gray(imread('../images/lena.jpg'))*255).astype(np.uint8)
noise = np.random.random(noisy_image.shape)
noisy_image[noise > 0.9] = 255
noisy_image[noise < 0.1] = 0
fig, axes = pylab.subplots(2, 2, figsize=(10, 10), sharex=True, sharey=True)
axes1, axes2, axes3, axes4 = axes.ravel()
plot_gray_image(axes1, noisy_image, 'Noisy image')
plot_gray_image(axes2, median(noisy_image, disk(1)), 'Median $r=1$')
plot_gray_image(axes3, median(noisy_image, disk(5)), 'Median $r=5$')
plot_gray_image(axes4, median(noisy_image, disk(20)), 'Median $r=20$')
```

The output of the previous code block is shown in the following screenshot. As can be seen, the output gets more patchy or blurred as the disk radius is increased, although more noise gets removed at the same time:

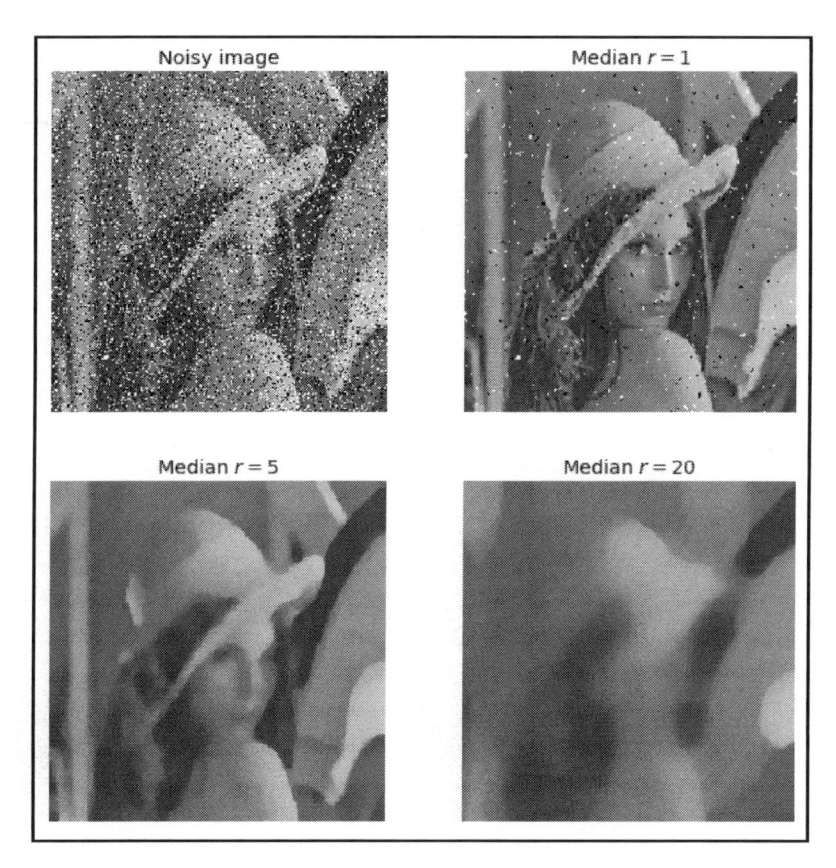

Computing the local entropy

Entropy is a measure of uncertainty or randomness in an image. It is mathematically defined as follows:

$$H = -\sum_{i=0}^{255} p_i \log_2 p_i$$

In the previous formula, p_i is the probability (obtained from the normalized histogram of the image) associated with the gray-level, i. This formula computes the global entropy of an image. In a similar manner, we can define local entropy too, to define local image complexity, and it can be computed from the local histograms.

The `skimage.rank.entropy()` function computes the local entropy (the minimum number of bits required to encode local gray-level distribution) of an image on a given structuring element. The following example shows how to apply this filter on a grayscale image. The function returns 10x entropy for 8-bit images:

```
from skimage.morphology import disk
from skimage.filters.rank import entropy
image = rgb2gray(imread('../images/birds.png'))
fig, (axes1, axes2) = pylab.subplots(1, 2, figsize=(18, 10), sharex=True,
sharey=True)
fig.colorbar(axes1.imshow(image, cmap=pylab.cm.gray), ax=axes1)
axes1.axis('off'), axes1.set_title('Image', size=20),
axes1.set_adjustable('box-forced')
fig.colorbar(axes2.imshow(entropy(image, disk(5)), cmap=pylab.cm.inferno),
ax=axes2)
axes2.axis('off'), axes2.set_title('Entropy', size=20),
axes2.set_adjustable('box-forced')
pylab.show()
```

The following screenshot shows the output. The regions with higher entropy (in other words, with higher information content such as the bird's nest) are represented with brighter colors:

The SciPy ndimage.morphology module

The SciPy `ndimage.morphology` module also provides the previously discussed functions for morphological operations on binary and grayscale images, and a few of them are demonstrated in the following sections.

Filling holes in binary objects

This function fills the holes in binary objects. The following code block demonstrates the application of the function with different structuring element sizes on an input binary image:

```
from scipy.ndimage.morphology import binary_fill_holes
im = rgb2gray(imread('../images/text1.png'))
im[im <= 0.5] = 0
im[im > 0.5] = 1
pylab.screenshot(figsize=(20,15))
pylab.subplot(221), pylab.imshow(im), pylab.title('original', size=20),
pylab.axis('off')
i = 2
for n in [3,5,7]:
 pylab.subplot(2, 2, i)
 im1 = binary_fill_holes(im, structure=np.ones((n,n)))
 pylab.imshow(im1), pylab.title('binary_fill_holes with structure square side ' + str(n), size=20)
 pylab.axis('off')
 i += 1
pylab.show()
```

Morphological Image Processing

The following screenshot shows the output of the previous code block. As can be seen, the larger the structuring element (square) side, the fewer number of holes are filled:

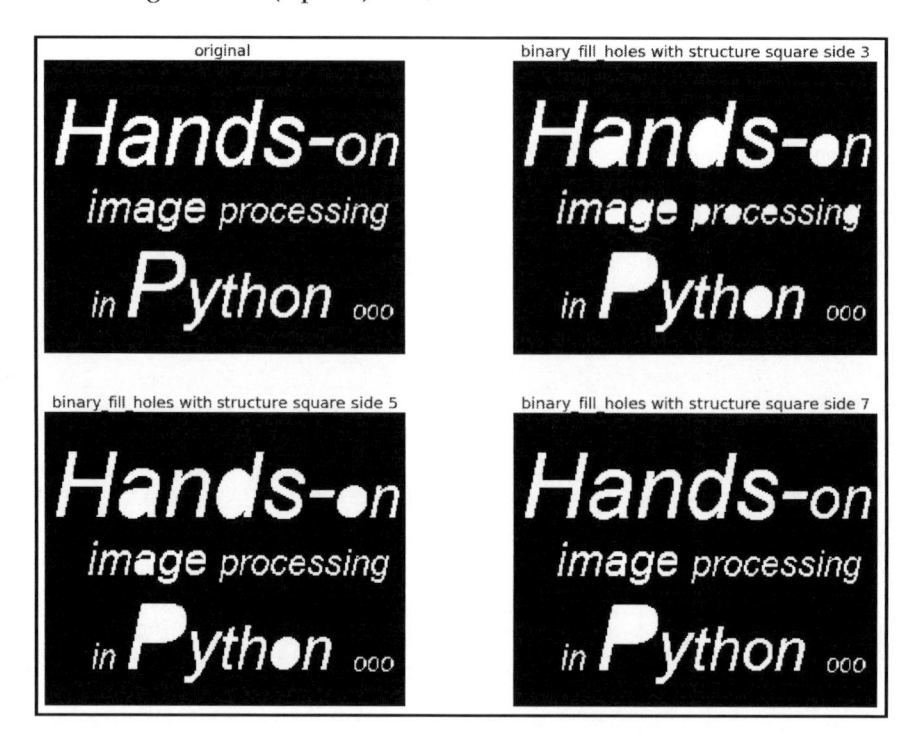

Using opening and closing to remove noise

The following code block shows how gray-level opening and closing can remove salt-and-pepper noise from a grayscale image, and how the successive application of opening and closing removes salt-and-pepper (impulse) noise from the input, a noisy mandrill grayscale image:

```
im = rgb2gray(imread('../images/mandrill_spnoise_0.1.jpg'))
im_o = ndimage.grey_opening(im, size=(2,2))
im_c = ndimage.grey_closing(im, size=(2,2))
im_oc = ndimage.grey_closing(ndimage.grey_opening(im, size=(2,2)), size=(2,2))
pylab.screenshot(figsize=(20,20))
pylab.subplot(221), pylab.imshow(im), pylab.title('original', size=20), pylab.axis('off')
pylab.subplot(222), pylab.imshow(im_o), pylab.title('opening (removes salt)', size=20), pylab.axis('off')
```

```
pylab.subplot(223), pylab.imshow(im_c), pylab.title('closing (removes
pepper)', size=20),pylab.axis('off')
pylab.subplot(224), pylab.imshow(im_oc), pylab.title('opening + closing
(removes salt + pepper)', size=20)
pylab.axis('off')
pylab.show()
```

The following shows the output of the previous code—how opening and closing removes the salt and the pepper noise from the grayscale noisy image of a mandrill:

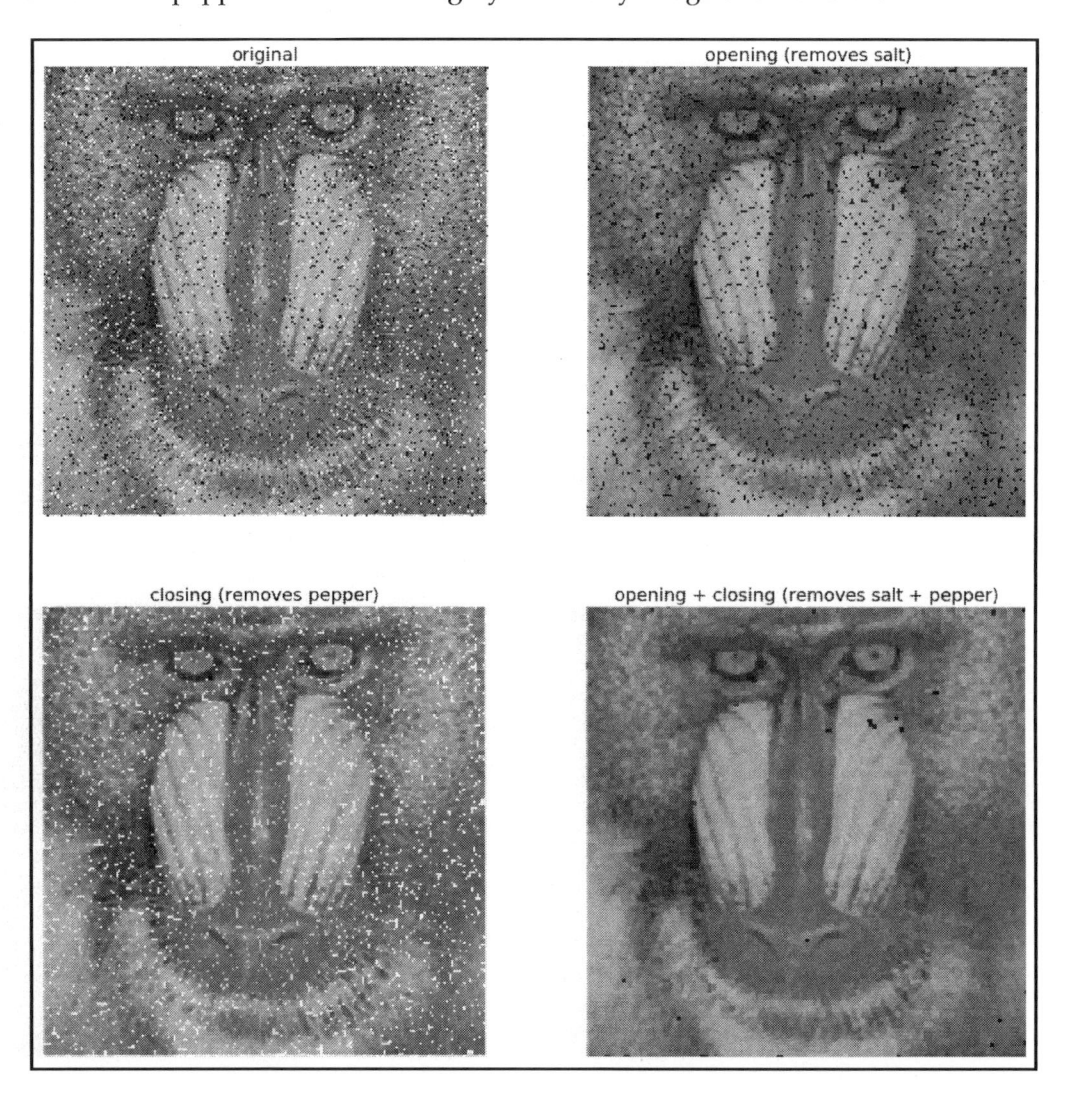

Computing the morphological Beucher gradient

The morphological Beucher gradient can be computed as a difference image of the dilated version and the eroded version of an input grayscale image. SciPy `ndimage` provides a function for computing the morphological gradient of a grayscale image. The following code block shows how these two produce the same output for an Einstein image:

```
from scipy import ndimage
im = rgb2gray(imread('../images/einstein.jpg'))
im_d = ndimage.grey_dilation(im, size=(3,3))
im_e = ndimage.grey_erosion(im, size=(3,3))
im_bg = im_d - im_e
im_g = ndimage.morphological_gradient(im, size=(3,3))
pylab.gray()
pylab.screenshot(figsize=(20,18))
pylab.subplot(231), pylab.imshow(im), pylab.title('original', size=20), pylab.axis('off')
pylab.subplot(232), pylab.imshow(im_d), pylab.title('dilation', size=20), pylab.axis('off')
pylab.subplot(233), pylab.imshow(im_e), pylab.title('erosion', size=20), pylab.axis('off')
pylab.subplot(234), pylab.imshow(im_bg), pylab.title('Beucher gradient (bg)', size=20), pylab.axis('off')
pylab.subplot(235), pylab.imshow(im_g), pylab.title('ndimage gradient (g)', size=20), pylab.axis('off')
pylab.subplot(236), pylab.title('diff gradients (bg - g)', size=20), pylab.imshow(im_bg - im_g) pylab.axis('off')
pylab.show()
```

The following screenshot shows the output—the SciPy morphological gradient function has the exact same output image as the Beucher gradient:

original	dilation	erosion

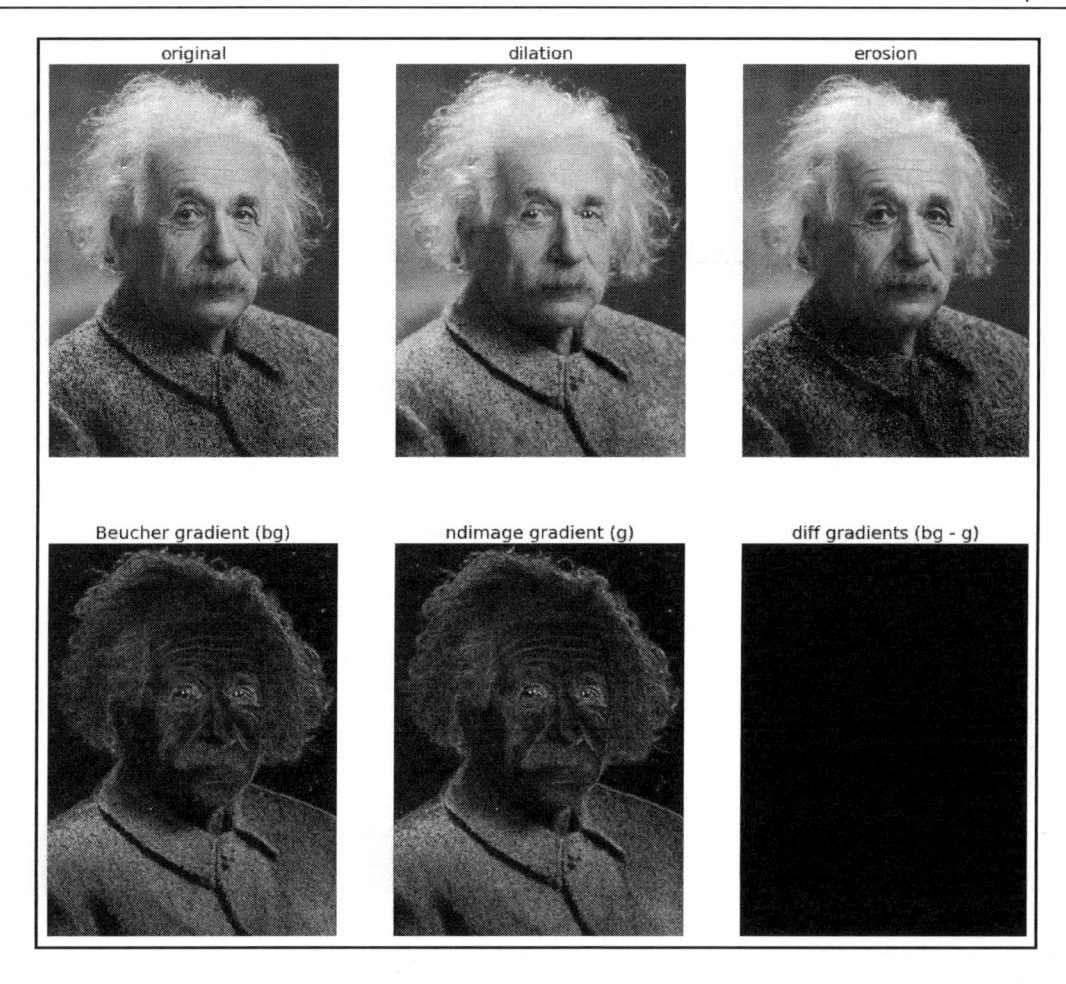

Beucher gradient (bg)	ndimage gradient (g)	diff gradients (bg - g)

Computing the morphological Laplace

The following code block demonstrates how to compute the morphological Laplace using the corresponding `ndimage` function with a binary image of Tagore, and compares it with the morphological gradient with structuring elements of different sizes, though as can be seen, for this image a smaller structuring element with gradient and a larger structuring element with Laplace yields better output images in terms of extracted edges:

```
im = imread('../images/tagore.png')[...,3]
im_g = ndimage.morphological_gradient(im, size=(3,3))
im_l = ndimage.morphological_laplace(im, size=(5,5))
pylab.screenshot(figsize=(15,10))
pylab.subplot(121), pylab.title('ndimage morphological laplace', size=20),
```

[249]

```
pylab.imshow(im_l)
pylab.axis('off')
pylab.subplot(122), pylab.title('ndimage morphological gradient', size=20),
pylab.imshow(im_g)
pylab.axis('off')
pylab.show()
```

The following screenshot shows the output of the previous code:

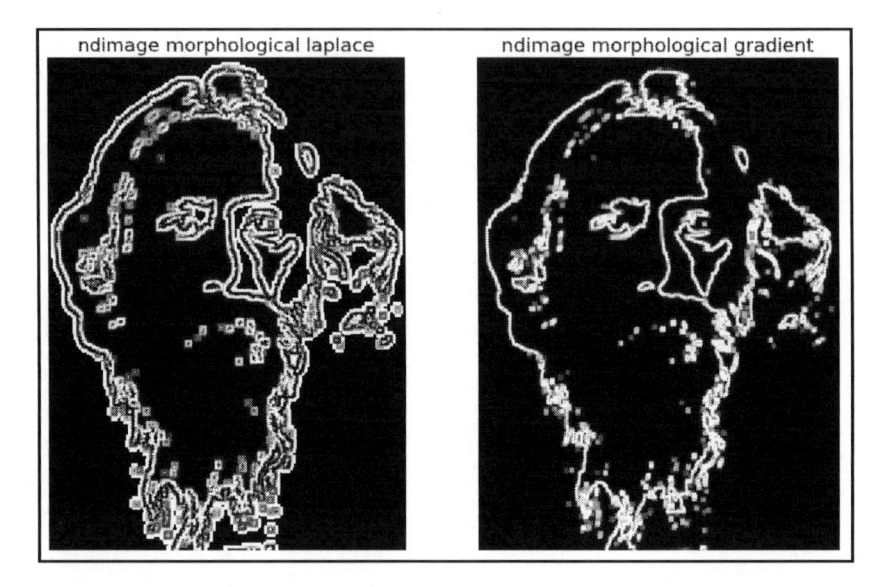

Summary

In this chapter, we discussed different image processing techniques based on mathematical morphology. We discussed morphological binary operations such as erosion, dilation, opening, closing, skeletonizing, and white and black top-hats. Then we discussed some applications such as computing the convex hull, removing small objects, extracting the boundary, fingerprint cleaning with opening and closing, filling holes in binary objects, and using opening and closing to remove noise. After that, we discussed extension of the morphological operations to grayscale operations and applications of morphological contrast enhancement, noise removal with the median filter, and computing local entropy. Also, we discussed how to compute the morphological (Beucher) gradient and the morphological Laplace. By the end of this chapter, the reader should be able to write Python code for morphological image processing (for example, opening, closing, skeletonizing, and computing the convex hull).

Questions

1. Show with a binary image that morphological opening and closing are dual operations. (Hint: apply opening on an image foreground and closing on the image background with the same structuring element)
2. Automatically crop an image using the convex hull of the object in it (the problem is taken from https://stackoverflow.com/questions/14211340/automatically-cropping-an-image-with-python-pil/51703287#51703287). Use the following image and crop the white background:

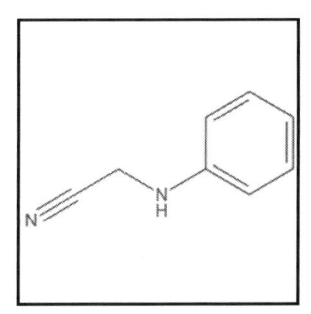

The desired output image is shown as follows—the bounding rectangle to crop the image is to be found automatically:

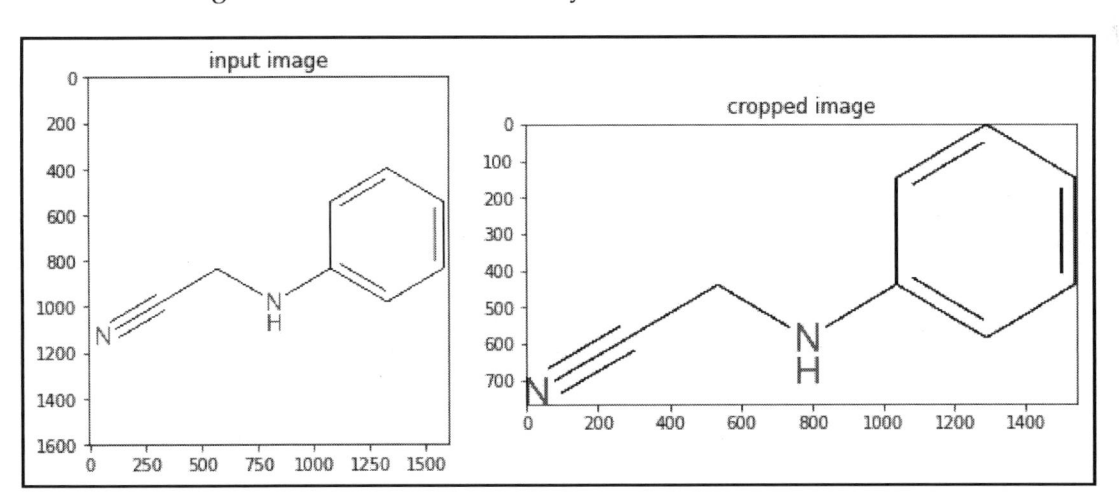

3. Use the `maximum()` and `minimum()` functions from `skimage.filters.rank` to implement morphological opening and closing with a grayscale image.

Further reading

- `https://www.idi.ntnu.no/emner/tdt4265/lectures/lecture3b.pdf`
- `https://www.uio.no/studier/emner/matnat/ifi/INF4300/h11/undervisningsmateriale/morfologi2011.pdf`
- `https://www.cis.rit.edu/class/simg782/lectures/lecture_03/lec782_05_03.pdf`
- `http://www.math.tau.ac.il/~turkel/notes/segmentation_morphology.pdf`
- `https://courses.cs.washington.edu/courses/cse576/book/ch3.pdf`
- `http://www.cse.iitd.ernet.in/~pkalra/csl783/Morphological.pdf`

7
Extracting Image Features and Descriptors

In this chapter, we will discuss feature detectors and descriptors, along with various applications of different types of feature detectors/extractors in image processing. We will start by defining feature detectors and descriptors. We will then continue our discussion on a few popular feature detectors such as Harris Corner/SIFT and HOG, and then their applications in important image processing problems such as image matching and object detection, respectively, with `scikit-image` and `python-opencv (cv2)` library functions.

The topics to be covered in this chapter are as follows:

- Feature detectors versus descriptors, to extract features/descriptors from images
- Harris Corner Detector and the application of Harris Corner features in image matching (with scikit-image)
- Blob detectors with LoG, DoG, and DoH (with `scikit-image`)
- Extraction of Histogram of Oriented Gradients features
- SIFT, ORB, and BRIEF features and their application in image matching
- Haar-like features and their application in face detection

Feature detectors versus descriptors

In image processing, (local) features refer to a group of key/salient points or information relevant to an image processing task, and they create an abstract, more general (and often robust) representation of an image. A family of algorithms that choose a set of interest points from an image based on some criterion (for example, cornerness, local maximum/minimum, and so on, that detect/extract the features from an image) are called **feature detectors/extractors**.

Extracting Image Features and Descriptors

On the contrary, a descriptor consists of a collection of values to represent the image with the features/interest points (for example, HOG features). Feature extraction can also be thought of as an operation that transforms an image into a set of feature descriptors, and, hence, a special form of dimensionality reduction. A local feature is usually formed by an interest point and its descriptor together.

Global features from the whole image (for example, image histogram) are often not desirable. A more practical approach is to describe an image as a collection of local features which correspond to interesting regions in the image such as corners, edges, and blobs. Each of these regions is characterized by a descriptor which captures the local distribution of certain photometric properties, such as intensities and gradients. Some properties of the local features are as follows:

- They should be repetitive (detect the same points independently in each image)
- They should be invariant to translation, rotation, scale (affine transformation)
- They should be robust to the presence of noise/blur/occlusion, clutter, and illumination change (locality)
- The region should contain interesting structures (distinctiveness), and suchlike

Many image processing tasks, such as image registration, image matching, image stitching (panoramas), and object detection/recognition use local features. The following diagram demonstrates the basic idea:

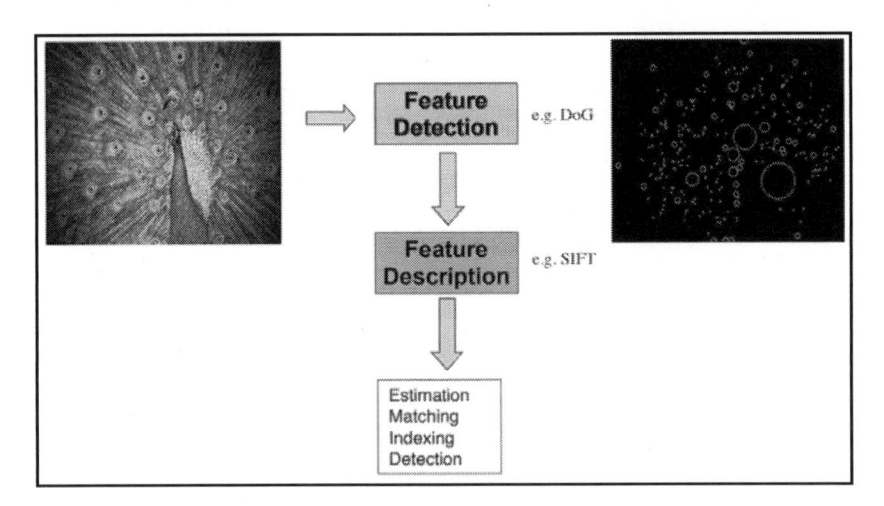

In this chapter, we are going to use `python-opencv` (the `cv2` library) for the first time. In order to install it properly, it is recommended you go through this link: https://opencv-python-tutroals.readthedocs.io/en/latest/py_tutorials/py_setup/py_setup_in_windows/py_setup_in_windows.html.

As usual, let's start by importing all the required libraries:

```
from matplotlib import pylab as pylab
from skimage.io import imread
from skimage.color import rgb2gray
from skimage.feature import corner_harris, corner_subpix, corner_peaks
from skimage.transform import warp, SimilarityTransform, AffineTransform, resize
import cv2
import numpy as np
from skimage import data
from skimage.util import img_as_float
from skimage.exposure import rescale_intensity
from skimage.measure import ransac
```

Harris Corner Detector

This algorithm explores the intensity changes within a window as the window changes location inside an image. Unlike an edge, for which intensity values change abruptly in only one direction, there is a significant change in intensity values at a corner in all directions. Hence, a large change in intensity value should result when the window is shifted in any direction at the corner (with good localization); this fact is exploited in the Harris Corner Detector algorithm. It is invariant to rotation, but not to scale (that is, the corner points found from an image remain unchanged when the image undergoes a rotation transformation, but change when the image is resized). In this section, we shall discuss how to implement a Harris Corner Detector with scikit-image.

With scikit-image

The next code snippet shows how to detect corner points in an image using the Harris Corner Detector with the corner_harris() function from the scikit-image feature module:

```
image = imread('../images/chess.png') # RGB image
image_gray = rgb2gray(image)
coordinates = corner_harris(image_gray, k =0.001)
image[coordinates>0.01*coordinates.max()]=[255,0,0,255]
pylab.figure(figsize=(20,10))
pylab.imshow(image), pylab.axis('off'), pylab.show()
```

The next screenshot shows the output of the code, with the corners detected as red points:

With sub-pixel accuracy

Sometimes, the corners may be needed to be found with maximum accuracy. With the `corner_subpix()` function from the scikit-image's feature module, the corners detected are refined with sub-pixel accuracy. The following code demonstrates how to use this function. The Louvre Pyramid in Paris is used as the input image. As usual, first the Harris Corners are computed with `corner_peaks()`, then the sub-pixel positions of corners are computed with the `corner_subpix()` function, which uses a statistical test to decide whether to accept/reject a corner point computed earlier with the `corner_peaks()` function. We need to define the size of neighborhood (window) the function will use to search for corners:

```
image = imread('../images/pyramids2.jpg')
image_gray = rgb2gray(image)
coordinates = corner_harris(image_gray, k =0.001)
coordinates[coordinates > 0.03*coordinates.max()] = 255 # threshold for an
optimal value, depends on the image
corner_coordinates = corner_peaks(coordinates)
coordinates_subpix = corner_subpix(image_gray, corner_coordinates,
window_size=11)
pylab.figure(figsize=(20,20))
pylab.subplot(211), pylab.imshow(coordinates, cmap='inferno')
pylab.plot(coordinates_subpix[:, 1], coordinates_subpix[:, 0], 'row.',
markersize=5, label='subpixel')
pylab.legend(prop={'size': 20}), pylab.axis('off')
pylab.subplot(212), pylab.imshow(image, interpolation='nearest')
pylab.plot(corner_coordinates[:, 1], corner_coordinates[:, 0], 'bo',
markersize=5)
pylab.plot(coordinates_subpix[:, 1], coordinates_subpix[:, 0], 'row+',
markersize=10), pylab.axis('off')
pylab.tight_layout(), pylab.show()
```

The next couple of screenshots show the output of the code. In the first screenshot, the Harris Corners are marked in yellow pixels and the refined sub-pixel corners are marked with red pixels. In the second screenshot, the corners detected are plotted on top of the original input image with blue pixels and the sub-pixel, again with red pixels:

An application – image matching

Once we have detected the interest points in an image, it would be good to know how to match the points across different images of the same object. For example, the following list shows the general approach to matching two such images:

- Compute the points of interest (for example, corner points with the Harris Corner Detector)
- Consider a region (window) around each of the key-points
- From the region, compute a local feature descriptor, for each key point for each image and normalize
- Match the local descriptors computed in two images (using Euclidean distance, for example)

Harris Corner points can be used to match two images; the next section gives an example.

Robust image matching using the RANSAC algorithm and Harris Corner features

In this example, we will match an image with its affine transformed version; they can be considered as if they were taken from different view points. The following steps describe the image matching algorithm:

1. First, we will compute the interest points or the Harris Corners in both the images.
2. A small space around the points will be considered, and the correspondences in-between the points will then be computed using a weighted sum of squared differences. This measure is not very robust, and it's only usable with slight viewpoint changes.
3. A set of source and corresponding destination coordinates will be obtained once the correspondences are found; they are used to estimate the geometric transformations between both the images.
4. A simple estimation of the parameters with the coordinates is not enough—many of the correspondences are likely to be faulty.

5. The RANdom SAmple Consensus (RANSAC) algorithm is used to robustly estimate the parameters, first by classifying the points into `inliers` and `outliers`, and then by fitting the model to `inliers` while ignoring the `outliers`, in order to find matches consistent with an affine transformation.

The next code block shows how to implement the image matching using the Harris Corner features:

```
temple = rgb2gray(img_as_float(imread('../images/temple.jpg')))
image_original = np.zeros(list(temple.shape) + [3])
image_original[..., 0] = temple
gradient_row, gradient_col = (np.mgrid[0:image_original.shape[0],
0:image_original.shape[1]] / float(image_original.shape[0]))
image_original[..., 1] = gradient_row
image_original[..., 2] = gradient_col
image_original = rescale_intensity(image_original)
image_original_gray = rgb2gray(image_original)
affine_trans  = AffineTransform(scale=(0.8, 0.9), rotation=0.1,
translation=(120, -20))
image_warped  = warp(image_original, affine_trans .inverse,
output_shape=image_original.shape)
image_warped_gray = rgb2gray(image_warped)
```

Extract corners using the Harris Corner measure:

```
coordinates = corner_harris(image_original_gray)
coordinates[coordinates > 0.01*coordinates.max()] = 1
coordinates_original = corner_peaks(coordinates, threshold_rel=0.0001,
min_distance=5)
coordinates = corner_harris(image_warped_gray)
coordinates[coordinates > 0.01*coordinates.max()] = 1
coordinates_warped = corner_peaks(coordinates, threshold_rel=0.0001,
min_distance=5)
```

Determine the sub-pixel corner position:

```
coordinates_original_subpix = corner_subpix(image_original_gray,
coordinates_original, window_size=9)
coordinates_warped_subpix = corner_subpix(image_warped_gray,
coordinates_warped, window_size=9)

def gaussian_weights(window_ext, sigma=1):
 y, x = np.mgrid[-window_ext:window_ext+1, -window_ext:window_ext+1]
 g_w = np.zeros(y.shape, dtype = np.double)
 g_w[:] = np.exp(-0.5 * (x**2 / sigma**2 + y**2 / sigma**2))
 g_w /= 2 * np.pi * sigma * sigma
 return g_w
```

Extracting Image Features and Descriptors

```
def match_corner(coordinates, window_ext=3):
  row, col = np.round(coordinates).astype(np.intp)
  window_original = image_original[row-window_ext:row+window_ext+1, col-window_ext:col+window_ext+1, :]
```

Weight pixels depending on the distance to the center pixel:

```
weights = gaussian_weights(window_ext, 3)
weights = np.dstack((weights, weights, weights))
```

Compute the sum of squared differences to all corners in the warped image:

```
SSDs = []
for coord_row, coord_col in coordinates_warped:
window_warped = image_warped[coord_row-window_ext:coord_row+window_ext+1,
coord_col-window_ext:coord_col+window_ext+1, :]
if window_original.shape == window_warped.shape:
SSD = np.sum(weights * (window_original - window_warped)**2)
SSDs.append(SSD)
```

Use the corner with the minimum SSD as correspondence:

```
min_idx = np.argmin(SSDs) if len(SSDs) > 0 else -1
return coordinates_warped_subpix[min_idx] if min_idx >= 0 else [None]
```

Find the correspondences using the simple weighted sum of the squared differences:

```
source, destination = [], []
for coordinates in coordinates_original_subpix:
  coordinates1 = match_corner(coordinates)
  if any(coordinates1) and len(coordinates1) > 0 and not
all(np.isnan(coordinates1)):
  source.append(coordinates)
  destination.append(coordinates1)
source = np.array(source)
destination = np.array(destination)
```

Estimate the affine transform model using all the coordinates:

```
model = AffineTransform()
model.estimate(source, destination)
```

Robustly estimate the affine transform model with RANSAC:

```
model_robust, inliers = ransac((source, destination), AffineTransform,
min_samples=3, residual_threshold=2, max_trials=100)
outliers = inliers == False
```

Compare the True and estimated transform parameters:

```
print(affine_trans.scale, affine_trans.translation, affine_trans.rotation)
# (0.8, 0.9) [ 120. -20.] 0.09999999999999999
print(model.scale, model.translation, model.rotation)
# (0.8982412101241938, 0.8072777593937368) [ -20.45123966 114.92297156]
-0.10225420334222493
print(model_robust.scale, model_robust.translation, model_robust.rotation)
# (0.9001524425730119, 0.8000362790749188) [ -19.87491292 119.83016533]
-0.09990858564132575
```

Visualize the correspondence:

```
fig, axes = pylab.subplots(nrows=2, ncols=1, figsize=(20,15))
pylab.gray()
inlier_idxs = np.nonzero(inliers)[0]
plot_matches(axes[0], image_original_gray, image_warped_gray, source,
destination, np.column_stack((inlier_idxs, inlier_idxs)),
matches_color='b')
axes[0].axis('off'), axes[0].set_title('Correct correspondences', size=20)
outlier_idxs = np.nonzero(outliers)[0]
plot_matches(axes[1], image_original_gray, image_warped_gray, source,
destination, np.column_stack((outlier_idxs, outlier_idxs)),
matches_color='row')
axes[1].axis('off'), axes[1].set_title('Faulty correspondences', size=20)
fig.tight_layout(), pylab.show()
```

The next screenshots show the output of the code block. The correct correspondences found are shown with blue lines, whereas the wrong correspondences are shown with red lines:

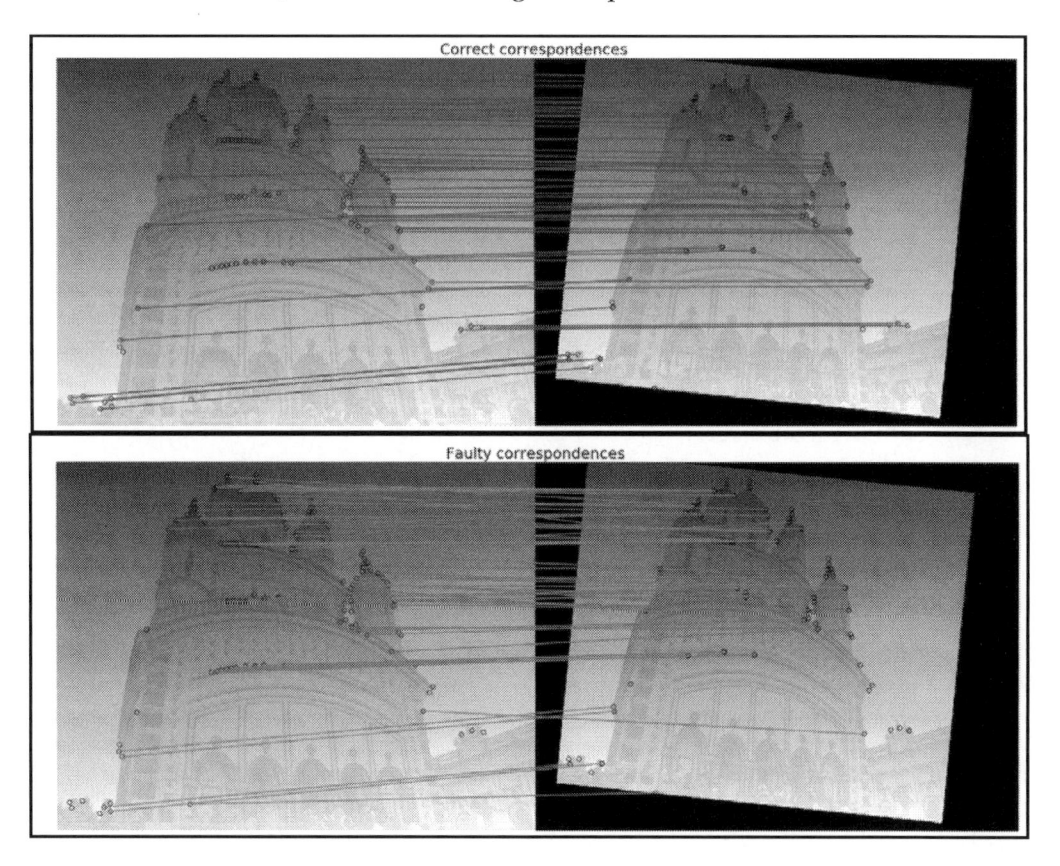

Blob detectors with LoG, DoG, and DoH

In an image, a blob is defined as either a bright on a dark region, or a dark on a bright region. In this section, we will discuss how to implement blob features detection in an image using the following three algorithms. The input image is a colored (RGB) butterfly image.

Laplacian of Gaussian (LoG)

In the `Chapter 3`, *Convolution and Frequency Domain Filtering*, we saw that the cross correlation of an image with a filter can be viewed as pattern matching; that is, comparing a (small) template image (of what we want to find) against all local regions in the image. The key idea in blob detection comes from this fact. We have already seen how an LoG filter with zero crossing can be used for edge detection in the last chapter. LoG can also be used to find scale invariant regions by searching 3D (location + scale) extrema of the LoG with the concept of Scale Space. If the scale of the Laplacian (σ of the LoG filter) gets matched with the scale of the blob, the magnitude of the Laplacian response attains a maximum at the center of the blob. With this approach, the LoG-convolved images are computed with gradually increasing σ and they are stacked up in a cube. The blobs correspond to the local maximums in this cube. This approach only detects the bright blobs on the dark backgrounds. It is accurate, but slow (particularly for detecting larger blobs).

Difference of Gaussian (DoG)

The LoG approach is approximated by the DoG approach, and hence it is faster. The image is smoothed (using Gaussians) with increasing σ values, and the difference between two consecutive smoothed images is stacked up in a cube. This approach again detects the bright blobs on the dark backgrounds. It is faster than LoG but less accurate, although the larger blobs detection is still expensive.

Determinant of Hessian (DoH)

The DoH approach is the fastest of all these approaches. It detects the blobs by computing maximums in the matrix of the Determinant of Hessian of the image. The size of blobs does not have any impact on the speed of detection. Both the bright blobs on the dark background and the dark blobs on the bright backgrounds are detected by this approach, but the small blobs are not detected accurately.

The next code block demonstrates how to implement these aforementioned three algorithms using scikit-image:

```
from numpy import sqrt
from skimage.feature import blob_dog, blob_log, blob_doh

im = imread('../images/butterfly.png')
im_gray = rgb2gray(im)
log_blobs = blob_log(im_gray, max_sigma=30, num_sigma=10, threshold=.1)
log_blobs[:, 2] = sqrt(2) * log_blobs[:, 2] # Compute radius in the 3rd
```

Extracting Image Features and Descriptors

```
column
dog_blobs = blob_dog(im_gray, max_sigma=30, threshold=0.1)
dog_blobs[:, 2] = sqrt(2) * dog_blobs[:, 2]
doh_blobs = blob_doh(im_gray, max_sigma=30, threshold=0.005)
list_blobs = [log_blobs, dog_blobs, doh_blobs]
color, titles = ['yellow', 'lime', 'red'], ['Laplacian of Gaussian',
'Difference of Gaussian', 'Determinant of Hessian']
sequence = zip(list_blobs, colors, titles)
fig, axes = pylab.subplots(2, 2, figsize=(20, 20), sharex=True,
sharey=True)
axes = axes.ravel()
axes[0].imshow(im, interpolation='nearest')
axes[0].set_title('original image', size=30), axes[0].set_axis_off()
for idx, (blobs, color, title) in enumerate(sequence):
 axes[idx+1].imshow(im, interpolation='nearest')
 axes[idx+1].set_title('Blobs with ' + title, size=30)
 for blob in blobs:
    y, x, row = blob
    col = pylab.Circle((x, y), row, color=color, linewidth=2, fill=False)
    axes[idx+1].add_patch(col),   axes[idx+1].set_axis_off()
pylab.tight_layout(), pylab.show()
```

The next screenshots show the output of the code which is the blobs detected with different algorithms:

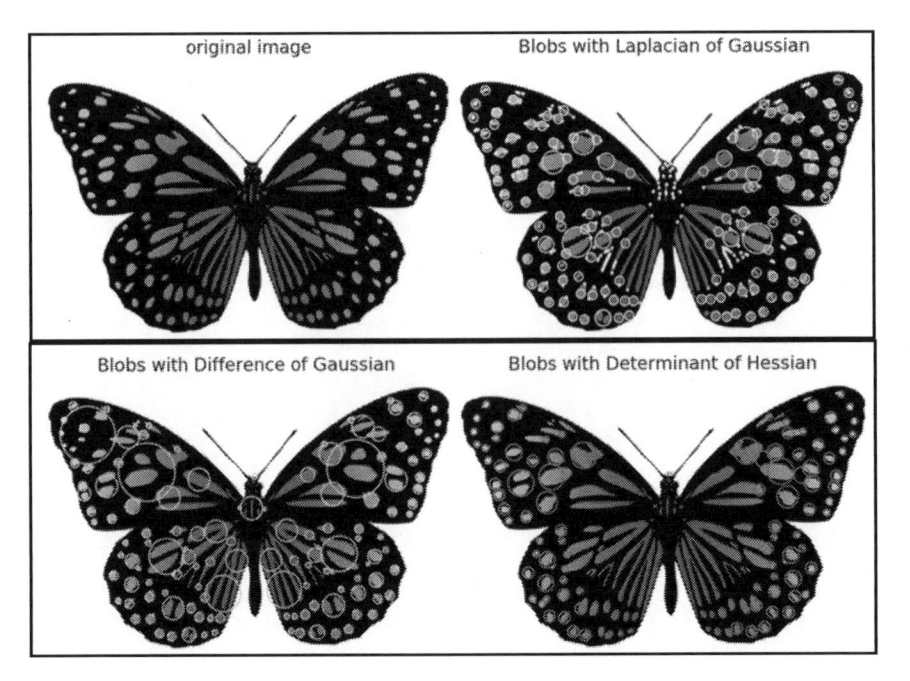

Both the corner and blob features possess repeatability, saliency, and locality properties.

Histogram of Oriented Gradients

A popular feature descriptor for object detection is the **Histogram of Oriented Gradients (HOG)**. In this section, we will discuss how HOG descriptors can be computed from an image.

Algorithm to compute HOG descriptors

The following steps describe the algorithm:

1. If you wish to, you can globally normalize the image
2. Compute the horizontal and vertical gradient images
3. Compute the gradient histograms
4. Normalize across blocks
5. Flatten into a feature descriptor vector

HOG descriptors are the normalized block descriptors finally obtained by using the algorithm.

Compute HOG descriptors with scikit-image

Let's now compute the HOG descriptors using the scikit-image feature module's `hog()` function and visualize them:

```
from skimage.feature import hog
from skimage import exposure
image = rgb2gray(imread('images/cameraman.jpg'))
fd, hog_image = hog(image, orientations=8, pixels_per_cell=(16, 16),
cells_per_block=(1, 1), visualize=True)
print(image.shape, len(fd))
# ((256L, 256L), 2048)
fig, (axes1, axes2) = pylab.subplots(1, 2, figsize=(15, 10), sharex=True,
sharey=True)
axes1.axis('off'), axes1.imshow(image, cmap=pylab.cm.gray),
axes1.set_title('Input image')
```

Let's now rescale the histogram for a better display:

```
hog_image_rescaled = exposure.rescale_intensity(hog_image, in_range=(0,
10))
axes2.axis('off'), axes2.imshow(hog_image_rescaled, cmap=pylab.cm.gray),
axes2.set_title('Histogram of Oriented Gradients')
pylab.show()
```

Here's the output that you should get—notice the visualization of the HOG features computed:

In `Chapter 9`, *Classical Machine Learning Methods in Image Processing*, we will discuss how to use the HOG descriptors to detect objects from an image.

Scale-invariant feature transform

Scale-invariant feature transform (SIFT) descriptors provide an alternative representation for image regions. They are very useful for matching images. As demonstrated earlier, simple corner detectors work well when the images to be matched are similar in nature (with respect to *scale, orientation*, and so on). But if they have different scales and rotations, the SIFT descriptors are needed to be used to match them. SIFT is not only just scale invariant, but it still obtains good results when rotation, illumination, and viewpoints of the images change as well.

Let's discuss the primary steps involved in the SIFT algorithm that transforms image content into local feature coordinates that are invariant to translation, rotation, scale, and other imaging parameters.

Algorithm to compute SIFT descriptors

- **Scale-space extrema detection**: Search over multiple scales and image locations, the location and characteristic scales are given by DoG detector
- **Keypoint localization:** Select keypoints based on a measure of stability, keep only the strong interest points by eliminating the low-contrast and edge keypoints
- **Orientation assignment**: Compute the best orientation(s) for each keypoint region, which contributes to the stability of matching
- **Keypoint descriptor computation**: Use local image gradients at selected scale and rotation to describe each keypoint region

As discussed, SIFT is robust with regard to small variations in illumination (due to gradient and normalization), pose (small affine variation due to orientation histogram), scale (by DoG), and intra-class variability (small variations due to histograms).

With opencv and opencv-contrib

In order to be able to use the SIFT functions with `python-opencv`, we first need to install `opencv-contrib` by following the instructions from this link: https://pypi.org/project/opencv-contrib-python/. The next code block demonstrates how to detect the SIFT keypoints and draws them using the input Mona Lisa image.

We will first construct a SIFT object and then use the `detect()` method to compute the keypoints in an image. Every keypoint is a special feature, and has several attributes. For example, its (x, y) coordinates, angle (orientation), response (strength of keypoints), size of the meaningful neighborhood, and so on.

Extracting Image Features and Descriptors

We will then use the `drawKeyPoints()` function from `cv2` to draw the small circles around the detected keypoints. If the `cv2.DRAW_MATCHES_FLAGS_DRAW_RICH_KEYPOINTS` flag is applied to the function, it will draw a circle with the size of a keypoint, along with its orientation. In order to compute the keypoints and the descriptor together, we will use the function `detectAndCompute()`:

```
img = cv2.imread('../images/monalisa.jpg')
gray= cv2.cvtColor(img,cv2.COLOR_BGR2GRAY)

sift = cv2.xfeatures2d.SIFT_create()
kp = sift.detect(gray,None)              # detect SIFT keypoints

img = cv2.drawKeypoints(img,kp, None,
flags=cv2.DRAW_MATCHES_FLAGS_DRAW_RICH_KEYPOINTS)
cv2.imshow("Image", img);
cv2.imwrite('me5_keypoints.jpg',img)

kp, des = sift.detectAndCompute(gray,None) # compute the SIFT descriptor
```

Here is the output of the code, the input Mona Lisa image, along with the computed SIFT keypoints drawn on it, and with the orientations:

Application – matching images with BRIEF, SIFT, and ORB

In the last section, we discussed how to detect SIFT keypoints. In this section, we will introduce a couple more feature descriptors for an image, namely BRIEF (a short binary descriptor) and ORB (an efficient alternative to SIFT). All of these descriptors can also be used for image matching and object detection, as we will see shortly.

Matching images with BRIEF binary descriptors with scikit-image

The BRIEF descriptor has comparatively few bits, and can be computed using a set of intensity difference tests. Being a short binary descriptor, it has a low memory footprint, and the matching using this descriptor turns out to be very efficient with the Hamming distance metric. With BRIEF, the desired scale-invariance can be obtained by detecting features at different scales, although it does not provide rotation-invariance. The next code block demonstrates how to compute the BRIEF binary descriptors with scikit-image functions. The input images for matching used are the gray-scale Lena image and its affine transformed versions.

Let's now code this:

```
from skimage import transform as transform
from skimage.feature import (match_descriptors, corner_peaks,
corner_harris, plot_matches, BRIEF)
img1 = rgb2gray(imread('images/lena.jpg')) #data.astronaut()
affine_trans = transform.AffineTransform(scale=(1.2, 1.2), translation=(0,
-100))
img2 = transform.warp(img1, affine_trans)
img3 = transform.rotate(img1, 25)
coords1, coords2, coords3 = corner_harris(img1), corner_harris(img2),
corner_harris(img3)
coords1[coords1 > 0.01*coords1.max()] = 1
coords2[coords2 > 0.01*coords2.max()] = 1
coords3[coords3 > 0.01*coords3.max()] = 1
keypoints1 = corner_peaks(coords1, min_distance=5)
keypoints2 = corner_peaks(coords2, min_distance=5)
keypoints3 = corner_peaks(coords3, min_distance=5)
extractor = BRIEF()
extractor.extract(img1, keypoints1)
keypoints1, descriptors1 = keypoints1[extractor.mask],
extractor.descriptors
extractor.extract(img2, keypoints2)
```

Extracting Image Features and Descriptors

```
keypoints2, descriptors2 = keypoints2[extractor.mask],
extractor.descriptors
extractor.extract(img3, keypoints3)
keypoints3, descriptors3 = keypoints3[extractor.mask],
extractor.descriptors
pylab.subplot(211), pylab.imshow(descriptors1)
pylab.subplot(212), pylab.imshow(descriptors2)
pylab.show()
#print(descriptors1.shape, descriptors2.shape)
matches12 = match_descriptors(descriptors1, descriptors2, cross_check=True)
matches13 = match_descriptors(descriptors1, descriptors3, cross_check=True)
fig, axes = pylab.subplots(nrows=2, ncols=1)
pylab.gray(), plot_matches(axes[0], img1, img2, keypoints1, keypoints2,
matches12)
axes[0].axis('off'), axes[0].set_title("Original Image vs. Transformed
Image")
plot_matches(axes[1], img1, img3, keypoints1, keypoints3, matches13)
axes[1].axis('off'), axes[1].set_title("Original Image vs. Transformed
Image"), pylab.show()
```

The next screenshots show the output of the code block and how the BRIEF keypoints match in-between the two images:

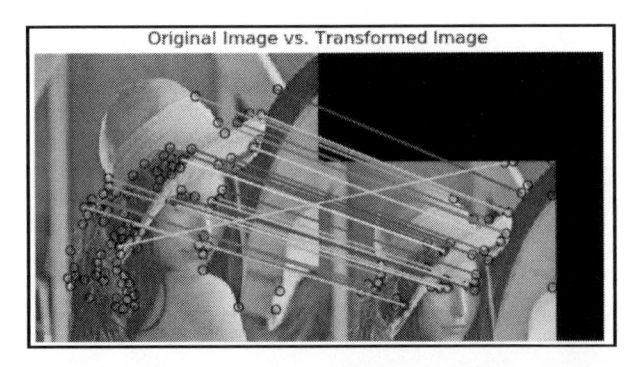

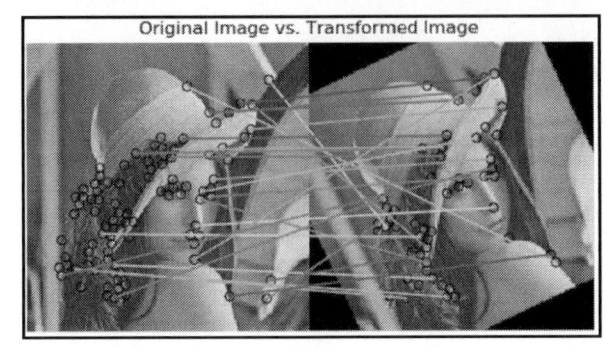

Matching with ORB feature detector and binary descriptor using scikit-image

Let's write a code that demonstrates the ORB feature detection and binary descriptor algorithm. An oriented FAST detection method and the rotated BRIEF descriptors are used by this algorithm. As compared to BRIEF, ORB is more scale and rotation invariant, but even this applies the Hamming distance metric for matching, which is more efficient. Hence, this method is preferred over BRIEF when considering real-time applications:

```
from skimage import transform as transform
from skimage.feature import (match_descriptors, ORB, plot_matches)

img1 = rgb2gray(imread('../images/me5.jpg'))
img2 = transform.rotate(img1, 180)
affine_trans = transform.AffineTransform(scale=(1.3, 1.1), rotation=0.5,
translation=(0, -200))
img3 = transform.warp(img1, affine_trans)
img4 = transform.resize(rgb2gray(imread('images/me6.jpg')), img1.shape,
anti_aliasing=True)

descriptor_extractor = ORB(n_keypoints=200)
descriptor_extractor.detect_and_extract(img1)
keypoints1, descriptors1 = descriptor_extractor.keypoints,
descriptor_extractor.descriptors

descriptor_extractor.detect_and_extract(img2)
keypoints2, descriptors2 = descriptor_extractor.keypoints,
descriptor_extractor.descriptors

descriptor_extractor.detect_and_extract(img3)
keypoints3, descriptors3 = descriptor_extractor.keypoints,
descriptor_extractor.descriptors

descriptor_extractor.detect_and_extract(img4)
keypoints4, descriptors4 = descriptor_extractor.keypoints,
descriptor_extractor.descriptors

matches12 = match_descriptors(descriptors1, descriptors2, cross_check=True)
matches13 = match_descriptors(descriptors1, descriptors3, cross_check=True)
matches14 = match_descriptors(descriptors1, descriptors4, cross_check=True)

fig, axes = pylab.subplots(nrows=3, ncols=1, figsize=(20,30))
pylab.gray()
plot_matches(axes[0], img1, img2, keypoints1, keypoints2, matches12)
axes[0].axis('off'), axes[0].set_title("Original Image vs. Transformed
Image")
plot_matches(axes[1], img1, img3, keypoints1, keypoints3, matches13)
```

Extracting Image Features and Descriptors

```
axes[1].axis('off'), axes[1].set_title("Original Image vs. Transformed
Image")
plot_matches(axes[2], img1, img4, keypoints1, keypoints4, matches14)
axes[2].axis('off'), axes[2].set_title("Image1 vs. Image2")
pylab.show()
```

You can see the output and how we matched it with an ORB detector and binary descriptor:

The next screenshots show the output images of the code block and the ORB keypoints for the images to be matched, along with the matches shown with lines. First the algorithm tries to match an image with its affine transformed version, and then two different images with a same object.

Orientation 1:

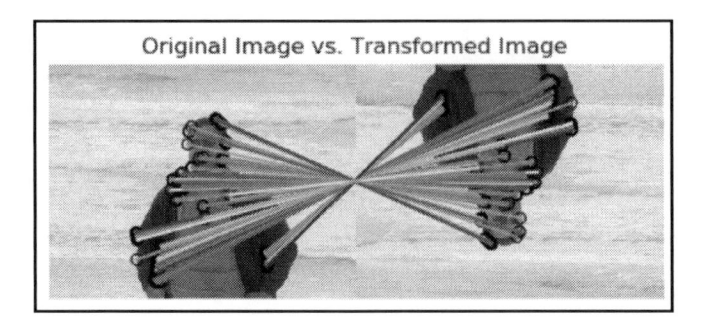

Orientation 2:

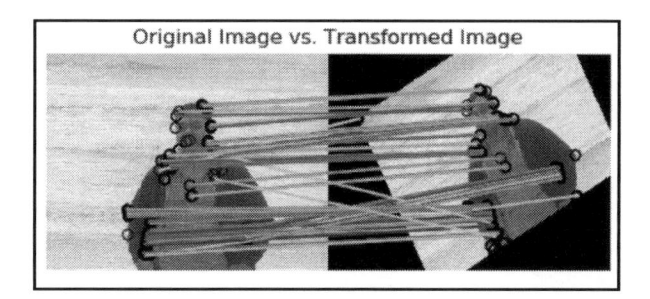

Original Image vs. Transformed Image

Orientation 3:

Image1 vs. Image2

Matching with ORB features using brute-force matching with python-opencv

In this section, we will demonstrate how two image descriptors can be matched using the brute-force matcher of opencv. In this, a descriptor of a feature from one image is matched with all the features in another image (using some distance metric), and the closest one is returned. We will use the BFMatcher() function with ORB descriptors to match two images of books:

```
img1 = cv2.imread('images/books.png',0) # queryImage
img2 = cv2.imread('images/book.png',0) # trainImage

# Create a ORB detector object
orb = cv2.ORB_create()
# find the keypoints and descriptors
kp1, des1 = orb.detectAndCompute(img1,None)
kp2, des2 = orb.detectAndCompute(img2,None)
# create a BFMatcher object
bf = cv2.BFMatcher(cv2.NORM_HAMMING, crossCheck=True)
# Match descriptors.
```

```
matches = bf.match(des1, des2)
# Sort them in the order of their distance.
matches = sorted(matches, key = lambda x:x.distance)
# Draw first 20 matches.
img3 = cv2.drawMatches(img1,kp1,img2,kp2,matches[:20], None, flags=2)
pylab.imshow(img3), pylab.show()
```

The following screenshots show the input images used in the code block:

The following screenshot shows the top 20 ORB keypoint matches computed by the code block:

Brute-force matching with SIFT descriptors and ratio test with OpenCV

The SIFT keypoints between two images are matched by identifying their nearest neighbors. But in some cases, because of factors such as noise, the second closest match may seem to be closer to the first. In this case, we compute the ratio of closest distance to the second closest distance and check if it is above 0.8. If the ratio is more than 0.8, it means they are rejected.

This efficiently eliminates approximately 90% of false matches, and only around 5% correct matches (as per the SIFT paper). Let's use the `knnMatch()` function to get k=2 best matches for a keypoint; we will also apply the ratio test:

```
img1 = cv2.imread('images/books.png',0) # queryImage
img2 = cv2.imread('images/book.png',0) # trainImage
# Create a SIFT detector object
sift = cv2.xfeatures2d.SIFT_create()
# find the keypoints and descriptors with SIFT
kp1, des1 = sift.detectAndCompute(img1,None)
```

```
kp2, des2 = sift.detectAndCompute(img2,None)
bf = cv2.BFMatcher()
matches = bf.knnMatch(des1, des2, k=2)
# Apply ratio test
good_matches = []
for m1, m2 in matches:
 if m1.distance < 0.75*m2.distance:
  good_matches.append([m1])
img3 = cv2.drawMatchesKnn(img1, kp1, img2, kp2,good_matches, None, flags=2)
pylab.imshow(img3),pylab.show()
```

The next screenshot shows the output of the preceding code block, and how the keypoint matches between the images with the k-nearest neighbor matcher:

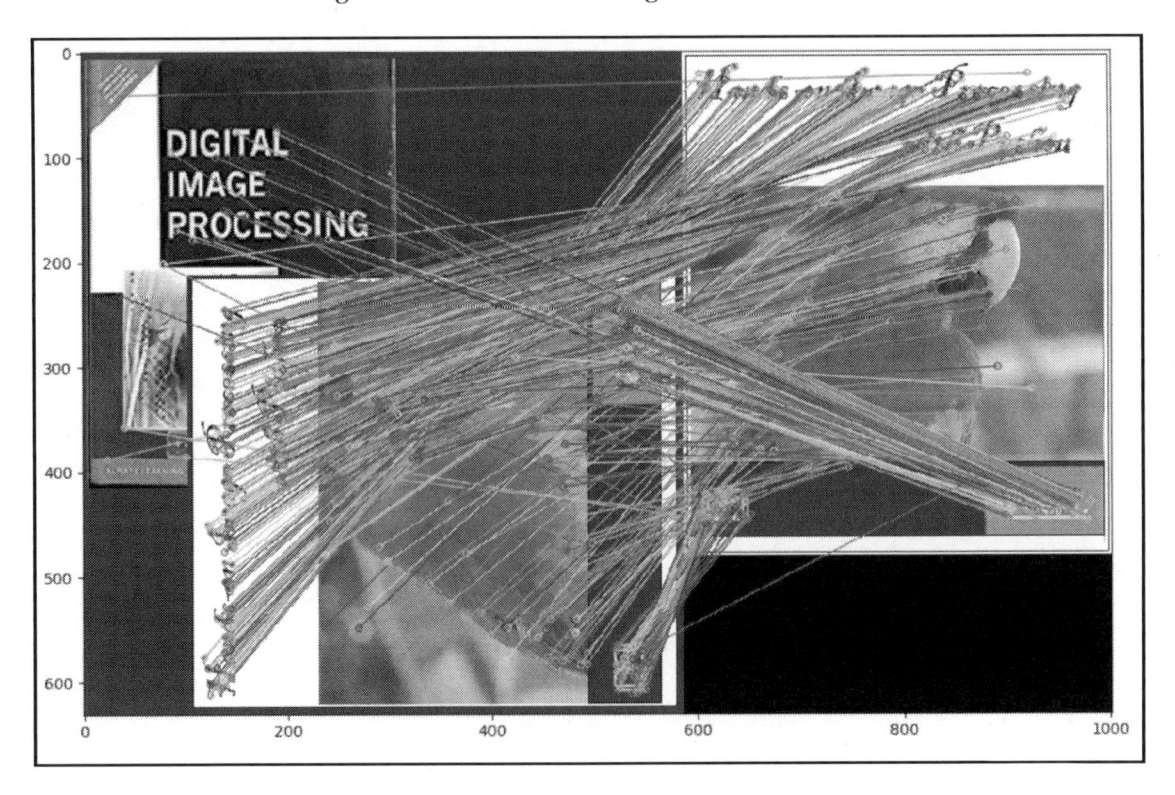

Haar-like features

Haar-like features are very useful image features used in object detection. They were introduced in the first real-time face detector by Viola and Jones. Using integral images, Haar-like features of any size (scale) can be efficiently computed in constant time. The computation speed is the key advantage of a Haar-like feature over most other features. These features are just like the convolution kernels (rectangle filters) introduced in `Chapter 3`, *Convolution and Frequency Domain Filtering*. Each feature corresponds to a single value computed by subtracting a sum of pixels under a white rectangle from a sum of pixels under a black rectangle. The next diagram shows different types of Haar-like features, along with the important Haar-like features for face detection:

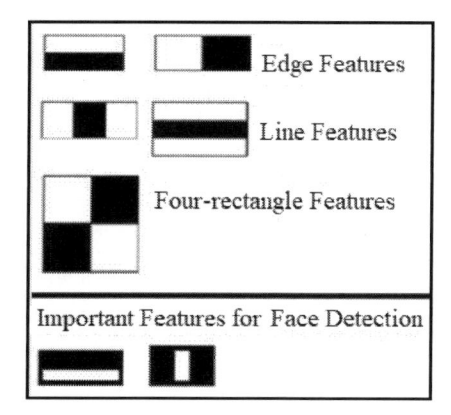

The first and the second important feature for face detection shown here seems to focus on the fact that the region of the eyes is often darker than the region of the nose and cheeks, and that the eyes are darker than the bridge of the nose, respectively. The next section visualizes the Haar-like features using scikit-image.

Haar-like feature descriptor with scikit-image

In this section, we are going to visualize different types of Haar-like feature descriptors, of which there are five different types. The value of the descriptor is equal to the difference between the sum of intensity values in the blue and the red one.

Extracting Image Features and Descriptors

The next code block shows how to use the scikit-image feature module's `haar_like_feature_coord()` and `draw_haar_like_feature()` functions to visualize different types of Haar feature descriptors:

```
from skimage.feature import haar_like_feature_coord
from skimage.feature import draw_haar_like_feature
images = [np.zeros((2, 2)), np.zeros((2, 2)), np.zeros((3, 3)),
np.zeros((3, 3)), np.zeros((2, 2))]
feature_types = ['type-2-x', 'type-2-y', 'type-3-x', 'type-3-y', 'type-4']
fig, axes = pylab.subplots(3, 2, figsize=(5,7))
for axes, img, feat_t in zip(np.ravel(axes), images, feature_types):
 coordinates, _ = haar_like_feature_coord(img.shape[0], img.shape[1],
feat_t)
 haar_feature = draw_haar_like_feature(img, 0, 0, img.shape[0],
img.shape[1],
 coordinates, max_n_features=1, random_state=0, color_positive_block=(1.0,
0.0, 0.0),
 color_negative_block=(0.0, 0.0, 1.0), alpha=0.8)
 axes.imshow(haar_feature), axes.set_title(feat_t),  axes.set_axis_off()
fig.suptitle('Different Haar-like feature descriptors')
pylab.axis('off'), pylab.tight_layout(), pylab.show()
```

The following screenshot shows the output of the preceding code block:

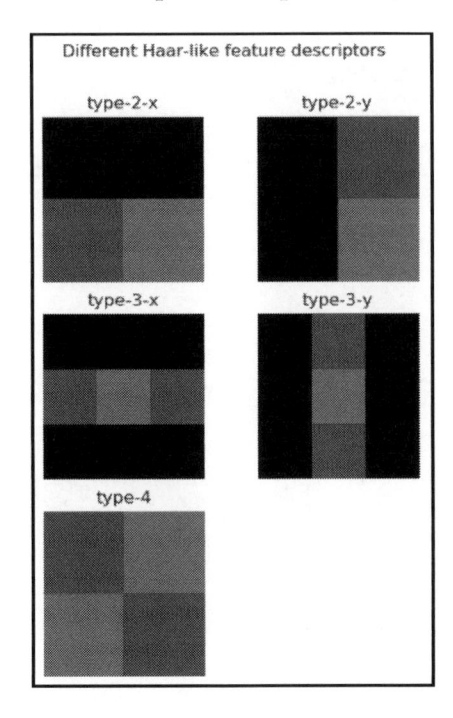

Application – face detection with Haar-like features

Using the Viola—Jones face detection algorithm, faces can be detected in an image using these Haar-like features. Each Haar-like feature is only a weak classifier, and hence a large number of Haar-like features are required to detect a face with good accuracy. A huge number of Haar-like features are computed for all possible sizes and locations of each Haar-like kernel using the integral images. Then an AdaBoost ensemble classifier is used to select important features from the huge number of features and combine them into a strong classifier model during the training phase. The model learned is then used to classify a face region with the selected features.

Most of the regions in an image is a non-face region in general. So, first it is checked whether a window is not a face region. If it is not, it is discarded in a single shot and a different region is inspected where a face is likely to be found. This ensures that more time is dedicated to checking a possible face region. In order to implement this idea, the concept of cascade of classifiers is introduced. Instead of applying all the huge number of features on a window, the features are grouped into different stages of classifiers and applied one-by-one. (The first few stages contain very few features). If a window fails at the first stage it is discarded, and the remaining features on it are not considered. If it passes, the second stage of features are applied, and so on and so forth. A face region corresponds to the window that passes all the stages. These concepts will be discussed more in Chapter 9, *Classical Machine Learning Methods in Image Processing*.

Face/eye detection with OpenCV using pre-trained classifiers with Haar-cascade features

OpenCV comes with a trainer as well as a detector. In this section, we will demonstrate the detection (skip training a model) with the pre-trained classifiers for face, eyes, smile, and so on. OpenCV already contains many such models already trained; we are going to use them instead of training a classifier from scratch. These pre-trained classifiers are serialized as XML files and come with an OpenCV installation (this can be found in the opencv/data/haarcascades/ folder).

In order to detect a face from an input image, first we need to load the required XML classifiers, and then load the input image (in grayscale mode). The faces in the image can be found using the `detectMultiScale()` function, with the pre-trained cascade classifier. This function accepts the following parameters:

- `scaleFactor`: A parameter that specifies how much the image size is reduced at each image scale and used to create a scale pyramid (for example, scale factor 1.2 means reduce the size by 20%). The smaller the `scaleFactor`, the more chance a matching size with the model for detection is found.
- `minNeighbors`: A parameter that specifies how many neighbors each candidate rectangle needs to retain. This parameter affects the quality of the detected faces; a higher value results in less detection, but with higher quality.
- `minSize` and `maxSize`: These are the minimum and maximum possible object size, respectively. Objects of sizes beyond these values will be ignored.

If faces are found, the function returns the positions of detected faces as `Rect(x, y, w, h)`. Once these locations are obtained, a ROI (region of interest) for the face can be created, and then the eye detection on this ROI is applied (since eyes are always on the face). The following code block demonstrates how to create a face and eye detector with python-opencv using different pre-trained classifiers (suitable for face detection with classifiers pre-trained using frontal faces, upper bodies, or pre-trained classifiers for eye detection, trained using eyes with/without glasses):

```
opencv_haar_path = 'C:/opencv/data/haarcascades/' # provide proper opencv installation path
face_cascade = cv2.CascadeClassifier(opencv_haar_path + 'haarcascade_frontalface_default.xml')
eye_cascade = cv2.CascadeClassifier(opencv_haar_path + 'haarcascade_eye.xml')
#eye_cascade = cv2.CascadeClassifier(opencv_haar_path + 'haarcascade_eye_tree_eyeglasses.xml') # eye with glasses

img = cv2.imread('images/lena.jpg')
gray = cv2.cvtColor(img, cv2.COLOR_BGR2GRAY)

faces = face_cascade.detectMultiScale(gray, 1.2, 5) # scaleFactor=1.2, minNbr=5
print(len(faces)) # number of faces detected
# 1
for (x,y,w,h) in faces:
  img = cv2.rectangle(img, (x,y), (x+w,y+h), (255,0,0), 2)
  roi_gray = gray[y:y+h, x:x+w]
  roi_color = img[y:y+h, x:x+w]
  eyes = eye_cascade.detectMultiScale(roi_gray)
```

```
print(eyes) # location of eyes detected
# [[11 14 23 23]
#  [38 16 21 21]]
for (ex,ey,ew,eh) in eyes:
    cv2.rectangle(roi_color,(ex,ey),(ex+ew,ey+eh),(0,255,0),2)
cv2.imwrite('me_face_detected.jpg', img)
```

The following two screenshots show the output of the preceding code block, with different pre-trained Haar cascade classifiers (`eye` and `eye_tree_glass` classifiers, respectively) and a couple of different input face images, the first one without and the second one with glasses:

Summary

In this chapter, we discussed a few important feature detection and extraction techniques to compute different types of feature descriptors from an image using Python's `scikit-image` and `cv2 (python-opencv)` libraries. We started with the basic concepts of local feature detectors and descriptors for an image, along with their desirable properties. Then we discussed the Harris Corner Detectors to detect corner interest points of an image and use them to match two images (with the same object captured from different viewpoints). Next, we discussed blob detection using LoG/DoG/DoH filters. Next, we discussed HOG, SIFT, ORB, BRIEF binary detectors/descriptors and how to match images with these features. Finally, we discussed Haar-like features and face detection with the Viola—Jones algorithm. By the end of this chapter, you should be able to compute different features/descriptors of an image with Python libraries. Also, you should be able to match images with different types of feature descriptors (for example, SIFT, ORB, and so on) and detect faces from images containing faces with Python.

In the next chapter, we will discuss image segmentation.

Questions

1. Implement the Harris Corner Detector with sub-pixel accuracy with `cv2`.
2. Play with a few different pre-trained Haar Cascade classifiers with `cv2` and try to detect multiple faces from images.
3. Use the FLANN-based approximate nearest-neighborhood matcher instead of `BFMatcher` to match the images with books with `cv2`.
4. Compute the SURF keypoints and use them for image matching with `cv2`.

Further reading

- http://scikit-image.org/docs/dev/api/skimage.feature.html
- https://docs.opencv.org/3.1.0/da/df5/tutorial_py_sift_intro.html
- https://sandipanweb.wordpress.com/2017/10/22/feature-detection-with-harris-corner-detector-and-matching-images-with-feature-descriptors-in-python/
- https://sandipanweb.wordpress.com/2018/06/30/detection-of-a-human-object-with-hog-descriptor-features-using-svm-primal-quadprog-implementation-using-cvxopt-in-python/

- http://vision.stanford.edu/teaching/cs231b_spring1213/slides/HOG_2011_Stanford.pdf
- http://cvgl.stanford.edu/teaching/cs231a_winter1415/lecture/lecture10_detector_descriptors_2015.pdf
- https://www.cis.rit.edu/~cnspci/references/dip/feature_extraction/harris1988.pdf
- https://www.cs.ubc.ca/~lowe/papers/ijcv04.pdf
- https://www.cs.cmu.edu/~efros/courses/LBMV07/Papers/viola-cvpr-01.pdf
- https://lear.inrialpes.fr/people/triggs/pubs/Dalal-cvpr05.pdf

8
Image Segmentation

In this chapter, we will discuss a key concept in image processing, namely *segmentation*. We will start by introducing the basic concepts of image segmentation and why it is so important. We will continue our discussion with a number of different image segmentation techniques along with their implementations in `scikit-image` and `python-opencv` (`cv2`) library functions.

The topics to be covered in this chapter are as follows:

- Hough transform—circle and line detection in an image (with `scikit-image`)
- Thresholding and Otsu's segmentation (with `scikit-image`)
- Edges-based/region-based segmentation techniques (with `scikit-image`)
- Felzenszwalb, SLIC, QuickShift, and Compact Watershed algorithms (with `scikit-image`)
- Active contours, morphological snakes, and GrabCut algorithms (with `scikit-image` and `python-opencv`)

What is image segmentation?

Image segmentation is the partitioning of an image into distinct regions or categories that correspond to different objects or parts of objects. Each region contains pixels with similar attributes, and each pixel in an image is allocated to one of these categories. A good segmentation is typically one in which pixels in the same category have similar intensity values and form a connected region, whereas the neighboring pixels that are in different categories have dissimilar values. The goal of this is to simplify/change the representation of an image into something more meaningful and easier to analyze.

If segmentation is done well, then all other stages in image analysis are made simpler. Hence, the quality and reliability of segmentation dictates whether an image analysis will be successful. But to partition an image into correct segments is often a very challenging problem.

Image Segmentation

Segmentation techniques can be either non-contextual (do not consider spatial relationships between features in an image and group pixels only with regard to some global attributes, for example, color/gray level) or contextual (additionally exploit spatial relationships; for example, group spatially close pixels with similar gray levels). In this chapter, we will discuss different segmentation techniques and demonstrate their Python-based implementations using `scikit-image`, `python-opencv` (`cv2`) and `SimpleITK` library functions. Let's start by importing the required libraries for this chapter:

```
import numpy as np
from skimage.transform import (hough_line, hough_line_peaks, hough_circle,
hough_circle_peaks)
from skimage.draw import circle_perimeter
from skimage.feature import canny
from skimage.data import astronaut
from skimage.io import imread
from skimage.color import rgb2gray, label2rgb
from skimage import img_as_float
import matplotlib.pyplot as pylab
from matplotlib import cm
from skimage.filters import sobel, threshold_otsu
from skimage.feature import canny
from skimage.segmentation import felzenszwalb, slic, quickshift, watershed
from skimage.segmentation import mark_boundaries, find_boundaries
```

Hough transform – detecting lines and circles

In image processing, **Hough transform** is a feature extraction technique that aims to find instances of objects of a certain shape using a *voting* procedure carried out in a parameter space. In its simplest form, the classical Hough transform can be used to detect *straight lines* in an image. We can represent a straight line using polar parameters (ρ, θ), where ρ is the length of the line segment and θ is the angle in between the line and the x axis. To explore (ρ, θ) parameter space, it first creates a 2D-histogram. Then, for each value of ρ and θ, it computes the number of non-zero pixels in the input image that are close to the corresponding line and increments the array at position (ρ, θ) accordingly. Hence, each non-zero pixel can be thought of as voting for potential line candidates. The most probable lines correspond to the parameter values that obtained the highest votes, that is, the local maxima in a 2D histogram. The method can be extended to detect circles (and other curves). A similar voting method can be used to find maximum values in the parameter space of circles. The more parameters a curve has, the more it will be spatially and computationally expensive to use the Hough transform to detect the curve.

The next code block demonstrates how to use `hough_line()` or `hough_line_peaks()` functions and also how to use `hough_circle()` or `hough_circle_peaks()` functions from `scikit-image` transform module to to detect straight lines/circles from an input image with lines and circles, respectively:

```
image = rgb2gray(imread('../images/triangle_circle.png'))
# Classic straight-line Hough transform
h, theta, d = hough_line(image)
fig, axes = pylab.subplots(2, 2, figsize=(20, 20))
axes = axes.ravel()
axes[0].imshow(image, cmap=cm.gray), axes[0].set_title('Input image', 
size=20), axes[0].set_axis_off()
axes[1].imshow(np.log(1 + h), 
 extent=[10*np.rad2deg(theta[-1]), np.rad2deg(theta[0]), d[-1], d[0]], 
 cmap=cm.hot, aspect=1/1.5)
axes[1].set_title('Hough transform', size=20)
axes[1].set_xlabel('Angles (degrees)', size=20),
axes[1].set_ylabel('Distance (pixels)', size=20)
axes[1].axis('image')
axes[2].imshow(image, cmap=cm.gray)
for _, angle, dist in zip(*hough_line_peaks(h, theta, d)):
 y0 = (dist - 0 * np.cos(angle)) / np.sin(angle)
 y1 = (dist - image.shape[1] * np.cos(angle)) / np.sin(angle)
 axes[2].plot((0, image.shape[1]), (y0, y1), '-r')
axes[2].set_xlim((0, image.shape[1])), axes[2].set_ylim((image.shape[0], 
0))
axes[2].set_axis_off(), axes[2].set_title('Detected lines', size=20)

# Circle Hough transform
hough_radii = np.arange(50, 100, 2)
hough_res = hough_circle(image, hough_radii)
# Select the most prominent 6 circles
accums, c_x, c_y, radii = hough_circle_peaks(hough_res, hough_radii, 
total_num_peaks=6)
segmented_image = np.zeros_like(image)
image = gray2rgb(image)
for center_y, center_x, radius in zip(c_y, c_x, radii):
 circ_y, circ_x = circle_perimeter(center_y, center_x, radius)
 image[circ_y, circ_x] = (1, 0, 0)
 segmented_image[circ_y, circ_x] = 1
axes[1].imshow(image, cmap=pylab.cm.gray), axes[1].set_axis_off()
axes[1].set_title('Detected Circles', size=20)
axes[2].imshow(segmented_image, cmap=pylab.cm.gray), axes[2].set_axis_off()
axes[2].set_title('Segmented Image', size=20)
pylab.tight_layout(), pylab.axis('off'), pylab.show()
```

Image Segmentation

The next screenshot shows the input image, the most probable (ρ, θ) pairs (the brightest points in the second subplot, the ones with the maximum votes) for the lines to be detected, the detected lines (in red) and the detected circles, respectively, obtained using the earlier code block:

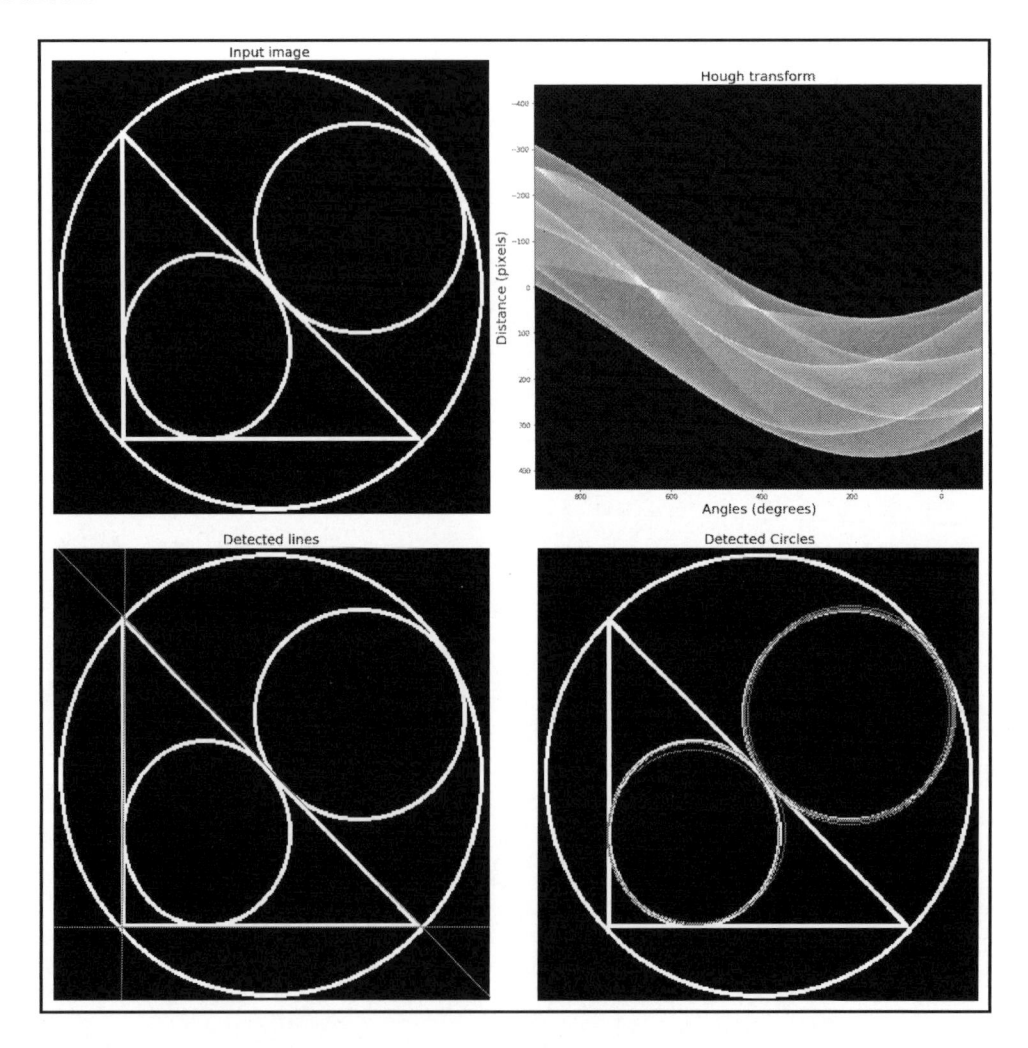

The following code block demonstrates how to use the Hough circle transform to segment the coin objects from the background in an image with coins:

```
image = rgb2gray(imread('images/coins.png'))
fig, axes = pylab.subplots(1, 2, figsize=(20, 10), sharex=True,
sharey=True)
axes = axes.ravel()
```

```
axes[0].imshow(image, cmap=pylab.cm.gray), axes[0].set_axis_off()
axes[0].set_title('Original Image', size=20)
hough_radii = np.arange(65, 75, 1)
hough_res = hough_circle(image, hough_radii)
# Select the most prominent 4 circles
accums, c_x, c_y, radii = hough_circle_peaks(hough_res, hough_radii,
total_num_peaks=4)
image = color.gray2rgb(image)
for center_y, center_x, radius in zip(c_y, c_x, radii):
  circ_y, circ_x = circle_perimeter(center_y, center_x, radius)
  image[circ_y, circ_x] = (1, 0, 0)
axes[1].imshow(image, cmap=pylab.cm.gray), axes[1].set_axis_off()
axes[1].set_title('Detected Circles', size=20)
pylab.tight_layout(), pylab.show()
```

The next screenshot shows the input coins image, the detected red circles with circle Hough transform and the segmented image, respectively, obtained using the previous code block:

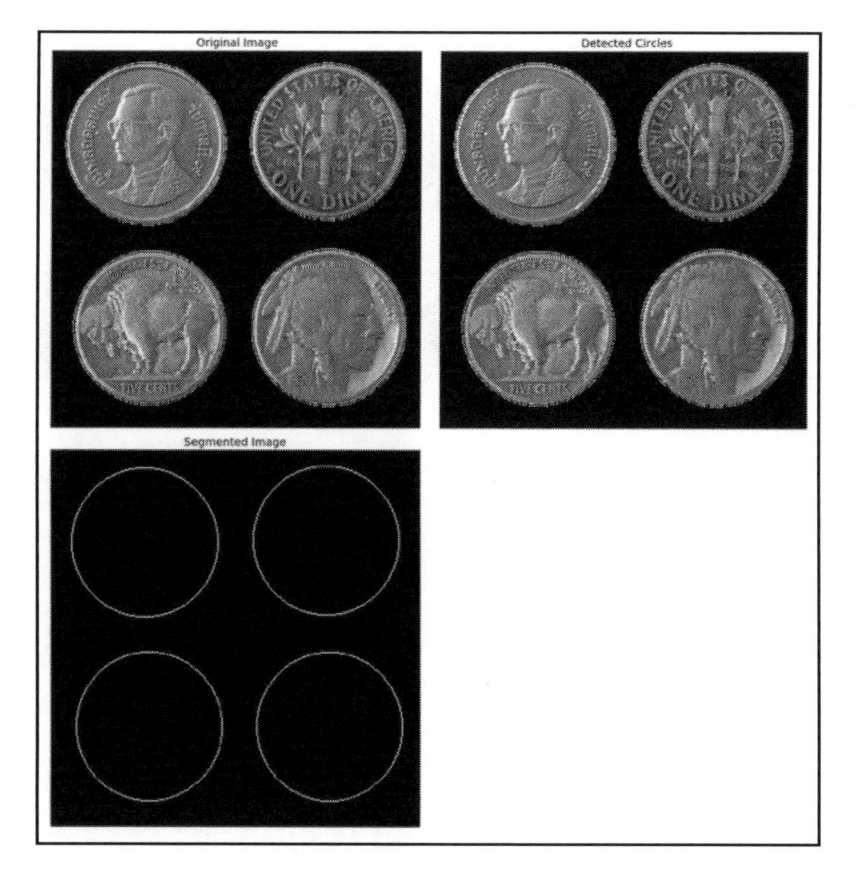

Thresholding and Otsu's segmentation

Thresholding refers to a family of algorithms that use a pixel value as a threshold to create a binary image (an image with only black-and-white pixels) from a grayscale image. It provides the simplest way to segment objects from a background in an image. The threshold can be chosen manually (by looking at the histogram of pixel values) or automatically using algorithm. In `scikit-image`, there are two categories of thresholding algorithm implementations, namely histogram-based (a pixel intensity histogram is used with some assumptions of the properties of this histogram, for example bimodal) and local (only the neighboring pixels are used to process a pixel; it makes these algorithms more computationally expensive).

In this section, we shall only discuss a popular histogram-based thresholding method known as **Otsu's method** (with the assumption of a bimodal histogram). It computes an optimal threshold value by simultaneously maximizing the inter-class variance and minimizing the intra-class variance between two classes of pixels (which are separated by that threshold value). The next code block demonstrates an implementation of Otsu's segmentation with the horse input image and computes the optimal threshold to separate out the foreground from the background:

```
image = rgb2gray(imread('../images/horse.jpg'))
thresh = threshold_otsu(image)
binary = image > thresh

fig, axes = pylab.subplots(nrows=2, ncols=2, figsize=(20, 15))
axes = axes.ravel()
axes[0], axes[1] = pylab.subplot(2, 2, 1), pylab.subplot(2, 2, 2)
axes[2] = pylab.subplot(2, 2, 3, sharex=axes[0], sharey=axes[0])
axes[3] = pylab.subplot(2, 2, 4, sharex=axes[0], sharey=axes[0])
axes[0].imshow(image, cmap=pylab.cm.gray)
axes[0].set_title('Original', size=20), axes[0].axis('off')
axes[1].hist(image.ravel(), bins=256, normed=True)
axes[1].set_title('Histogram', size=20), axes[1].axvline(thresh, color='r')
axes[2].imshow(binary, cmap=pylab.cm.gray)
axes[2].set_title('Thresholded (Otsu)', size=20), axes[2].axis('off')
axes[3].axis('off'), pylab.tight_layout(), pylab.show()
```

The next screenshot shows the output of the previous code block; the optimal threshold computed by Otsu's method is marked by a red line in the histogram as follows:

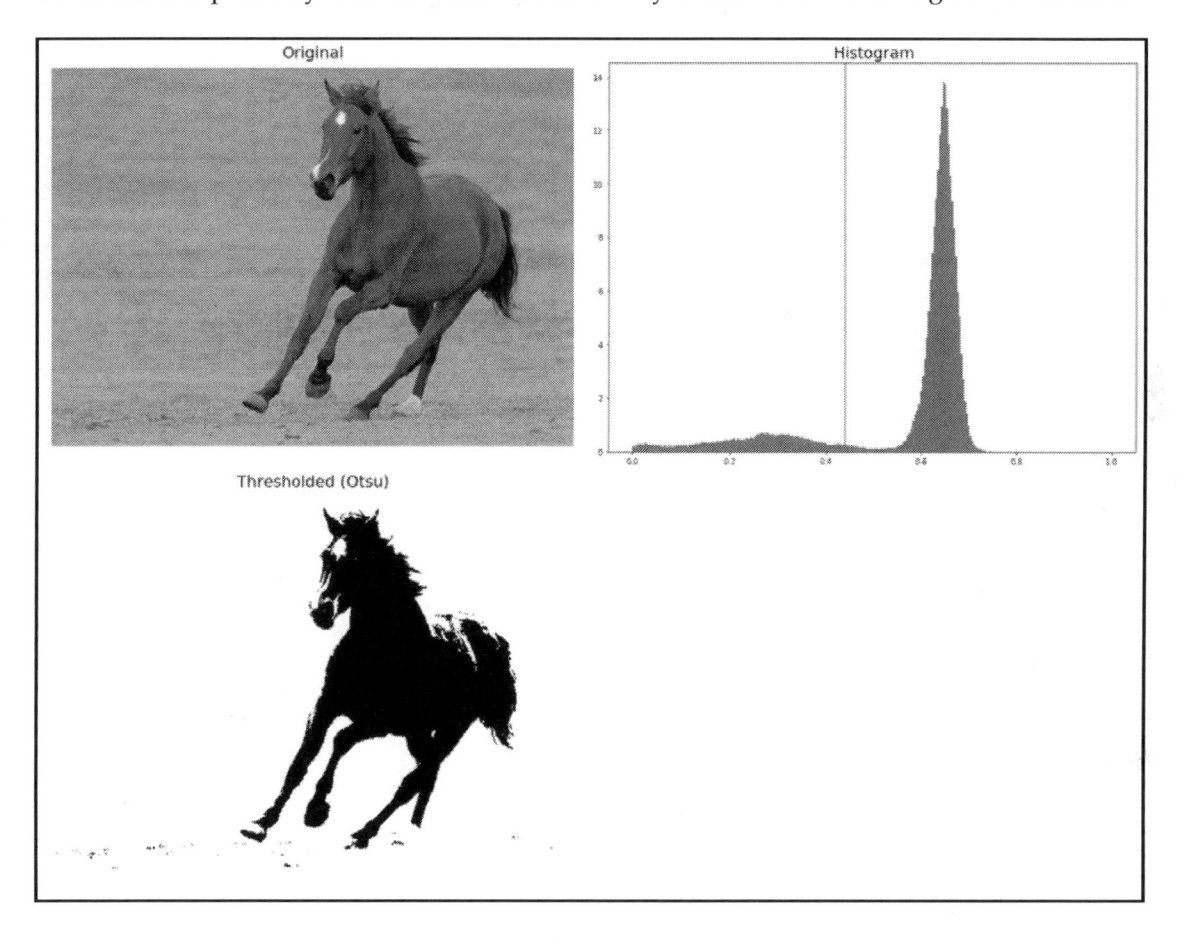

Edges-based/region-based segmentation

This example, taken from the examples in the `scikit-image` documentation, demonstrates how to segment objects from a background by first using edge-based and then using region-based segmentation algorithms. The coins image from `skimage.data` is used as the input image, which shows several coins outlined against a darker background. The next code block displays the grayscale image and its intensity histogram:

```
coins = data.coins()
hist = np.histogram(coins, bins=np.arange(0, 256), normed=True)
fig, axes = pylab.subplots(1, 2, figsize=(20, 10))
axes[0].imshow(coins, cmap=pylab.cm.gray, interpolation='nearest')
axes[0].axis('off'), axes[1].plot(hist[1][:-1], hist[0], lw=2)
axes[1].set_title('histogram of gray values')
pylab.show()
```

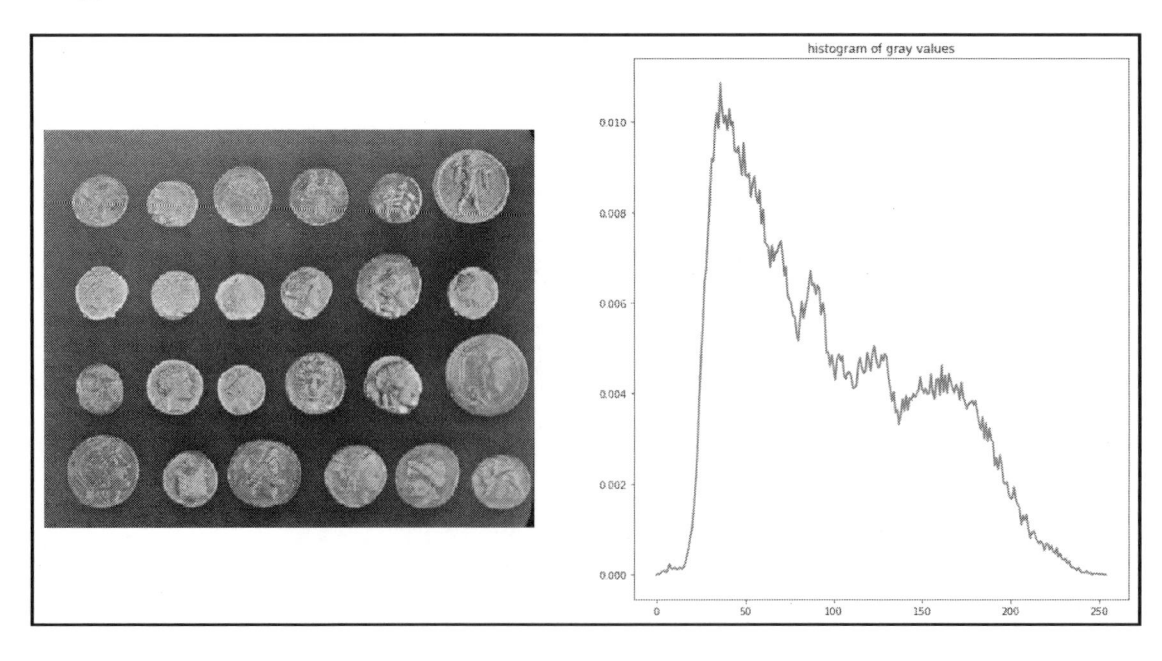

Edge-based segmentation

In this example, we will try to delineate the contours of the coins using *edge-based segmentation*. To do this, the first step is to get the edges of features using the Canny edge detector, demonstrated by the following code block:

```
edges = canny(coins, sigma=2)
fig, axes = pylab.subplots(figsize=(10, 6))
axes.imshow(edges, cmap=pylab.cm.gray, interpolation='nearest')
axes.set_title('Canny detector'), axes.axis('off'), pylab.show()
```

The next screenshot shows the output of the earlier code, the contours of the coins obtained using the Canny edge detector:

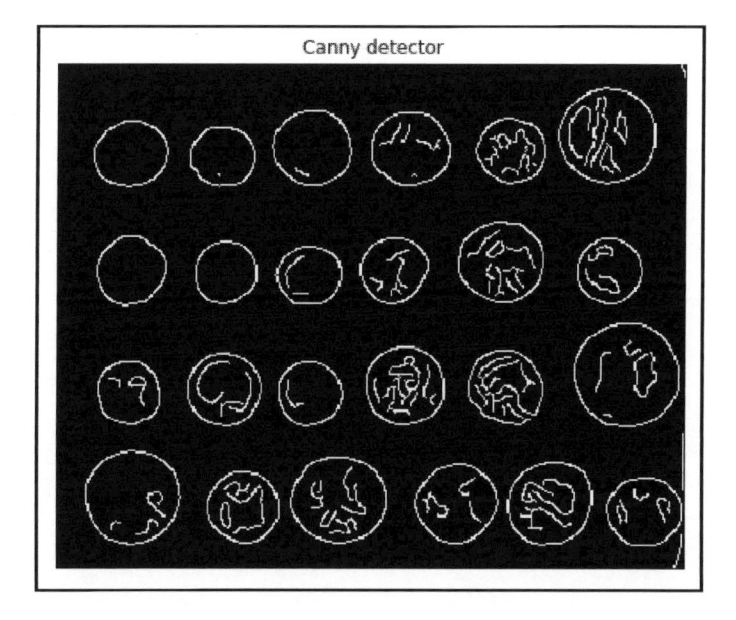

The next step is to fill these contours using the `morphological` function `binary_fill_holes()` from the `scipy ndimage` module, as shown in the next code block:

```
from scipy import ndimage as ndi
fill_coins = ndi.binary_fill_holes(edges)
fig, axes = pylab.subplots(figsize=(10, 6))
axes.imshow(fill_coins, cmap=pylab.cm.gray, interpolation='nearest')
axes.set_title('filling the holes'), axes.axis('off'), pylab.show()
```

The next screenshot shows the output of the earlier code block, the filled contours of the coins:

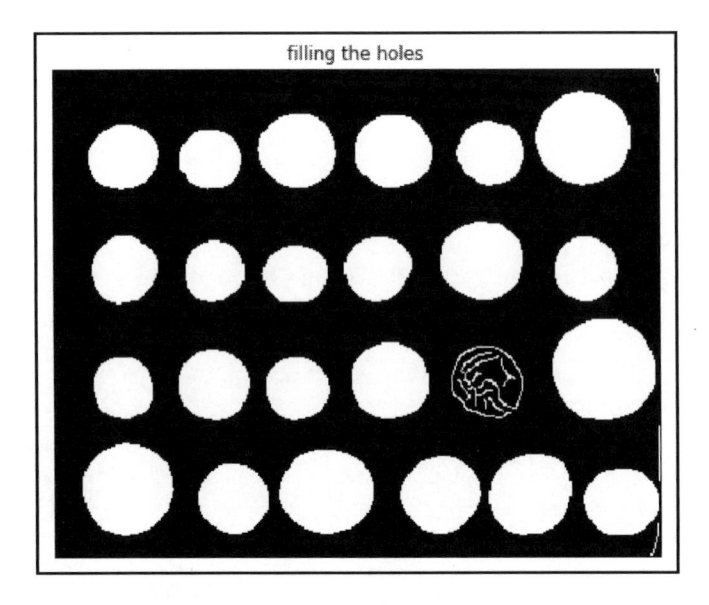

filling the holes

As can be seen from the screenshot, there is a coin whose contour did not get filled with the operation. In the next step, the small spurious objects such as this one are then removed by setting a minimum size for valid objects and again using `morphological` functions, this time with the function `remove_small_objects()` from `scikit-image` **morphology** module:

```
from skimage import morphology
coins_cleaned = morphology.remove_small_objects(fill_coins, 21)
fig, axes = pylab.subplots(figsize=(10, 6))
axes.imshow(coins_cleaned, cmap=pylab.cm.gray, interpolation='nearest')
axes.set_title('removing small objects'), axes.axis('off'), pylab.show()
```

The next screenshot shows the output of the earlier code block:

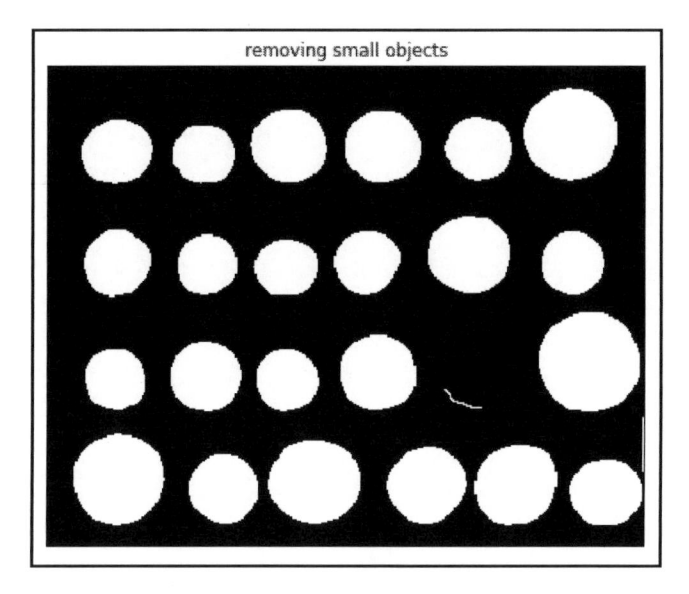

However, this method is not very robust, since the contours that are not perfectly closed are not filled correctly, as is the case for one unfilled coin, as can be seen from the previous screenshot.

Region-based segmentation

In this section, we will apply a region-based segmentation method to the same image using the morphological watershed algorithm. First, let's intuitively discuss the basic steps the watershed algorithm.

Morphological watershed algorithm

Any grayscale image can be considered as a topographic surface. If this surface is flooded from its minima, and the merging of waters from different sources are prevented, and the image will be partitioned into two different sets, namely the catchment basins and the watershed lines. If this transform is applied to the image gradient, the catchment basins should theoretically correspond to the homogeneous gray-level regions (segments) of this image.

However, the image gets over-segmented using this transform in practice, because of noise or local irregularities in the gradient image. To prevent over-segmentation, a pre-defined set of markers are used and the flooding of the surface starts from these markers. Hence, the following are the steps in segmentation of an image by the watershed transformation:

- Find the markers and the segmentation criterion (the function that is to be used to split the regions, often it is the contrast/gradient)
- Run a marker-controlled watershed algorithm with these two elements

Now let's use the `scikit-image` implementation of the morphological watershed algorithm to separate the foreground coins from the background. The first step is to find an elevation map using the `sobel` gradient of the image, as demonstrated in the following code block:

```
elevation_map = sobel(coins)
fig, axes = pylab.subplots(figsize=(10, 6))
axes.imshow(elevation_map, cmap=pylab.cm.gray, interpolation='nearest')
axes.set_title('elevation map'), axes.axis('off'), pylab.show()
```

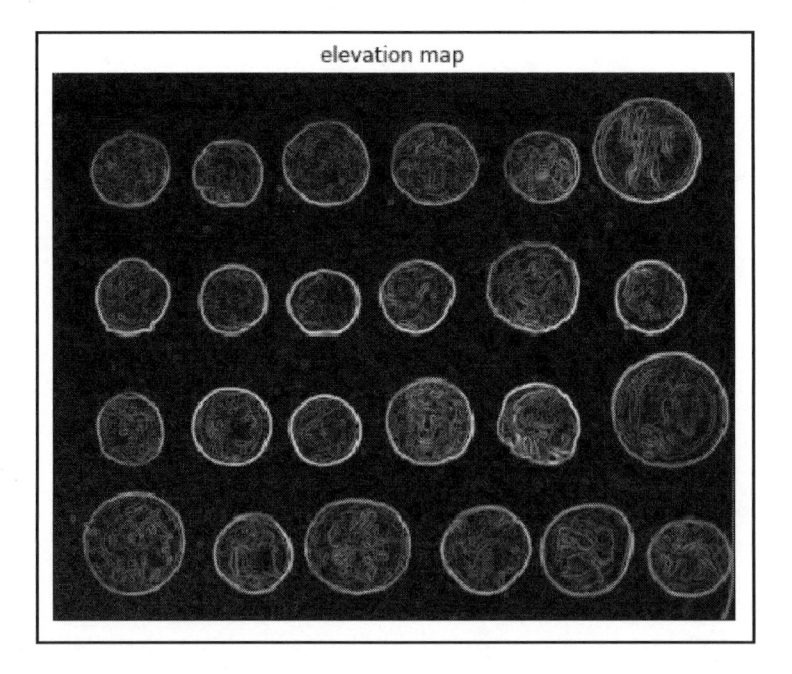

Next, the markers of the background and the coins are computed, based on the extreme parts of the histogram of gray values, as demonstrated in the following code block:

```
markers = np.zeros_like(coins)
markers[coins < 30] = 1
markers[coins > 150] = 2
print(np.max(markers), np.min(markers))
fig, axes = pylab.subplots(figsize=(10, 6))
a = axes.imshow(markers, cmap=plt.cm.hot, interpolation='nearest')
plt.colorbar(a)
axes.set_title('markers'), axes.axis('off'), pylab.show()
```

The next screenshot shows the output of the earlier code block, the heatmap of the markers array:

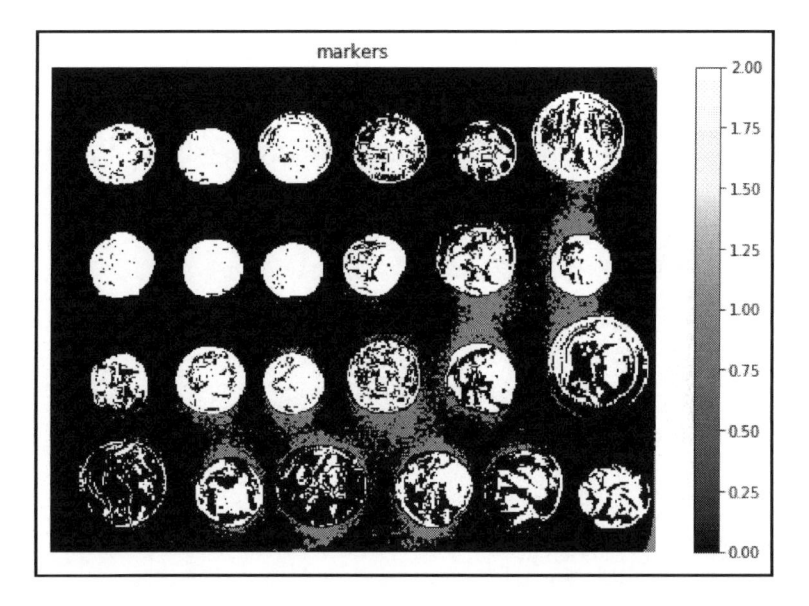

Finally, the watershed transform is used to fill regions of the elevation map starting from the markers determined, as demonstrated in the next code block:

```
segmentation = morphology.watershed(elevation_map, markers)
fig, axes = pylab.subplots(figsize=(10, 6))
axes.imshow(segmentation, cmap=pylab.cm.gray, interpolation='nearest')
axes.set_title('segmentation'), axes.axis('off'), pylab.show()
```

Image Segmentation

The following image shows the output of the code block, the resulting segmented binary image using the morphological watershed algorithm:

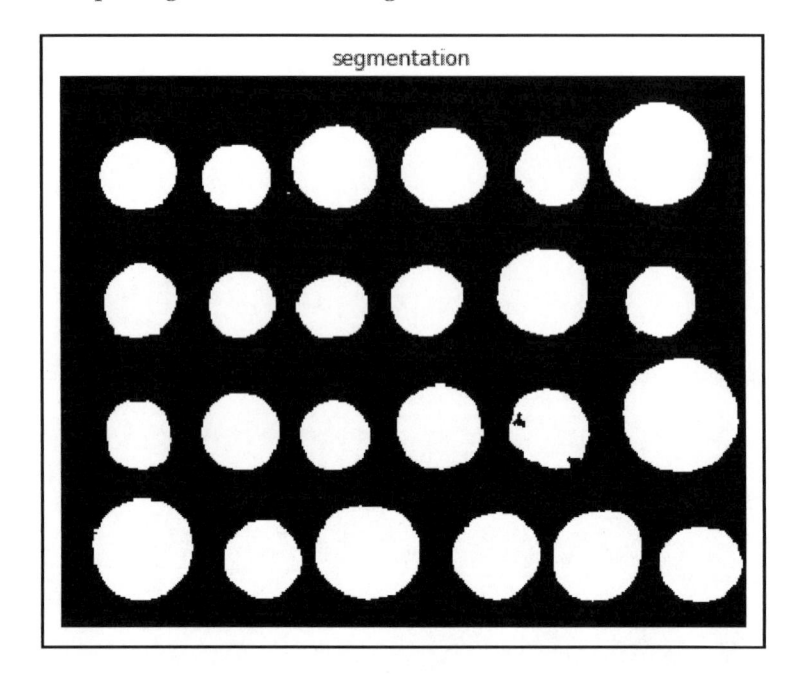

This last method works even better, and the coins can be segmented and labeled individually, as shown in the following code block:

```
segmentation = ndi.binary_fill_holes(segmentation - 1)
labeled_coins, _ = ndi.label(segmentation)
image_label_overlay = label2rgb(labeled_coins, image=coins)
fig, axes = pylab.subplots(1, 2, figsize=(20, 6), sharey=True)
axes[0].imshow(coins, cmap=pylab.cm.gray, interpolation='nearest')
axes[0].contour(segmentation, [0.5], linewidths=1.2, colors='y')
axes[1].imshow(image_label_overlay, interpolation='nearest')
for a in axes:
 a.axis('off')
pylab.tight_layout(), pylab.show()
```

The next screenshot shows the output of this code block, the segmented coins with the watershed lines (contours), and the labeled coins, respectively:

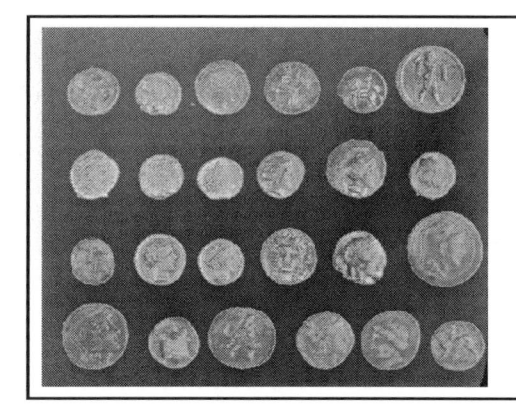

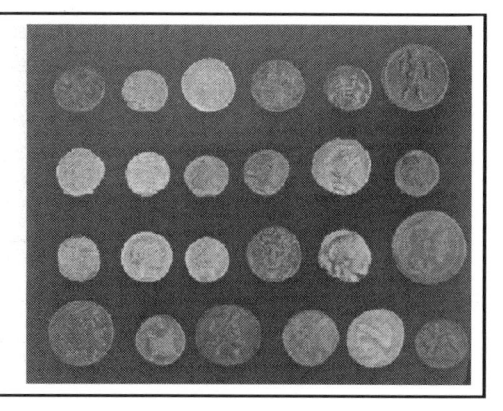

Felzenszwalb, SLIC, QuickShift, and Compact Watershed algorithms

In this section, we will discuss four popular low-level image segmentation methods and then compare the results obtained by those methods with an input image. The definition of good segmentation often depends on the application, and thus it is difficult to obtain a good segmentation. These methods are generally used for obtaining an over-segmentation, also known as **superpixels**. These superpixels then serve as a basis for more sophisticated algorithms such as merging with a region adjacency graph or conditional random fields.

Felzenszwalb's efficient graph-based image segmentation

Felzenszwalb's algorithm takes a graph-based approach to segmentation. It first constructs an undirected graph with the image pixels as vertices (the set to be segmented) and the weight of an edge between the two vertices being some measure of the dissimilarity (for example, the difference in intensity). In the graph-based approach, the problem of partitioning an image into segments translates to finding a connected components in the constructed graph. The edges between two vertices in the same component should have relatively low weights, and edges between vertices in different components should have higher weights.

The algorithm runs in time nearly linear in the number of graph edges and is also fast in practice. This technique preserves the details in low-variability image regions while ignores the details in high-variability regions. The algorithm has a single-scale parameter that influences the size of the segments. The actual size and the number of the segments can vary greatly, depending on local contrast. The following code block demonstrates how to use the `scikit-image` segmentation module's implementation of this algorithm and the output segmented images obtained using a few input images:

```
from matplotlib.colors import LinearSegmentedColormap
for imfile in ['../images/eagle.png', '../images/horses.png',
'../images/flowers.png', '../images/bisons.png']:
  img = img_as_float(imread(imfile)[::2, ::2, :3])
  pylab.figure(figsize=(20,10))
  segments_fz = felzenszwalb(img, scale=100, sigma=0.5, min_size=400)
  borders = find_boundaries(segments_fz)
  unique_colors = np.unique(segments_fz.ravel())
  segments_fz[borders] = -1
  colors = [np.zeros(3)]
  for color in unique_colors:
     colors.append(np.mean(img[segments_fz == color], axis=0))
  cm = LinearSegmentedColormap.from_list('pallete', colors, N=len(colors))
  pylab.subplot(121), pylab.imshow(img), pylab.title('Original', size=20),
pylab.axis('off')
  pylab.subplot(122), pylab.imshow(segments_fz, cmap=cm),
  pylab.title('Segmented with Felzenszwalbs\'s method', size=20),
pylab.axis('off')
  pylab.show()
```

The next screenshots show the output of the code block, the input images, and the corresponding segmented output images with the algorithm:

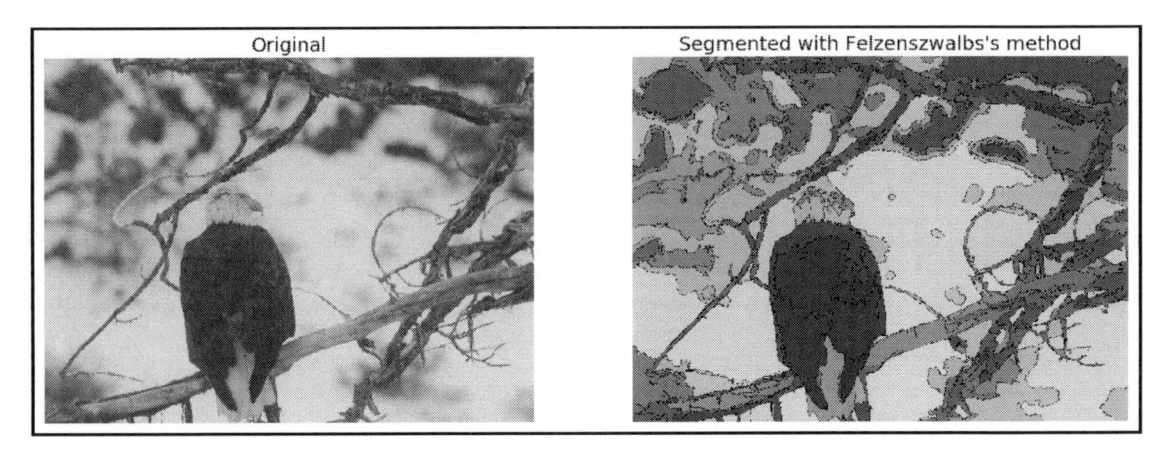

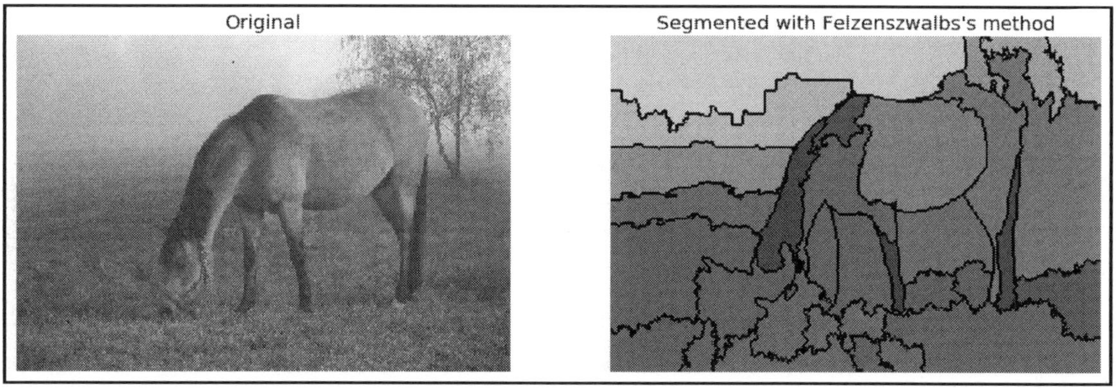
Original
Segmented with Felzenszwalbs's method

Original
Segmented with Felzenszwalbs's method

Original
Segmented with Felzenszwalbs's method

Image Segmentation

The following code block demonstrates how the result of the algorithm changes when the scale parameter is varied:

```
def plot_image(img, title):
  pylab.imshow(img), pylab.title(title, size=20), pylab.axis('off')

img = imread('../images/fish.jpg')[::2, ::2, :3]
pylab.figure(figsize=(15,10))
i = 1
for scale in [50, 100, 200, 400]:
   plt.subplot(2,2,i)
   segments_fz = felzenszwalb(img, scale=scale, sigma=0.5, min_size=200)
   plot_image(mark_boundaries(img, segments_fz, color=(1,0,0)), 'scale=' + str(scale))
   i += 1
pylab.suptitle('Felzenszwalbs\'s method', size=30),
pylab.tight_layout(rect=[0, 0.03, 1, 0.95])
pylab.show()
```

The next screenshot shows the input fish image used for segmentation:

The next screenshot shows the output of the earlier code block. As can be seen, the number of segments in the output image decreases with the increase in the value of the `scale` parameter:

scale=200 scale=400

SLIC

The SLIC algorithm simply performs k-means clustering (we will explore more on this clustering algorithm in Chapter 9, *Classical Machine Learning Methods in Image Processing*) in the five-dimensional space of color space (RGB or Lab) and image location (that is, pixel coordinates: *x, y*). This algorithm is very efficient, since the clustering method is simpler. To obtain good results with this algorithm, it is essential to work in Lab color space. The algorithm has quickly gained momentum and is now widely used. The compactness parameter trades off color-similarity and proximity, while n_segments parameter chooses the number of centers for k-means. The next code block demonstrates how to implement this algorithm using the scikit-image segmentation module. It also shows how the output varies with the compactness parameter value:

```
pylab.figure(figsize=(15,10))
i = 1
for compactness in [0.1, 1, 10, 100]:
 pylab.subplot(2,2,i)
 segments_slic = slic(img, n_segments=250, compactness=compactness, sigma=1)
 plot_image(mark_boundaries(img, segments_slic, color=(1,0,0)), 'compactness=' + str(compactness))
 i += 1
pylab.suptitle('SLIC', size=30), pylab.tight_layout(rect=[0, 0.03, 1, 0.95]), pylab.show()
```

The following screenshot shows the output of the code block. As can be seen from the next segmentation results, higher values give more weight to space proximity, making superpixel shapes more square/cubic:

RAG merging

In this section, we discuss how the **Region Adjacency Graph** (**RAG**) can be used to combine the over-segmented regions of an image, to obtain a better segmentation. It uses the SLIC algorithm to first segment the input image and obtain the region labels. Then, it constructs a RAG and progressively merges the over-segmented regions that are similar in color. Merging two adjacent regions produces a new region with all the pixels from the merged regions. Regions are merged until no highly similar region pairs remain:

```
from skimage import segmentation
from skimage.future import graph

def _weight_mean_color(graph, src, dst, n):
    diff = graph.node[dst]['mean color'] - graph.node[n]['mean color']
    diff = np.linalg.norm(diff)
    return {'weight': diff}
```

```
def merge_mean_color(graph, src, dst):
 graph.node[dst]['total color'] += graph.node[src]['total color']
 graph.node[dst]['pixel count'] += graph.node[src]['pixel count']
 graph.node[dst]['mean color'] = (graph.node[dst]['total color'] /
graph.node[dst]['pixel count'])

img = imread('../images/me12.jpg')
labels = segmentation.slic(img, compactness=30, n_segments=400)
g = graph.rag_mean_color(img, labels)
labels2 = graph.merge_hierarchical(labels, g, thresh=35, rag_copy=False,
 in_place_merge=True,
 merge_func=merge_mean_color,
 weight_func=_weight_mean_color)
out = label2rgb(labels2, img, kind='avg')
out = segmentation.mark_boundaries(out, labels2, (0, 0, 0))
pylab.figure(figsize=(20,10))
pylab.subplot(121), pylab.imshow(img), pylab.axis('off')
pylab.subplot(122), pylab.imshow(out), pylab.axis('off')
pylab.tight_layout(), pylab.show()
```

The next screenshot shows the output of the code, the input image, and the output image obtained using RAG, merging the SLIC segments:

QuickShift

QuickShift is a 2D image segmentation algorithm that is based on an approximation of the kernelized mean-shift algorithm and is relatively recent. It belongs to the family of local (non-parametric) mode-seeking algorithms (based on the idea of associating each data point to a mode of the underlying probability density function) and is applied to the 5D space consisting of color space and image location.

QuickShift actually computes a hierarchical segmentation of multiple scales simultaneously, which is one of the benefits of this algorithm. QuickShift has two main parameters: the parameter sigma controls the scale of the local density approximation, where the parameter `max_dist` selects a level in the hierarchical segmentation that is produced. There is also a trade-off between distance in color-space and distance in image-space, given by ratio. The next code snippet demonstrates how to use the `scikit-image` implementation of the algorithm. It also shows the impact of varying the `max_distance` and ratio parameters on the segmentation output obtained:

```
pylab.figure(figsize=(12,10))
i = 1
for max_dist in [5, 500]:
  for ratio in [0.1, 0.9]:
   pylab.subplot(2,2,i)
   segments_quick = quickshift(img, kernel_size=3, max_dist=max_dist, ratio=ratio)
   plot_image(mark_boundaries(img, segments_quick, color=(1,0,0)), 
'max_dist=' + str(max_dist) + ', ratio=' + str(ratio))
   i += 1
pylab.suptitle('Quickshift', size=30), pylab.tight_layout(rect=[0, 0.03, 1, 0.95]), pylab.show()
```

The next screenshot shows the output of the code block. As can be seen, the `max_dist` parameter works as a cut-off point for data distances: the higher the value of the parameter, the fewer the number of clusters. On the contrary, the parameter `ratio` balances color-space proximity and image-space proximity: higher values of this parameter give more weight to color-space:

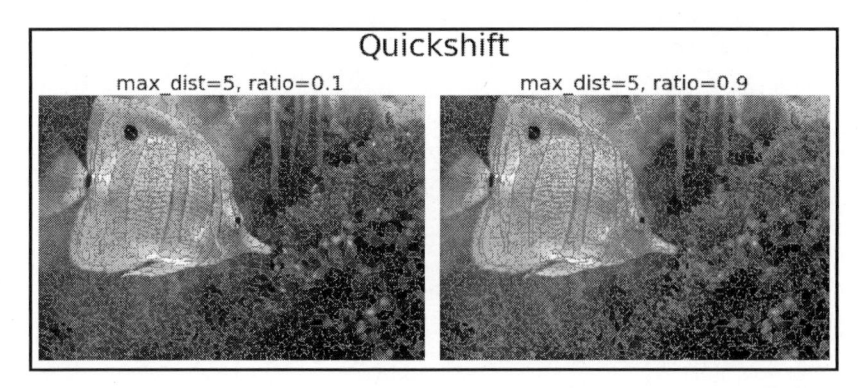

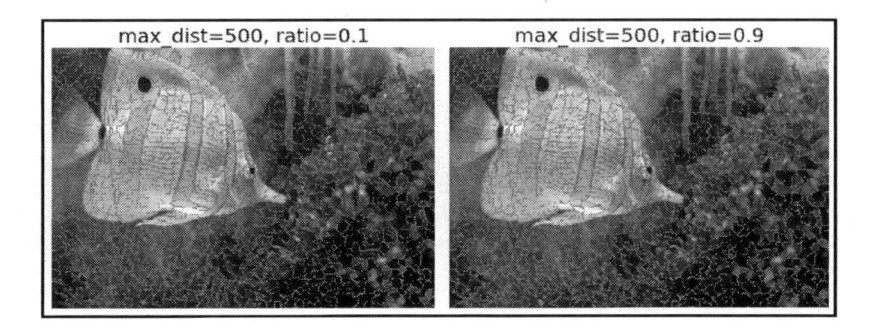

Compact Watershed

As discussed earlier, the watershed algorithm computes watershed catchment basins in an image flooded from given markers, apportioning the pixels into marked basins. The algorithm requires a grayscale gradient image as input (viewing the image as a landscape), where the bright pixels indicate a boundary (forming high peaks) between the regions. From the given markers, this landscape is then flooded until different flood basins meet at the peaks. A different image segment is formed by each distinct basin. As we had with SLIC, there is an additional compactness argument that makes it harder for markers to flood faraway pixels. Higher values of compactness make the watershed regions more regularly shaped. The next code block demonstrates how the `scikit-image` implementation of this algorithm can be used. It also shows the impact of changing the markers and compactness parameters on the segmentation results:

```
from skimage.segmentation import watershed
gradient = sobel(rgb2gray(img))
pylab.figure(figsize=(15,10))
i = 1
for markers in [200, 1000]:
 for compactness in [0.001, 0.0001]:
    pylab.subplot(2,2,i)
    segments_watershed = watershed(gradient, markers=markers, compactness=compactness)
    plot_image(mark_boundaries(img, segments_watershed, color=(1,0,0),
'markers=' + str(markers) + '.compactness=' + str(compactness))
    i += 1
pylab.suptitle('Compact watershed', size=30), pylab.tight_layout(rect=[0, 0.03, 1, 0.95]), pylab.show()
```

The next screenshot shows the output of the code block. As can be seen, the higher value of the compactness results in more regularly-shaped watershed basins, whereas the higher value of the `markers` parameter leads to over-segmentation:

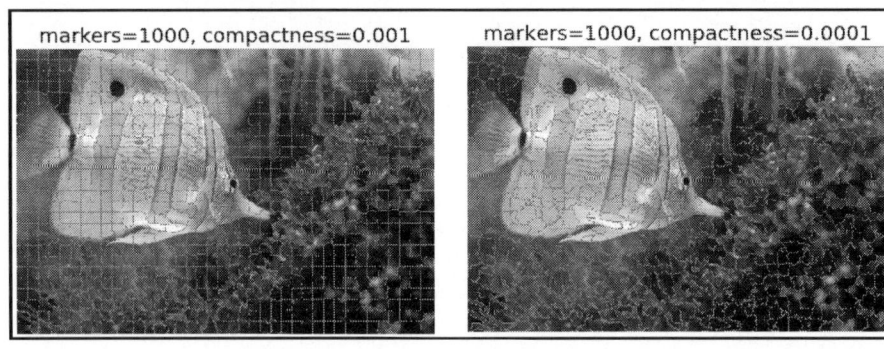

Region growing with SimpleITK

Region growing refers to a class of segmentation algorithms where a pixel's neighbor is considered to be in the same segment if its intensity is similar to the current pixel. How the similarity is defined varies across algorithms. The initial set of pixels are called **seed points** that are usually manually selected. The next code block demonstrates how to use the `SimpleITK` library's implementation of the `ConnectedThreshold` (on variant of the region growing segmentation algorithm). A cranial MRI scan (`T1`) medical image is used as the input image. In the case of the `ConnectedThreshold` algorithm, a voxel's (volume pixel) neighbor is considered to be in the same segment if the neighboring voxel's intensity is within two explicitly specified lower and upper thresholds.

A fixed seed point is used to start the algorithm, and the upper threshold is varied (by keeping the lower threshold fixed), to see the effects of the resulting segmentation:

```
import SimpleITK as sitk
def show_image(img, title=None):
 nda = sitk.GetArrayViewFromImage(img)
 pylab.imshow(nda, cmap='gray'), pylab.axis('off')
 if(title):
    pylab.title(title, size=20)

img = 255*rgb2gray(imread('../images/mri_T1.png'))
img_T1 = sitk.GetImageFromArray(img)
img_T1_255 = sitk.Cast(sitk.RescaleIntensity(img_T1), sitk.sitkUInt8)

seed = (100,120)
for upper in [80, 85, 90]:
    pylab.figure(figsize=(18,20)), pylab.subplot(221), show_image(img_T1,
"Original Image")
    pylab.scatter(seed[0], seed[1], color='red', s=50)
    pylab.subplot(222)
    seg = sitk.ConnectedThreshold(img_T1, seedList=[seed], lower=40,
                                  upper=upper)
    show_image(seg, "Region Growing")
    pylab.subplot(223), show_image(sitk.LabelOverlay(img_T1_255, seg),
"Connected Threshold")
    pylab.axis('off'), pylab.tight_layout(), pylab.show()
```

The following screenshots show the output of the region—growing `ConnectedThreshold` algorithm with different values of the upper threshold. The seed voxel to start with is indicated by a red point.

Image Segmentation

As can be seen from the next screenshot, the higher the upper-threshold value, the larger the size of the segmented region obtained using the `ConnectedThreshold` algorithm, which is as expected:

With upper threshold value = 80

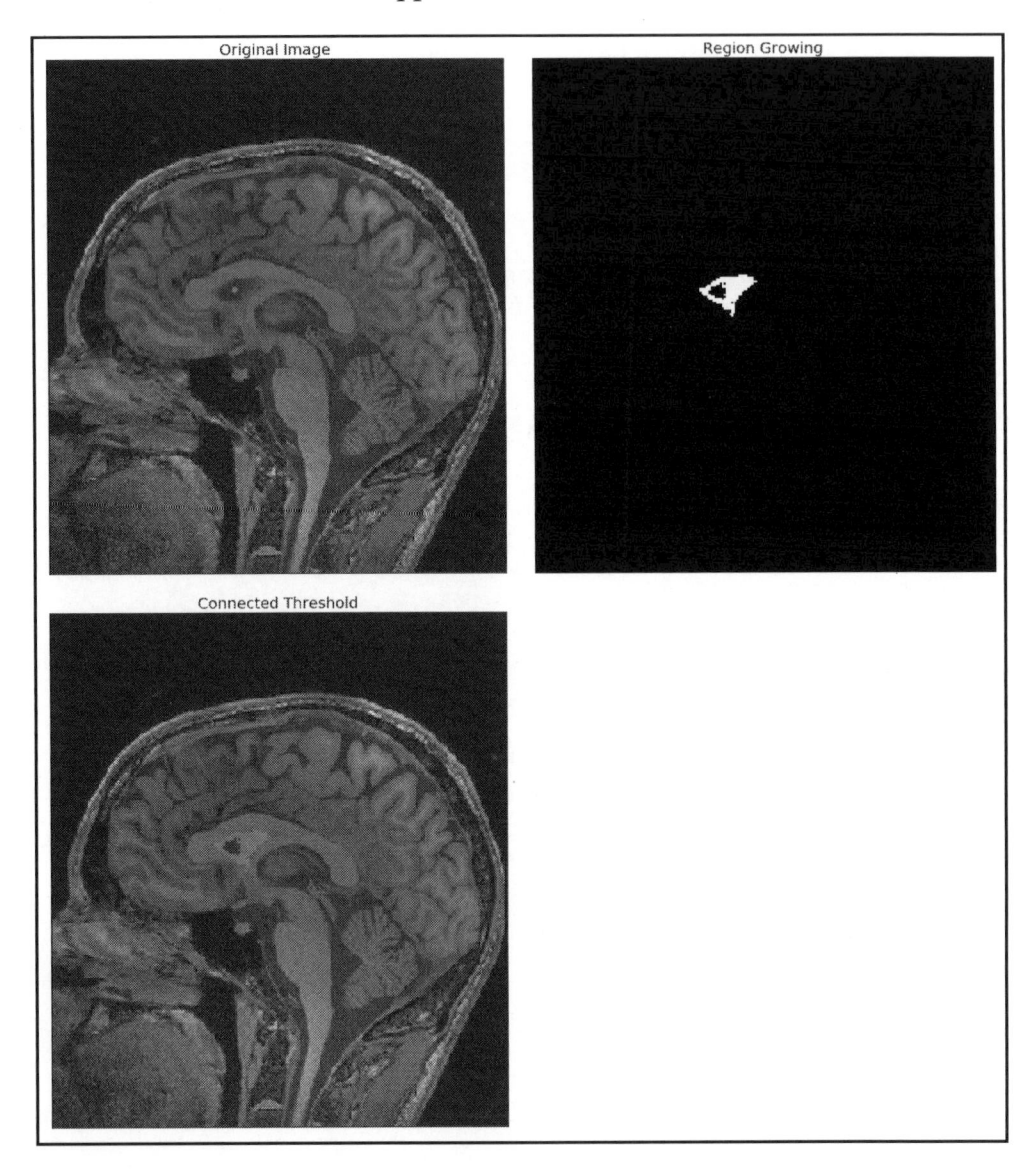

Chapter 8

With upper threshold value = 85

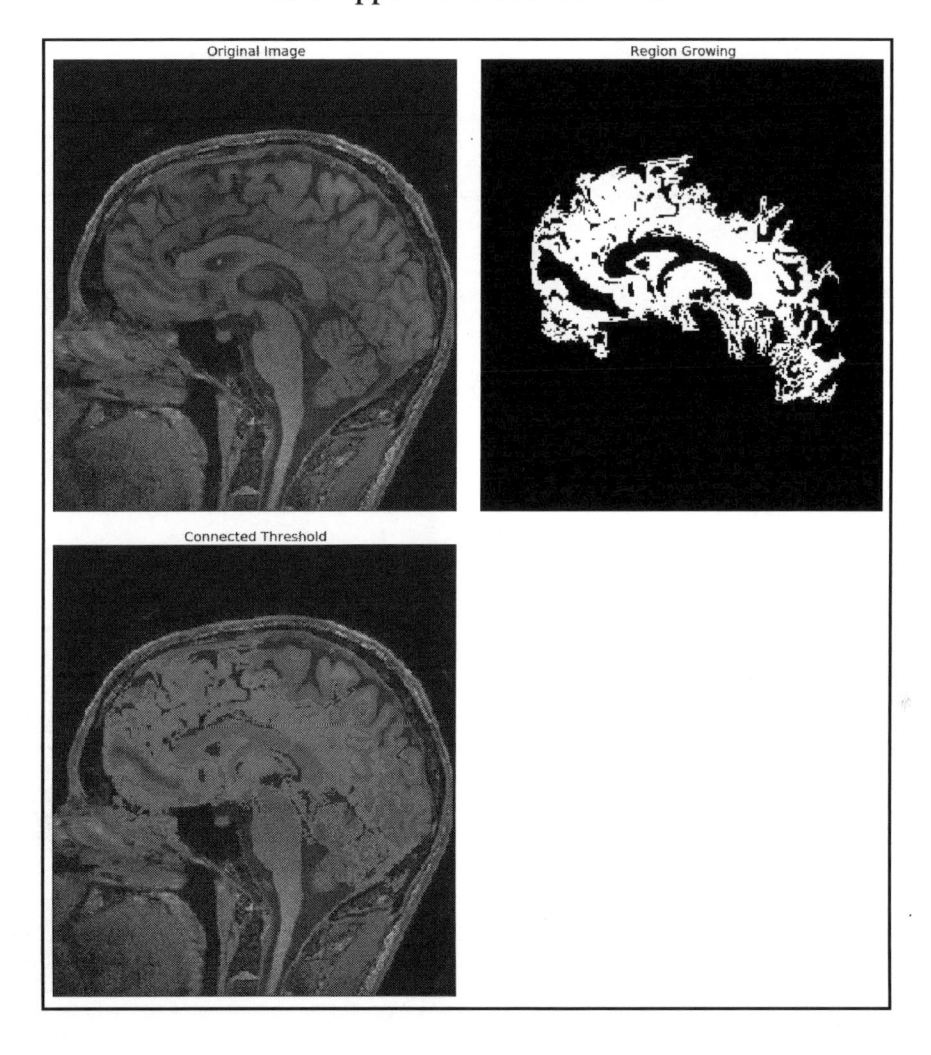

Image Segmentation

With upper threshold value = 90

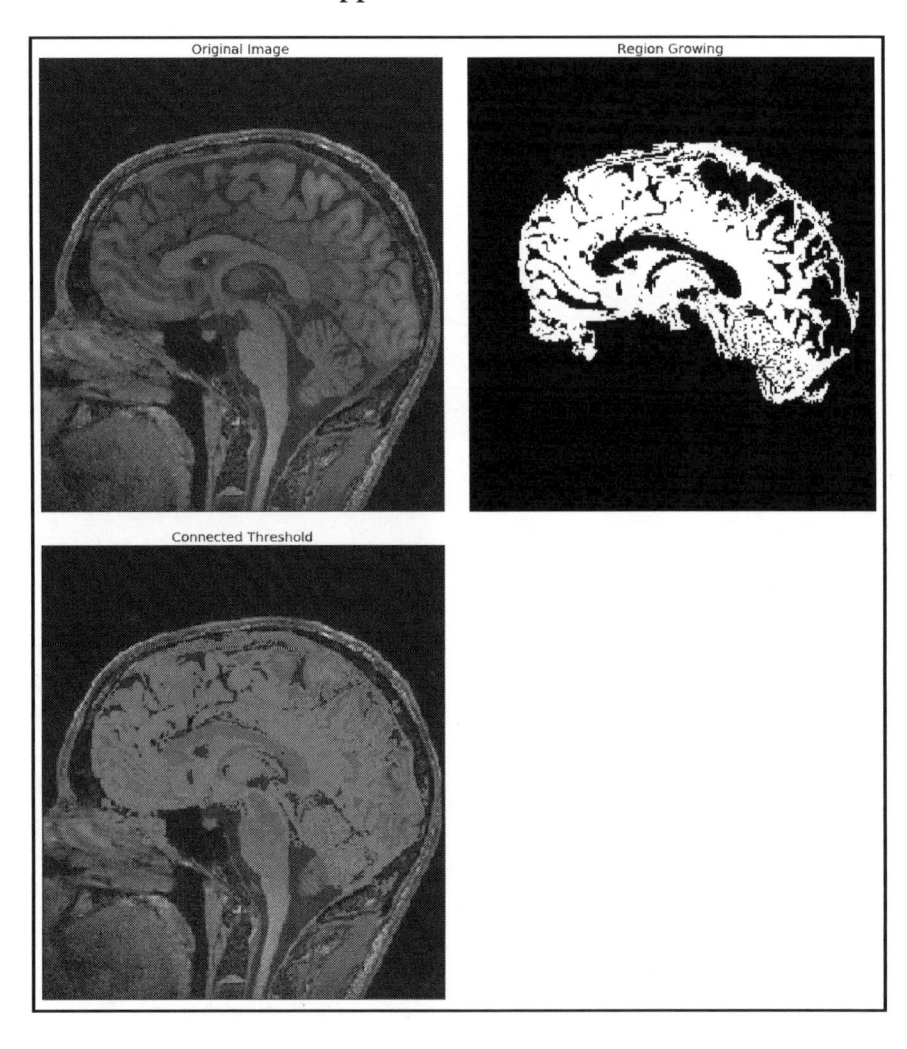

Active contours, morphological snakes, and GrabCut algorithms

In this section, we will discuss some more sophisticated segmentation algorithms and demonstrate them with `scikit-image` or `python-opencv` (cv2) library functions. We will start with segmentation using the active contours.

Active contours

The **active contour model** (also known as **snakes**) is a framework that fits open or closed splines to lines or edges in an image. A snake is an energy-minimizing, deformable spline influenced by constraint, image, and internal forces. Hence, it works by minimizing an energy that is partially defined by the image and partially by the spline's shape, length, and smoothness. The constraint and image forces pull the snake toward object contours and internal forces resist the deformation. The algorithm accepts an initial snake (around the object of interest) and to fit the closed contour to the object of interest, it shrinks/expands. The minimization is done explicitly in the image energy and implicitly in the shape energy. As the number of points is constant, we need to ensure that the initial snake has enough points to capture the details of the final contour.

In the following example, taken from the `scikit-image` documentation, the active contour model is going to be used to segment the face of a person (the astronaut) from the rest of an image by fitting a spline to the edges of the face. The image is smoothed a bit as a preprocessing step. First, a circle is initialized around the astronaut's face and the default boundary condition `bc='periodic'` is used to fit a closed curve. To make the curve search toward edges (for example, the boundaries of the face), the default parameter values `w_line=0, w_edge=1` are used. The next code block demonstrates how to use the `active_contour()` function for segmentation (which runs an iterative algorithm with a maximum number of iterations that can be specified by a parameter to the function), and shows the closed contour line obtained by running the algorithm internally for a different number of iterations:

```
from skimage import data
from skimage.filters import gaussian
from skimage.segmentation import active_contour
img = data.astronaut()
img_gray = rgb2gray(img)
s = np.linspace(0, 2*np.pi, 400)
x = 220 + 100*np.cos(s)
y = 100 + 100*np.sin(s)
init = np.array([x, y]).T
```

```
i = 1
pylab.figure(figsize=(20,20))
for max_it in [20, 30, 50, 100]:
   snake = active_contour(gaussian(img_gray, 3), init, alpha=0.015, beta=10,
gamma=0.001, max_iterations=max_it)
   pylab.subplot(2,2,i), pylab.imshow(img), pylab.plot(init[:, 0], init[:,
1], '--b', lw=3)
   pylab.plot(snake[:, 0], snake[:, 1], '-r', lw=3)
   pylab.axis('off'), pylab.title('max_iteration=' + str(max_it), size=20)
   i += 1
pylab.tight_layout(), pylab.show()
```

The next screenshot shows the output of the code. The initial circle to start with was the dotted blue circle. The active contour algorithm iteratively shrinks the contour (denoted by the red lines) starting from the circle toward the face, and finally, at `max_iteration=100`, fits itself to the boundary of the face, thereby segmenting the face out from the image:

Morphological snakes

Morphological snakes refers to a family of methods (similar to the active contours) for image segmentation. However, the morphological snakes are faster and numerically more stable than the active contours, since they use morphological operators (for example, dilation/erosion) over a binary array, whereas the active contours solve PDEs over a floating-point array. There are a couple of morphological snakes methods available in the scikit-image implementation, namely **Morphological Geodesic Active Contours (MorphGAC** with morphological_geodesic_active_contour()) and **Morphological Active Contours without Edges (MorphACWE** with morphological_chan_vese()). MorphGAC is suitable for images with visible (may be noisy, cluttered, or partially unclear) contours and requires that the image is preprocessed to highlight the contours. This preprocessing can be done using the function inverse_gaussian_gradient(). This preprocessing step has a great impact on the quality of the MorphGAC segmentation. On the contrary, when the pixel values of the inside and the outside regions of the object to segment have different averages, MorphACWE works well. It works with the original image without any preprocessing and does not need the contours of the object to be defined. For this reason, MorphACWE is easier to use and tune than MorphGAC. The next code block demonstrates how to implement morphological snakes using these functions. It also shows the evolution of the algorithms and the segmentation obtained at different iterations:

```
from skimage.segmentation import (morphological_chan_vese,
morphological_geodesic_active_contour,
  inverse_gaussian_gradient, checkerboard_level_set)

def store_evolution_in(lst):
 """Returns a callback function to store the evolution of the level sets in
  the given list.
 """

 def _store(x):
  lst.append(np.copy(x))
  return _store

# Morphological ACWE
image = imread('../images/me14.jpg')
image_gray = rgb2gray(image)
# initial level set
init_lvl_set = checkerboard_level_set(image_gray.shape, 6)
# list with intermediate results for plotting the evolution
evolution = []
callback = store_evolution_in(evolution)
lvl_set = morphological_chan_vese(image_gray, 30,
init_level_set=init_lvl_set, smoothing=3, iter_callback=callback)
```

Image Segmentation

```python
fig, axes = pylab.subplots(2, 2, figsize=(8, 6))
axes = axes.flatten()
axes[0].imshow(image, cmap="gray"), axes[0].set_axis_off(),
axes[0].contour(lvl_set, [0.5], colors='r')
axes[0].set_title("Morphological ACWE segmentation", fontsize=12)
axes[1].imshow(lvl_set, cmap="gray"), axes[1].set_axis_off()
contour = axes[1].contour(evolution[5], [0.5], colors='g')
contour.collections[0].set_label("Iteration 5")
contour = axes[1].contour(evolution[10], [0.5], colors='y')
contour.collections[0].set_label("Iteration 10")
contour = axes[1].contour(evolution[-1], [0.5], colors='r')
contour.collections[0].set_label("Iteration " + str(len(evolution)-1))
axes[1].legend(loc="upper right"), axes[1].set_title("Morphological ACWE evolution", fontsize=12)

# Morphological GAC
image = imread('new images/fishes4.jpg')
image_gray = rgb2gray(image)
gimage = inverse_gaussian_gradient(image_gray)
# initial level set
init_lvl_set = np.zeros(image_gray.shape, dtype=np.int8)
init_lvl_set[10:-10, 10:-10] = 1
# list with intermediate results for plotting the evolution
evolution = []
callback = store_evolution_in(evolution)
lvl_set = morphological_geodesic_active_contour(gimage, 400, init_lvl_set,
smoothing=1, balloon=-1,
 threshold=0.7, iter_callback=callback)
axes[2].imshow(image, cmap="gray"), axes[2].set_axis_off(),
axes[2].contour(lvl_set, [0.5], colors='r')
axes[2].set_title("Morphological GAC segmentation", fontsize=12)
axes[3].imshow(lvl_set, cmap="gray"), axes[3].set_axis_off()
contour = axes[3].contour(evolution[100], [0.5], colors='g')
contour.collections[0].set_label("Iteration 100")
contour = axes[3].contour(evolution[200], [0.5], colors='y')
contour.collections[0].set_label("Iteration 200")
contour = axes[3].contour(evolution[-1], [0.5], colors='r')
contour.collections[0].set_label("Iteration " + str(len(evolution)-1))
axes[3].legend(loc="upper right"), axes[3].set_title("Morphological GAC evolution", fontsize=12)
fig.tight_layout(), pylab.show()
```

The next screenshot shows the output of the code:

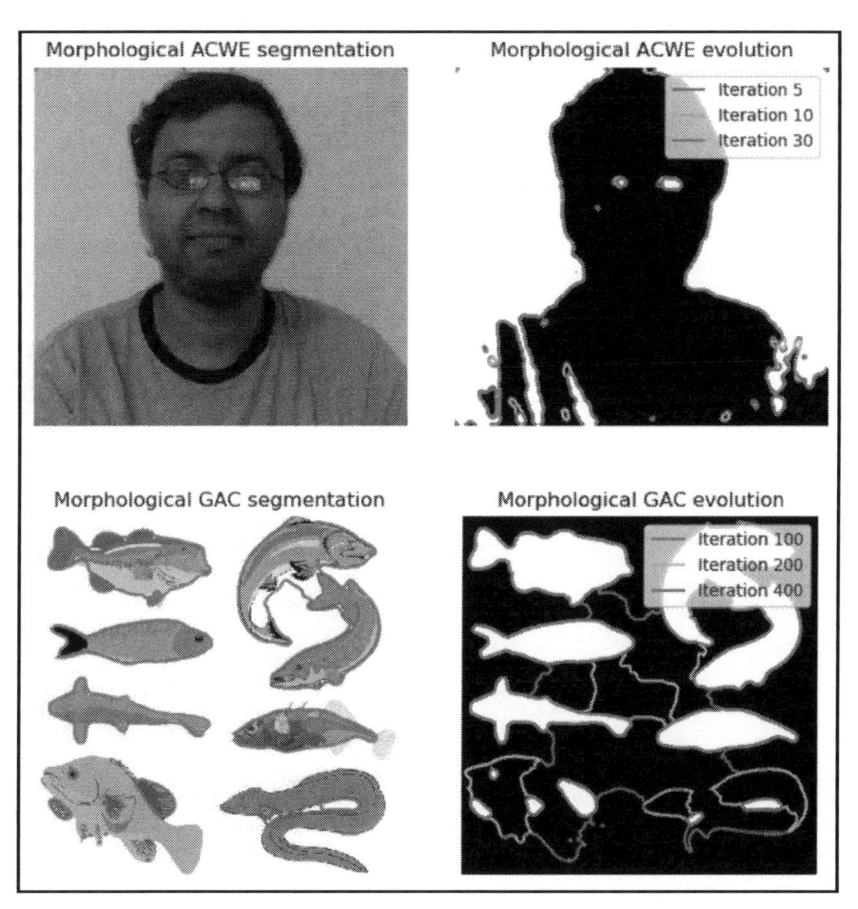

GrabCut with OpenCV

GrabCut is an interactive segmentation method that extracts the foreground from the background in an image using the graph-theoretic max-flow/min-cut algorithm. Before the algorithm can start, the user first needs to provide some hint by specifying the foreground region in the input image roughly with minimum possible interaction (for example, by drawing a rectangle around the foreground region). The algorithm then segments the image iteratively to get the best possible result. In some cases, the segmentation may not be the desired one (for example, the algorithm may have marked some foreground region as background and vice versa).

Image Segmentation

In that case, the user needs to do fine touch-ups again by giving some strokes on the images (by marking some more pixels as foreground or background) where there are some wrongly segmented pixels. This results in better segmentation in the next iteration.

The next code snippet demonstrates how the foreground whale object can be extracted from the input image by just drawing a rectangle around the whale (by providing a hint to the algorithm that the foreground object needs to be found inside the rectangle) and calling the `grabCut()` function from `cv2` on the input image. The mask image is an image through which we can specify which regions in the image are surely background, surely foreground, or probable background/foreground, using the following flags, 0 (`cv2.GC_BGD`), 1 (`cv2.GC_FGD`), 2 (`cv2.GC_PR_BGD`), 3 (`cv2.GC_PR_FGD`). Since in this case a rectangle is used (instead of the mask) to indicate the foreground, the mode parameter to the `cv2.grabCut()` function needs to be `cv2.GC_INIT_WITH_RECT`, and the mask image is set to zeros, initially. The algorithm is run for five iterations, and it modifies the mask image where the pixels are marked with four flag values denoting background/foreground. Next, we modify the mask so that all 0/2 valued pixels are set to 0 (background) and all 1/3 valued pixels are set to 1 (foreground); after this, we obtain the final mask that we need to multiply with the input image to obtain the segmented image:

```
img = cv2.imread('../images/whale.jpg')
mask = np.zeros(img.shape[:2],np.uint8)
bg_model = np.zeros((1,65),np.float64)
fg_model = np.zeros((1,65),np.float64)
rect = (80,50,720,420)
cv2.grabCut(img, mask, rect, bg_model, fg_model, 5, cv2.GC_INIT_WITH_RECT)
mask2 = np.where((mask==2)|(mask==0),0,1).astype('uint8')
img = img*mask2[:,:,np.newaxis]
pylab.imshow(img), pylab.colorbar(), pylab.show()
```

The next screenshot shows the input image along with the bounding box rectangle drawn around the foreground object. Notice that the rectangle misses a small part of the fin of the whale at the top and includes a part of the white ocean foam at the bottom of the image:

The following screenshot shows the output of the code block. As can be seen, a part of the upper fin is missed out and the white foam at the bottom is included as part of the foreground object since the bounding rectangle was a little incorrect (the entire foreground was not inside the bounding rectangle). This can be corrected by providing the hint bounding rectangle correctly, which is left as an exercise for you:

Image Segmentation

Another way to initialize the segmentation is to provide some hint to the algorithm by inputting a mask. For example, in this case, the mask image is of the same shape as the whale image. Some green and red strokes are drawn on the mask to provide some hint to the algorithm that these pixels surely belong to foreground and background pixels, respectively:

```
newmask = cv2.imread('../images/whale_mask.jpg')
# whereever it is marked green(sure foreground), change mask=1
# whereever it is marked red (sure background), change mask=0
```

The next screenshot shows what the mask looks like when drawn on the input image:

Now the algorithm needs to be run with this mask. The next code block shows how to run the algorithm with the mask:

```
mask = 2*np.ones(img.shape[:2],np.uint8) # initialize all pixels to be
probably backgrounds
mask[(newmask[...,0] <= 20)&(newmask[...,1] <= 20)&(newmask[...,2] >= 200)]
= 0 # red pixels are backgrounds
mask[(newmask[...,0] <= 20)&(newmask[...,1] >= 200)&(newmask[...,2] <= 20)]
= 1 # green pixels are foregrounds
mask, bg_model, fg_model =
cv2.grabCut(img,mask,None,bg_model,fg_model,5,cv2.GC_INIT_WITH_MASK)
mask = np.where((mask==2)|(mask==0),0,1).astype('uint8')
img = img*mask[:,:,np.newaxis]
pylab.imshow(img),pylab.colorbar(),pylab.show()
```

The following screenshot shows the output of the code block, the correctly segmented foreground object with the algorithm, with just the strokes in the mask as hints:

Summary

In this chapter, we discussed image segmentation and demonstrated different algorithms with Python libraries such as `scikit-image`, `opencv (cv2)` and `SimpleITK`. We started with line and circle detection in an image with Hough transform and also showed an example of how it can be used for image segmentation. Next, we discussed Otsu's thresholding algorithm to find the optimal threshold for segmentation. Then edge-based and region-based segmentation algorithms were demonstrated along with the morphological watershed algorithm for image segmentation. In the next section, some more segmentation algorithms such as Felzenszwalb's graph-based algorithm, region growing, SLIC, and QuickShift were discussed, along with the implementations using `scikit-image`. Finally, we discussed some more sophisticated segmentation algorithms, such as GrabCut, active contours, and morphological snakes.

In the next chapter, we shall discuss machine learning techniques in image processing, and we will discuss more on image segmentation with k-means clustering and mean-shift algorithms as unsupervised machine learning algorithms. We will also discuss semantic segmentation techniques later in the deep-learning chapters.

Questions

1. Use Hough transform to detect *ellipses* from an image with ellipses with `scikit-image`.
2. Use `scikit-image` transform module's `probabilistic_hough_line()` function to detect lines from images. How is it different than the `hough_line()`?
3. Use `scikit-image` filter module's `try_all_threshold()` function to compare different types of local thresholding techniques to segment a gray-scale image into a binary image.
4. Use the `ConfidenceConnected` and `VectorConfidenceConnected` algorithms for the MRI-scan image segmentation using `SimpleITK`.
5. Use the correct bounding rectangle around the foreground object to segment the whale image with the GrabCut algorithm.
6. Use `scikit-image` segmentation module's `random_walker()` function to segment an image starting from a few marked locations defined by markers.

Further reading

- http://scikit-image.org/docs/dev/user_guide/tutorial_segmentation.html
- https://www.scipy-lectures.org/packages/scikit-image/index.html
- http://scikit-image.org/docs/dev/auto_examples/
- https://web.stanford.edu/class/ee368/Handouts/Lectures/2014_Spring/Combined_Slides/6-Image-Segmentation-Combined.pdf
- https://courses.csail.mit.edu/6.869/lectnotes/lect19/lect19-slides-6up.pdf
- http://cmm.ensmp.fr/~beucher/publi/WTS_residues.pdf
- http://cmm.ensmp.fr/~beucher/wtshed.html
- https://sandipanweb.wordpress.com/2018/02/25/graph-based-image-segmentation-in-python/
- https://sandipanweb.wordpress.com/2018/02/11/interactive-image-segmentation-with-graph-cut/
- http://people.cs.uchicago.edu/~pff/papers/seg-ijcv.pdf
- http://www.kev-smith.com/papers/SMITH_TPAMI12.pdf

9
Classical Machine Learning Methods in Image Processing

In this chapter, we will discuss the application of machine learning techniques in image processing. We will define machine learning and learn about two of its algorithms, supervised and unsupervised. Then, we will continue our discussion on the application of a few popular unsupervised machine learning techniques, such as clustering, and problems such as image segmentation.

We will also be looking at applications of supervised machine learning techniques for problems such as image classification and object detection. We will be using a very popular library, scikit-learn, along with scikit-image and Python-OpenCV (cv2) to implement machine learning algorithms for image processing. This chapter is going to give you insight into machine learning algorithms and the problems they solve.

The topics to be covered in this chapter are as follows:

- Supervised versus unsupervised learning
- Unsupervised machine learning—clustering, PCA, and eigenfaces
- Supervised machine learning—image classification with the handwritten digits dataset
- Supervised machine learning—object detection

Supervised versus unsupervised learning

Machine learning algorithms can primarily be of two types:

- **Supervised learning**: In this type of learning, we are given an input dataset along with the correct labels, and we need to learn the the relationship (as a function) between the input and the output. The handwritten-digit classification problem is an example of a supervised (classification) problem.
- **Unsupervised learning**: In this type of learning, we have little or no idea what our output should look like. We can derive structure from data where we don't necessarily know the effect of the variables. An example is clustering, which can also be thought of as segmentation, in image processing technique where we do not have any prior knowledge of which pixel belongs to which segment.

A computer program is said to learn from experience, E, with respect to some task, T, and some performance measure, P, if its performance on T, as measured by P, improves with experience, E.

For example, let's say that we are given a set of handwritten digit images along with their labels (digits from zero to nine) and we need to write a Python program that learns the association between the images and labels (as experience E) and then automatically labels a set of new handwritten digit images.

In this case, the task, T, is the assignment of labels to the image (that is, classifying or identifying the digit image). The proportion of the set of new images correctly identified will be the performance, P, (accuracy). of the program. In this case, the program can be said to be a learning program.

In this chapter, we will describe a few image processing problems that can be solved using machine learning algorithms (unsupervised or supervised). We will start with learning the applications of a couple of unsupervised machine learning techniques in solving image processing problems.

Unsupervised machine learning – clustering, PCA, and eigenfaces

In this section, we will discuss a few popular machine learning algorithms along with their applications in image processing. Let's start with a couple of clustering algorithms and their applications in color quantization and the segmentation of images. We will use the scikit-learn library's implementation for these clustering algorithms.

K-means clustering for image segmentation with color quantization

In this section, we will demonstrate how to perform a pixel-wise **Vector Quantization** (**VQ**) of the pepper image, reducing the number of colors required to show the image from 250 unique colors down to four colors, while preserving the overall appearance quality. In this example, pixels are represented in a 3D space and k-means is used to find four color clusters.

In image processing literature, the codebook is obtained from k-means (the cluster centers) and is called the **color palette**. In a color palette, using a single byte, up to 256 colors can be addressed, whereas an RGB encoding requires 3 bytes per pixel. The GIF file format uses such a palette. For comparison, we will also see a quantized image using a random codebook (colors picked up randomly).

Let's use k-means clustering to segment an image:

```
import numpy as np
import matplotlib.pyplot as pylab
from sklearn.cluster import KMeans
from sklearn.metrics import pairwise_distances_argmin
from skimage.io import imread
from sklearn.utils import shuffle
from skimage import img_as_float

pepper = imread("../images/pepper.jpg")
# Convert to floats instead of the default 8 bits integer coding, so that
# pylab.imshow behaves works well on float data (need to be in the range
[0-1])
pepper = img_as_float(pepper)
# Load Image and transform to a 3D numpy array.
w, h, d = original_shape = tuple(pepper.shape)
assert d == 3
image_array = np.reshape(pepper, (w * h, d))
```

```python
def recreate_image(codebook, labels, w, h):
    """Recreate the (compressed) image from the code book & labels"""
    d = codebook.shape[1]
    image = np.zeros((w, h, d))
    label_idx = 0
    for i in range(w):
        for j in range(h):
            image[i][j] = codebook[labels[label_idx]]
            label_idx += 1
    return image

# Display all results, alongside original image
pylab.screenshot(1), pylab.clf()
ax = pylab.axes([0, 0, 1, 1])
pylab.axis('off'), pylab.title('Original image (%d colors)' 
%(len(np.unique(pepper)))), pylab.imshow(pepper)

pylab.screenshot(2, figsize=(10,10)), pylab.clf()
i = 1
for k in [64, 32, 16, 4]:
    # run kmeans on a random sample of 1000 pixels from the image
    image_array_sample = shuffle(image_array, random_state=0)[:1000]
    kmeans = KMeans(n_clusters=k, random_state=0).fit(image_array_sample)
    # predicting color indices on the full image (k-means)
    labels = kmeans.predict(image_array)
    pylab.subplot(2,2,i), pylab.axis('off'), pylab.title('Quantized image (' + 
str(k) + ' colors, K-Means)')
    pylab.imshow(recreate_image(kmeans.cluster_centers_, labels, w, h))
    i += 1
pylab.show()

pylab.screenshot(3, figsize=(10,10)), pylab.clf()
i = 1
for k in [64, 32, 16, 4]:
    codebook_random = shuffle(image_array, random_state=0)[:k + 1]
    # predicting color indices on the full image (random)
    labels_random = pairwise_distances_argmin(codebook_random, image_array, 
axis=0)
    pylab.subplot(2,2,i), pylab.title('Quantized image (' + str(k) + ' colors, 
Random)'), pylab.axis('off')
    pylab.imshow(recreate_image(codebook_random, labels_random, w, h))
    i += 1
pylab.show()
```

This is the original image and the output generated by the preceding code block, respectively:

Original image (250 colors)

As can be seen, k-means clustering always does a better job color quantization than using a random codebook, in terms of the preserved image quality:

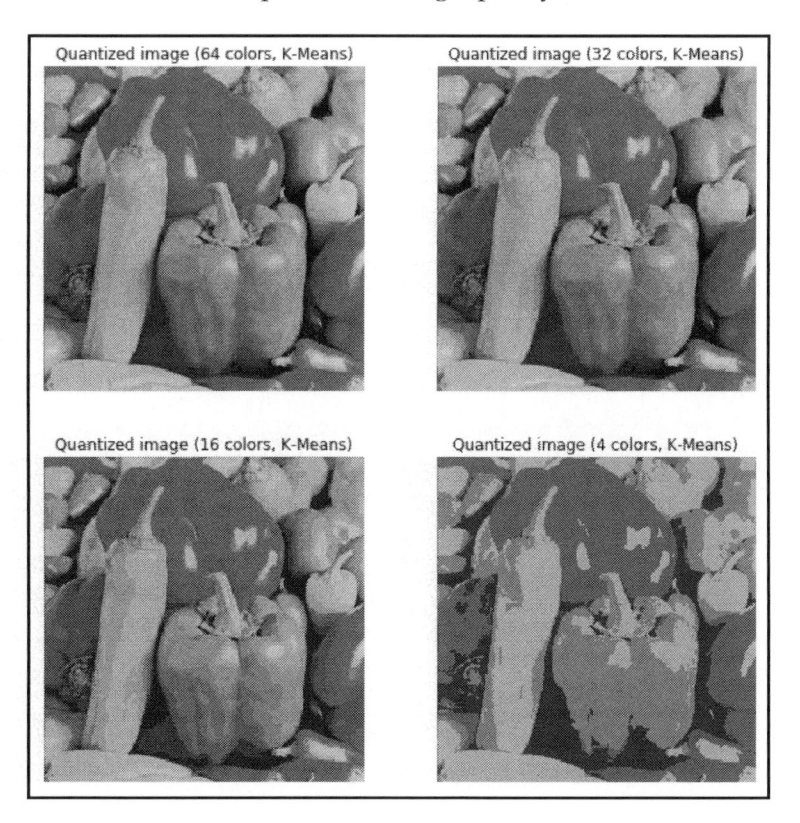

Quantized image (64 colors, K-Means)

Quantized image (32 colors, K-Means)

Quantized image (16 colors, K-Means)

Quantized image (4 colors, K-Means)

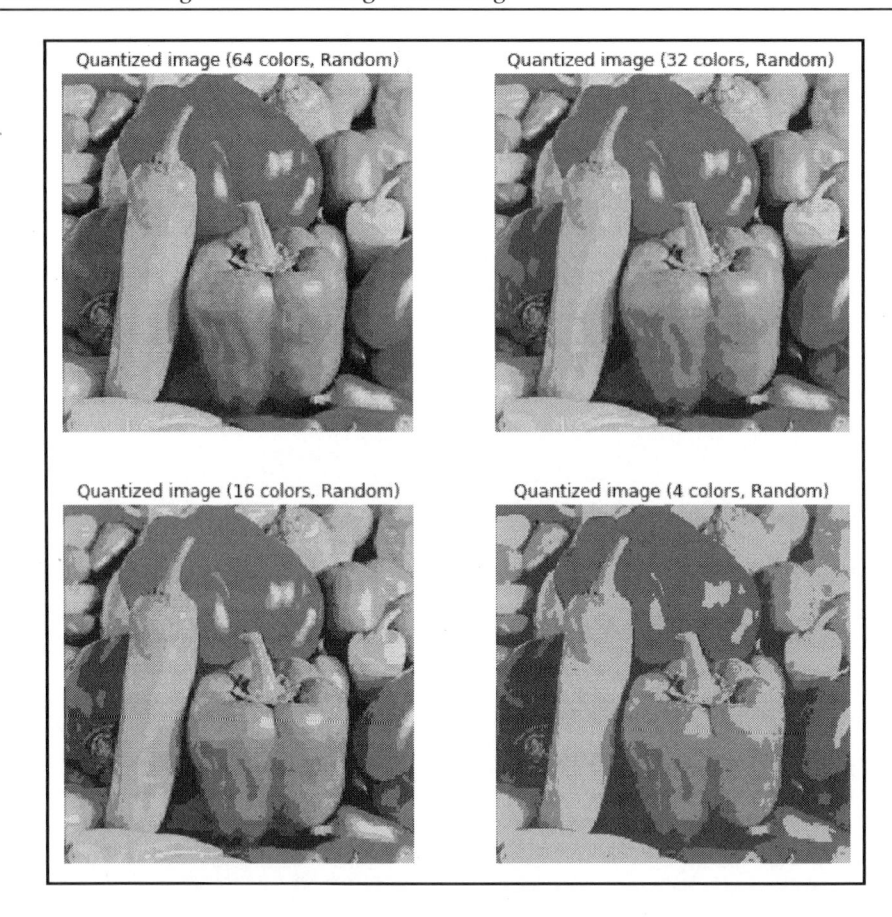

Spectral clustering for image segmentation

In this section, we will demonstrate how the spectral clustering technique can be used for image segmentation. In these settings, the spectral clustering approach solves the problem known as normalized graph cuts—the image is seen as a graph of connected pixels and the spectral clustering algorithm amounts to choosing graph cuts defining regions while minimizing the ratio of the gradient along the cut and the volume of the region. `SpectralClustering()` from the scikit-learn cluster module will be used to segment the image into foreground and background.

The result is compared with binary segmentation obtained using k-means clustering, as demonstrated in the following code:

```
from sklearn import cluster
from skimage.io import imread
from skimage.color import rgb2gray
from scipy.misc import imresize
im = imresize(imread('../images/me14.jpg'), (100,100,3))
img = rgb2gray(im)
k = 2 # binary segmentation, with 2 output clusters / segments
X = np.reshape(im, (-1, im.shape[-1]))
two_means = cluster.MiniBatchKMeans(n_clusters=k, random_state=10)
two_means.fit(X)
y_pred = two_means.predict(X)
labels = np.reshape(y_pred, im.shape[:2])
pylab.screenshot(figsize=(20,20))
pylab.subplot(221), pylab.imshow(np.reshape(y_pred, im.shape[:2])),
pylab.title('k-means segmentation (k=2)', size=30)
pylab.subplot(222), pylab.imshow(im), pylab.contour(labels == 0,
contours=1, colors='red'), pylab.axis('off')
pylab.title('k-means contour (k=2)', size=30)
spectral = cluster.SpectralClustering(n_clusters=k, eigen_solver='arpack',
affinity="nearest_neighbors", n_neighbors=100, random_state=10)
spectral.fit(X)
y_pred = spectral.labels_.astype(np.int)
labels = np.reshape(y_pred, im.shape[:2])
pylab.subplot(223), pylab.imshow(np.reshape(y_pred, im.shape[:2])),
pylab.title('spctral segmentation (k=2)', size=30)
pylab.subplot(224), pylab.imshow(im), pylab.contour(labels == 0,
contours=1, colors='red'), pylab.axis('off'), pylab.title('spectral contour
(k=2)', size=30), pylab.tight_layout()
pylab.show()
```

The following screenshot shows the output of the preceding code. As can be seen, the spectral clustering does a better job in segmenting the image than the k-means clustering:

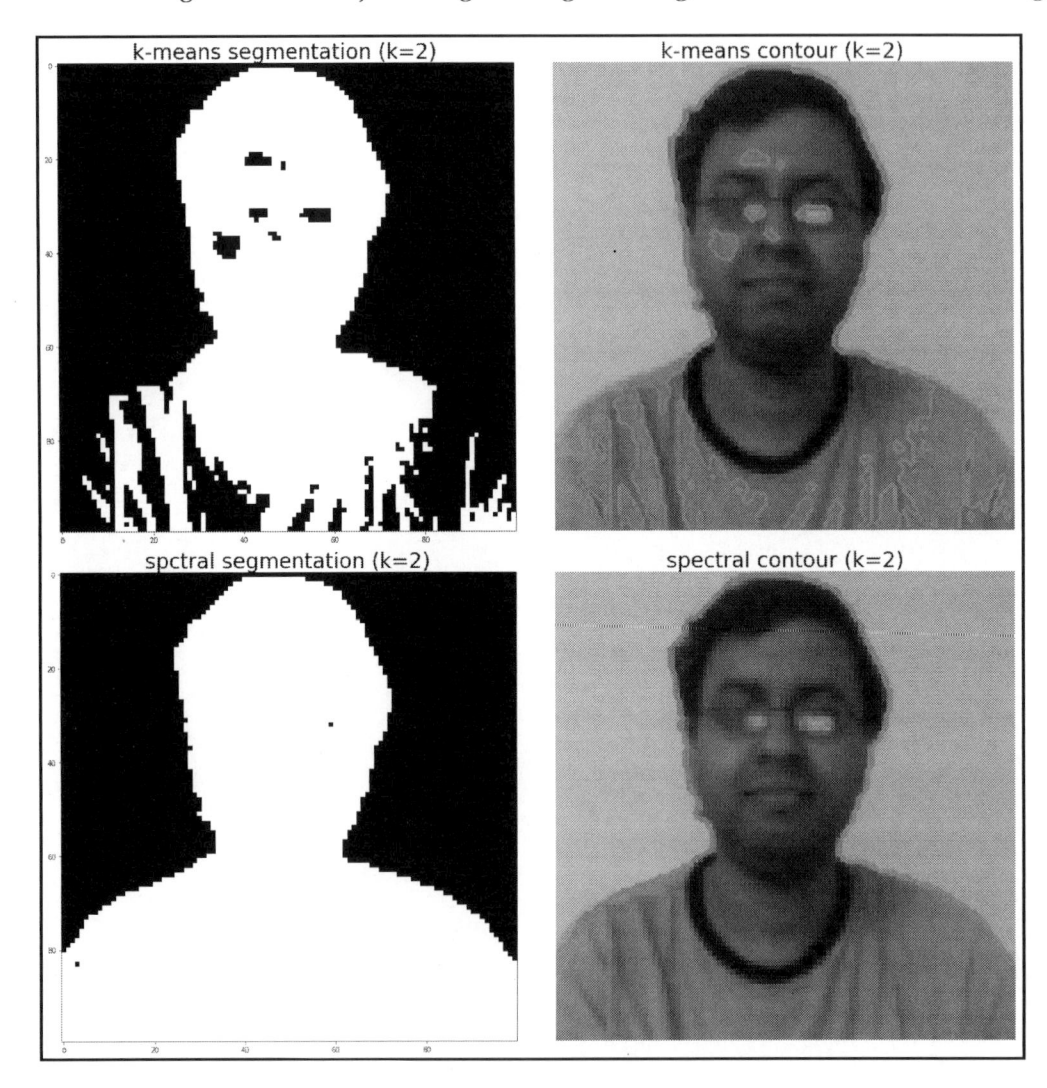

PCA and eigenfaces

Principal Component Analysis (PCA) is a statistical/unsupervised machine learning technique that uses an orthogonal transformation to convert a set of observations of possibly correlated variables into a set of values of linearly uncorrelated variables called principal components, thereby finding the maximum directions of variances in the dataset (along the principal components).

This can be used for (linear) dimensionality reduction (only a few dominant principal components captures almost all of the variance in a dataset most of the time) and visualization (in 2D) of datasets having many dimensions. One application of PCA is eigenfaces, to find a set of faces that can (theoretically) represent any face (as a linear combination of those eigenfaces).

Dimension reduction and visualization with PCA

In this section, we will use the scikit-learn's digits dataset that contains 1,797 images (each of 8 x 8 pixels) of handwritten digits. Each row represents an image in the data matrix. Let's first load and display the first 25 digits from the dataset with the following code block:

```
from sklearn.datasets import load_digits
digits = load_digits()
print(digits.data.shape)
# (1797, 64)
j = 1
np.random.seed(1)
fig = pylab.screenshot(figsize=(3,3))
fig.subplots_adjust(left=0, right=1, bottom=0, top=1, hspace=0.05, wspace=0.05)
for i in np.random.choice(digits.data.shape[0], 25):
 pylab.subplot(5,5,j), pylab.imshow(np.reshape(digits.data[i,:], (8,8)), cmap='binary'), pylab.axis('off')
 j += 1
pylab.show()
```

The following screenshot shows the output of the preceding code block, the first 25 handwritten digits from the dataset:

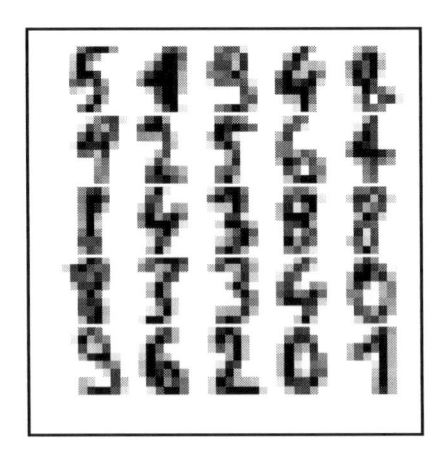

2D projection and visualization

As we can see from the loaded dataset, it's a 64-dimensional dataset. Now let's use scikit-learn's PCA() function to find the two dominant principal components of this dataset and project the dataset along these two dimensions, followed by scatter-plotting the projected data with Matplotlib and with each data point representing an image (a digit), with the digits label represented by a unique color, using the following code block:

```
pca_digits = PCA(2)
digits.data_proj = pca_digits.fit_transform(digits.data)
pylab.screenshot(figsize=(15,10))
pylab.scatter(digits.data_proj[:, 0], digits.data_proj[:, 1], lw=0.25,
    c=digits.target, edgecolor='k', s=100, cmap=pylab.cm.get_cmap('cubehelix',
    10))
pylab.xlabel('PC1', size=20), pylab.ylabel('PC2', size=20), pylab.title('2D
Projection of handwritten digits with PCA', size=25)
pylab.colorbar(ticks=range(10), label='digit value')
pylab.clim(-0.5, 9.5)
```

The following screenshot shows the output. As can be seen, the digits are somewhat separated (although there is some overlap) even in the 2D projection along the PCs, with same digit values appearing nearby in clusters:

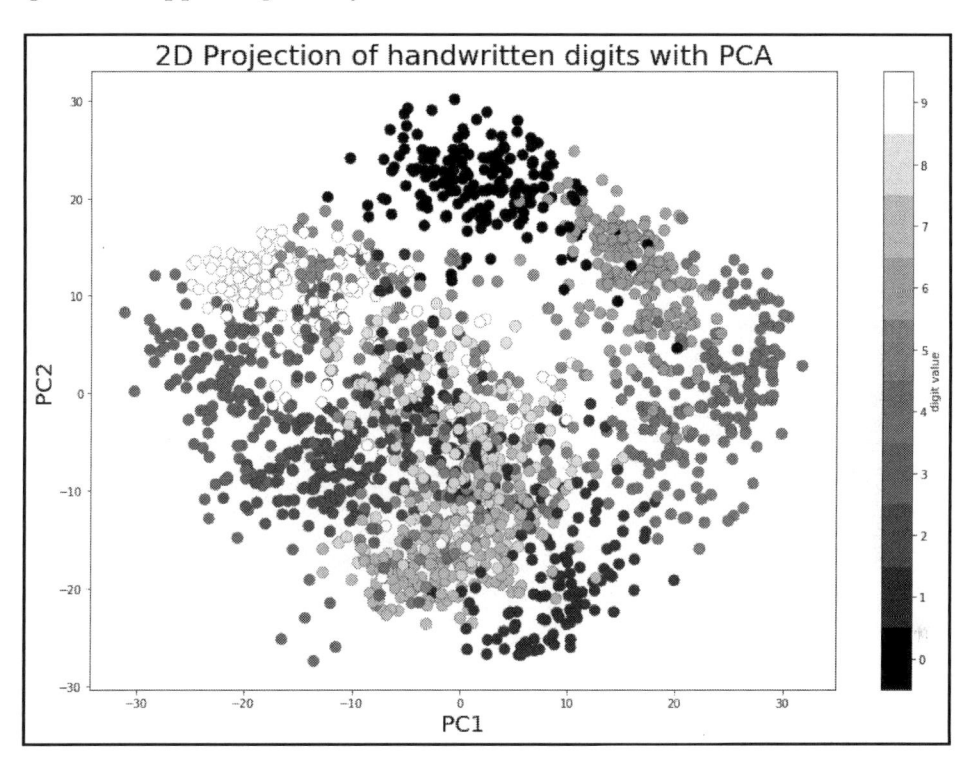

Eigenfaces with PCA

Let's start by loading the olivetti face dataset from scikit-learn; it contains 400 face images, each with a dimension of 64 x 64 pixels.

The following code block shows a few random faces from the dataset:

```
from sklearn.datasets import fetch_olivetti_faces
faces = fetch_olivetti_faces().data
print(faces.shape) # there are 400 faces each of them is of 64x64=4096
pixels
# (400, 4096)
fig = pylab.screenshot(figsize=(5,5))
fig.subplots_adjust(left=0, right=1, bottom=0, top=1, hspace=0.05,
wspace=0.05)
# plot 25 random faces
```

```
j = 1
np.random.seed(0)
for i in np.random.choice(range(faces.shape[0]), 25):
    ax = fig.add_subplot(5, 5, j, xticks=[], yticks=[])
    ax.imshow(np.reshape(faces[i,:],(64,64)), cmap=pylab.cm.bone,
interpolation='nearest')
    j += 1
pylab.show()
```

The following screenshot shows the output of the preceding code—25 face images randomly selected from the dataset:

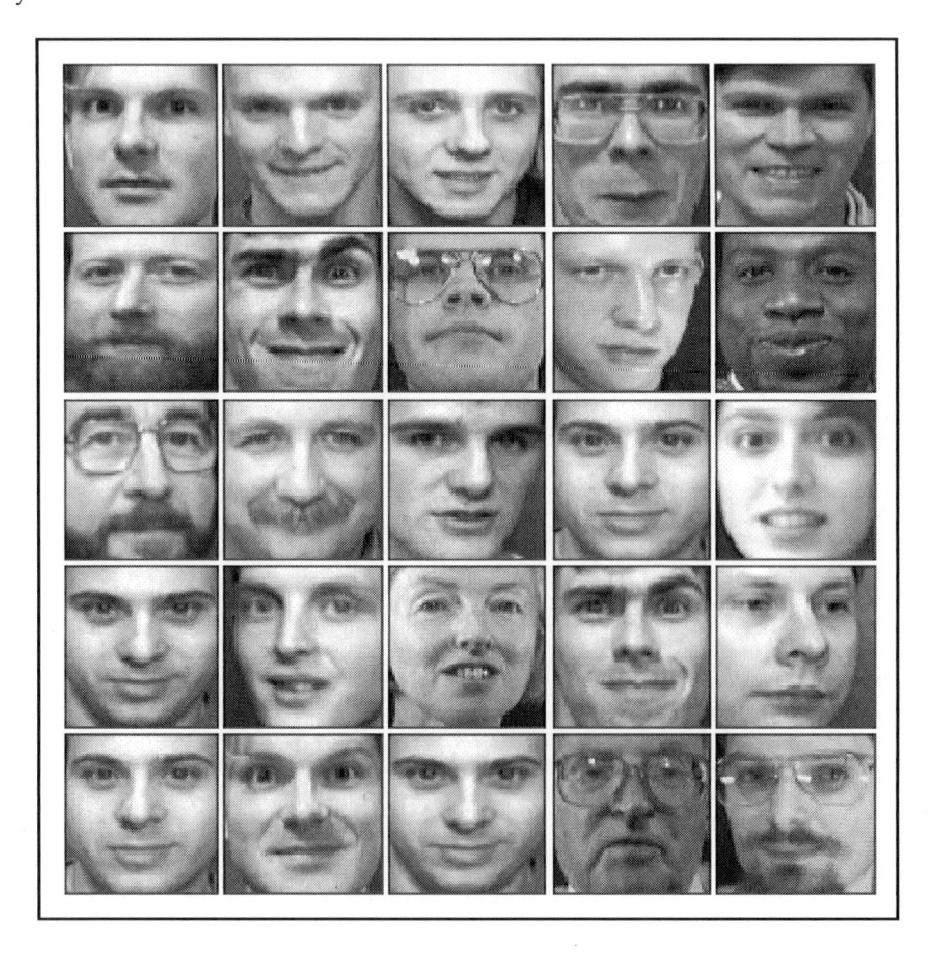

Next, let's pre-process the dataset to perform a z-score normalization (subtracting the mean face from all the faces and dividing by the standard deviation); this is a necessary step before we apply PCA on the images. Next, the principal components are computed with `PCA()` and only the 64 (instead of 4,096) dominant principal components are chosen; the dataset is projected onto these PCs. The following code block shows how to do it and visualizes how much variance of the image dataset is captured by choosing more and more principal components:

```
from sklearn.preprocessing import StandardScaler
from sklearn.decomposition import PCA
from sklearn.pipeline import Pipeline
n_comp =64
pipeline = Pipeline([('scaling', StandardScaler()), ('pca',
PCA(n_components=n_comp))])
faces_proj = pipeline.fit_transform(faces)
print(faces_proj.shape)
# (400, 64)
mean_face = np.reshape(pipeline.named_steps['scaling'].mean_, (64,64))
sd_face = np.reshape(np.sqrt(pipeline.named_steps['scaling'].var_),
(64,64))
pylab.screenshot(figsize=(8, 6))
pylab.plot(np.cumsum(pipeline.named_steps['pca'].explained_variance_ratio_)
, linewidth=2)
pylab.grid(), pylab.axis('tight'), pylab.xlabel('n_components'),
pylab.ylabel('cumulative explained_variance_ratio_')
pylab.show()
pylab.screenshot(figsize=(10,5))
pylab.subplot(121), pylab.imshow(mean_face, cmap=pylab.cm.bone),
pylab.axis('off'), pylab.title('Mean face')
pylab.subplot(122), pylab.imshow(sd_face, cmap=pylab.cm.bone),
pylab.axis('off'), pylab.title('SD face')
pylab.show()
```

The following diagram shows the output. As can be seen, around 90% of the variances are explained by only the first 64 principal components:

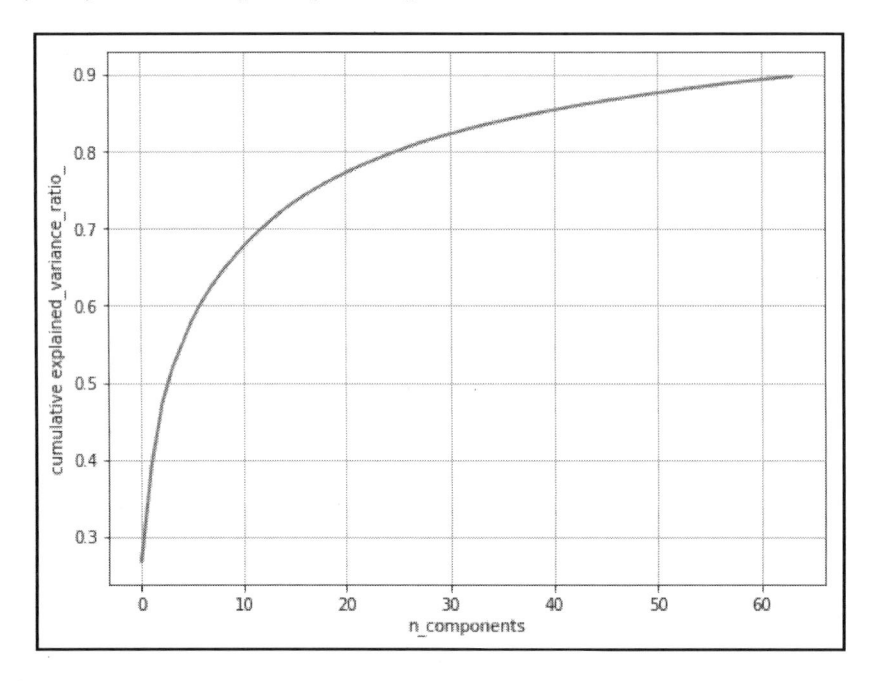

The following screenshot shows the mean and the standard deviation face images computed from the dataset, respectively:

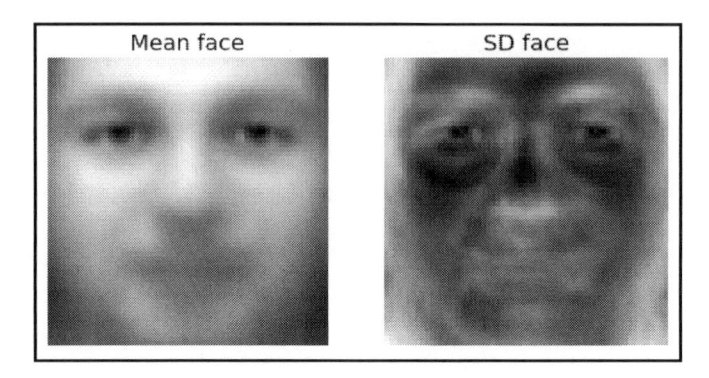

Chapter 9

Eigenfaces

Given the property of PCA, the PCs computed are orthogonal to each other and each of them contains 4,096 pixels—and can be reshaped to a 64 x 64 image. These principal components are known as eigenfaces (since they are also the eigenvectors). As can be seen, they represent certain properties of the faces. The following code block displays some of the computed eigenfaces:

```
fig = pylab.screenshot(figsize=(5,2))
fig.subplots_adjust(left=0, right=1, bottom=0, top=1, hspace=0.05,
wspace=0.05)
# plot the top 10 eigenfaces
for i in range(10):
  ax = fig.add_subplot(2, 5, i+1, xticks=[], yticks=[])
  ax.imshow(np.reshape(pipeline.named_steps['pca'].components_[i,:],
  (64,64)), cmap=pylab.cm.bone, interpolation='nearest')
```

The following screenshot shows the output of the preceding code block—the first 10 eigenfaces:

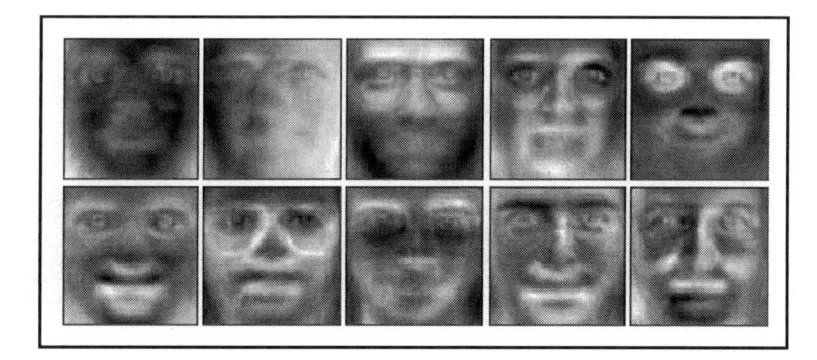

Reconstruction

The following code block demonstrates how each of the faces can be approximately represented as a linear combination of only those 64 dominant eigenfaces. The `inverse_transform()` function from scikit-learn is used to go back to the original space but only with these 64 dominant eigenfaces, discarding all other eigenfaces:

```
# face reconstruction
faces_inv_proj = pipeline.named_steps['pca'].inverse_transform(faces_proj)
#reshaping as 400 images of 64x64 dimension
fig = pylab.screenshot(figsize=(5,5))
fig.subplots_adjust(left=0, right=1, bottom=0, top=1, hspace=0.05,
wspace=0.05)
```

```
# plot the faces, each image is 64 by 64 dimension but 8x8 pixels
j = 1
np.random.seed(0)
for i in np.random.choice(range(faces.shape[0]), 25):
 ax = fig.add_subplot(5, 5, j, xticks=[], yticks=[])
 ax.imshow(mean_face + sd_face*np.reshape(faces_inv_proj,(400,64,64))
[i,:], cmap=pylab.cm.bone, interpolation='nearest')
 j += 1
```

The following screenshot shows the output of the preceding code block—25 randomly chosen face images reconstructed from the 64 eigenfaces. As can be seen, they look pretty much like the original faces (without many visible errors):

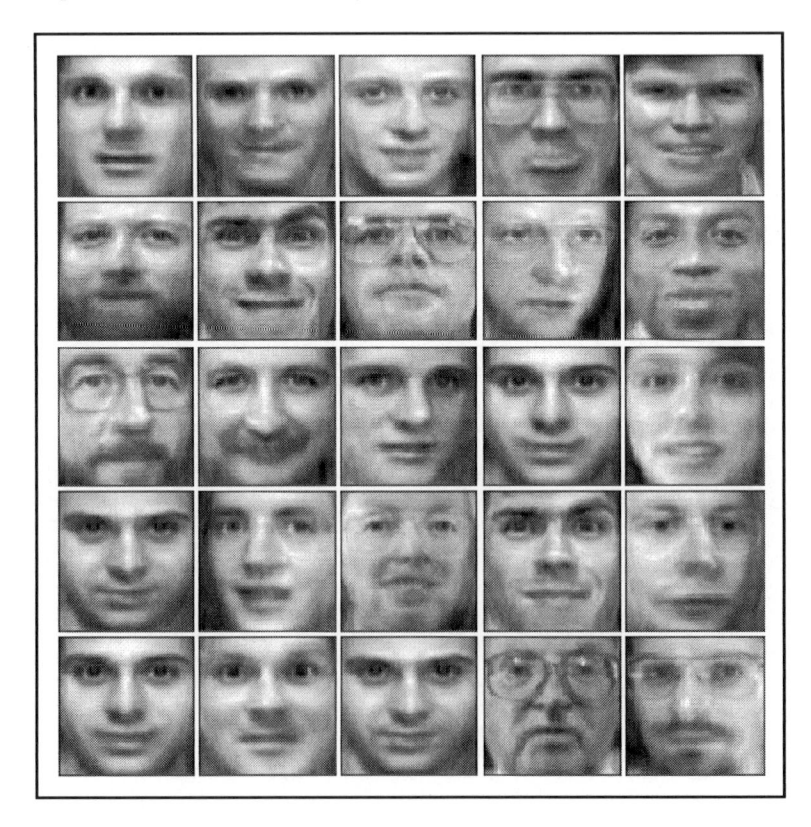

The following code block helps us to take a closer look and compares an original face with its reconstructed version:

```
orig_face = np.reshape(faces[0,:], (64,64))
reconst_face =
np.reshape(faces_proj[0,:]@pipeline.named_steps['pca'].components_,
(64,64))
reconst_face = mean_face + sd_face*reconst_face
pylab.screenshot(figsize=(10,5))
pylab.subplot(121), pylab.imshow(orig_face, cmap=pylab.cm.bone,
interpolation='nearest'), pylab.axis('off'), pylab.title('original',
size=20)
pylab.subplot(122), pylab.imshow(reconst_face, cmap=pylab.cm.bone,
interpolation='nearest'), pylab.axis('off'), pylab.title('reconstructed',
size=20)
pylab.show()
```

The following screenshot shows the output. As can be seen, the reconstructed face approximates the original face with some distortion:

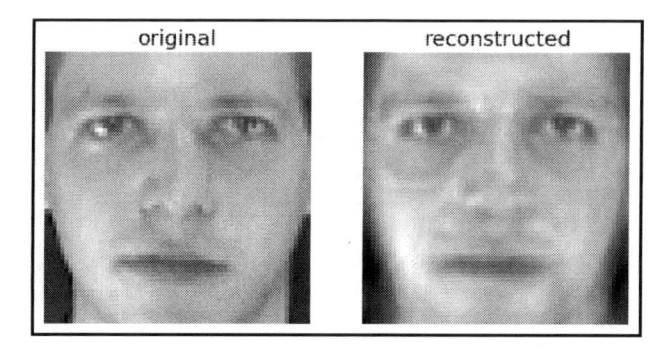

Eigen decomposition

Each face can be represented as a linear combination of the 64 eigenfaces. Each eigenface will have different weights (loadings) for different face image. The following screenshot shows how a face can be represented with the eigenfaces and shows the first few corresponding weights.

The code is left as an exercise to the reader:

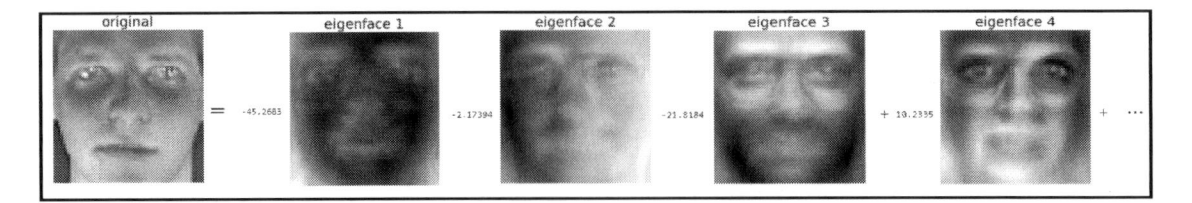

Supervised machine learning – image classification

In this section, we will discuss the image classification problem. The input dataset that we will use is MNIST (`http://yann.lecun.com/exdb/mnist/`), which is a classic dataset in machine learning, consisting of 28 x 28 grayscale images of handwritten digits. The original training dataset contains 60,000 examples (the handwritten digit images along with the labels to train machine learning models), and the test dataset contains 10,000 examples (the handwritten digit images along with the labels as ground-truths, to test the accuracy of the models learned). Given a set of handwritten digits and images along with their labels (0-9), the goal will be to learn a machine learning model that can automatically identify the digit from an unseen image and assign a label (0-9) to the image:

1. A few supervised machine learning (multi-class classification) models (classifiers) will be trained using the training dataset
2. Then, they will be used to predict the labels of the images from the test dataset
3. The predicted labels will be subsequently compared with the ground-truth labels to evaluate the performance of the classifiers

The following screenshot describes the steps in the training, prediction, and evaluation of a basic classification model. When we train many more different models (possibly with different algorithms or the same algorithm with different values of hyper-parameters) on the training dataset, in order to select the best one, we need a third dataset, which is called a validation dataset (the training dataset is split into two parts, one to train and another to hold out for validation) and is used for model selection and hyper-parameter tuning:

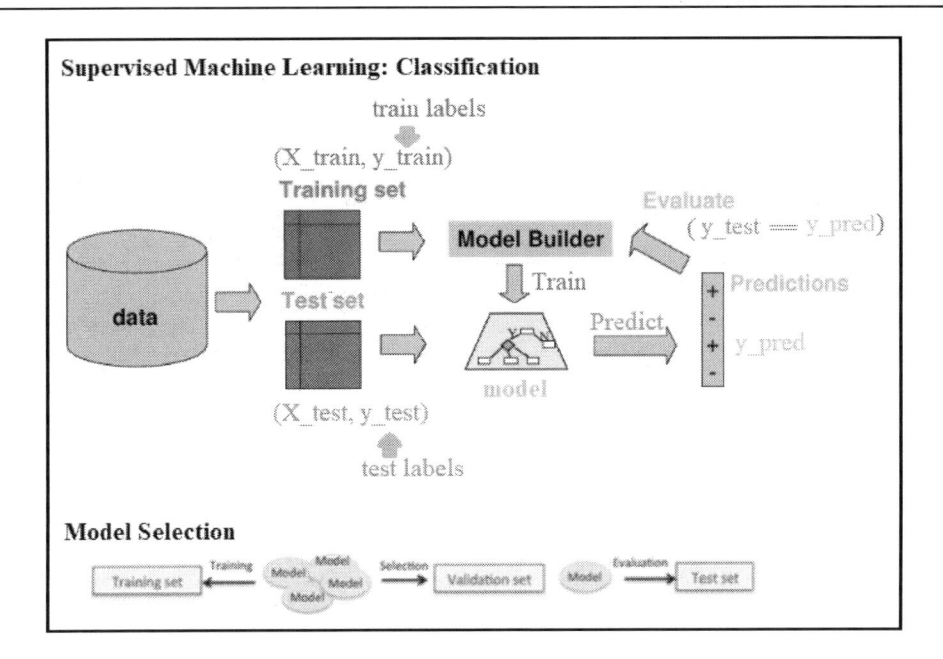

![Supervised Machine Learning: Classification diagram showing training set (X_train, y_train) and test set (X_test, y_test) flowing into Model Builder which trains a model to produce predictions y_pred, evaluated against y_test. Below is Model Selection flow: Training set → Training → Models → Selection → Validation set → Model → Evaluation → Test set.]

Again, let's start importing the required libraries, as follows:

```
%matplotlib inline
import gzip, os, sys
import numpy as np
from scipy.stats import multivariate_normal
from urllib.request import urlretrieve
import matplotlib.pyplot as pylab
```

Downloading the MNIST (handwritten digits) dataset

Let's start by downloading the MNIST dataset. The following Python code shows you how to download the training and test datasets:

```
# Function that downloads a specified MNIST data file from Yann Le Cun's
website
def download(filename, source='http://yann.lecun.com/exdb/mnist/'):
    print("Downloading %s" % filename)
    urlretrieve(source + filename, filename)

# Invokes download() if necessary, then reads in images
def load_mnist_images(filename):
```

Classical Machine Learning Methods in Image Processing

```
        if not os.path.exists(filename):
            download(filename)
        with gzip.open(filename, 'rb') as f:
            data = np.frombuffer(f.read(), np.uint8, offset=16)
        data = data.reshape(-1,784)
        return data

    def load_mnist_labels(filename):
        if not os.path.exists(filename):
            download(filename)
        with gzip.open(filename, 'rb') as f:
            data = np.frombuffer(f.read(), np.uint8, offset=8)
        return data

    ## Load the training set
    train_data = load_mnist_images('train-images-idx3-ubyte.gz')
    train_labels = load_mnist_labels('train-labels-idx1-ubyte.gz')
    ## Load the testing set
    test_data = load_mnist_images('t10k-images-idx3-ubyte.gz')
    test_labels = load_mnist_labels('t10k-labels-idx1-ubyte.gz')

    print(train_data.shape)
    # (60000, 784)          ## 60k 28x28 handwritten digits
    print(test_data.shape)
    # (10000, 784)          ## 10k 28x28 handwritten digits
```

Visualizing the dataset

Each data point is stored as 784-dimensional vector. To visualize a data point, we first need to reshape it to a 28 x 28 image. The following code snippet shows how to display a few handwritten digits from the test dataset:

```
    ## Define a function that displays a digit given its vector representation
    def show_digit(x, label):
     pylab.axis('off')
     pylab.imshow(x.reshape((28,28)), cmap=pylab.cm.gray)
     pylab.title('Label ' + str(label))

    pylab.screenshot(figsize=(10,10))
    for i in range(25):
     pylab.subplot(5, 5, i+1)
     show_digit(test_data[i,], test_labels[i])
    pylab.tight_layout()
    pylab.show()
```

The following screenshot shows the first 25 handwritten digits from the test dataset along with their ground-truth (true) labels. The kNN classifier trained on the training dataset will be used to predict the labels of this unseen test dataset and the predicted labels will be compared with the true labels to evaluate the accuracy of the classifier:

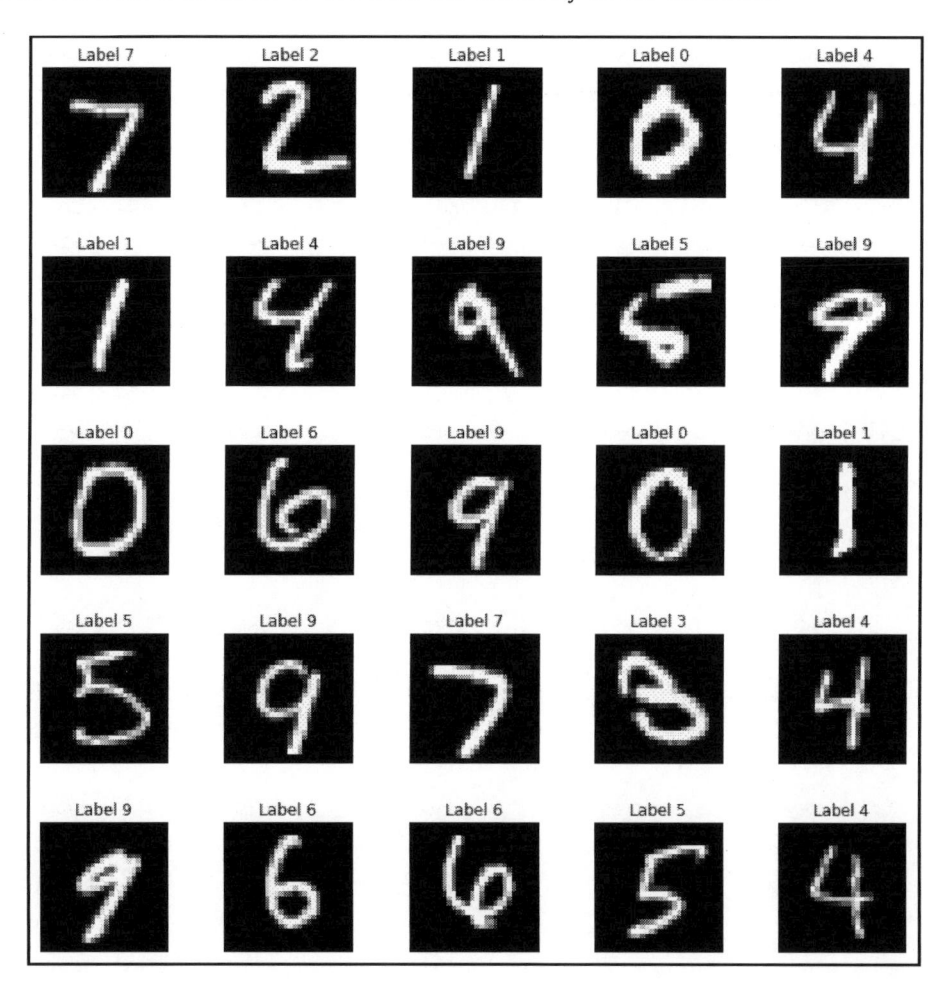

Training kNN, Gaussian Bayes, and SVM models to classify MNIST

We will use scikit-learn library functions to implement the following set of classifiers:

- k-nearest neighbors
- The Gaussian Bayes classifier (a generative model)
- The **Support Vector Machine (SVM)** classifier

Let's start with the k-nearest neighbors classifier.

k-nearest neighbors (KNN) classifier

In this section, we will build a classifier that takes an image of a handwritten digit and outputs a label (0-9) using a particularly simple strategy for this problem known as the **nearest neighbor classifier**. The idea to predict an unseen test digit image is pretty simple. First, we need to find the *k* instances from the training dataset that are nearest to this test image. Next, we need to simply use majority-voting to compute the label of the test image, that is, the label that most of the data points from the k nearest training data points have will be be assigned to the test image (breaking ties arbitrarily).

Squared Euclidean distance

To compute the nearest neighbors in our dataset, we need to first be able to compute distances between data points. A natural distance function is Euclidean distance; for two vectors $x, y \in R^d$, their Euclidean distance is defined as follows:

$$\|x - y\| = \sum_{i=1}^{d}(x_i - y_i)^2$$

Often, we omit the square root and simply compute the squared Euclidean distance. For the purposes of nearest neighbor computations, the two are equivalent: for three vectors x, y, z $\in R^d$, we have ‖x–y‖ ≤ ‖x–z‖ if and only if ‖x–y‖² ≤ ‖x–z‖². Now we just need to be able to compute the squared Euclidean distance.

Computing the nearest neighbors

A naive implementation of k-nearest neighbor will scan through each of the training images for each test image. Performing nearest neighbor classification in this way will require a full pass through the training set in order to classify a single point. If there are N training points in R^d, this takes $O(Nd)$ time, which will be quite slow. Fortunately, there are faster methods to perform nearest neighbor lookup if we are willing to spend some time pre-processing the training set. The scikit-learn library has fast implementations of two useful nearest neighbor data structures: the ball tree and the k-d tree. The following code shows how to create a ball tree data structure at training time and then use it for fast nearest neighbor computation during testing for *1-NN (k=1)*:

```
import time
from sklearn.neighbors import BallTree

## Build nearest neighbor structure on training data
t_before = time.time()
ball_tree = BallTree(train_data)
t_after = time.time()

## Compute training time
t_training = t_after - t_before
print("Time to build data structure (seconds): ", t_training)

## Get nearest neighbor predictions on testing data
t_before = time.time()
test_neighbors = np.squeeze(ball_tree.query(test_data, k=1,
return_distance=False))
test_predictions = train_labels[test_neighbors]
t_after = time.time()

## Compute testing time
t_testing = t_after - t_before
print("Time to classify test set (seconds): ", t_testing)
# Time to build data structure (seconds): 0.3269999027252197
# Time to classify test set (seconds): 6.457000017166138
```

Evaluating the performance of the classifier

Next, we need to evaluate the performance of the classifier on the test dataset. The following code snippet shows how to do that:

```
# evaluate the classifier
t_accuracy = sum(test_predictions == test_labels) / float(len(test_labels))
t_accuracy
# 0.9690999999999996

import pandas as pd
import seaborn as sn
from sklearn import metrics

cm=metrics.confusion_matrix(test_labels,test_predictions)
df_cm = pd.DataFrame(cm, range(10), range(10))
#pylab.screenshot(figsize = (10,7))
sn.set(font_scale=1.2)#for label size
sn.heatmap(df_cm, annot=True,annot_kws={"size": 16}, fmt="g") #,
cmap='viridis')# font size
```

The following screenshot shows the confusion matrix for the classification; we can see there are a few misclassified test images and the overall accuracy of the training dataset is 96.9%:

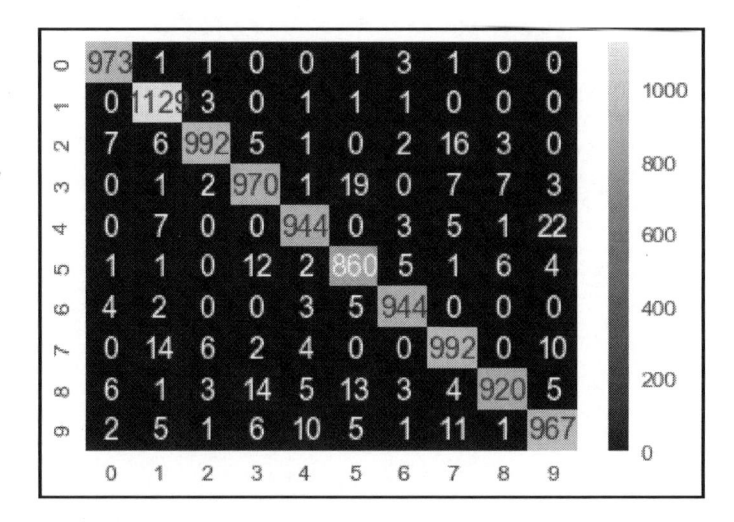

The following screenshot shows:

- **A success case**: *1-NN prediction label = True label = 0*
- **A failure case**: *1-NN prediction label = 2, True label = 3*

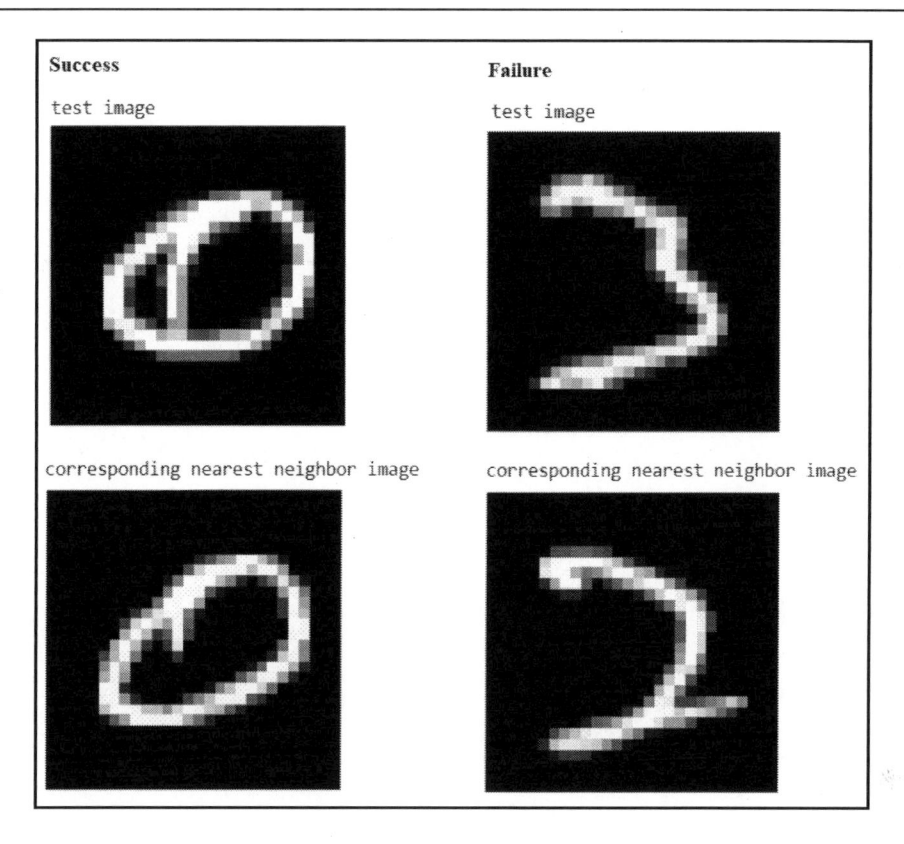

Success	Failure
test image	test image
corresponding nearest neighbor image	corresponding nearest neighbor image

The code to find a success and a failure case for prediction is left as an exercise for the reader.

Bayes classifier (Gaussian generative model)

As we have seen in the last section, the 1-NN classifier yielded a 3.09% test error rate on the MNIST data set of handwritten digits. In this section, we will build a Gaussian generative model that does almost as well, while being significantly faster and more compact. Again, we need to load the MNIST training and test dataset first, as we did last time. Next, let's fit a Gaussian generative model to the training dataset.

Training the generative model – computing the MLE of the Gaussian parameters

The following code block defines a function, `fit_generative_model()`, that takes as input a training set (x data and y labels) and fits a Gaussian generative model to it. It returns the following parameters of this generative model—for each label, $j = 0,1,...,9$, we have the following:

- πj: The frequency of the label (that is, the prior)
- μj: The 784-dimensional mean vector
- Σj: The 784 x 784 covariance matrix

This means that π is a 10 x 1, μ is a 10 x 784, and Σ is a 10 x 784 x 784 matrix. The **Maximum Likelihood Estimates (MLE)** for the parameters are the empirical estimates, as shown in the following diagram:

$$I_j(x) = \begin{cases} 1 & \text{if } y = j \\ 0 & \text{otherwise} \end{cases}$$

Assumption: $P(x|y=j) \sim \mathcal{N}(\mu_j, \Sigma_j)$

MLE for the parameters

$$\mu_j = \frac{\sum_{n=1}^{N} I_j(x_n) x_n}{\sum_{n=1}^{N} I_j(x_n)} \qquad \Sigma_j = \frac{\sum_{n=1}^{N} I_j(x_n)(x_n - \mu_j)(x_n - \mu_j)^\top}{\sum_{n=1}^{N} I_j(x_n)}$$

$$P(y=j) = \pi_j = \frac{1}{N} \sum_{n=1}^{N} I_j(x_n)$$

The empirical covariances are very likely to be singular (or close to singular), which means that we won't be able to do calculations with them. Hence, it is important to regularize these matrices. The standard way of doing this is to add $c*I$ to them, where c is some constant and I is the 784-dimensional identity matrix (to put it another way, we compute the empirical covariances and then increase their diagonal entries by some constant c).

This modification is guaranteed to yield covariance matrices that are non-singular, for any $c > 0$, no matter how small. Now, c becomes a (regularization) parameter and, by setting it appropriately, we can improve the performance of the model. We should choose a good value of c. Crucially, this needs to be done using the training set alone, by setting aside part of the training set as a validation set or using some kind of cross-validation—we leave this as an exercise for the reader to complete. In particular, the `displaychar()` function will be used to visualize the means of the Gaussians for the first three digits:

```
def fit_generative_model(x,y):
  k = 10 # labels 0,1,...,k-1
  d = (x.shape)[1] # number of features
  mu = np.zeros((k,d))
  sigma = np.zeros((k,d,d))
  pi = np.zeros(k)
  c = 3500 # parameter for regularization, exercise: choose the best c with cross-validation
  for label in range(k):
    indices = (y == label)
    pi[label] = sum(indices) / float(len(y))
    mu[label] = np.mean(x[indices,:], axis=0)
    sigma[label] = np.cov(x[indices,:], rowvar=0, bias=1) + c*np.eye(d) # regularization
  # return parameters
  return mu, sigma, pi

def displaychar(image):
  pylab.imshow(np.reshape(image, (28,28)), cmap=pylab.cm.gray)
  pylab.axis('off')
  pylab.show()

mu, sigma, pi = fit_generative_model(train_data, train_labels)
displaychar(mu[0])
displaychar(mu[1])
displaychar(mu[2])
```

The following screenshot shows the output of the preceding code block—the MLE of the means for the first three digits:

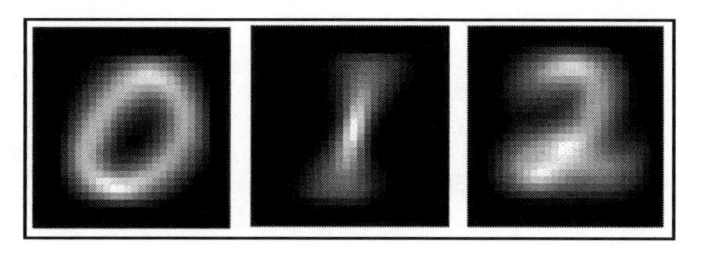

Classical Machine Learning Methods in Image Processing

Computing the posterior probabilities to make predictions on test data and model evaluation

In order to predict the label of a new image, x, we need to find the label, j, for which the posterior probability, *Pr(y=j|x)*, is maximum. It can be computed using the Bayes rule, as follows:

$$\max_j P(y=j|x) \propto \max_j P(x|y=j)P(y=j) = \max_j \mathcal{N}(x; \mu_j, \Sigma_j)\pi_j$$

$$\max_j \log P(y=j|x) \propto \max_j \left(\log \mathcal{N}(x; \mu_j, \Sigma_j) + \log \pi_j\right)$$

The following code block shows how to predict the labels of the test dataset using the generative model and how to compute the number of errors the model makes on the test dataset. As can be seen, the accuracy of the test dataset is 95.6%, which is a little less than the 1-NN classifier:

```
# Compute log Pr(label|image) for each [test image,label] pair.
k = 10
score = np.zeros((len(test_labels),k))
for label in range(0,k):
 rv = multivariate_normal(mean=mu[label], cov=sigma[label])
 for i in range(0,len(test_labels)):
    score[i,label] = np.log(pi[label]) + rv.logpdf(test_data[i,:])
test_predictions = np.argmax(score, axis=1)
# Finally, tally up score
errors = np.sum(test_predictions != test_labels)
print("The generative model makes " + str(errors) + " errors out of 10000")
# The generative model makes 438 errors out of 10000
t_accuracy = sum(test_predictions == test_labels) / float(len(test_labels)
t_accuracy
# 0.95620000000000005
```

SVM classifier

In this section, we will train the (multi-class) SVM classifier with the MNIST training dataset and then use it to predict the labels of the images from the MNIST test dataset.

SVM is a pretty complex binary classifier that uses quadratic programming to maximize the margin between the separating hyper-planes. The binary SVM classifier is extended to handle multi-class classification problems using the 1-vs-all or 1-vs-1 technique. We are going to use scikit-learn's implementation, `SVC()`, with polynomial kernel (of degree 2) to fit (train) the soft-margin (kernelized) SVM classifier with the training dataset and then predict the labels of the test images using the `score()` function.

The following code shows how to train, predict, and evaluate the SVM classifier using the MNIST dataset. As can be seen, the accuracy obtained on the test dataset has increased to 98% using this classifier:

```
from sklearn.svm import SVC
clf = SVC(C=1, kernel='poly', degree=2)
clf.fit(train_data,train_labels)
print(clf.score(test_data,test_labels))
# 0.9806
test_predictions = clf.predict(test_data)
cm=metrics.confusion_matrix(test_labels,test_predictions)
df_cm = pd.DataFrame(cm, range(10), range(10))
sn.set(font_scale=1.2)
sn.heatmap(df_cm, annot=True,annot_kws={"size": 16}, fmt="g")
```

The following screenshot shows the output—the confusion matrix for classification:

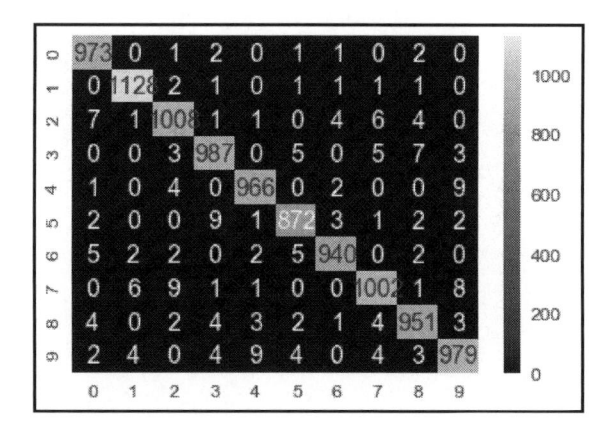

	0	1	2	3	4	5	6	7	8	9
0	973	0	1	2	0	1	1	0	2	0
1	0	1128	2	1	0	1	1	1	1	0
2	7	1	1008	1	1	0	4	6	4	0
3	0	0	3	987	0	5	0	5	7	3
4	1	0	4	0	966	0	2	0	0	9
5	2	0	0	9	1	872	3	1	2	2
6	5	2	2	0	2	5	940	0	2	0
7	0	6	9	1	1	0	0	1002	1	8
8	4	0	2	4	3	2	1	4	951	3
9	2	4	0	4	9	4	0	4	3	979

Next, let's find a test image for which the SVM classifier has predicted the wrong label (different from the ground-truth label).

The following code finds such an image and displays it along with the predicted and true labels:

```
wrong_indices = test_predictions != test_labels
wrong_digits, wrong_preds, correct_labs = test_data[wrong_indices],
test_predictions[wrong_indices], test_labels[wrong_indices]
print(len(wrong_pred))
# 194
pylab.title('predicted: ' + str(wrong_preds[1]) + ', actual: ' +
str(correct_labs[1]))
displaychar(wrong_digits[1])
```

The following screenshot shows the output. As can be seen, the test image has the true label **2**, but the image looks more like **7** and hence SVM predicted it to be **7**:

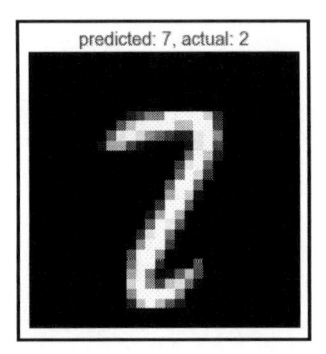

Supervised machine learning – object detection

So far, we have demonstrated how to use the classification model to classify an image, for example, to use binary classification to find if an image contains the handwritten digit 1 or not. In the next section, we will see how to use supervised machine learning models, not only to check whether an object is in an image or not, but also to find the location of the object in the image (for example, in terms of a bounding box—a rectangle the object is contained in).

Face detection with Haar-like features and cascade classifiers with AdaBoost – Viola-Jones

As we have discussed briefly in `Chapter 7`, *Extracting Image Features and Descriptors*, (in the context of Haar-like feature extraction), the Viola-Jones' object detection technique can be used for face detection in images. It is a classical machine learning approach, where a cascade function is trained using a training set of positive and negative images, by using the hand-crafted Haar-like features extracted from the images.

The Viola-Jones algorithm typically uses a base patch size (for example, 24 x 24 pixels) that it slides across and down an image and computes a huge number of Haar-like features (160,000 possible features for a 24 x 24 patch, although they have achieved 95% accuracy with an appropriately chosen 6,000 feature subset); these can be extracted, but to run even 6,000 features on every patch is a lot of effort. So, once the features have been decided on and assembled, a number of fast rejectors are built. This is based on the idea that, in a complete image, most of the possible positions we check will not contain a face—therefore, it is faster overall to reject quickly than to invest too much in it. If the location doesn't contain a face, we discard it and move on before investing more computational checks. This is another of the tricks used by Viola-Jones to achieve its performance, as shown in the following diagram:

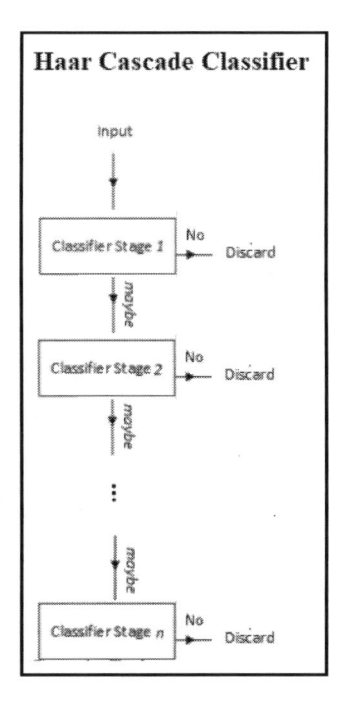

Instead of applying all 6,000 features on a window, the features are grouped into different stages of weak classifiers through the use of the AdaBoost ensemble classifier (to perform adaptive boosting of the performance of the cascade of feature), and these weak classifiers are run one by one in a cascade. If the patch window under consideration fails at any stage, the window is rejected. A patch that passes all stages is considered a valid detection.

A nice benefit of Haar-like features being so quick to calculate (due to the integral image technique) leads to the final aspect of the Viola-Jones performance. The base patch itself can be scaled and the features in the final cascade evaluated very quickly to search for objects of different sizes without the requirement for an image pyramid. Putting it all together, the Viola-Jones workflow for training looks like the one shown in the following diagram:

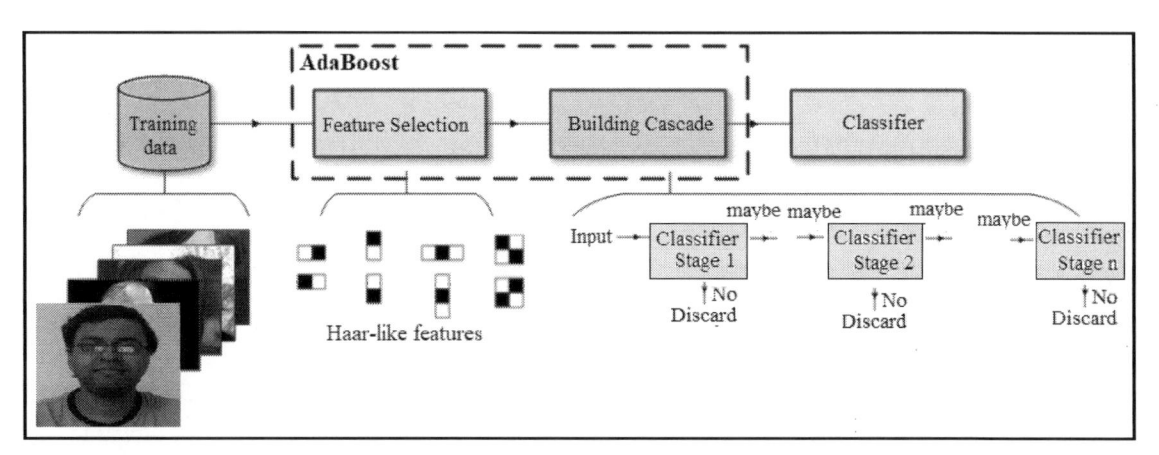

This algorithm is blazingly fast, but has obvious accuracy limitations.

Face classification using the Haar-like feature descriptor

The first real-time face detector was implemented using Haar-like feature descriptors by Viola-Jones. The following example is taken from the scikit-image's example that illustrates the extraction, selection, and classification of Haar-like features to detect faces versus non-faces. Clearly, this is a binary classification problem.

The scikit-learn library for feature selection and classification. Although the original implementation for face detection used the AdaBoost ensemble classifier, in this example, a different ensemble classifier, random forest, will be used, primarily to find important Haar-like features useful for the classification.

In order to extract the Haar-like features for an image, first a **Region Of Interest (ROI)** is defined for which all possible features are extracted. The integral image of this ROI is then computed to compute all possible features very fast.

A subset of the LFW image dataset, which is composed of 100 face images (positive examples) and 100 non-face images (negative examples), is used as input. Each image is resized to an ROI of 19 x 19 pixels. A traditional machine learning validation process is used to divide the images into 75% (that is, 75 images from each group) training and 25% (that is, the remaining 25 from each class) and validation datasets in order to train a classifier, check which extracted features are the most salient, and check the performance of the classifier, respectively.

The following code block demonstrates the extraction of the Haar-like features from the image and displays a few positive examples (face images) from the dataset:

```
from time import time
import numpy as np
import matplotlib.pyplot as pylab
from dask import delayed
from sklearn.ensemble import RandomForestClassifier
from sklearn.model_selection import train_test_split
from sklearn.metrics import roc_auc_score
from skimage.data import lfw_subset
from skimage.transform import integral_image
from skimage.feature import haar_like_feature
from skimage.feature import haar_like_feature_coord
from skimage.feature import draw_haar_like_feature

@delayed
def extract_feature_image(img, feature_type, feature_coord=None):
    """Extract the haar feature for the current image"""
    ii = integral_image(img)
    return haar_like_feature(ii, 0, 0, ii.shape[0], ii.shape[1],
    feature_type=feature_type,
            feature_coord=feature_coord)

images = lfw_subset()
print(images.shape)
# (200, 25, 25)
```

```
fig = pylab.screenshot(figsize=(5,5))
fig.subplots_adjust(left=0, right=0.9, bottom=0, top=0.9, hspace=0.05,
wspace=0.05)
for i in range(25):
    pylab.subplot(5,5,i+1), pylab.imshow(images[i,:,:], cmap='bone'),
pylab.axis('off')
pylab.suptitle('Faces')
pylab.show()
```

The following screenshot shows the output of the preceding code—the first 25 face images:

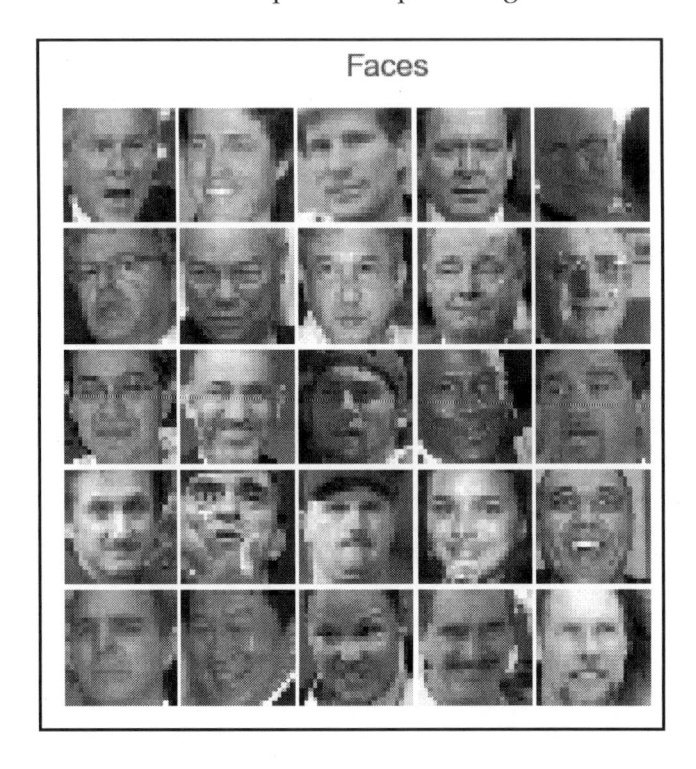

The following code block displays a few images from the negative examples (non-face images) from the dataset:

```
fig = pylab.screenshot(figsize=(5,5))
fig.subplots_adjust(left=0, right=0.9, bottom=0, top=0.9, hspace=0.05, wspace=0.05)
for i in range(100,125):
  pylab.subplot(5,5,i-99), pylab.imshow(images[i,:,:], cmap='bone'), pylab.axis('off')
pylab.suptitle('Non-Faces')
pylab.show()
```

The following screenshot shows the output of the preceding code—the first 25 non-face images:

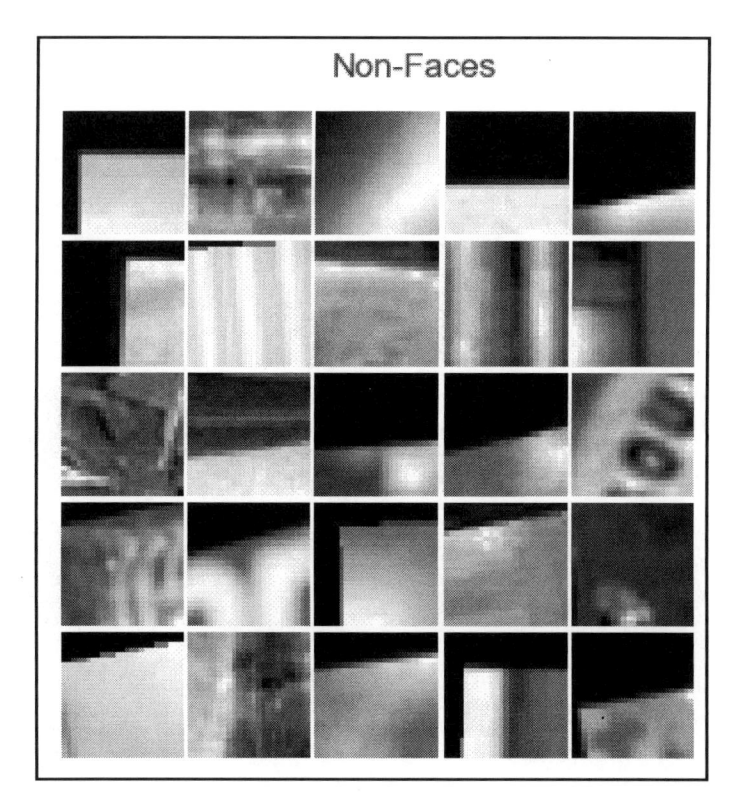

Finding the most important Haar-like features for face classification with the random forest ensemble classifier

A random forest classifier is trained in order to select the most salient features for face classification. The idea is to check which features are the most often used by the ensemble of trees. By using only the most salient features in subsequent steps, computation speed can be increased, while retaining accuracy. The following code snippet shows how to compute the feature importance for the classifier and displays the top 25 most important Haar-like features:

```
# For speed, only extract the two first types of features
feature_types = ['type-2-x', 'type-2-y']
# Build a computation graph using dask. This allows using multiple CPUs for
# the computation step
X = delayed(extract_feature_image(img, feature_types)
    for img in images)
# Compute the result using the "processes" dask backend
t_start = time()
X = np.array(X.compute(scheduler='processes'))
time_full_feature_comp = time() - t_start
y = np.array([1] * 100 + [0] * 100)
X_train, X_test, y_train, y_test = train_test_split(X, y, train_size=150,
random_state=0, stratify=y)
print(time_full_feature_comp)
# 104.87986302375793
print(X.shape, X_train.shape)
# (200, 101088) (150, 101088)

from sklearn.metrics import roc_curve, auc, roc_auc_score
# Extract all possible features to be able to select the most salient.
feature_coord, feature_type = \
        haar_like_feature_coord(width=images.shape[2],
height=images.shape[1],
                                feature_type=feature_types)
# Train a random forest classifier and check performance
clf = RandomForestClassifier(n_estimators=1000, max_depth=None,
                             max_features=100, n_jobs=-1, random_state=0)
t_start = time()
clf.fit(X_train, y_train)
time_full_train = time() - t_start
print(time_full_train)
# 1.6583366394042969
auc_full_features = roc_auc_score(y_test, clf.predict_proba(X_test)[:, 1])
print(auc_full_features)
# 1.0

# Sort features in order of importance, plot six most significant
```

Chapter 9

```
idx_sorted = np.argsort(clf.feature_importances_)[::-1]

fig, axes = pylab.subplots(5, 5, figsize=(10,10))
for idx, ax in enumerate(axes.ravel()):
 image = images[1]
 image = draw_haar_like_feature(image, 0, 0, images.shape[2],
images.shape[1],
                                  [feature_coord[idx_sorted[idx]]])
 ax.imshow(image), ax.set_xticks([]), ax.set_yticks([])
fig.suptitle('The most important features', size=30)
```

The following screenshot shows the output of the preceding code block—the top 25 most important Haar-like features for face detection:

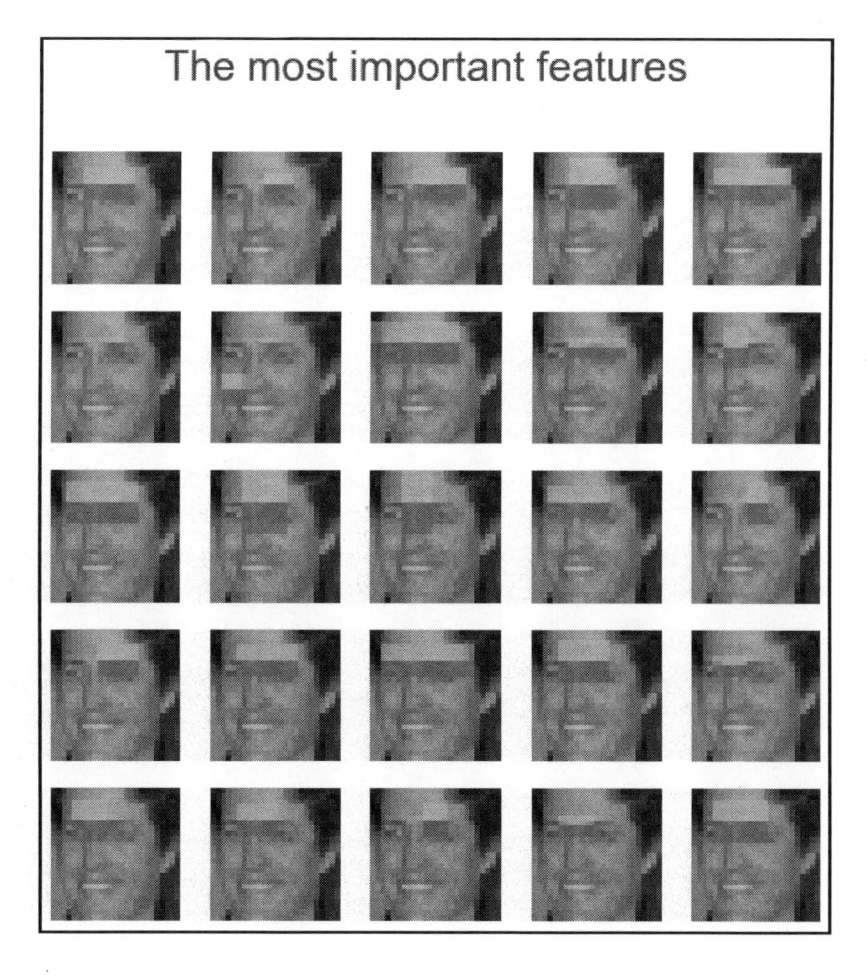

By, keeping only a few of the most important features (~3% of all of the features), most (~70%) feature importance can be preserved and by training the `RandomForest` classifier only with those features we should be able to retain the accuracy of the validation dataset (that we obtained by training the classifier with all the features), but with a much smaller time required for feature extraction and to train the classifier. The code is left as an exercise for the reader.

Detecting objects with SVM using HOG features

As discussed in `Chapter 7`, *Extracting Image Features and Descriptors*, a **Histogram of Oriented Gradients** (**HOG**) is a feature descriptor used in a variety of computer vision and image processing applications for the purposes of object detection. HOG descriptors were first used along with the SVM classifier for pedestrian detection by Navneet Dalal and Bill Triggs. The use of HOG descriptors has been a particularly successful technique in detecting, among other things, humans, animals, faces, and text. For example, an object detection system can be considered for generating HOG descriptors that describe features of objects in an input image.

We already described how to compute a HOG descriptor from an image. At first, an SVM model is trained with a number of positive and negative training example images. Positive images are examples that contain the object we want to detect. The negative training set can be any images that do not contain the object we want to detect. Positive and negative source images are converted into HOG block descriptors.

HOG training

The SVM trainer selects the best hyperplane to separate positive and negative examples from the training set. These block descriptors are concatenated, converted into the input format for the SVM trainer, and labelled appropriately as positive or negative. The trainer typically outputs a set of support vectors—that is, examples from the training set that best describe the hyperplane. The hyperplane is the learned decision boundary separating positive examples from negative examples. These support vectors are used later by the SVM model to classify a HOG-descriptor block from a test image to detect the presence/absence of an object.

Classification with the SVM model

This HOG computation is traditionally performed by repeatedly stepping a window of, say, 64 pixels wide by 128 pixels high across a test image frame and computing the HOG descriptors. As the HOG calculation contains no intrinsic sense of scale and objects can occur at multiple scales within an image, the HOG calculation is stepped and repeated across each level of a scale pyramid. The scaling factor between each level in the scale pyramid is commonly between 1.05 and 1.2 and the image is repeatedly scaled down until the scaled source frame can no longer accommodate a complete HOG window. If the SVM classifier predicts the detection of an object at any scale, the corresponding bounding box is returned. The following diagram shows a typical HOG object (pedestrian) detection workflow:

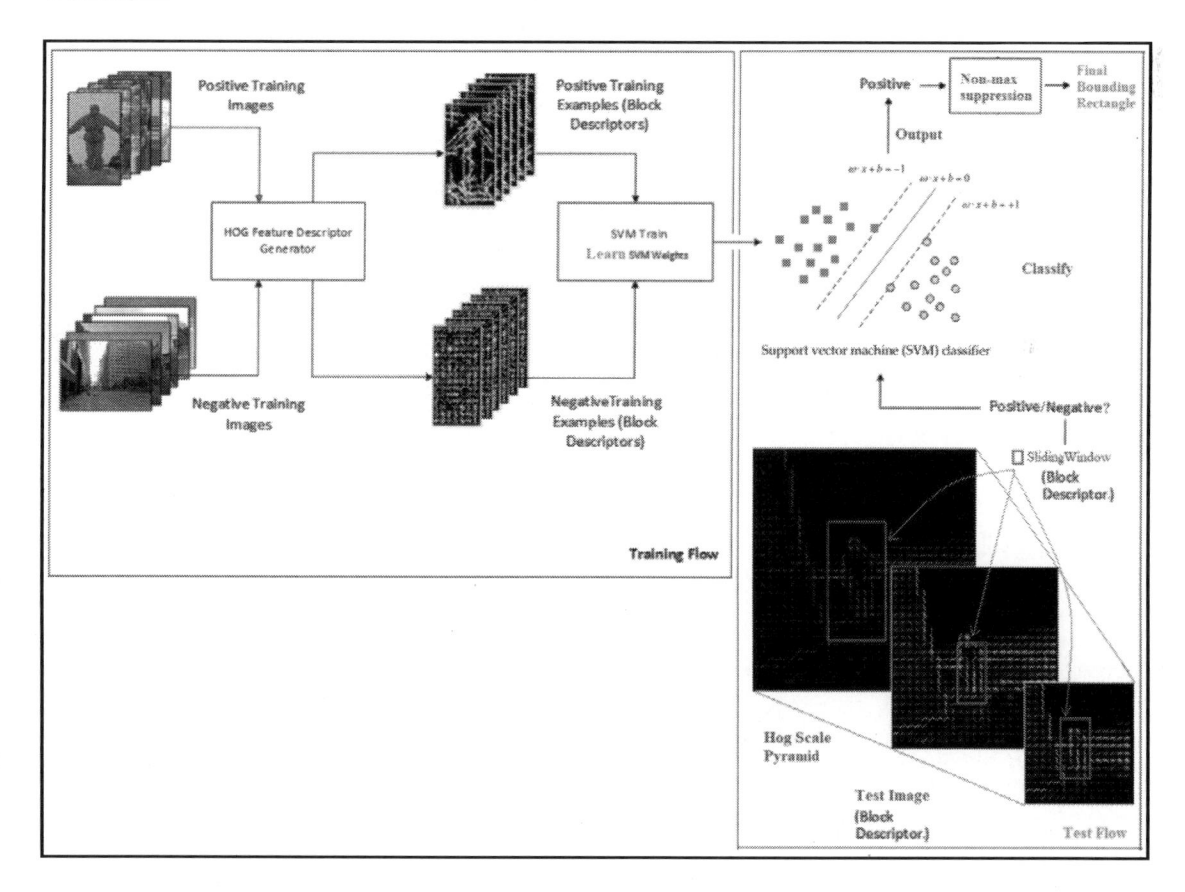

This technique is more accurate but more computationally complex than Viola-Jones object detection.

Computing BoundingBoxes with HOG-SVM

In this section, we will demonstrate how the python-opencv library functions can be used to detect people in an image using HOG-SVM. The following code shows how to compute the HOG descriptors from an image and use the descriptors to feed into a pre-trained SVM classifier (with cv2's HOGDescriptor_getDefaultPeopleDetector()), which will predict the presence or absence of a person in from an image block at multiple scales with the detectMultiScale() function from python-opencv:

```python
import cv2
import matplotlib.pylab as pylab
img = cv2.imread("../images/me16.jpg")
# create HOG descriptor using default people (pedestrian) detector
hog = cv2.HOGDescriptor()
hog.setSVMDetector(cv2.HOGDescriptor_getDefaultPeopleDetector())
# run detection, using a spatial stride of 4 pixels (horizontal and vertical), a scale stride of 1.02, and # zero grouping of rectangles (to demonstrate that HOG will detect at potentially multiple places in the
# scale pyramid)
(foundBoundingBoxes, weights) = hog.detectMultiScale(img, winStride=(4, 4), padding=(8, 8), scale=1.02, finalThreshold=0)
print(len(foundBoundingBoxes)) # number of boundingboxes
# 357
# copy the original image to draw bounding boxes on it for now, as we'll use it again later
imgWithRawBboxes = img.copy()
for (hx, hy, hw, hh) in foundBoundingBoxes:
    cv2.rectangle(imgWithRawBboxes, (hx, hy), (hx + hw, hy + hh), (0, 0, 255), 1)
pylab.screenshot(figsize=(20, 12))
imgWithRawBboxes = cv2.cvtColor(imgWithRawBboxes, cv2.COLOR_BGR2RGB)
pylab.imshow(imgWithRawBboxes, aspect='auto'), pylab.axis('off'),
pylab.show()
```

The following screenshot shows the output, the image along with the detected object(s) at different scales indicated by bounding boxes (red rectangles):

The preceding screenshot illustrates some interesting properties and problems with HOG—we can see in the preceding screenshot that there are many extraneous detections (a total of 357 of them), which need to be fused together using non-maximal suppression. Additionally, we may see some false positives too.

Non-max suppression

Next, a non-max suppression function needs to be invoked to avoid detection of the same object at multiple times and scales. The following code block shows how to implement it with the `cv2` library functions:

```
from imutils.object_detection import non_max_suppression
# convert our bounding boxes from format (x1, y1, w, h) to (x1, y1, x2, y2)
rects = np.array([[x, y, x + w, y + h] for (x, y, w, h) in
foundBoundingBoxes])
# run non-max suppression on these based on an overlay op 65%
nmsBoundingBoxes = non_max_suppression(rects, probs=None,
overlapThresh=0.65)
print(len(rects), len(nmsBoundingBoxes))
# 357 1
# draw the final bounding boxes
for (x1, y1, x2, y2) in nmsBoundingBoxes:
  cv2.rectangle(img, (x1, y1), (x2, y2), (0, 255, 0), 2)
pylab.screenshot(figsize=(20, 12))
img = cv2.cvtColor(img, cv2.COLOR_BGR2RGB)
pylab.imshow(img, aspect='auto'), pylab.axis('off'), pylab.show()
```

The following screenshot shows the output; before suppression, we had 357 bounding boxes and, after suppression, we have one:

Summary

In this chapter, we discussed a few classical machine learning techniques and their applications in solving image processing problems. We started with unsupervised machine learning algorithms such as clustering and principal component analysis. We demonstrated k-means and spectral clustering algorithms with scikit-learn and showed you how they can be used in vector quantization and segmentation. Next, we saw how PCA can be used in dimension reduction and the visualization of high-dimensional datasets such as the scikit-learn handwritten digits images dataset. Also, how the PCA can be used to implement eigenfaces using a scikit-learn face dataset was illustrated.

Then, we discussed a few supervised machine learning classification models, such as kNN, the Gaussian Bayes generative model, and SVM to solve problems such as the classification of the handwritten digits dataset. Finally, we discussed a couple of classical machine learning techniques for object detection in images, namely Viola-Jones' AdaBoost cascade classifier with Haar-like features for face detection (and finding the most important features with random forest classifier) and HOG-SVM for pedestrian detection.

In the next chapter, we are going to start discussing recent advances in image processing with deep learning techniques.

Questions

1. Use k-means clustering for thresholding an image (use `number of clusters=2`) and compare the result with Otsu's.
2. Use scikit-learn's `cluster.MeanShift()` and `mixture.GaussianMixture()` functions to segment an image with mean shift and GMM-EM clustering methods, respectively—another two popular clustering algorithms.
3. Use Isomap (from `sklearn.manifold`) for non-linear dimension reduction and visualize 2-D projections. Is it better than linear dimension reduction with PCA? Repeat the exercise with TSNE (again from `sklearn.manifold`).
4. Write a Python program to show that the weighted linear combination of a few dominating eigenfaces indeed approximates a face.
5. Show that eigenfaces can also be used for naive face-detection (and recognition) and write Python code to implement this (hint—refer to this article: https://sandipanweb.wordpress.com/2018/01/06/eigenfaces-and-a-simple-face-detector-with-pca-svd-in-python/).
6. Use PCA to compute eigendigit-based vectors from the MNIST dataset (this is similar to eigenfaces; refer to this article: https://sandipanweb.wordpress.com/2016/06/25/using-pca-to-represnt-digits-in-the-eigen-digits-space/) and show that an handwritten digit image can be reconstructed with small errors from a small subspace of the eigendigit-based vectors.
7. Try to fit the KNN models with different k values (3, 5, and 9) for MNIST classification and observe the impact on the accuracy of classification on the test dataset. With higher values of k, does the model overfit/underfit the training dataset?
8. While fitting the generative model to classify handwritten digits, what happens if we do not regularize the covariance matrices? What value of c did you end up using (with cross-validation)? How many errors did the model make on the training set? What happens if the value of c high (for example, one billion) or too low (for example, between 3 and 10) and why? We have talked about using the same regularization constant c for all ten classes. What about using a different value of c for each class? How would you go about choosing these? Can you get better performance in this way?

9. For the face classification problem, write code to show that, by keeping only ~3% of all the features (only the top important ones), ~70% of the total feature importance can be preserved. Train a `RandomForest` classifier only with those features and predict the class labels on the validation dataset. Show the the accuracy on the validation dataset remains the same and, at the same time, a much smaller time required for feature extraction and to train the classifier.

Further reading

- Viola, Paul, and Michael J. Jones, *Robust real-time face detection. International journal of computer vision*: `http://www.merl.com/publications/docs/TR2004-043.pdf`
- Navneet Dalal and Bill Triggs, *Histograms of Oriented Gradients for Human Detection*: `https://lear.inrialpes.fr/people/triggs/pubs/Dalal-cvpr05.pdf`

10
Deep Learning in Image Processing - Image Classification

In this chapter, we shall discuss recent advances in image processing with deep learning. We'll start by differentiating between classical and deep learning techniques, followed by a conceptual section on **convolutional neural networks** (**CNN**), the deep neural net architectures particularly useful for image processing. Then we'll continue our discussion on the image classification problem with a couple of image datasets and how to implement it with TensorFlow and Keras, two very popular deep learning libraries. Also, we'll see how to train deep CNN architectures and use them for predictions.

The topics to be covered in this chapter are as follows:

- Deep learning in image processing
- CNNs
- Image classification with TensorFlow or Keras with the handwritten digits images dataset
- Some popular deep CNNs (VGG-16/19, InceptionNet, ResNet) with an application in classifying the cats versus dogs images with the VGG-16 network

Deep learning in image processing

The main goal of **Machine Learning** (ML) is **generalization**; that is, we train an algorithm on a training dataset and we want the algorithm to work with high performance (accuracy) on an unseen dataset. In order to solve a complex image processing task (such as image classification), the more training data we have, we may expect better generalization—ability of the ML model learned, provided we have taken care of overfitting (for example, with regularization). But with traditional ML techniques, not only does it become computationally very expensive with huge training data, but also, the learning (improvement in generalization) often stops at a certain point. Also, the traditional ML algorithms often need lots of domain expertise and human intervention and they are only capable of what they are designed for—nothing more and nothing less. This is where deep learning models are very promising.

What is deep learning?

Some of the well-known and widely accepted definitions of deep learning are as follows:

- It is a subset of ML.
- It uses a cascade of multiple layers of (non-linear) processing units, called an **artificial neural network (ANN)**, and algorithms inspired by the structure and function of the brain (neurons). Each successive layer uses the output from the previous layer as input.
- It uses ANN for feature extraction and transformation, to process data, find patterns, and develop abstractions.
- It can be supervised (for example, classification) or unsupervised (for example, pattern analysis).
- It uses gradient-descent algorithms to learn multiple levels of representations that correspond to different levels of abstraction and the levels form a hierarchy of concepts.
- It achieves great power and flexibility by learning to represent the world as a nested hierarchy of concepts, with each concept defined in relation to simpler concepts, and more abstract representations computed in terms of less abstract ones.

For example, for an image classification problem, a deep learning model learns the image classes in an incremental manner using its hidden layer architecture.

First, it automatically extracts low-level features such as identifying light or dark regions, and then it extracts high-level features such as edges. Later, it extracts the highest-level features, such as shapes, so that they can be classified.

Every node or neuron represents a small aspect of the whole image. When put together, they depict the whole image. They are capable of representing the image fully. Moreover, every node and every neuron in the network is assigned weights. These weights represent the actual weight of the neuron with respect to the strength of its relationship with the output. These weights can be adjusted while the models are developed.

Classical versus deep learning

- **Handcrafted versus automated feature extraction**: In order to solve image processing problems with traditional ML techniques, the most important preprocessing step is the handcrafted feature (for example, HOG and SIFT) extraction in order to reduce the complexity of an image and make patterns more visible for learning algorithms to work. The biggest advantage of deep learning algorithms is that they try to learn low-level and high-level features from training images in an incremental manner. This eliminates the need for handcrafted feature in extraction or engineering.
- **By parts versus end-to-end solution**: Traditional ML techniques solve the problem statement by breaking down the problem, solving different parts first, and then aggregating the results finally to give output, whereas deep learning techniques solve the problem using an end-to-end approach. For example, in an object detection problem, classical ML algorithms such as SVM require a bounding box object detection algorithm that will first identify all of the possible objects that will need to have HOG as input to the ML algorithm in order to recognize correct objects. But a deep learning method, such as the YOLO network, takes the image as input and provides the location and name of the object as output. Clearly end-to-end, isn't it?
- **Training time and advanced hardware**: Unlike traditional ML algorithms, deep learning algorithms take a long time to get trained because of the huge number of parameters and relatively huge datasets. Hence, we should always train a deep learning model on high-end hardware such as GPUs and remember to train for a reasonable time, as time is a very important aspect in training the models effectively.

- **Adaptable and transferable**: Classical ML techniques are quite restrictive, whereas deep learning techniques can be applied to a wide range of applications and various domains. A big share of it goes to the transfer learning that allows us to use pre-trained deep networks for different applications within the same domains. For example, here, in image processing, pre-trained image classification networks are generally used as a feature extraction frontend to detect objects and segmentation networks.

Let's now see the differences between a ML and a deep learning model when used in image classification diagrammatically (cat versus dog images).

Traditional ML will have feature extraction and a classifier to give a solution to any problem:

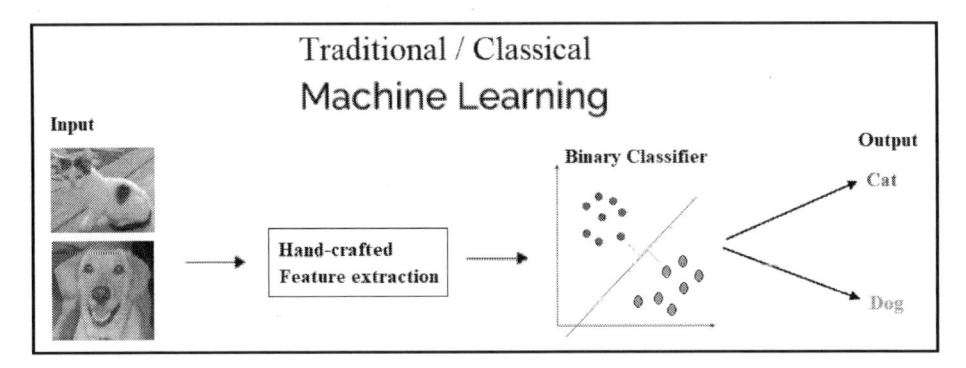

With deep learning, you can see the hidden layers that we talked about and the decision making in action:

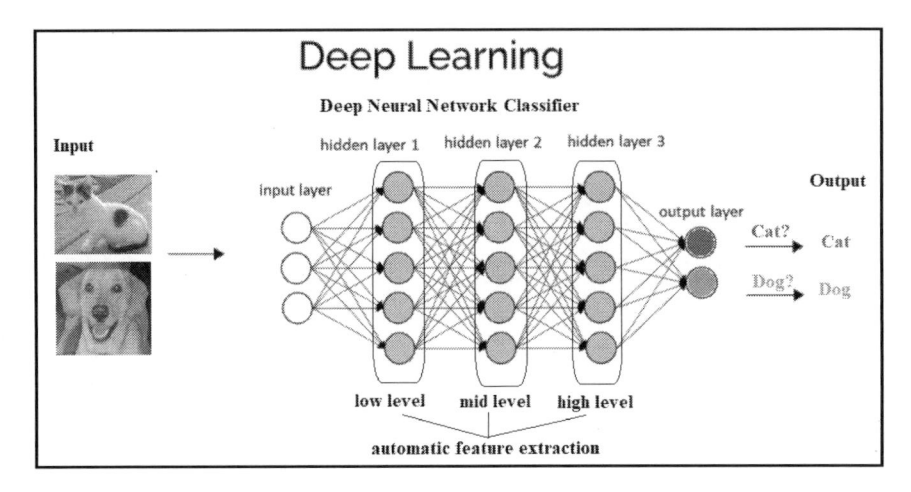

Why deep learning?

As discussed earlier, if you have more data, the best choice would be deep networks that perform much better with ample data. Many a time, the more data used, the more accurate the result. The classical ML method needs a complex set of ML algorithms and more data is only going to hamper its accuracy. Complex methods then need to be applied to make up for the less accuracy. Moreover, even learning is affected—it is almost stopped at some point in time when more training data is added to train the model.

This is how this can be depicted graphically:

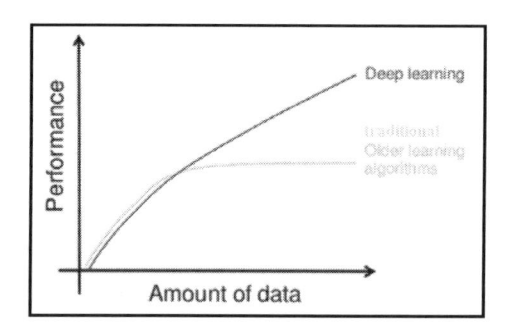

CNNs

CNNs are deep neural networks for which the primarily used input is images. CNNs learn the filters (features) that are hand-engineered in traditional algorithms. This independence from prior knowledge and human effort in feature design is a major advantage. They also reduce the number of parameters to be learned with their shared-weights architecture and possess translation invariance characteristics. In the next subsection, we'll discuss the general architecture of a CNN and how it works.

Conv or pooling or FC layers – CNN architecture and how it works

The next screenshot shows the typical architecture of a CNN. It consists of one or more convolutional layer, followed by a nonlinear ReLU activation layer, a pooling layer, and, finally, one (or more) **fully connected** (**FC**) layer, followed by an FC softmax layer, for example, in the case of a CNN designed to solve an image classification problem.

There can be multiple convolution ReLU pooling sequences of layers in the network, making the neural network deeper and useful for solving complex image processing tasks, as seen in the following diagram:

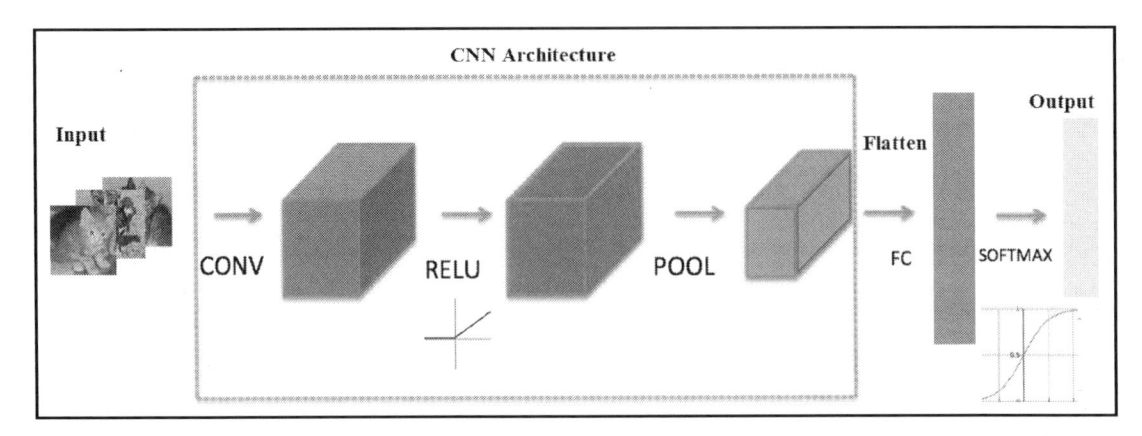

The next few sections describe each of the layers and how they work.

Convolutional layer

The main building block of CNN is the convolutional layer. The convolutional layer consists of a bunch of convolution filters (kernels), which we already discussed in detail in Chapter 2, *Sampling, Fourier Transform, and Convolution*. The convolution is applied on the input image using a convolution filter to produce a feature map. On the left side is the input to the convolutional layer; for example, the input image. On the right is the convolution filter, also called the **kernel**. As usual, the convolution operation is performed by sliding this filter over the input. At every location, the sum of element-wise matrix multiplication goes into the feature map. A convolutional layer is represented by its width, height (the size of a filter is width x height), and depth (number of filters). **Stride** specifies how much the convolution filter will be moved at each step (the default value is 1). **Padding** refers to the layers of zeros to surround the input (generally used to keep the input and output image size the same, also known as **same padding**). The following screenshot shows how 3 x 3 x 3 convolution filters are applied on an RGB image, the first with valid padding and the second with the computation with two such filters with the size of the **stride=padding=1**:

input	convolution	output
$n \times n$ image	$f \times f$ filter padding p stride s	$\left\lfloor \frac{n+2p-f}{s} + 1 \right\rfloor \times \left\lfloor \frac{n+2p-f}{s} + 1 \right\rfloor$ image

Convolution with RGB images : valid (zero) padding

Convolution with 3-channel input with two 3x3 filters: padding=stride=1

figure taken from *http://cs231n.github.io/convolutional-networks/*

Pooling layer

After a convolution operation, a pooling operation is generally performed to reduce dimensionality and the number of parameters to be learned, which shortens the training time, requires less data to train, and combats overfitting. Pooling layers downsample each feature map independently, reducing the height and width, but keeping the depth intact. The most common type of pooling is **max pooling**, which just takes the maximum value in the pooling window. Contrary to the convolution operation, pooling has no parameters. It slides a window over its input and simply takes the max value in the window. Similar to a convolution, the window size and stride for pooling can be specified.

Non-linearity – ReLU layer

For any kind of neural network to be powerful, it needs to contain non-linearity. The result of the convolution operation is hence passed through the non-linear activation function. ReLU activation is used in general to achieve non-linearity (and to combat the vanishing gradient problem with sigmoid activation). So, the values in the final feature maps are not actually the sums, but the `relu` function applied to them.

FC layer

After the convolutional and pooling layers, generally a couple of FC layers are added to wrap up the CNN architecture. The output of both convolutional and pooling layers are 3D volumes, but an FC layer expects a 1D vector of numbers. So, the output of the final pooling layer needs to be flattened to a vector, and that becomes the input to the FC layer. Flattening is simply arranging the 3D volume of numbers into a 1D vector.

Dropout

Dropout is the most popular regularization technique for deep neural networks. Dropout is used to prevent overfitting, and it is typically used to increase the performance (accuracy) of the deep learning task on the unseen dataset. During training time, at each iteration, a neuron is temporarily dropped or disabled with some probability, p. This means all the input and output to this neuron will be disabled at the current iteration. This hyperparameter p is called the **dropout rate**, and it's typically a number around 0.5, corresponding to 50% of the neurons being dropped out.

Image classification with TensorFlow or Keras

In this section, we shall revisit the problem of handwritten digits classification (with the MNIST dataset), but this time with deep neural networks. We are going to solve the problem using two very popular deep learning libraries, namely TensorFlow and Keras. **TensorFlow** (**TF**) is the most famous library used in production for deep learning models. It has a very large and awesome community. However, TensorFlow is not that easy to use. On the other hand, Keras is a high level API built on TensorFlow. It is more user-friendly and easy to use compared to TF, although it provides less control over low-level structures. Low-level libraries provide more flexibility. Hence TF can be tweaked much more as compared to Keras.

Classification with TF

First, we shall start with a very simple deep neural network, one containing only a single FC hidden layer (with ReLU activation) and a softmax FC layer, with no convolutional layer. The next screenshot shows the network upside down. The input is a flattened image containing 28 x 28 nodes and 1,024 nodes in the hidden layer and 10 output nodes, corresponding to each of the digits to be classified:

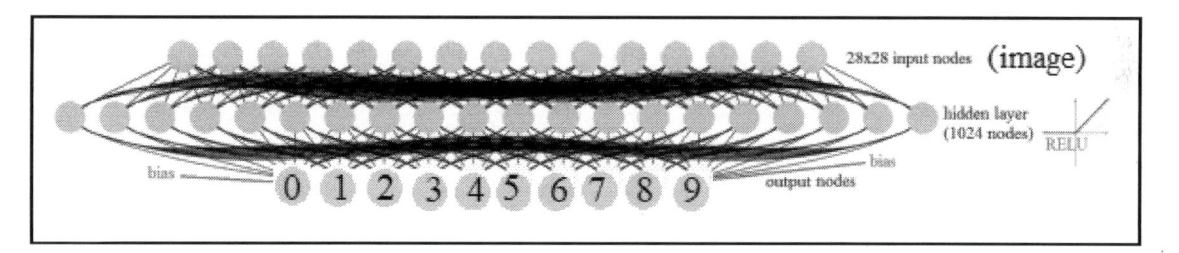

Now let's implement the deep learning image classification with TF. First, we need to load the `mnist` dataset and divide the training images into two parts, the first one being the larger (we use 50k images) for training, and the second one (10k images) to be used for validation. Let's reformat the labels to represent the image classes with one-hot encoded binary vectors. Then the `tensorflow` graph needs to be initialized along with the variable, constant, and placeholder tensors. A mini-batch **stochastic gradient descent** (**SGD**) optimizer is to be used as the learning algorithm with a batch size of 256, to minimize the softmax cross-entropy logit loss function with L2 regularizers on the couple of weights layers (with hyperparameter values of $\lambda1=\lambda2=1$). Finally, the TensorFlow `session` object will be run for 6k steps (mini-batches) and the forward/backpropagation will be run to update the model (weights) learned, with subsequent evaluation of the model on the validation dataset. As can be seen, the accuracy obtained after the final batch completes is 96.5%:

```
%matplotlib inline
import numpy as np
# import data
from keras.datasets import mnist
import tensorflow as tf

# load data
(X_train, y_train), (X_test, y_test) = mnist.load_data()
np.random.seed(0)
train_indices = np.random.choice(60000, 50000, replace=False)
valid_indices = [i for i in range(60000) if i not in train_indices]
X_valid, y_valid = X_train[valid_indices,:,:], y_train[valid_indices]
X_train, y_train = X_train[train_indices,:,:], y_train[train_indices]
print(X_train.shape, X_valid.shape, X_test.shape)
# (50000, 28, 28) (10000, 28, 28) (10000, 28, 28)
image_size = 28
num_labels = 10

def reformat(dataset, labels):
  dataset = dataset.reshape((-1, image_size * image_size)).astype(np.float32)
  # one hot encoding: Map 1 to [0.0, 1.0, 0.0 ...], 2 to [0.0, 0.0, 1.0 ...]
  labels = (np.arange(num_labels) == labels[:,None]).astype(np.float32)
  return dataset, labels

X_train, y_train = reformat(X_train, y_train)
X_valid, y_valid = reformat(X_valid, y_valid)
X_test, y_test = reformat(X_test, y_test)
print('Training set', X_train.shape, X_train.shape)
print('Validation set', X_valid.shape, X_valid.shape)
print('Test set', X_test.shape, X_test.shape)
# Training set (50000, 784) (50000, 784) # Validation set (10000, 784)
```

```python
(10000, 784) # Test set (10000, 784) (10000, 784)

def accuracy(predictions, labels):
 return (100.0 * np.sum(np.argmax(predictions, 1) == np.argmax(labels, 1))
/ predictions.shape[0])

batch_size = 256
num_hidden_units = 1024
lambda1 = 0.1
lambda2 = 0.1

graph = tf.Graph()
with graph.as_default():

 # Input data. For the training data, we use a placeholder that will be fed
 # at run time with a training minibatch.
 tf_train_dataset = tf.placeholder(tf.float32,
 shape=(batch_size, image_size * image_size))
 tf_train_labels = tf.placeholder(tf.float32, shape=(batch_size,
num_labels))
 tf_valid_dataset = tf.constant(X_valid)
 tf_test_dataset = tf.constant(X_test)

 # Variables.
 weights1 = tf.Variable(tf.truncated_normal([image_size * image_size,
num_hidden_units]))
 biases1 = tf.Variable(tf.zeros([num_hidden_units]))

 # connect inputs to every hidden unit. Add bias
 layer_1_outputs = tf.nn.relu(tf.matmul(tf_train_dataset, weights1) +
biases1)

 weights2 = tf.Variable(tf.truncated_normal([num_hidden_units,
num_labels]))
 biases2 = tf.Variable(tf.zeros([num_labels]))

 # Training computation.
 logits = tf.matmul(layer_1_outputs, weights2) + biases2
 loss =
tf.reduce_mean(tf.nn.softmax_cross_entropy_with_logits(labels=tf_train_labe
ls, logits=logits) + \
 lambda1*tf.nn.l2_loss(weights1) + lambda2*tf.nn.l2_loss(weights2))

 # Optimizer.
 optimizer = tf.train.GradientDescentOptimizer(0.008).minimize(loss)

 # Predictions for the training, validation, and test data.
 train_prediction = tf.nn.softmax(logits)
```

```python
  layer_1_outputs = tf.nn.relu(tf.matmul(tf_valid_dataset, weights1) + biases1)
  valid_prediction = tf.nn.softmax(tf.matmul(layer_1_outputs, weights2) + biases2)
  layer_1_outputs = tf.nn.relu(tf.matmul(tf_test_dataset, weights1) + biases1)
  test_prediction = tf.nn.softmax(tf.matmul(layer_1_outputs, weights2) + biases2)

num_steps = 6001

ll = []
atr = []
av = []

import matplotlib.pylab as pylab

with tf.Session(graph=graph) as session:
 #tf.global_variables_initializer().run()
 session.run(tf.initialize_all_variables())
 print("Initialized")
 for step in range(num_steps):
 # Pick an offset within the training data, which has been randomized.
 # Note: we could use better randomization across epochs.
  offset = (step * batch_size) % (y_train.shape[0] - batch_size)
 # Generate a minibatch.
  batch_data = X_train[offset:(offset + batch_size), :]
  batch_labels = y_train[offset:(offset + batch_size), :]
 # Prepare a dictionary telling the session where to feed the minibatch.
 # The key of the dictionary is the placeholder node of the graph to be fed,
 # and the value is the numpy array to feed to it.
  feed_dict = {tf_train_dataset : batch_data, tf_train_labels : batch_labels}
  _, l, predictions = session.run([optimizer, loss, train_prediction], feed_dict=feed_dict)
  if (step % 500 == 0):
  ll.append(l)
  a = accuracy(predictions, batch_labels)
  atr.append(a)
  print("Minibatch loss at step %d: %f" % (step, l))
  print("Minibatch accuracy: %.1f%%" % a)
  a = accuracy(valid_prediction.eval(), y_valid)
  av.append(a)
  print("Validation accuracy: %.1f%%" % a)
  print("Test accuracy: %.1f%%" % accuracy(test_prediction.eval(), y_test))

# Initialized
```

```
# Minibatch loss at step 0: 92091.781250
# Minibatch accuracy: 9.0%
# Validation accuracy: 21.6%
#
# Minibatch loss at step 500: 35599.835938
# Minibatch accuracy: 50.4%
# Validation accuracy: 47.4%
#
# Minibatch loss at step 1000: 15989.455078
# Minibatch accuracy: 46.5%
# Validation accuracy: 47.5%
#
# Minibatch loss at step 1500: 7182.631836
# Minibatch accuracy: 59.0%
# Validation accuracy: 54.7%
#
# Minibatch loss at step 2000: 3226.800781
# Minibatch accuracy: 68.4%
# Validation accuracy: 66.0%
#
# Minibatch loss at step 2500: 1449.654785
# Minibatch accuracy: 79.3%
# Validation accuracy: 77.7%
#
# Minibatch loss at step 3000: 651.267456
# Minibatch accuracy: 89.8%
# Validation accuracy: 87.7%
#
# Minibatch loss at step 3500: 292.560272
# Minibatch accuracy: 94.5%
# Validation accuracy: 91.3%
#
# Minibatch loss at step 4000: 131.462219
# Minibatch accuracy: 95.3%
# Validation accuracy: 93.7%
#
# Minibatch loss at step 4500: 59.149700
# Minibatch accuracy: 95.3%
# Validation accuracy: 94.3%
#
# Minibatch loss at step 5000: 26.656094
# Minibatch accuracy: 94.9%
# Validation accuracy: 95.5%
#
# Minibatch loss at step 5500: 12.033947
# Minibatch accuracy: 97.3%
# Validation accuracy: 97.0%
#
```

Deep Learning in Image Processing - Image Classification

```
# Minibatch loss at step 6000: 5.521026
# Minibatch accuracy: 97.3%
# Validation accuracy: 96.6%
#
# Test accuracy: 96.5%
```

Let's visualize the layer 1 weights at each step with the following code block:

```
images = weights1.eval()
pylab.screenshot(figsize=(18,18))
indices = np.random.choice(num_hidden_units, 225)
for j in range(225):
    pylab.subplot(15,15,j+1)
    pylab.imshow(np.reshape(images[:,indices[j]], (image_size,image_size)), cmap='gray')
    pylab.xticks([],[]), pylab.yticks([],[])
    pylab.subtitle('SGD after Step ' + str(step) + ' with lambda1=lambda2=' + str(lambda1))
pylab.show()
```

The preceding visualizes the weights learned for 225 (randomly chosen) hidden nodes in the FC layer 1 of the network after 4,000 steps. Observe that the weights are already learned some features from the input images the model was trained on:

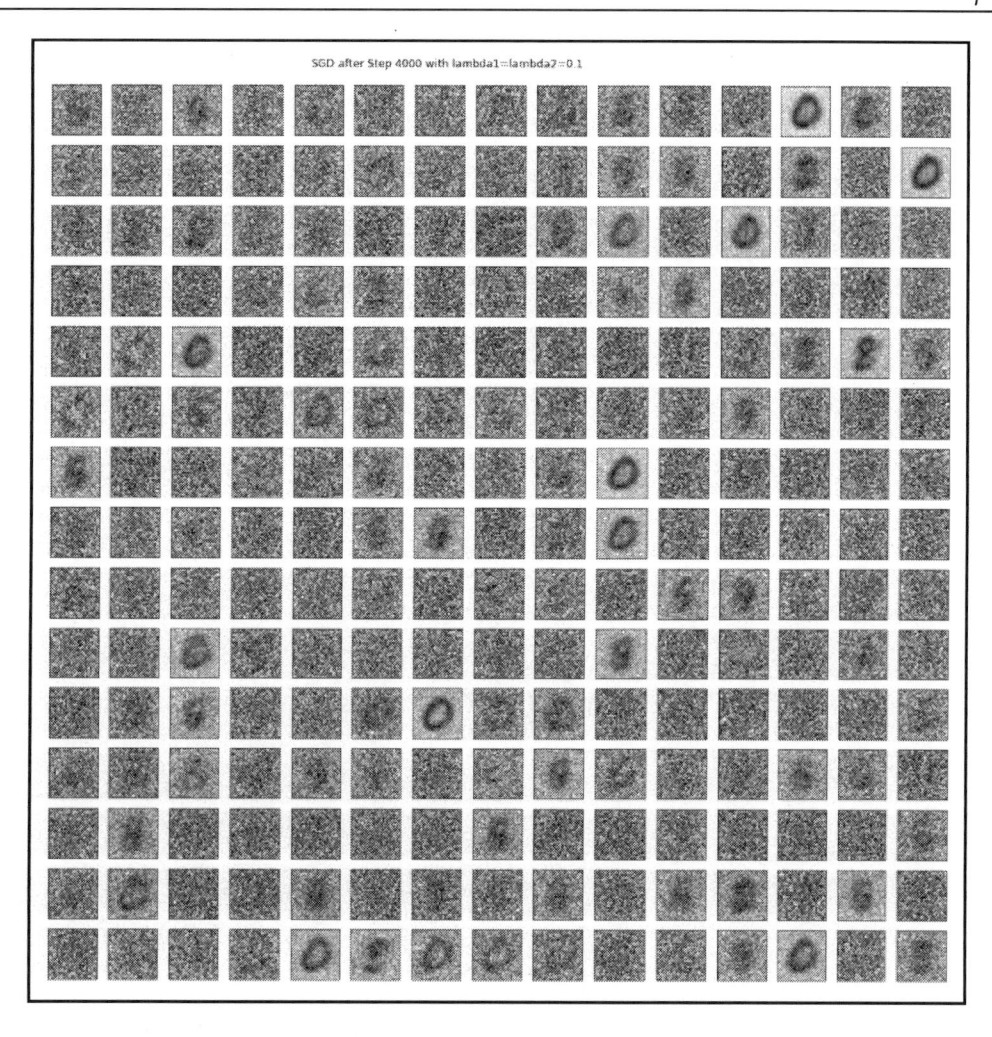

The following code snippet plots the training accuracy and validation accuracy at different steps:

```
pylab.screenshot(figsize=(8,12))
pylab.subplot(211)
pylab.plot(range(0,3001,500), atr, '.-', label='training accuracy')
pylab.plot(range(0,3001,500), av, '.-', label='validation accuracy')
pylab.xlabel('GD steps'), pylab.ylabel('Accuracy'), pylab.legend(loc='lower right')
pylab.subplot(212)
pylab.plot(range(0,3001,500), ll, '.-')
pylab.xlabel('GD steps'), pylab.ylabel('Softmax Loss')
pylab.show()
```

Deep Learning in Image Processing - Image Classification

The next screenshot shows the output of the previous code block; observe that the accuracies keep on increasing in general, but become almost constant in the end, which means learning no longer happens:

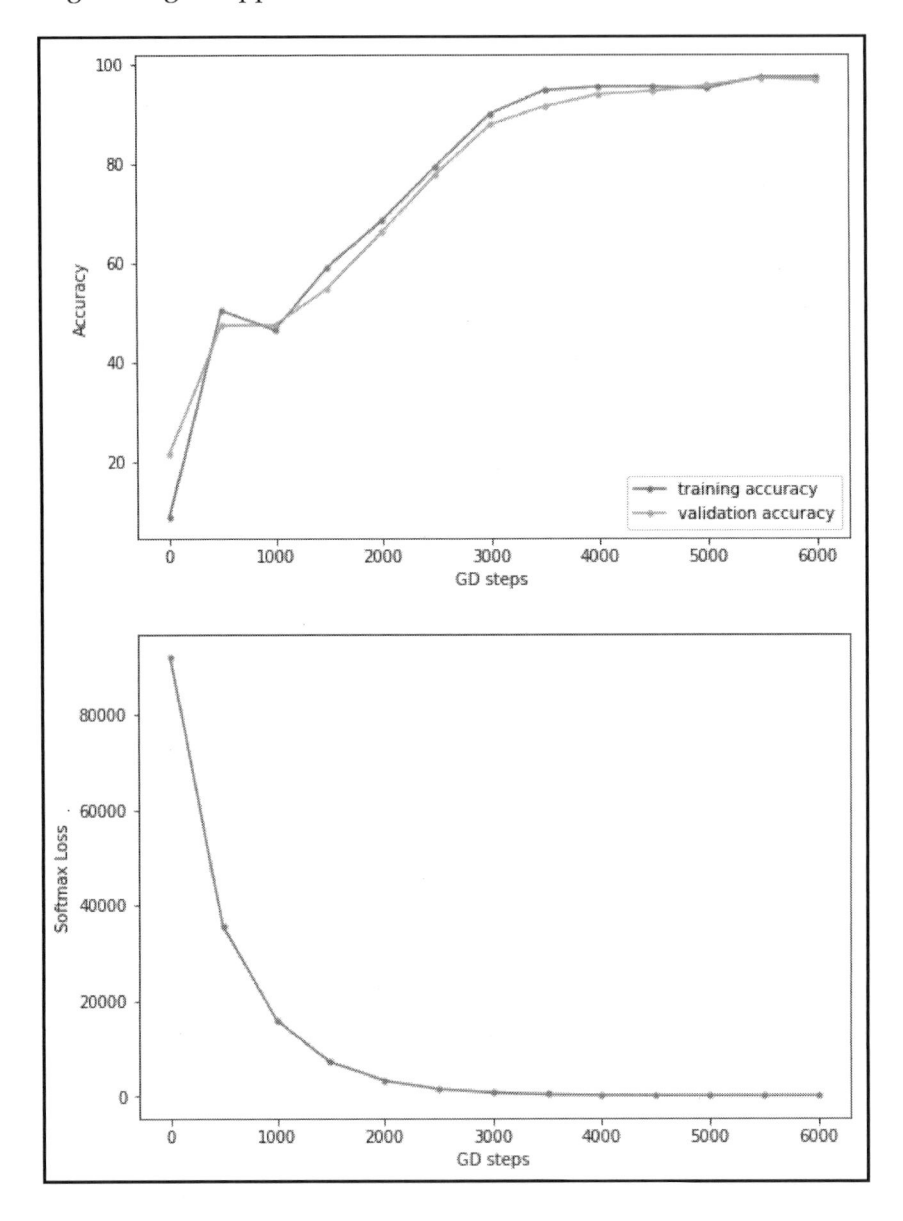

Classification with dense FC layers with Keras

Let's implement the handwritten digits classification with Keras, again using dense FC layers only. This time we shall use one more hidden layer, along with a dropout layer. The next code block shows how to implement the classifier with a few lines of code using the `keras.models Sequential()` function. We can simply add the layers sequentially to the model. There are a couple of hidden layers introduced, with each of them having 200 nodes along with a dropout in between, with 15% dropout rate. This time, let's use the **Adam** optimizer (which uses **momentum** to accelerate SGD). Let's fit the model on the training dataset with 10 `epochs` (one pass over the entire input dataset). As can be seen, with this simple change in the architecture, an accuracy of 98.04% is obtained on the test images of MNIST:

```python
import keras
from keras.models import Sequential
from keras.layers import Dense, Flatten, Dropout
from keras.utils import to_categorical

# import data
from keras.datasets import mnist
# load data
(X_train, y_train), (X_test, y_test) = mnist.load_data()
print(X_train.shape, X_test.shape)
# (60000, 28, 28) (10000, 28, 28)
# reshape to be [samples][pixels][width][height]
X_train = X_train.reshape(X_train.shape[0], 28, 28, 1).astype('float32')
X_test = X_test.reshape(X_test.shape[0], 28, 28, 1).astype('float32')
X_train = X_train / 255 # normalize training data
X_test = X_test / 255 # normalize test data
y_train = to_categorical(y_train) # to one-hot-encoding of the labels
y_test = to_categorical(y_test)
num_classes = y_test.shape[1] # number of categories

def FC_model():
    # create model
    model = Sequential()
    model.add(Flatten(input_shape=(28, 28, 1)))
    model.add(Dense(200, activation='relu'))
    model.add(Dropout(0.15))
    model.add(Dense(200, activation='relu'))
    model.add(Dense(num_classes, activation='softmax'))
    # compile model
```

```
        model.compile(optimizer='adam', loss='categorical_crossentropy',
metrics=['accuracy'])
        return model

# build the model
model = FC_model()
model.summary()
# fit the model
model.fit(X_train, y_train, validation_data=(X_test, y_test), epochs=10,
batch_size=200, verbose=2)
# evaluate the model
scores = model.evaluate(X_test, y_test, verbose=0)
print("Accuracy: {} \n Error: {}".format(scores[1], 100-scores[1]*100))

#  _____
# Layer (type)              Output Shape              Param #
# ===============================================================
# flatten_1 (Flatten)       (None, 784)               0
# _____
# dense_1 (Dense)           (None, 200)               157000
# _____
# dropout_1 (Dropout)       (None, 200)               0
# _____
# dense_2 (Dense)           (None, 200)               40200
# _____
# dense_3 (Dense)           (None, 10)                2010
# ===============================================================
# Total params: 199,210
# Trainable params: 199,210
# Non-trainable params: 0
# _____
# Train on 60000 samples, validate on 10000 samples
# Epoch 1/10
#  - 3s - loss: 0.3487 - acc: 0.9010 - val_loss: 0.1474 - val_acc: 0.9562
# Epoch 2/10
#  - 2s - loss: 0.1426 - acc: 0.9580 - val_loss: 0.0986 - val_acc: 0.9700
# Epoch 3/10
#  - 2s - loss: 0.0976 - acc: 0.9697 - val_loss: 0.0892 - val_acc: 0.9721
# Epoch 4/10
#  - 2s - loss: 0.0768 - acc: 0.9762 - val_loss: 0.0829 - val_acc: 0.9744
# Epoch 5/10
#  - 2s - loss: 0.0624 - acc: 0.9806 - val_loss: 0.0706 - val_acc: 0.9774
# Epoch 6/10
#  - 2s - loss: 0.0516 - acc: 0.9838 - val_loss: 0.0655 - val_acc: 0.9806
# Epoch 7/10
#  - 2s - loss: 0.0438 - acc: 0.9861 - val_loss: 0.0692 - val_acc: 0.9788
# Epoch 8/10
#  - 2s - loss: 0.0387 - acc: 0.9874 - val_loss: 0.0623 - val_acc: 0.9823
```

```
# Epoch 9/10
#  - 2s - loss: 0.0341 - acc: 0.9888 - val_loss: 0.0695 - val_acc: 0.9781
# Epoch 10/10
#  - 2s - loss: 0.0299 - acc: 0.9899 - val_loss: 0.0638 - val_acc: 0.9804
# Accuracy: 0.9804
# Error: 1.9599999999999937
```

Visualizing the network

Let's visualize the architecture of the neural network we designed with Keras. The following code snippet will allow us to save the model (network) architecture in an image:

```
# pip install pydot_ng ## install pydot_ng if not already installed
import pydot_ng as pydot
from keras.utils import plot_model
plot_model(model, to_file='model.png')
```

The following screenshot shows the output of the previous code block, the neural network architecture:

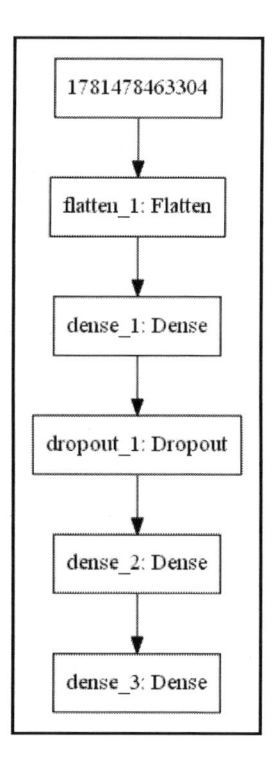

Visualizing the weights in the intermediate layers

Now, let's visualize the weights learned in the intermediate layers. The following Python code visualizes the weights learned for the first 200 hidden units at the first dense layer:

```
from keras.models import Model
import matplotlib.pylab as pylab
import numpy as np
W = model.get_layer('dense_1').get_weights()
print(W[0].shape)
print(W[1].shape)
fig = pylab.screenshot(figsize=(20,20))
fig.subplots_adjust(left=0, right=1, bottom=0, top=0.95, hspace=0.05, wspace=0.05)
pylab.gray()
for i in range(200):
    pylab.subplot(15, 14, i+1), pylab.imshow(np.reshape(W[0][:, i], (28,28))), pylab.axis('off')
pylab.suptitle('Dense_1 Weights (200 hidden units)', size=20)
pylab.show()
```

This results in the following output:

Chapter 10

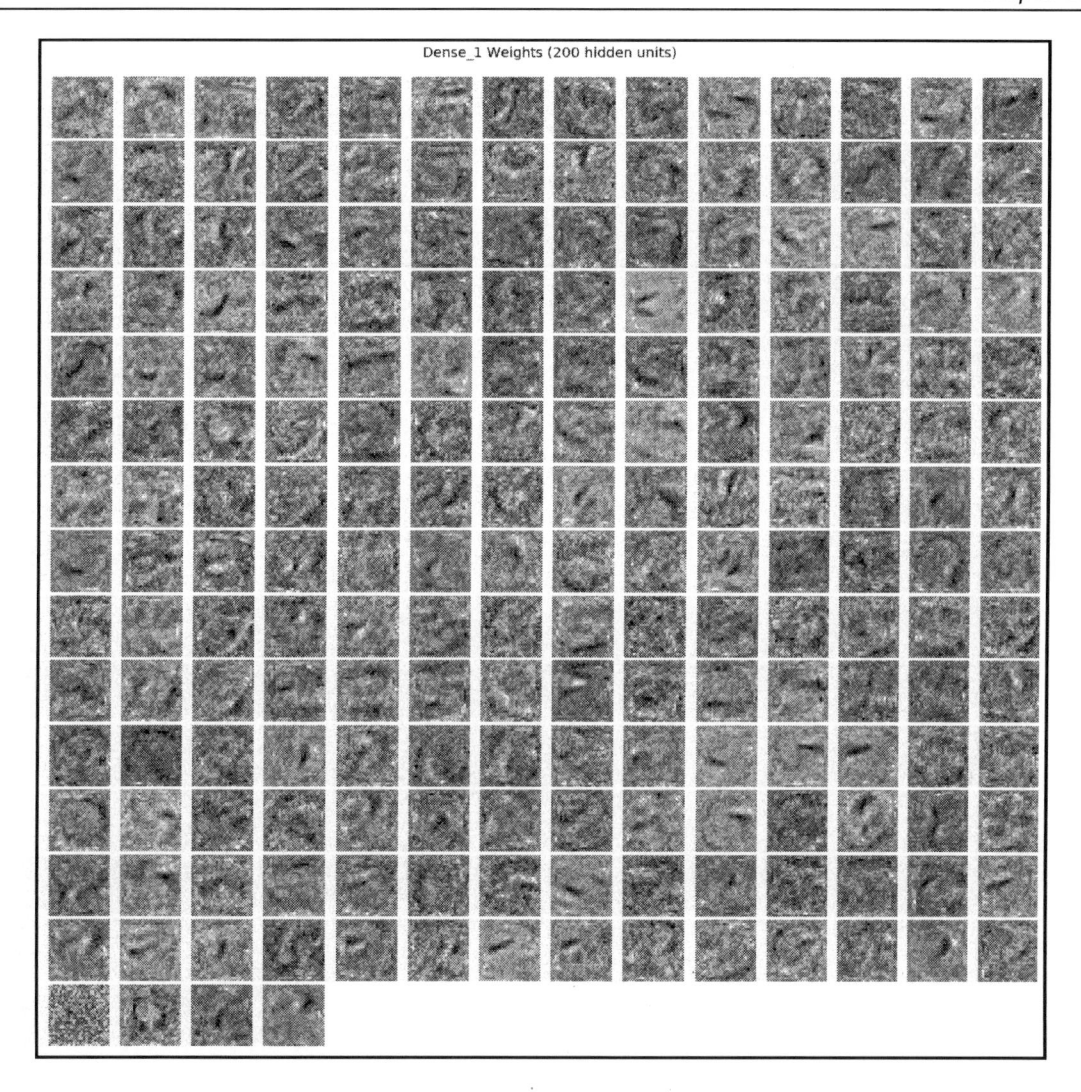

Dense_1 Weights (200 hidden units)

The following screenshot shows what the neural network sees in the output layer, the code being left as an exercise to the reader:

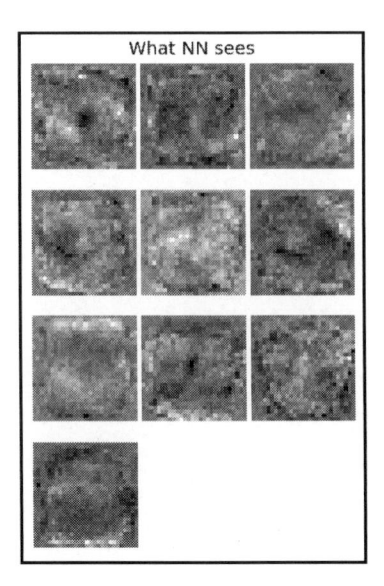

CNN for classification with Keras

Now, let's implement a CNN with Keras. We need to introduce the convolutional, pooling, and flatten layers. The next subsection shows how to implement and use a CNN for MNIST classification again. As we shall see, the accuracy on the test dataset increases.

Classifying MNIST

This time, let's introduce a 5 x 5 convolutional layer with 64 filters with ReLU activation, followed by a 2 x 2 max pooling layer with a stride of 2. This needs to be followed by a flattened layer and then a single hidden dense layer with 100 nodes, followed by the output softmax dense layer. As can be seen, the accuracy on the test dataset increased to `98.77%` after training the model for 10 epochs:

```
import keras
from keras.models import Sequential
from keras.layers import Dense
from keras.utils import to_categorical
from keras.layers.convolutional import Conv2D # to add convolutional layers
from keras.layers.convolutional import MaxPooling2D # to add pooling layers
from keras.layers import Flatten # to flatten data for fully connected
```

layers

```python
# import data
from keras.datasets import mnist
# load data
(X_train, y_train), (X_test, y_test) = mnist.load_data()
print(X_train.shape, X_test.shape)
# (60000, 28, 28) (10000, 28, 28)
# reshape to be [samples][pixels][width][height]
X_train = X_train.reshape(X_train.shape[0], 28, 28, 1).astype('float32')
X_test = X_test.reshape(X_test.shape[0], 28, 28, 1).astype('float32')
X_train = X_train / 255 # normalize training data
X_test = X_test / 255 # normalize test data
y_train = to_categorical(y_train)
y_test = to_categorical(y_test)
num_classes = y_test.shape[1] # number of categories

def convolutional_model():

    # create model
    model = Sequential()
    model.add(Conv2D(64, (5, 5), strides=(1, 1), activation='relu', input_shape=(28, 28, 1)))
    model.add(MaxPooling2D(pool_size=(2, 2), strides=(2, 2)))
    model.add(Flatten())
    model.add(Dense(100, activation='relu'))
    model.add(Dense(num_classes, activation='softmax'))
    # compile model
    model.compile(optimizer='adam', loss='categorical_crossentropy', metrics=['accuracy'])
    return model

# build the model
model = convolutional_model()
model.summary()
# _____
# Layer (type)                 Output Shape              Param #
# =================================================================
# conv2d_1 (Conv2D)            (None, 24, 24, 64)        1664
# _____
# max_pooling2d_1 (MaxPooling2D) (None, 12, 12, 64)      0
# _____
# flatten_1 (Flatten)          (None, 9216)              0
# _____
# dense_1 (Dense)              (None, 100)               921700
# _____
# dense_2 (Dense)              (None, 10)                1010
# =================================================================
```

```
# Total params: 924,374
# Trainable params: 924,374
# Non-trainable params: 0
#_____

# fit the model
model.fit(X_train, y_train, validation_data=(X_test, y_test), epochs=10,
batch_size=200, verbose=2)
# evaluate the model
scores = model.evaluate(X_test, y_test, verbose=0)
print("Accuracy: {} \n Error: {}".format(scores[1], 100-scores[1]*100))
#Train on 60000 samples, validate on 10000 samples
#Epoch 1/10
# - 47s - loss: 0.2161 - acc: 0.9387 - val_loss: 0.0733 - val_acc: 0.9779
#Epoch 2/10
# - 46s - loss: 0.0611 - acc: 0.9816 - val_loss: 0.0423 - val_acc: 0.9865
#Epoch 3/10
# - 46s - loss: 0.0417 - acc: 0.9876 - val_loss: 0.0408 - val_acc: 0.9871
#Epoch 4/10
# - 41s - loss: 0.0315 - acc: 0.9904 - val_loss: 0.0497 - val_acc: 0.9824
#Epoch 5/10
# - 40s - loss: 0.0258 - acc: 0.9924 - val_loss: 0.0445 - val_acc: 0.9851
#Epoch 6/10
# - 39s - loss: 0.0188 - acc: 0.9943 - val_loss: 0.0368 - val_acc: 0.9890
#Epoch 7/10
# - 39s - loss: 0.0152 - acc: 0.9954 - val_loss: 0.0391 - val_acc: 0.9874
#Epoch 8/10
# - 42s - loss: 0.0114 - acc: 0.9965 - val_loss: 0.0408 - val_acc: 0.9884
#Epoch 9/10
# - 41s - loss: 0.0086 - acc: 0.9976 - val_loss: 0.0380 - val_acc: 0.9893
#Epoch 10/10
# - 47s - loss: 0.0070 - acc: 0.9980 - val_loss: 0.0434 - val_acc: 0.9877
# Accuracy: 0.9877
# Error: 1.230000000000004
```

The next screenshot shows the distribution of predicted probability that the output class is 0 for the test instances with the ground truth label 0. The code is left as an exercise to the reader:

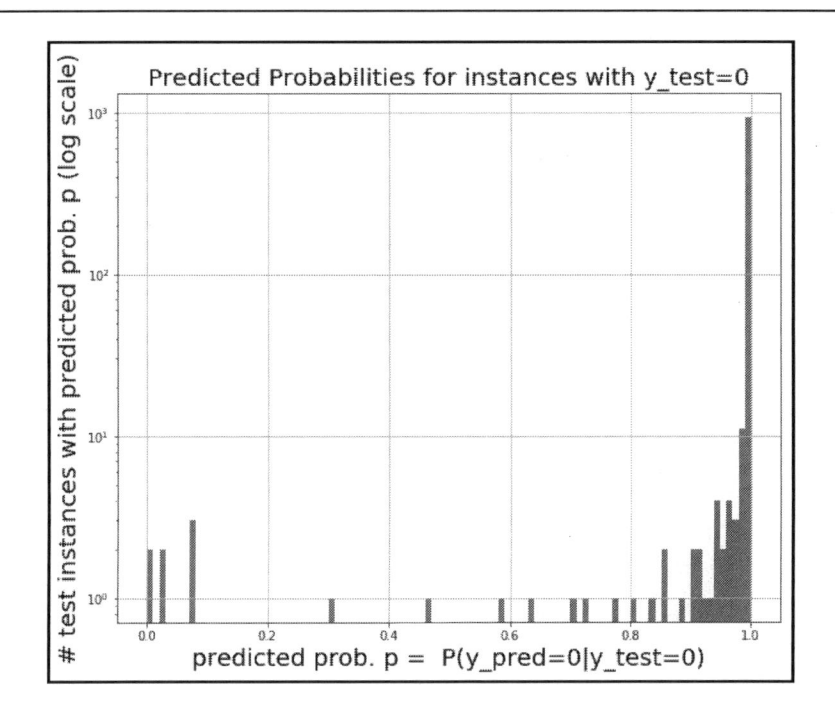

Visualizing the intermediate layers

Now let's visualize the image feature maps (64 features with 64 filters) that are learned with the convolutional layer for a couple of images using the following code block:

```
from keras.models import Model
import matplotlib.pylab as pylab
import numpy as np
intermediate_layer_model = Model(inputs=model.input,
outputs=model.get_layer('conv2d_1').output)
intermediate_output = intermediate_layer_model.predict(X_train)
print(model.input.shape, intermediate_output.shape)
fig = pylab.screenshot(figsize=(15,15))
fig.subplots_adjust(left=0, right=1, bottom=0, top=1, hspace=0.05,
wspace=0.05)
pylab.gray()
i = 1
for c in range(64):
    pylab.subplot(8, 8, c+1), pylab.imshow(intermediate_output[i,:,:,c]),
pylab.axis('off')
pylab.show()
```

The following screenshot shows the feature maps learned by the convolutional layer for a handwritten digit image with the label 0 from the training dataset:

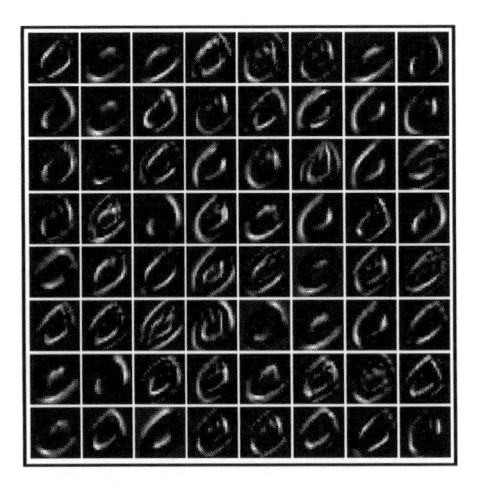

By changing the index of the image from the training dataset to 2 and running the previous code again, we get the following output:

```
i - 2
```

The following screenshot shows the feature maps learned by the convolutional layer for a handwritten digit image with the label 4 from the MNIST training dataset:

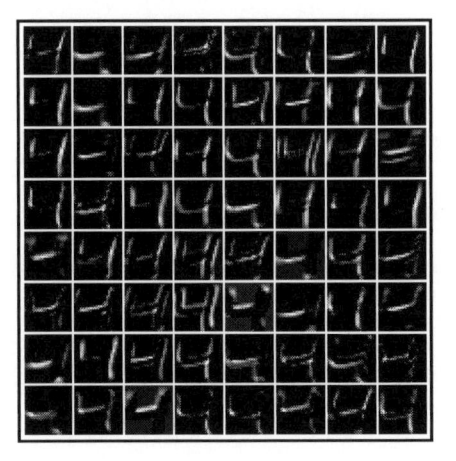

Some popular deep CNNs

In this section, let's discuss popular deep CNNs (for example, VGG-18/19, ResNet, and InceptionNet) used for image classification. The following screenshot shows single-crop accuracies (**top-1 accuracy**: how many times the correct label has the highest probability predicted by the CNN) of the most relevant entries submitted to the ImageNet challenge, from **AlexNet** (Krizhevsky et al., 2012), on the far left, to the best performing, **Inception-v4** (Szegedy et al., 2016):

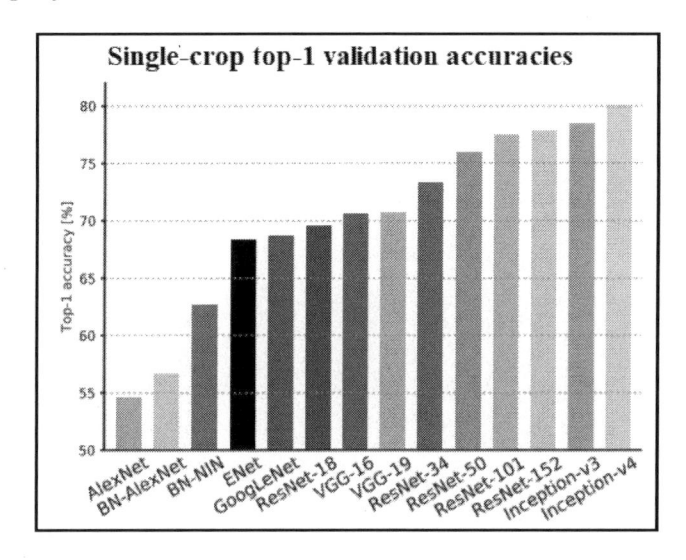

Also, we shall train a VGG-16 CNN with Keras to classify the cat images against the dog images.

VGG-16/19

The following screenshot shows the architecture of a popular CNN called VGG-16/19. The remarkable thing about the VGG-16 net is that, instead of having so many hyper-parameters, it lets you use a much simpler network where you focus on just having convolutional layers that are just 3 x 3 filters with a stride of 1 and that always use the same padding and make all the max pooling layers 2 x 2 with a stride of 2. It is a really deep network.

This network has a total of about 138 million parameters, as seen in the following diagram:

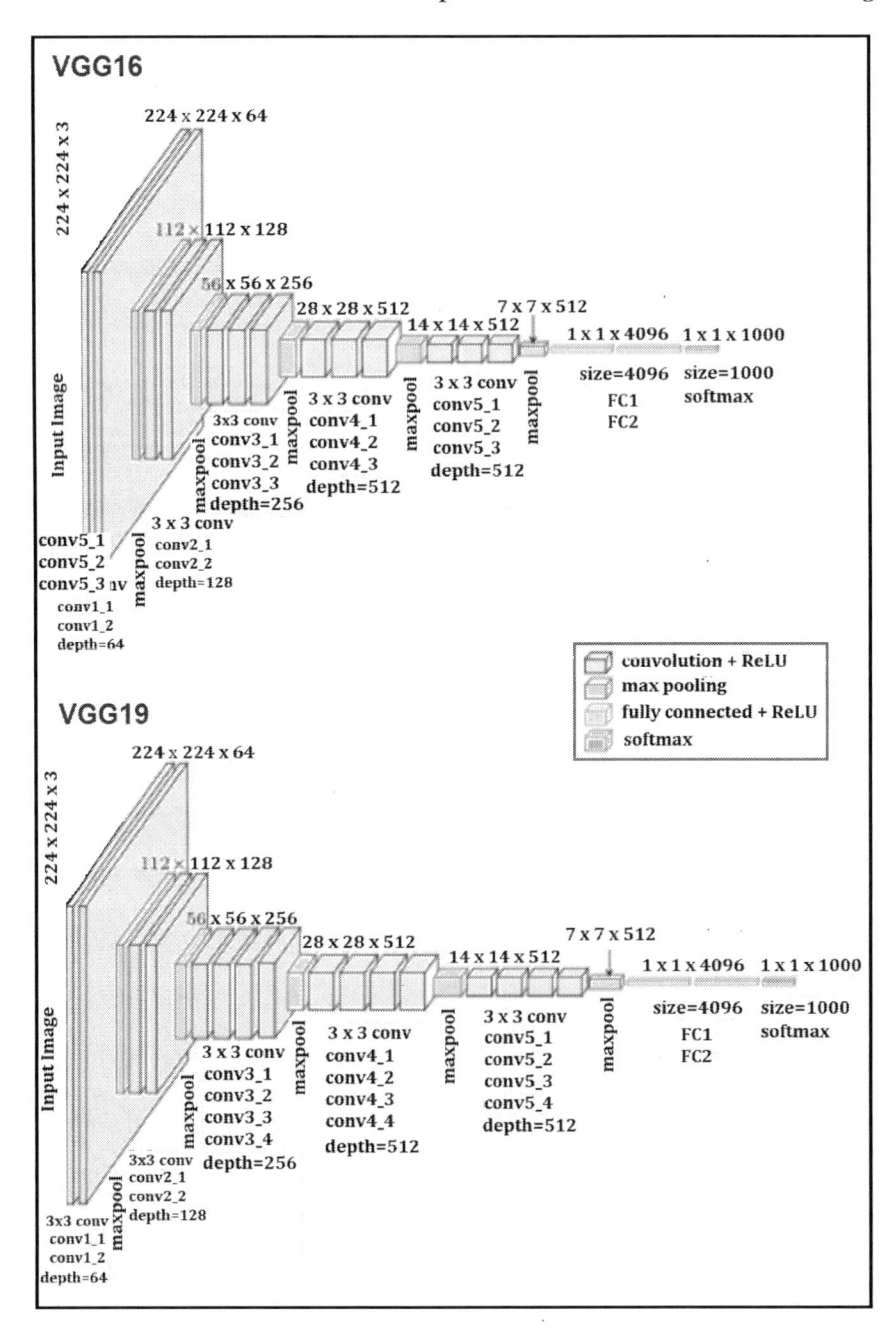

Classifying cat/dog images with VGG-16 in Keras

In this section, let's use the Keras VGG-16 implementation to classify cat and dog images from the Kaggle *Dogs vs. Cats* competition. Let's download the training and the test images dataset (https://www.kaggle.com/c/dogs-vs-cats) first. Then let's train the VGG-16 network from scratch on the training images.

Training phase

The following code block shows how to fit the model on the training dataset. Let's use 20k images from the training dataset to train the VGG-16 model and 5k images as validation dataset to evaluate the model while training. The `weights=None` parameter value must be passed to the `VGG16()` function to ensure that the network is trained from scratch. Note, this will take a long time if not run on a GPU, so a GPU is recommended.

> For installing TensorFlow with a GPU, refer to this article: https://medium.com/@raza.shahzad/setting-up-tensorflow-gpu-keras-in-conda-on-windows-10-75d4fd498198.

With 20 epochs, the accuracy achieved on the validation dataset is 78.38%. We can tune the hyperparameters to increase the accuracy of the model further, which is left as an exercise to the reader:

```
import cv2 # working with, mainly resizing, images
import numpy as np # dealing with arrays
import os # dealing with directories
from random import shuffle # mixing up or currently ordered data that might
lead our network astray in training.
from tqdm import tqdm # a nice pretty percentage bar for tasks.
from keras.utils import to_categorical

TRAIN_DIR = 'C:\Courses\My Book\Chapter10\\train' # point to the right path
for the training images
TEST_DIR = 'C:\Courses\My Book\Chapter10\\test'   # point to the right path
for the test images
IMG_SIZE = 64
LR = 1e-5

MODEL_NAME = 'dogsvscats-{}-{}.model'.format(LR, '2conv-basic') # just so
we remember which saved model is which, sizes must match

def label_img(img):
```

```python
    word_label = img.split('.')[-3]
    # conversion to one-hot array [cat,dog]
    # [much cat, no dog]
    if word_label == 'cat': return 0
    # [no cat, very doggo]
    elif word_label == 'dog': return 1

def create_train_data():
    training_data = []
    for img in tqdm(os.listdir(TRAIN_DIR)):
    label = label_img(img)
    path = os.path.join(TRAIN_DIR,img)
    img = cv2.imread(path)
    img = cv2.resize(img, (IMG_SIZE,IMG_SIZE))
    training_data.append([np.array(img),np.array(label)])
    shuffle(training_data)
    np.save('train_data.npy', training_data)
    return training_data

train_data = create_train_data()
#
100%|████████████████████████████████████████| 1100/1100 [00:00<00:00,
1133.86it/s]

from keras.applications.vgg16 import VGG16
from keras.optimizers import Adam

train = train_data[:-5000]
test = train_data[-5000:]
X_train = np.array([i[0] for i in train]).reshape(-1,IMG_SIZE,IMG_SIZE,3)
y_train = [i[1] for i in train]
y_train = to_categorical(y_train)
print(X_train.shape, y_train.shape)

X_test = np.array([i[0] for i in test]).reshape(-1,IMG_SIZE,IMG_SIZE,3)
y_test = [i[1] for i in test]
y_test = to_categorical(y_test)

num_classes = y_test.shape[1] # number of categories

model = VGG16(weights=None, input_shape=(IMG_SIZE,IMG_SIZE,3),
classes=num_classes)
model.compile(Adam(lr=LR), "categorical_crossentropy",
metrics=["accuracy"]) # "adam"
model.summary()
# fit the model
```

```
model.fit(X_train, y_train, validation_data=(X_test, y_test), epochs=10,
batch_size=256, verbose=2)
# evaluate the model
scores = model.evaluate(X_test, y_test, verbose=0)
print("Accuracy: {} \n Error: {}".format(scores[1], 100-scores[1]*100))
#_____
#Layer (type)                 Output Shape              Param
#=================================================================
# input_5 (InputLayer)         (None, 50, 50, 3)         0
#_____
# block1_conv1 (Conv2D)        (None, 50, 50, 64)        1792
#_____
# block1_conv2 (Conv2D)        (None, 50, 50, 64)        36928
#_____
# block1_pool (MaxPooling2D)   (None, 25, 25, 64)        0
#_____
# block2_conv1 (Conv2D)        (None, 25, 25, 128)       73856
#_____
# block2_conv2 (Conv2D)        (None, 25, 25, 128)       147584
#_____
# block2_pool (MaxPooling2D)   (None, 12, 12, 128)       0
#_____
# block3_conv1 (Conv2D)        (None, 12, 12, 256)       295168
#_____
# block3_conv2 (Conv2D)        (None, 12, 12, 256)       590080
#_____
# block3_conv3 (Conv2D)        (None, 12, 12, 256)       590080
#_____
# block3_pool (MaxPooling2D)   (None, 6, 6, 256)         0
#_____
# block4_conv1 (Conv2D)        (None, 6, 6, 512)         1180160
#_____
# block4_conv2 (Conv2D)        (None, 6, 6, 512)         2359808
#_____
# block4_conv3 (Conv2D)        (None, 6, 6, 512)         2359808
#_____
# block4_pool (MaxPooling2D)   (None, 3, 3, 512)         0
#_____
# block5_conv1 (Conv2D)        (None, 3, 3, 512)         2359808
#_____
# block5_conv2 (Conv2D)        (None, 3, 3, 512)         2359808
#_____
# block5_conv3 (Conv2D)        (None, 3, 3, 512)         2359808
#_____
# block5_pool (MaxPooling2D)   (None, 1, 1, 512)         0
#_____
# flatten (Flatten)            (None, 512)               0
#_____
```

```
# fc1 (Dense)                    (None, 4096)              2101248
#
# fc2 (Dense)                    (None, 4096)              16781312
#
# predictions (Dense)            (None, 2)                 8194
# =================================================================
# Total params: 33,605,442
# Trainable params: 33,605,442
# Non-trainable params: 0
#
#
# Train on 20000 samples, validate on 5000 samples
# Epoch 1/10
#  - 92s - loss: 0.6878 - acc: 0.5472 - val_loss: 0.6744 - val_acc: 0.5750
# Epoch 2/20
#  - 51s - loss: 0.6529 - acc: 0.6291 - val_loss: 0.6324 - val_acc: 0.6534
# Epoch 3/20
#  - 51s - loss: 0.6123 - acc: 0.6649 - val_loss: 0.6249 - val_acc: 0.6472
# Epoch 4/20
#  - 51s - loss: 0.5919 - acc: 0.6842 - val_loss: 0.5902 - val_acc: 0.6828
# Epoch 5/20
#  - 51s - loss: 0.5709 - acc: 0.6992 - val_loss: 0.5687 - val_acc: 0.7054
# Epoch 6/20
#  - 51s - loss: 0.5564 - acc: 0.7159 - val_loss: 0.5620 - val_acc: 0.7142
# Epoch 7/20
#  - 51s - loss: 0.5539 - acc: 0.7137 - val_loss: 0.5698 - val_acc: 0.6976
# Epoch 8/20
#  - 51s - loss: 0.5275 - acc: 0.7371 - val_loss: 0.5402 - val_acc: 0.7298
# Epoch 9/20
#  - 51s - loss: 0.5072 - acc: 0.7536 - val_loss: 0.5240 - val_acc: 0.7444
# Epoch 10/20
#  - 51s - loss: 0.4880 - acc: 0.7647 - val_loss: 0.5127 - val_acc: 0.7544
# Epoch 11/20
#  - 51s - loss: 0.4659 - acc: 0.7814 - val_loss: 0.5594 - val_acc: 0.7164
# Epoch 12/20
#  - 51s - loss: 0.4584 - acc: 0.7813 - val_loss: 0.5689 - val_acc: 0.7124
# Epoch 13/20
#  - 51s - loss: 0.4410 - acc: 0.7952 - val_loss: 0.4863 - val_acc: 0.7704
# Epoch 14/20
#  - 51s - loss: 0.4295 - acc: 0.8022 - val_loss: 0.5073 - val_acc: 0.7596
# Epoch 15/20
#  - 51s - loss: 0.4175 - acc: 0.8084 - val_loss: 0.4854 - val_acc: 0.7688
# Epoch 16/20
#  - 51s - loss: 0.3914 - acc: 0.8259 - val_loss: 0.4743 - val_acc: 0.7794
# Epoch 17/20
#  - 51s - loss: 0.3852 - acc: 0.8286 - val_loss: 0.4721 - val_acc: 0.7810
# Epoch 18/20
#  - 51s - loss: 0.3692 - acc: 0.8364 - val_loss: 0.6765 - val_acc: 0.6826
# Epoch 19/20
```

```
# - 51s - loss: 0.3752 - acc: 0.8332 - val_loss: 0.4805 - val_acc: 0.7760
# Epoch 20/20
# - 51s - loss: 0.3360 - acc: 0.8586 - val_loss: 0.4711 - val_acc: 0.7838
# Accuracy: 0.7838
# Error: 21.61999999999999
```

The next code block visualizes the features learned for a dog image with the first 64 filters in the second convolutional layer of the first block:

```
intermediate_layer_model = Model(inputs=model.input,
outputs=model.get_layer('block1_conv2').output)
intermediate_output = intermediate_layer_model.predict(X_train)
fig = pylab.screenshot(figsize=(10,10))
fig.subplots_adjust(left=0, right=1, bottom=0, top=1, hspace=0.05,
wspace=0.05)
pylab.gray()
i = 3
for c in range(64):
    pylab.subplot(8, 8, c+1), pylab.imshow(intermediate_output[i,:,:,c]),
pylab.axis('off')
pylab.show()
```

Deep Learning in Image Processing - Image Classification

The following screenshot shows the output of the previous code, the feature maps learned for the dog image with the model:

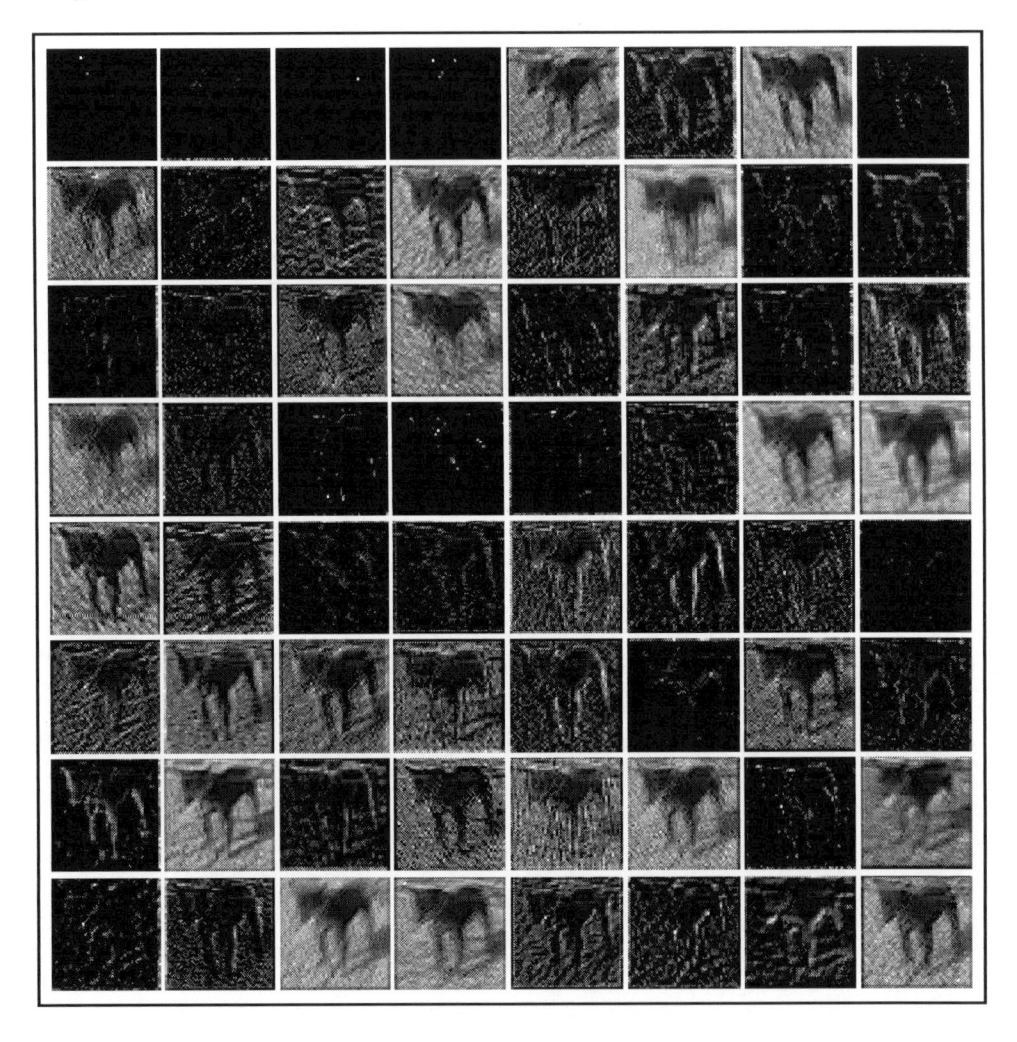

By changing the single line in the previous code snippet, we can visualize the features learned for the same dog image with the first 64 filters in the second convolutional layer of the second block:

```
intermediate_layer_model = Model(inputs=model.input,
outputs=model.get_layer('block2_conv2').output)
```

The following screenshot shows the output of the previous code, the feature maps learned for the same dog image with the model:

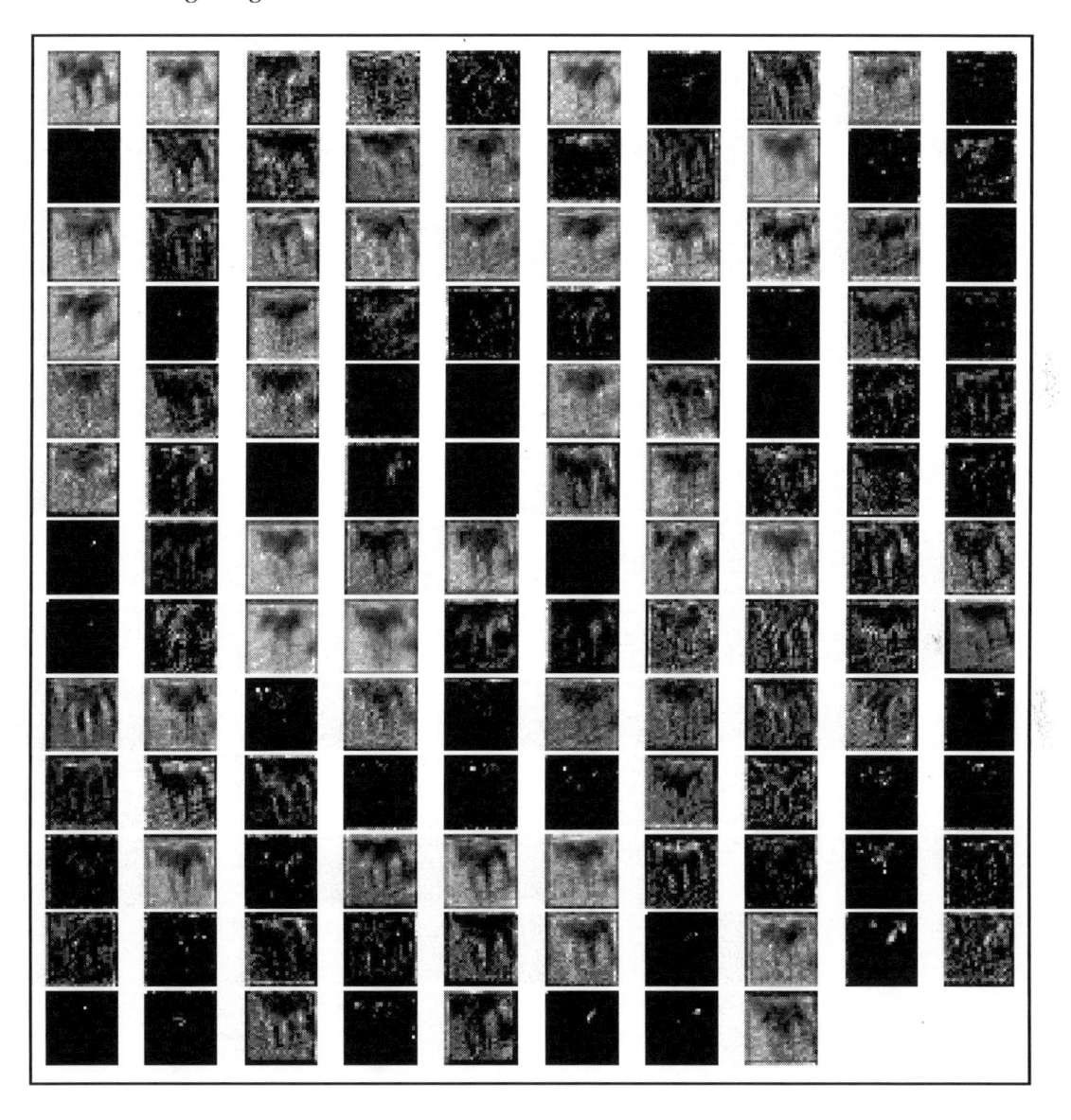

Testing (prediction) phase

The next code block show how to use the VGG-16 model learned to predict the probability of whether an image is dog or cat from the `test` images dataset:

```
test_data = process_test_data()
len(test_data)
X_test = np.array([i for i in test_data]).reshape(-1,IMG_SIZE,IMG_SIZE,3)
probs = model.predict(X_test)
probs = np.round(probs,2)
pylab.screenshot(figsize=(20,20))
for i in range(100):
    pylab.subplot(10,10,i+1), pylab.imshow(X_test[i,:,:,::-1]),
pylab.axis('off')
    pylab.title("{}, prob={:0.2f}".format('cat' if probs[i][1] < 0.5 else 'dog', max(probs[i][0],probs[i][1])))
pylab.show()
```

The next screenshot shows the class predicted the first 100 test images along with the prediction probabilities. As can be seen in the following output, the labels for most of the images are predicted correctly, although there are quite a few wrong predictions too by the VGG-16 model learned:

cat, prob=0.89
dog, prob=1.00
dog, prob=0.93
dog, prob=0.76
dog, prob=0.83
dog, prob=0.64
dog, prob=0.96
cat, prob=0.71
dog, prob=0.53
dog, prob=0.62
cat, prob=0.61
cat, prob=0.93
dog, prob=1.00
dog, prob=1.00
cat, prob=0.77
dog, prob=1.00
cat, prob=0.99
dog, prob=0.97
dog, prob=0.94
dog, prob=0.92
cat, prob=0.98
cat, prob=0.53
dog, prob=0.84
dog, prob=0.87
cat, prob=0.64
cat, prob=0.95
cat, prob=0.92
cat, prob=0.60
dog, prob=0.71
cat, prob=0.89
dog, prob=0.58
dog, prob=0.84
cat, prob=0.77
dog, prob=0.59
cat, prob=0.98
cat, prob=0.97
cat, prob=0.91
dog, prob=0.92
dog, prob=0.50
dog, prob=0.64
dog, prob=0.94
dog, prob=0.96
cat, prob=0.96
cat, prob=0.96
dog, prob=0.61
cat, prob=0.88
cat, prob=0.92
dog, prob=0.77
dog, prob=0.88
cat, prob=0.89
cat, prob=0.96
cat, prob=0.55
dog, prob=0.50
dog, prob=0.82
dog, prob=0.99
cat, prob=0.97
dog, prob=0.82
dog, prob=0.80
cat, prob=0.65
cat, prob=0.84
dog, prob=0.68
dog, prob=1.00
dog, prob=0.89
dog, prob=0.96
dog, prob=0.55
dog, prob=0.95
cat, prob=0.92
cat, prob=0.73
dog, prob=0.62
dog, prob=0.70
dog, prob=0.57
cat, prob=0.91
cat, prob=0.75
cat, prob=0.69
dog, prob=1.00
cat, prob=0.52
dog, prob=0.73
dog, prob=0.71
cat, prob=0.52
cat, prob=0.84
cat, prob=0.81
cat, prob=0.81
dog, prob=0.72
cat, prob=0.99
cat, prob=0.59
cat, prob=0.90
cat, prob=0.70
cat, prob=0.93
cat, prob=0.56
cat, prob=0.88
dog, prob=0.99
dog, prob=0.99
cat, prob=0.75
dog, prob=0.99
cat, prob=0.77
cat, prob=0.62
cat, prob=0.57
cat, prob=0.77
dog, prob=0.66
dog, prob=0.81

InceptionNet

In the development of CNN classifiers, the inception network is a very important milestone. Before the inception network came into the picture, CNNs used to just stack the convolutional layers to the utmost depths in order to achieve better performance. Inception networks use complex techniques and tricks to meet performance both in terms of speed and accuracy.

Inception networks are evolving constantly and have led to the birth of several new versions of the network. Some of the popular versions are—Inception-v1, v2, v3, v4, and Inception-ResNet. Since there can be huge variations in salient parts and the location of information in images, choosing the right kernel size for the convolution operation becomes tough. A larger kernel is preferred for information that is distributed more globally, and a smaller kernel is preferred for information that is distributed more locally. Deep neural networks suffer from overfitting and vanishing gradient problems. Naively stacking large convolution operations will incur a lot of expenses.

The inception network solves all of the previous issues by adding filters that have multiple sizes that operate on the same level. This causes the network to become wider rather than deeper. The next screenshot shows an inception module with dimension reduction. It performs convolution on the input with three different sizes of filters (1 x 1, 3 x 3, and 5 x 5) and an additional max pooling. The output is concatenated and sent to the next inception module. To make it cheaper, the number of input channels were limited by adding an extra 1 x 1 convolution before the 3 x 3 and 5 x 5 convolutions. Using the dimension reduced inception module, a neural network architecture was built. This was popularly known as **GoogleNet** (**Inception v1**). The architecture is shown in the following—GoogleNet has nine such inception modules stacked linearly. It is 22 layers deep (27, including the pooling layers) and uses global average pooling at the end of the last inception module:

Inception module with dimension reductions

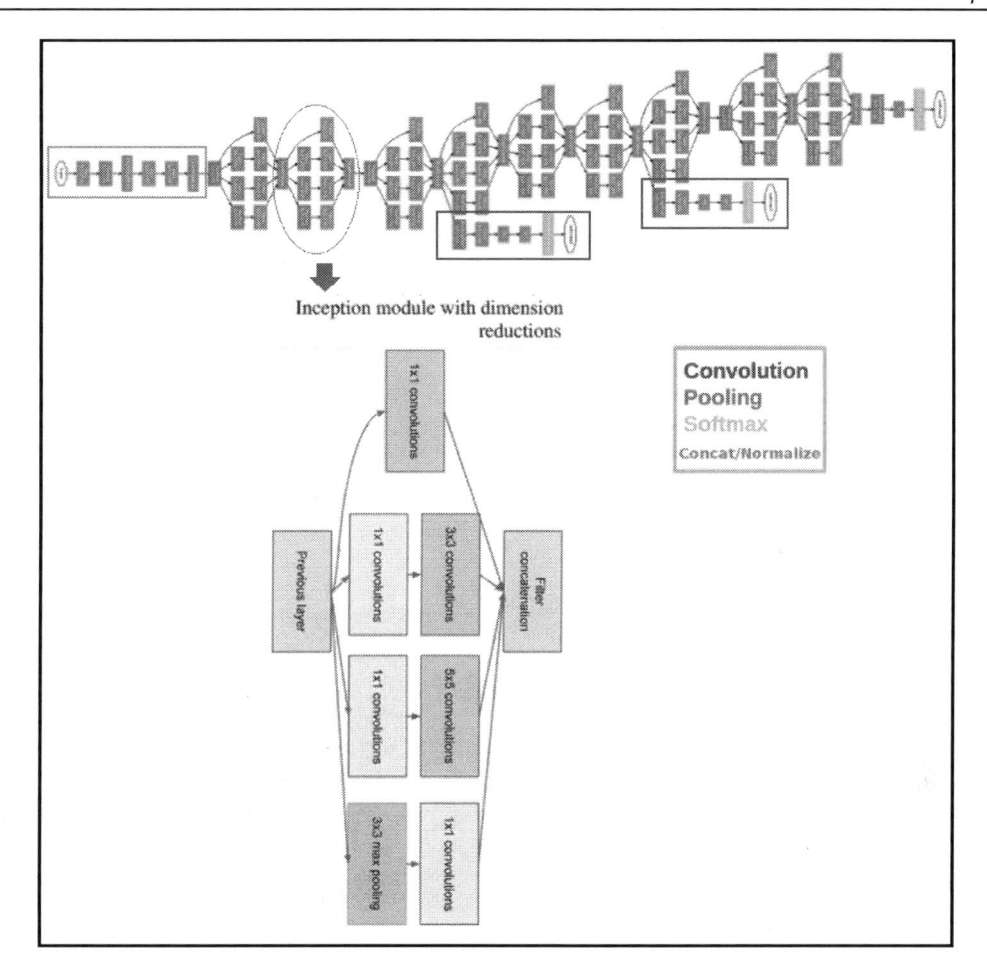

Convolution
Pooling
Softmax
Concat/Normalize

Several versions of the inception net have been introduced to the time of writing (V2, 3, and 4) that are extensions over the previous architecture. Keras provides Inception-v3 models that can be trained from scratch or a pre-trained version (with the weights obtained by training on ImageNet) can be used.

ResNet

Simply stacking the layers won't necessarily increase the network depth. They are difficult to train because of the **vanishing gradient problem** as well. It is an issue wherein the gradient is backpropagated to previous layers and if this happens repeatedly, the gradient may become infinitely small. Hence, as we get deeper, performance gets heavily affected.

Deep Learning in Image Processing - Image Classification

ResNet stands for **Residual Network** and it introduces shortcuts in the network, which we know by the name of identity shortcut connections. Shortcut connections abide by their name and do the job of skipping one or more layers, hence preventing the stacked layers from degrading performance. The identity layers that are stacked do nothing other than simply stacking identity mappings on the current network. The other architectures can then perform at their expected levels, meaning the deeper models will not produce a training error rate higher than its shallower counterparts.

Here is an example of a 34-layer plain versus residual network:

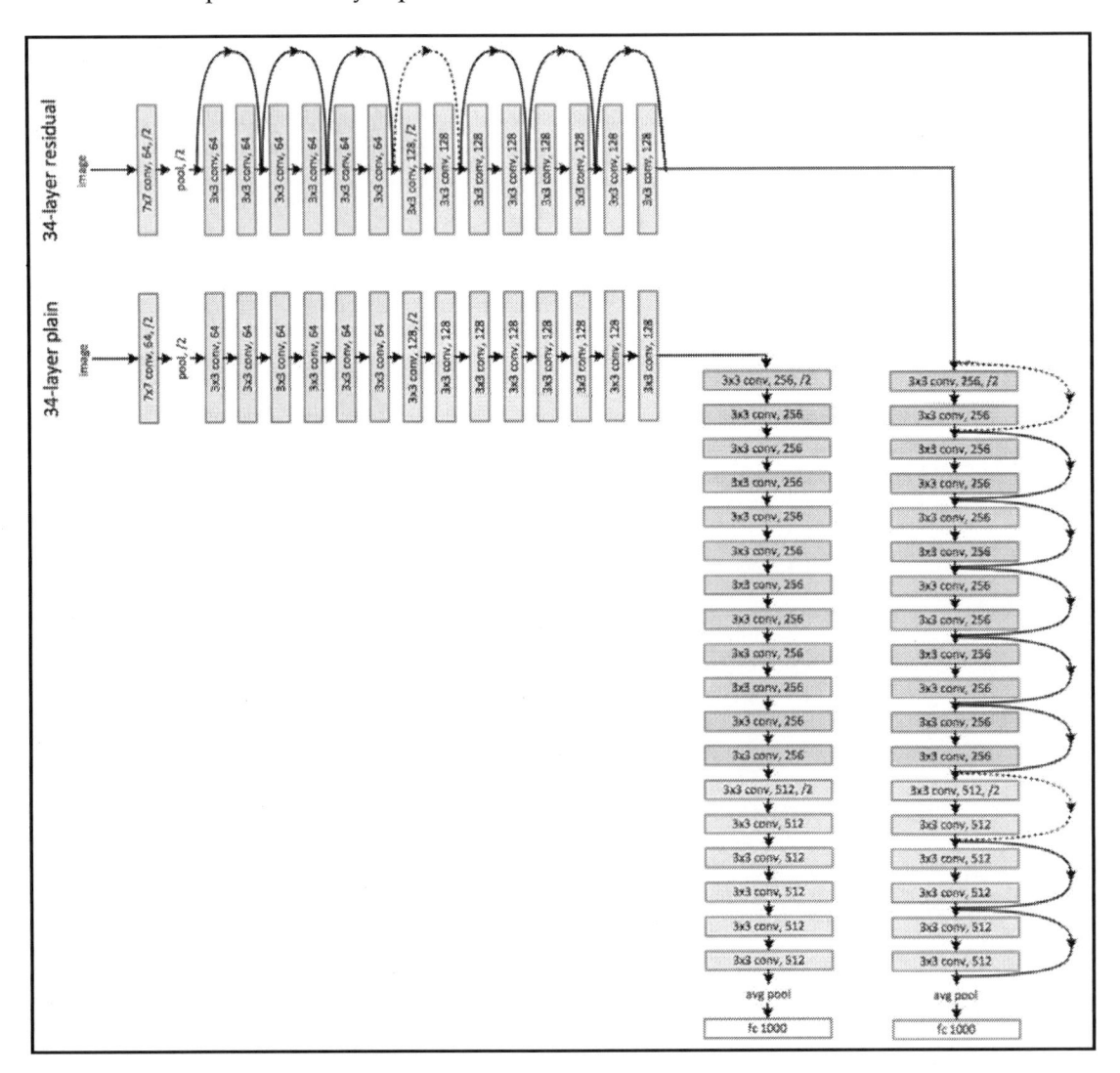

Keras provides the ResNet50 model that can be trained from scratch or a pre-trained network can be loaded.

There are a few more architectures, such as AlexNet and MobileNet, that the reader is encouraged to explore (for example, from here: `https://medium.com/@sidereal/cnns-architectures-lenet-alexnet-vgg-googlenet-resnet-and-more-666091488df5`).

Summary

In this chapter, the recent advances in image processing with deep learning models were introduced. We started by discussing the basic concepts of deep learning, how it's different from traditional ML, and why we need it. Then CNNs were introduced as deep neural networks designed particularly to solve complex image processing and computer vision tasks. The CNN architecture with convolutional, pooling, and FC layers were discussed. Next, we introduced TensorFlow and Keras, two popular deep learning libraries in Python. We showed how test accuracy on the MNIST dataset for handwritten digits classification can be increased with CNNs, then the same using FC layers only. Finally, we discussed a few popular networks such as VGG-16/19, GoogleNet, and ResNet. Kera's VGG-16 model was trained on Kaggle's Dogs vs. Cats competition images and we showed how it performs on the validation image dataset with decent accuracy.

In the next chapter, we'll discuss how to solve more complex image processing tasks (for example, object detection, segmentation, and style transfer) with deep learning models and how to use transfer learning to save training time.

Questions

1. For classification of the `mnist` dataset using an FC layer with Keras, write a Python code fragment to visualize the output layer (what the neural network sees).
2. For classification of the `mnist` dataset using the neural network with FC layers only and with the CNN with Keras, we have directly used the test dataset for evaluating the model while training it. Set aside a few thousand images from training images and create a validation dataset and train the model on the remaining images. Use the validation dataset to evaluate the model while training. At the end of training, use the model learned to predict the labels of the test dataset and evaluate the accuracy of the model. Does it increase?

3. Use VGG-16/19, Resnet-50, and Inception V3 models (from Keras) to train (from scratch) on the `mnist` training images. What is the maximum accuracy you get on the test images?

Further reading

- https://arxiv.org/pdf/1409.4842v1.pdf
- http://cs231n.github.io/convolutional-networks/
- https://arxiv.org/abs/1512.03385.pdf
- https://arxiv.org/pdf/1605.07678.pdf
- https://www.cs.toronto.edu/~frossard/post/vgg16/
- https://pythonprogramming.net/convolutional-neural-network-kats-vs-dogs-machine-learning-tutorial/

11
Deep Learning in Image Processing - Object Detection, and more

In this chapter, we'll continue our discussion on the recent advances in image processing with deep learning. We will be dealing with a few problems in particular, and shall try to solve them using deep learning with deep CNNs.

We will look at the object detection problem, understanding the basic concepts involved, then examine how to write code to solve the problem with object proposals and a **You Only Look On (YOLO)** v2 pre-trained deep neural network in Keras. You will be provided with resources that will help you in training the YOLO net.

Get ready to learn about transfer learning and solve deep segmentation problems using the `DeepLab` library. You will learn to specify which layers to train while training a deep learning model, and demonstrate a custom image classification problem by only learning the weights for the FC layers of a VGG16 network.

You may be surprised to learn how deep learning can be used in art generation, with deep style transfer models, where the content of one image and the style of another image can be used to obtain a final image.

The topics to be covered in this chapter are the following:

- A fully convolutional model for detecting objects: YOLO (v2)
- Deep segmentation with DeepLab (v3)
- Transfer learning: what is it and when to use it
- Deep style transfer with cv2 using a pretrained torch-based deep learning model

Introducing YOLO v2

YOLO, is a very popular and fully conventional algorithm that is used for detecting images. It gives a very high accuracy rate compared to other algorithms, and also runs in real time. As the name suggests, this algorithm looks only once at an image. This means that this algorithm requires only one forward propagation pass to make accurate predictions.

In this section, we will detect objects in images with a **fully convolutional network** (**FCN**) deep learning model. Given an image with some objects (for example, animals, cars, and so on), the goal is to detect objects in those images using a pre-trained YOLO model, with bounding boxes.

Many of the ideas are from the two original YOLO papers, available at `https://arxiv.org/abs/1506.02640` and `https://arxiv.org/abs/1612.08242`. But before diving into the YOLO model, let's first understand some prerequisite fundamental concepts.

Classifying and localizing images and detecting objects

Let's first understand the concepts
regarding classification, localization, detection, and object detection problems, how they can be transformed into supervised machine learning problems, and subsequently, how they can be solved using a deep convolution neural network.

Refer to the following diagram:

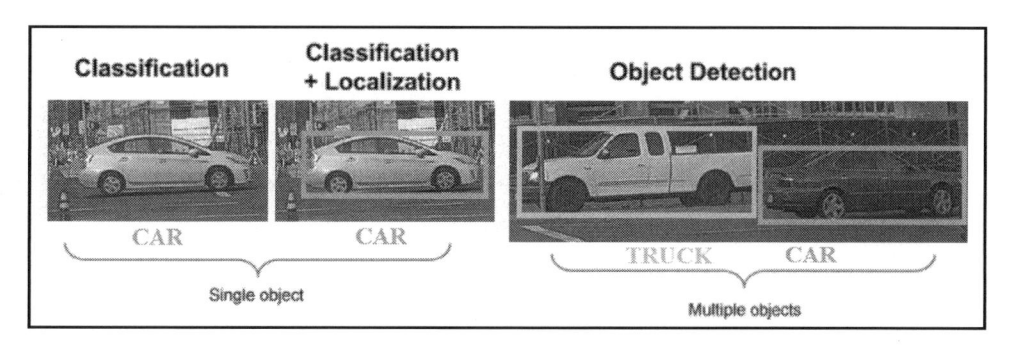

Here's what we can infer:

- In the image classification problem, there is generally a (big) central object in an image and we have to recognize the object by assigning a correct label to the image.
- Image classification with localization aims to find the location of an object in an image by not only assigning a label (*class*) the image (for example, a binary classification problem: whether there is a *car* in an image or not), but also finding a bounding box around the object, if there is one to be found.
- Detection goes a level further by aiming to identify multiple instances of same/different types of objects, by localizing all the objects (all instances) by marking their locations (the localization problem usually tries to find a single object location).
- The localization problem can be converted to a supervised machine learning multi-class classification and a regression problem in the following way: in addition to the class labels of the objects to be identified (with classification), the output vector corresponding to an input training image must also contain the location (bounding box coordinates relative to image size, with regression) of the object.

- A typical output data vector will contain eight entries for a 4-class classification. As shown in the following diagram, the first entry will correspond to whether or not an object of any from the three classes of objects (except the background). If one is present in an image, the next four entries will define the bounding box containing the object, followed by three binary values for the three class labels indicating the class of the object. If none of the objects are present, the first entry will be 0 and the others will be ignored:

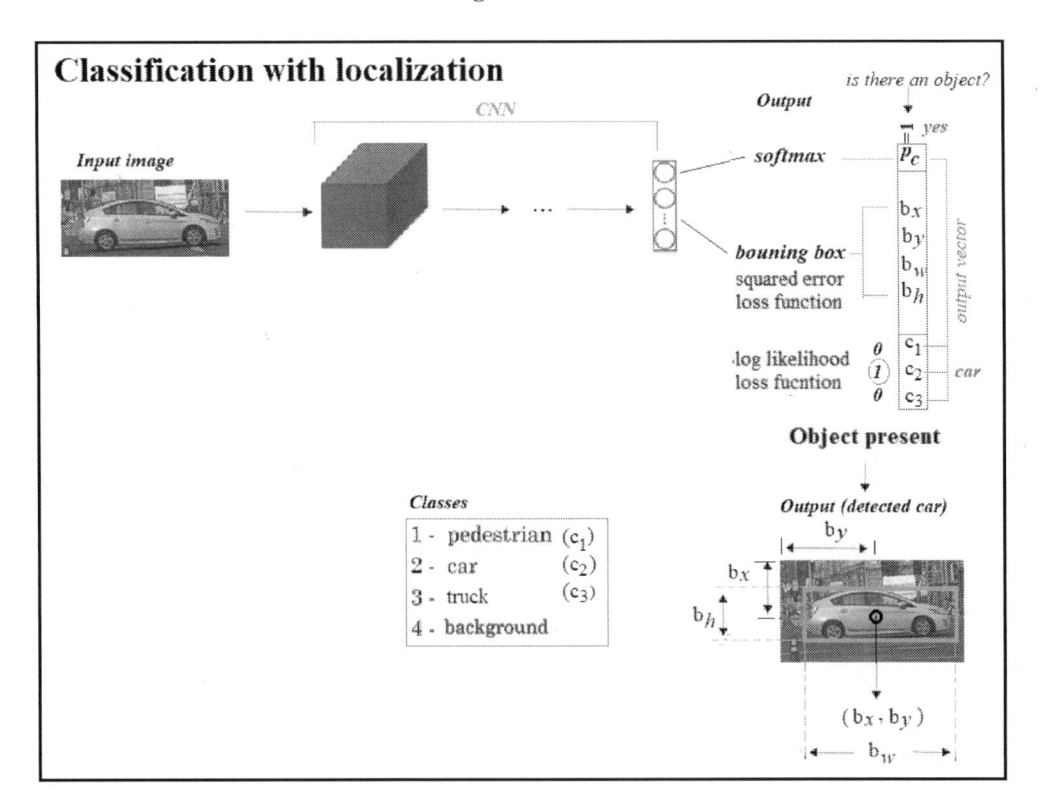

Proposing and detecting objects using CNNs

Moving from localization to detection, we can proceed in two steps, as shown in the following screenshot: first use small tightly cropped images to train a convolution neural net for image classification, and then use sliding windows of different window sizes (smaller to larger) to classify a test image within that window using the convnet learnt and run the windows sequentially through the entire image, but it's infeasibly slow computationally.

However, as shown in the next figure, the convolutional implementation of the sliding windows by replacing the fully connected layers with 1 × 1 filters makes it possible to simultaneously classify the image-subset inside all possible sliding windows parallelly, making it much more efficient computationally.

Using YOLO v2

The convolutional sliding windows, although computationally much more efficient, still has the problem of detecting bounding boxes accurately, since the boxes don't align with the sliding windows and the object shapes also tend to be different. The YOLO algorithm overcomes this limitation by dividing a training image into grids and assigning an object to a grid if and only if the center of the object falls inside the grid. This way, each object in a training image can get assigned to exactly one grid and then the corresponding bounding box is represented by the coordinates relative to the grid.

In the test images, multiple adjacent grids may think that an object actually belongs to them. In order to resolve this, the **intersection of union** (**iou**) measure is used to find the maximum overlap and the non-maximum-suppression algorithm is used to discard all the other bounding boxes with low-confidence of containing an object, keeping the one with the highest confidence among the competing ones, and discarding the others. Still, there is the problem of multiple objects falling in the same grid. Multiple anchor boxes (of different shapes) are used to resolve the problem, each anchor box of a particular shape being likely to eventually detect an object of a particular shape.

If we want YOLO to recognize 80 classes that we have, we will represent the class label c as an 80-dimensional vector, which means having 80 numbers out of these 80 numbers, one of the components is 0, whereas others are 1.

To reduce the computational expense in training the YOLO model, we will be using pre-trained weights. For more detail about the model, refer to the links provided at the end of the chapter.

Using a pre-trained YOLO model for object detection

The following are the steps that you must follow to be able to use the pre-trained model:

1. Clone this repository: go to `https://github.com/allanzelener/YAD2K/`, right-click on clone or download, and select the path where you want to download the ZIP. Then unzip the compressed file to `YAD2K-master` folder.

2. Download the weights and cfg file from `https://pjreddie.com/darknet/yolo/` by clicking on the yellow links on the page, marked by red boxes here:

Performance on the COCO Dataset

Model	Train	Test	mAP	FLOPS	FPS	Cfg	Weights
SSD300	COCO trainval	test-dev	41.2	-	46		link
SSD500	COCO trainval	test-dev	46.5	-	19		link
YOLOv2 608x608	COCO trainval	test-dev	48.1	62.94 Bn	40	cfg	weights

3. Save the `yolov2.cfg` and the `yolov2.weights` files downloaded inside the `YAD2K-master` folder.

4. Go inside the `YAD2K-master` folder, open a command prompt (you need to have Python3 installed and in path) and run the following command:

   `python yad2k.py yolov2.cfg yolov2.weights yolo/yolo.h5`

   If executed successfully, it will create two files inside the `YAD2K-master/model_data` folder, namely, `yolo.h5` and `yolo.anchors`.

5. Now go to the folder from where you want to run your code. Create a folder named `yolo` here and copy the four files (`coco_classes`, `pascal_classes`, `yolo.h5`, `yolo.anchors`) from the `YAD2K-master/model_data` folder to the `yolo` folder you created.

6. Copy the `yad2k` folder from the `YAD2K-master` folder to the current path. Your current path should have these two folders, `yad2k` and `yolo`, now.

7. Create a new folder named `images` in the current path and put your input images here.

8. Create another new empty folder named `output` in the current path. The YOLO model will save the output images (with objects detected) here.

9. Create a `.py` script in the current path and copy-paste the following code and run (or run in from Jupyter Notebook cell from the current path).

10. Double-check that the folder structure is exactly as shown in the following screenshot, with the required files present, before running the code:

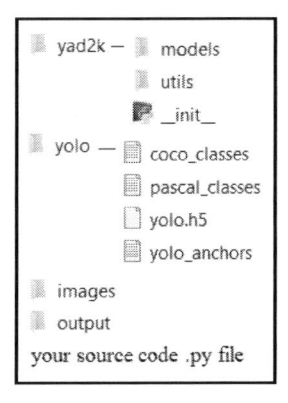

Let's first load all the required libraries, as shown in this code block:

```
import os
from matplotlib.pyplot import imshow
import scipy.io
import scipy.misc
import numpy as np
from PIL import Image
from keras import backend as K
from keras.models import load_model
# The following functions from the yad2k library will be used
# Note: it assumed that you have the yad2k folder in your current path, otherwise it will not work!
from yad2k.models.keras_yolo import yolo_head, yolo_eval
import colorsys
import imghdr
import os
import random
from keras import backend as K
import numpy as np
from PIL import Image, ImageDraw, ImageFont
```

Deep Learning in Image Processing - Object Detection, and more

Now implement a few functions to read the `classes` and `anchor` files, generate the color of the boxes, and scale the boxes predicted by YOLO:

```python
def read_classes(classes_path):
    with open(classes_path) as f:
        class_names = f.readlines()
    class_names = [c.strip() for c in class_names]
    return class_names

def read_anchors(anchors_path):
    with open(anchors_path) as f:
        anchors = f.readline()
        anchors = [float(x) for x in anchors.split(',')]
        anchors = np.array(anchors).reshape(-1, 2)
    return anchors

def generate_colors(class_names):
    hsv_tuples = [(x / len(class_names), 1., 1.) for x in range(len(class_names))]
    colors = list(map(lambda x: colorsys.hsv_to_rgb(*x), hsv_tuples))
    colors = list(map(lambda x: (int(x[0] * 255), int(x[1] * 255), int(x[2] * 255)), colors))
    random.seed(10101)  # Fixed seed for consistent colors across runs.
    random.shuffle(colors)  # Shuffle colors to decorrelate adjacent classes.
    random.seed(None)  # Reset seed to default.
    return colors

def scale_boxes(boxes, image_shape):
    """ scales the predicted boxes in order to be drawable on the image"""
    height = image_shape[0]
    width = image_shape[1]
    image_dims = K.stack([height, width, height, width])
    image_dims = K.reshape(image_dims, [1, 4])
    boxes = boxes * image_dims
    return boxes
```

In the following code snippet, we'll implement a couple of functions to preprocess an image and draw the boxes obtained from YOLO to detect the objects present in the image:

```python
def preprocess_image(img_path, model_image_size):
    image_type = imghdr.what(img_path)
    image = Image.open(img_path)
    resized_image = image.resize(tuple(reversed(model_image_size)), Image.BICUBIC)
    image_data = np.array(resized_image, dtype='float32')
    image_data /= 255.
    image_data = np.expand_dims(image_data, 0)  # Add batch dimension.
```

```
    return image, image_data

def draw_boxes(image, out_scores, out_boxes, out_classes, class_names,
colors):
    font = ImageFont.truetype(font='font/FiraMono-
Medium.otf',size=np.floor(3e-2 * image.size[1] + 0.5).astype('int32'))
    thickness = (image.size[0] + image.size[1]) // 300

    for i, c in reversed(list(enumerate(out_classes))):
        predicted_class = class_names[c]
        box = out_boxes[i]
        score = out_scores[i]
        label = '{} {:.2f}'.format(predicted_class, score)
        draw = ImageDraw.Draw(image)
        label_size = draw.textsize(label, font)
        top, left, bottom, right = box
        top = max(0, np.floor(top + 0.5).astype('int32'))
        left = max(0, np.floor(left + 0.5).astype('int32'))
        bottom = min(image.size[1], np.floor(bottom | 0.5).astype('int32'))
        right = min(image.size[0], np.floor(right + 0.5).astype('int32'))
        print(label, (left, top), (right, bottom))
        if top - label_size[1] >= 0:
            text_origin = np.array([left, top - label_size[1]])
        else:
            text_origin = np.array([left, top + 1])
        # My kingdom for a good redistributable image drawing library.
        for i in range(thickness):
            draw.rectangle([left + i, top + i, right - i, bottom - i],
outline=colors[c])
        draw.rectangle([tuple(text_origin), tuple(text_origin +
label_size)], fill=colors[c])
        draw.text(text_origin, label, fill=(0, 0, 0), font=font)
        del draw
```

Let's now load the input image, the classes file, and the anchors using our functions, then load the YOLO pretrained model and print the model summary using the next code block:

```
# provide the name of the image that you saved in the images folder to be
fed through the network
input_image_name = "giraffe_zebra.jpg"
input_image = Image.open("images/" + input_image_name)
width, height = input_image.size
width = np.array(width, dtype=float)
height = np.array(height, dtype=float)
image_shape = (height, width)
#Loading the classes and the anchor boxes that are copied to the yolo
folder
class_names = read_classes("yolo/coco_classes.txt")
```

```
anchors = read_anchors("yolo/yolo_anchors.txt")
#Load the pretrained model
yolo_model = load_model("yolo/yolo.h5")
#Print the summery of the model
yolo_model.summary()
#
#Layer (type) Output Shape Param # Connected to
#================================================================================
#input_1 (InputLayer) (None, 608, 608, 3) 0
#
#conv2d_1 (Conv2D) (None, 608, 608, 32) 864 input_1[0][0]
#
#batch_normalization_1 (BatchNor (None, 608, 608, 32) 128 conv2d_1[0][0]
#
#leaky_re_lu_1 (LeakyReLU) (None, 608, 608, 32) 0 batch_normalization_1[0][0]
#
#max_pooling2d_1 (MaxPooling2D) (Nonc, 304, 304, 32) 0 leaky_re_lu_1[0][0]
#
#conv2d_2 (Conv2D) (None, 304, 304, 64) 18432 max_pooling2d_1[0][0]
#
#batch_normalization_2 (BatchNor (None, 304, 304, 64) 256 conv2d_2[0][0]
#
#leaky_re_lu_2 (LeakyReLU) (None, 304, 304, 64) 0 batch_normalization_2[0][0]
#
#max_pooling2d_2 (MaxPooling2D) (None, 152, 152, 64) 0 leaky_re_lu_2[0][0]
#
#... ... ...
#
#concatenate_1 (Concatenate) (None, 19, 19, 1280) 0 space_to_depth_x2[0][0]
# leaky_re_lu_20[0][0]
#
```

```
#conv2d_22 (Conv2D)          (None, 19, 19, 1024) 11796480 concatenate_1[0][0]
#
#_____
#batch_normalization_22 (BatchNo (None, 19, 19, 1024) 4096 conv2d_22[0][0]
#
#_____
#leaky_re_lu_22 (LeakyReLU)  (None, 19, 19, 1024) 0
batch_normalization_22[0][0]
#
#_____
#conv2d_23 (Conv2D)          (None, 19, 19, 425) 435625 leaky_re_lu_22[0][0]
#=================================================================
#Total params: 50,983,561
#Trainable params: 50,962,889
#Non-trainable params: 20,672
```

Finally, the next code block extracts the bounding boxes from the YOLO prediction output and draws the boxes around the objects found with right labels, scores, and colors:

```
# convert final layer features to bounding box parameters
yolo_outputs = yolo_head(yolo_model.output, anchors, len(class_names))
#Now yolo_eval function selects the best boxes using filtering and non-max
suppression techniques.
# If you want to dive in more to see how this works, refer keras_yolo.py
file in yad2k/models
boxes, scores, classes = yolo_eval(yolo_outputs, image_shape)
# Initiate a session
sess = K.get_session()
#Preprocess the input image before feeding into the convolutional network
image, image_data = preprocess_image("images/" + input_image_name,
model_image_size = (608, 608))
#Run the session
out_scores, out_boxes, out_classes = sess.run([scores, boxes,
classes],feed_dict={yolo_model.input:image_data,K.learning_phase(): 0})
#Print the results
print('Found {} boxes for {}'.format(len(out_boxes), input_image_name))
#Found 5 boxes for giraffe_zebra.jpg
#zebra 0.83 (16, 325) (126, 477)
#giraffe 0.89 (56, 175) (272, 457)
#zebra 0.91 (370, 326) (583, 472)
#giraffe 0.94 (388, 119) (554, 415)
#giraffe 0.95 (205, 111) (388, 463)
#Produce the colors for the bounding boxs
colors = generate_colors(class_names)
#Draw the bounding boxes
```

```
draw_boxes(image, out_scores, out_boxes, out_classes, class_names, colors)
#Apply the predicted bounding boxes to the image and save it
image.save(os.path.join("output", input_image_name), quality=90)
output_image = scipy.misc.imread(os.path.join("output", input_image_name))
imshow(output_image)
```

The following image shows the output obtained by running the preceding code. The objects, giraffes and zebras, marked with bounding boxes were predicted using the YOLO model. The numbers above each bounding box is the probability score from the YOLO model:

Likewise, let's try using the following photo as input:

We'll get the following objects (cars, bus, person, umbrella) detected instead:

Deep semantic segmentation with DeepLab V3+

In this section, we'll discuss how to use a deep learning FCN to perform semantic segmentation of an image. Before diving into further details, let's clear the basic concepts.

Semantic segmentation

Semantic segmentation refers to an understanding of an image at pixel level; that is, when we want to assign each pixel in the image an object class (a semantic label). It is a natural step in the progression from coarse to fine inference. It achieves fine-grained inference by making dense predictions that infer labels for every pixel so that each pixel is labeled with the class of its enclosing object or region.

DeepLab V3+

DeepLab presents an architecture for controlling signal decimation and learning multi-scale contextual features. DeepLab uses an ResNet-50 model, pre-trained on the ImageNet dataset, as its main feature extractor network. However, it proposes a new residual block for multi-scale feature learning, as shown in the following diagram. Instead of regular convolutions, the last ResNet block uses atrous convolutions. Also, each convolution (within this new block) uses different dilation rates to capture multi-scale context. Additionally, on top of this new block, it uses **Atrous Spatial Pyramid Pooling** (**ASPP**). ASPP uses dilated convolutions with different rates as an attempt of classifying regions of an arbitrary scale. Hence, the DeepLab v3+ architecture contains three main components:

1. The ResNet architecture
2. Atrous convolutions
3. Atrous Spatial Pyramid Pooling

DeepLab v3 architecture

The image shows the parallel modules with atrous convolution:

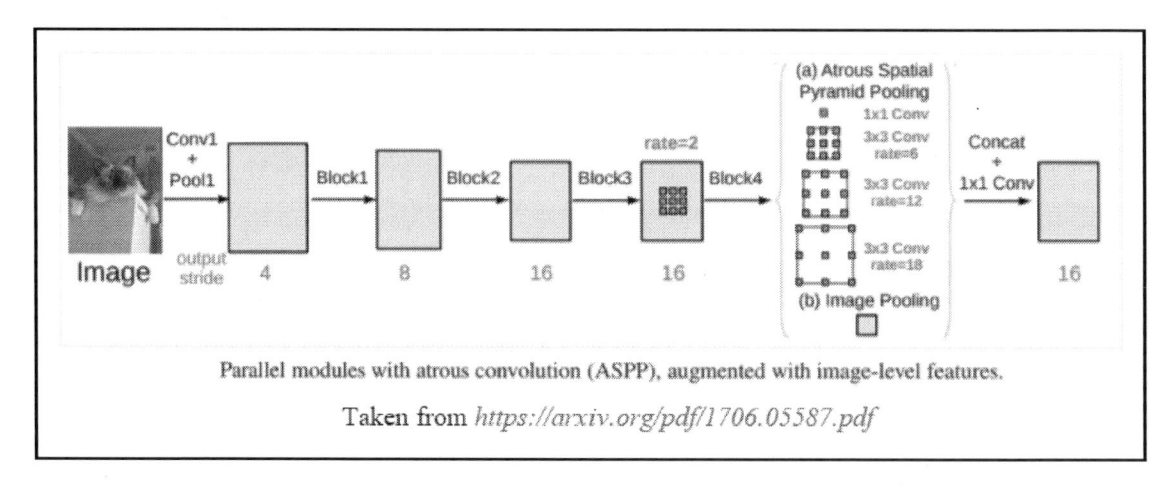

Parallel modules with atrous convolution (ASPP), augmented with image-level features.
Taken from https://arxiv.org/pdf/1706.05587.pdf

With DeepLab-v3+, the DeepLab-v3 model is extended by adding a simple, yet effective, decoder module to refine the segmentation results, especially along object boundaries. The depth-wise separable convolution is applied to both atrous spatial pyramid pooling and decoder modules, resulting in a faster and stronger encoder-decoder network for semantic segmentation. The architecture is shown in the following diagram:

Deeplab V3+ architecture

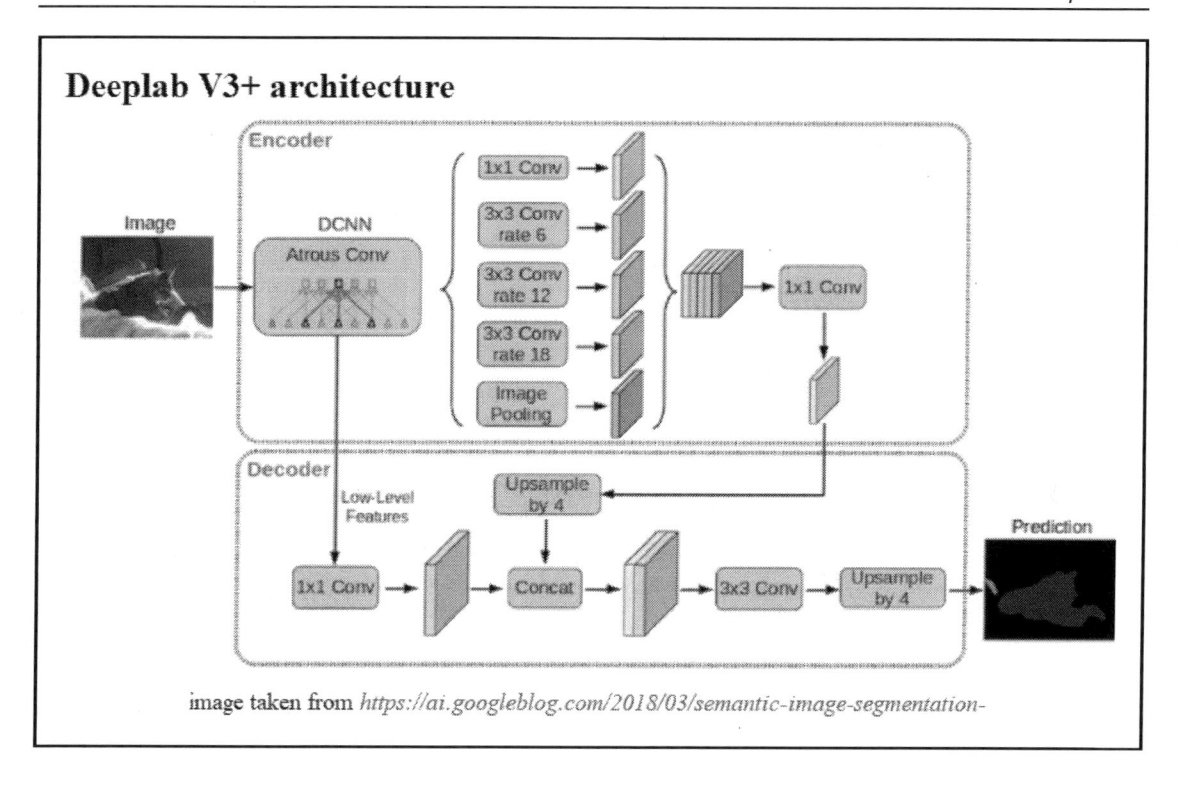

image taken from https://ai.googleblog.com/2018/03/semantic-image-segmentation-

Steps you must follow to use DeepLab V3+ model for semantic segmentation

Here are the steps that must be followed to be able to use the model to segment an image:

1. First, clone or download the repository from `https://github.com/bonlime/keras-deeplab-v3-plus`.
2. Extract the `ZIP` file downloaded to the `keras-deeplab-v3-plus-master` folder.
3. Navigate to the `keras-deeplab-v3-plus-master` folder; the following code needs to be run from inside the directory.

Before running the following code block, create an input folder and an empty output folder. Save your images you want to segment inside the input folder. The following code block shows how to use the Deeplabv3+ in Python to do semantic segmentation:

```python
% matplotlib inline
#import os
#os.chdir('keras-deeplab-v3-plus-master') # go to keras-deeplab-v3-plus-master

from matplotlib import pyplot as pylab
import cv2 # used for resize
import numpy as np
from model import Deeplabv3

deeplab_model = Deeplabv3()
pathIn = '../input' # path for the input image
pathOut = '../output' # output path for the segmented image
img = pylab.imread(pathIn + "/cycle.jpg")
w, h, _ = img.shape
ratio = 512. / np.max([w,h])
resized = cv2.resize(img,(int(ratio*h),int(ratio*w)))
resized = resized / 127.5 - 1.
pad_x = int(512 - resized.shape[0])
resized2 = np.pad(resized,((0,pad_x),(0,0),(0,0)),mode='constant')
res = deeplab_model.predict(np.expand_dims(resized2,0))
labels = np.argmax(res.squeeze(),-1)
pylab.imshow(labels[:-pad_x], cmap='inferno'), pylab.axis('off'),
pylab.colorbar()
pylab.savefig(pathOut + "\\segmented.jpg", bbox_inches='tight',
pad_inches=0)
pylab.close()
```

The following photo is the input image fed to the DeepLab v3+ model:

The following screenshot shows the output created after semantic segmentation of the previous photo, obtained by running the preceding code:

You can obtain the labels of the segments and create an overlay with yet another input image, as shown in the following diagram:

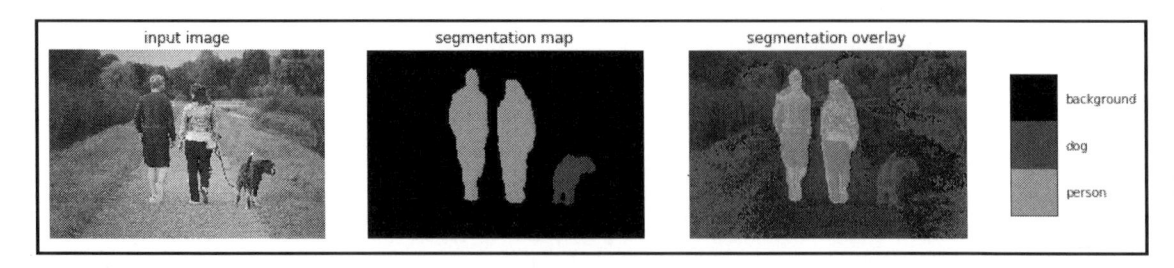

Transfer learning – what it is, and when to use it

Transfer learning is a deep learning strategy that reuses knowledge gained from solving one problem by applying it to a different, but related, problem. For example, let's say we have three types of flowers, namely, a rose, a sunflower, and a tulip. We can use the standard pre-trained models, such as VGG16/19, ResNet50, or InceptionV3 models (pre-trained on ImageNet with 1000 output classes, which can be found at `https://gist.github.com/yrevar/942d3a0ac09ec9e5eb3a`) to classify the flower images, but our model wouldn't be able to correctly identify them because these flower categories were not learned by the models. In other words, they are classes that the model is not aware of.

The following image shows how the flower images are classified wrongly by the pre-trained VGG16 model (the code is left to the reader as an exercise):

Chapter 11

Transfer learning with Keras

Training of pre-trained models is done on many comprehensive image classification problems. The convolutional layers act as a feature extractor, and the **fully connected** (**FC**) layers act as classifiers, as shown in the following diagram, in the context of cat vs. dog image classification with a conv net:

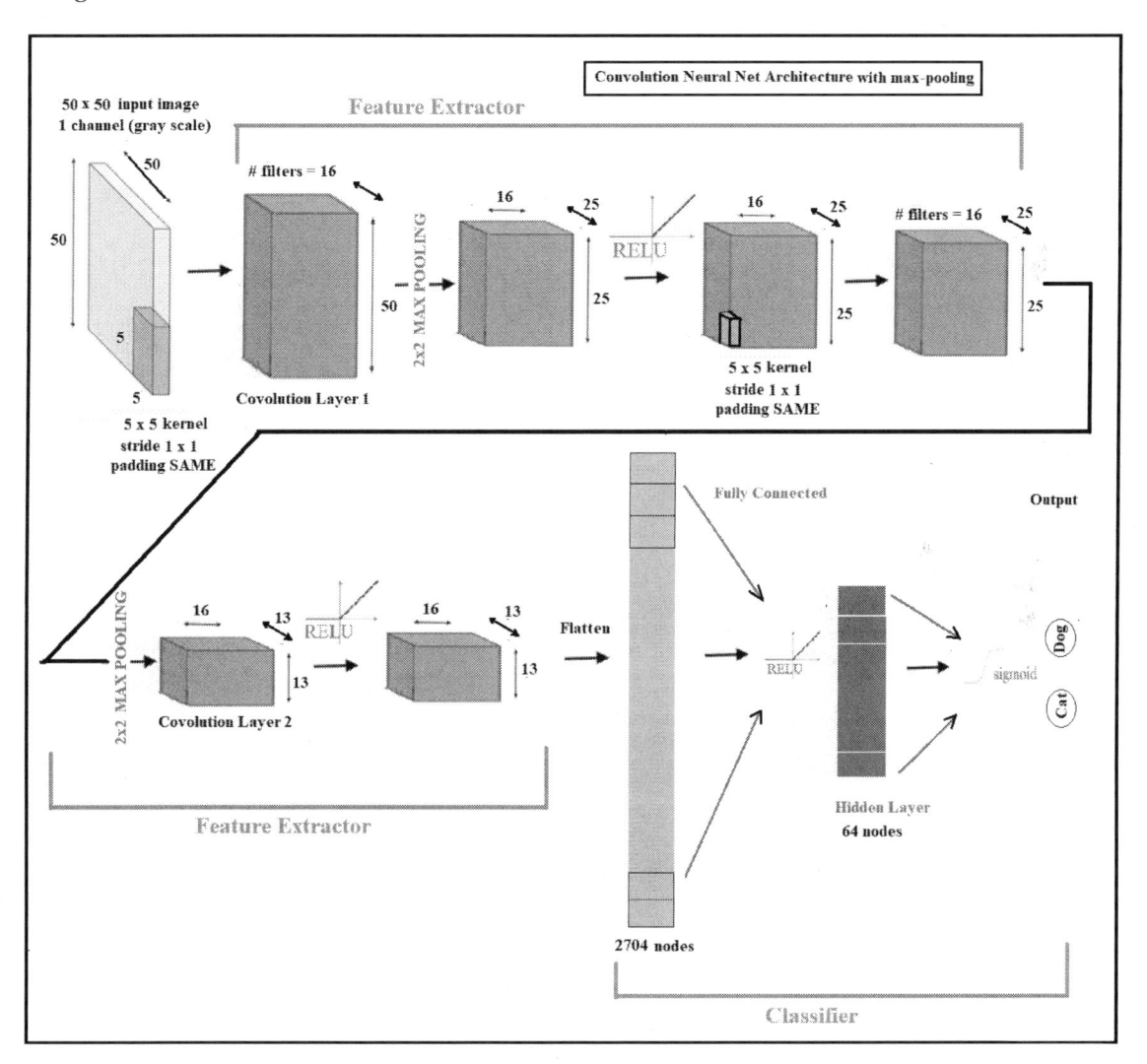

Since the standard models, such as VGG-16/19, are quite large and are trained on many images, they are capable of learning many different features for different classes. We can simply reuse the convolutional layers as a feature extractor that learns low and high level image features, and train only the FC layer weights (parameters). This is what transfer learning is.

We can use transfer learning when we have a training set that is concise, and the problem that we are dealing with is the same as that on which the pre-trained model was trained. We can tweak the convolutional layers if we have ample data, and learn all the model parameters from scratch so that we can train the models to learn more robust features relevant to our problem.

Now, let's use transfer learning to classify rose, sunflower and tulip flower images. These images are obtained from the TensorFlow sample image dataset, available at `http://download.tensorflow.org/example_images/flower_photos.tgz`. Let's use 550 images for each of the three classes, making a total of 1,650 images, which is a small number of images and the right place to use transfer learning. We'll use 500 images from each class for training, reserving the remaining 50 images from each class for validation. Also, let's create a folder called `flower_photos`, with two sub-folders, `train` and `valid`, inside it, and save our training and validation images inside those folders, respectively. The folder structure should look such as the following:

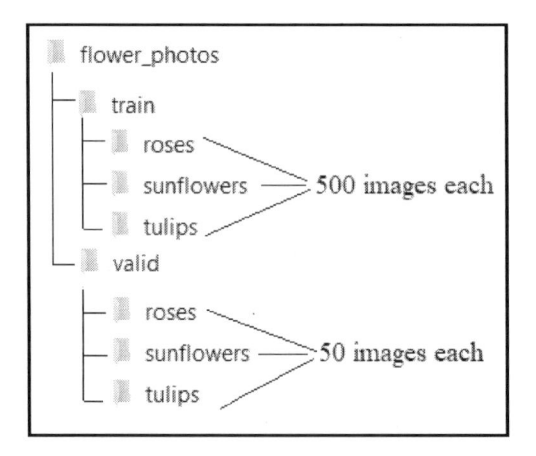

```
flower_photos
├── train
│   ├── roses
│   ├── sunflowers  ──→ 500 images each
│   └── tulips
└── valid
    ├── roses
    ├── sunflowers  ──→ 50 images each
    └── tulips
```

We will first load the weights of the convolution layers only for the pre-trained VGG16 model (with `include_top=False`, let's not load the last two FC layers), which will act as our classifier. Note that the last layer has a shape of 7 x 7 x 512.

We will use the `ImageDataGenerator` class to load the images, and the `flow_from_directory()` function to generate batches of images and labels. We will also use `model.predict()` function to pass the image through the network, giving us a 7 x 7 x 512 dimensional tensor and subsequently reshape the tensor into a vector. We will find the `validation_features` in the same way.

That being said, let's implement transfer learning with Keras to train the VGG16 model partially—that is, it will just learn the weights for the FC layers only on the training images we have, and then use it to predict the classes:

```
from keras.applications import VGG16
from keras.preprocessing.image import ImageDataGenerator
from keras import models, layers, optimizers
from keras.preprocessing.image import load_img

# train only the top FC layers of VGG16, use weights learnt with ImageNet
for the convolution layers
vgg_model = VGG16(weights='imagenet', include_top=False, input_shape=(224, 224, 3))
# the directory flower_photos is assumed to be on the current path
train_dir = './flower_photos/train'
validation_dir = './flower_photos/valid'

n_train = 500*3
n_val = 50*3
datagen = ImageDataGenerator(rescale=1./255)
batch_size = 25

train_features = np.zeros(shape=(n_train, 7, 7, 512))
train_labels = np.zeros(shape=(n_train,3))
train_generator = datagen.flow_from_directory(train_dir, target_size=(224, 224),
 batch_size=batch_size, class_mode='categorical', shuffle=True)
i = 0
for inputs_batch, labels_batch in train_generator:
 features_batch = vgg_model.predict(inputs_batch)
 train_features[i * batch_size : (i + 1) * batch_size] = features_batch
 train_labels[i * batch_size : (i + 1) * batch_size] = labels_batch
 i += 1
 if i * batch_size >= n_train: break
train_features = np.reshape(train_features, (n_train, 7 * 7 * 512))
```

```
validation_features = np.zeros(shape=(n_val, 7, 7, 512))
validation_labels = np.zeros(shape=(n_val,3))
validation_generator = datagen.flow_from_directory(validation_dir,
target_size=(224, 224),
 batch_size=batch_size, class_mode='categorical', shuffle=False)
i = 0
for inputs_batch, labels_batch in validation_generator:
 features_batch = vgg_model.predict(inputs_batch)
 validation_features[i * batch_size : (i + 1) * batch_size] =
features_batch
 validation_labels[i * batch_size : (i + 1) * batch_size] = labels_batch
 i += 1
 if i * batch_size >= n_val: break
validation_features = np.reshape(validation_features, (n_val, 7 * 7 * 512))
```

Next, create your own model with a simple feed-forward network with a softmax output layer that has three classes. Next, we have to train the model. As you have already seen, training a network in Keras is as simple as calling the `model.fit()` function. In order to check the performance of the model, let's visualize which images are wrongly classified:

```
# now learn the FC layer parameters by training with the images we have
model = models.Sequential()
model.add(layers.Dense(512, activation='relu', input_dim=7 * 7 * 512))
model.add(BatchNormalization())
model.add(layers.Dropout(0.5))
model.add(layers.Dense(3, activation='softmax'))
model.compile(optimizer=optimizers.Adam(lr=1e-5),
loss='categorical_crossentropy', metrics=['acc'])
history = model.fit(train_features, train_labels, epochs=20,
batch_size=batch_size,
 validation_data=(validation_features,validation_labels))

filenames = validation_generator.filenames
ground_truth = validation_generator.classes
label2index = validation_generator.class_indices
# Getting the mapping from class index to class label
idx2label = dict((v,k) for k,v in label2index.items())
predictions = model.predict_classes(validation_features)
prob = model.predict(validation_features)
errors = np.where(predictions != ground_truth)[0]
print("No of errors = {}/{}".format(len(errors),n_val))
# No of errors = 13/150
pylab.figure(figsize=(20,12))
for i in range(len(errors)):
    pred_class = np.argmax(prob[errors[i]])
    pred_label = idx2label[pred_class]
    original =
load_img('{}/{}'.format(validation_dir,filenames[errors[i]]))
```

```
    pylab.subplot(3,5,i+1), pylab.imshow(original), pylab.axis('off')
    pylab.title('Original
label:{}\nPrediction:{}\nconfidence:{:.3f}'.format(
        filenames[errors[i]].split('\\')[0], pred_label,
prob[errors[i]][pred_class]), size=15)
pylab.show()
```

The following diagram shows the output of the preceding code. As we can see, there are 13 images in the validation dataset out of 150 images that are classified wrongly by the transfer learning model, shown here:

The flower images we used initially (that were part of the validation dataset, not used for training the transfer learning model) are classified correctly now, as shown in the following photos (the code is again left as an exercise for the reader):

Neural style transfers with cv2 using a pre-trained torch model

In this section, we will discuss how to use deep learning to implement a **neural style transfer** (**NST**). You will be surprised at the kind of artistic images we can generate using it. Before diving into further details about the deep learning model, let's discuss some of the basic concepts.

Understanding the NST algorithm

The NST algorithm was first revealed in a paper on the subject by Gatys *et alia* in 2015. This technique involves a lot of fun! I am sure you will love implementing this, and will be amazed at the outputs that you'll create.

It attempts to merge two images based on the following parameters:

- A content image (C)
- A style image (S)

The NST algorithm uses these parameters to create a third, generated image (G).
The generated image G combines the content of the image C with the style of image S.

Here is an example of what we will actually be doing:

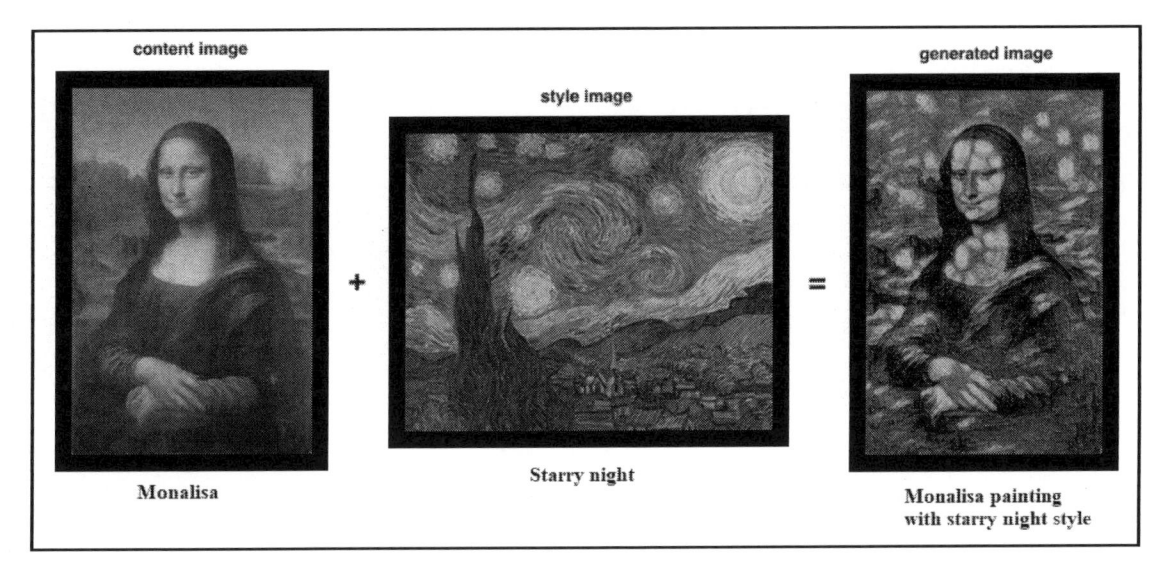

content image — Monalisa
style image — Starry night
generated image — Monalisa painting with starry night style

Surprised? I hope you liked the filter applied on the Mona Lisa! Excited to implement this? Let's do it with transfer learning.

Implementation of NST with transfer learning

Unlike most of the algorithms in deep learning, NST optimizes a cost function to get pixel values. An NST implementation generally uses a pre-trained convolutional network.

It is simply the idea of using a network trained on one task and putting it to use on an entirely new task.

The following are the three component loss functions:

- Content loss
- Style loss
- Total-variation loss

Each component is individually computed and then combined in a single meta-loss function. By minimizing the meta-loss function, we will be, in turn, jointly optimizing the content, style, and total-variation loss as well.

Ensuring NST with content loss

We now thoroughly know that top layers of a convolutional network detect lower level features and the deeper layers detect high-level features of an image. But what about the middle layers? They hold content. And as we want the *generated* image G to have similar contents as the input, our content image C, we would use some activation layers in between to represent content of an image.

We are going to get more visually pleasing outputs if we choose the middle layers of the network ourselves, meaning that it's neither too shallow, nor too deep.

The *content loss* or *feature reconstruction loss* (which we want to minimize) can be represented as the following:

$$J_{content}(C, G) = \frac{1}{4n_C n_W n_H} \sum_{all\ entries} (a^{(C)} - a^{(G)})^2$$

Here, n_W, n_H, and n_C are width, height, and number of channels in the chosen hidden layer, respectively. In practice, the following happens:

- The content cost takes a hidden layer activation of the neural network, and measures how different $a^{(C)}$ and $a^{(G)}$ are.
- When we minimize the content cost later, this will help make sure G has similar content to C.

Computing the style cost

We first need to compute the style, or Gram matrix, by computing the matrix of dot products from the unrolled filter matrix.

The style loss for the hidden layer *a* can be represented as the following:

$$J_{style}^{[l]}(S, G) = \frac{1}{4n_C^2 (n_W n_H)^2} \sum_{i=1}^{n_C} \sum_{j=1}^{n_C} (G_{ij}^{(S)} - G_{ij}^{(G)})^2$$

We want to minimize the distance between the Gram matrices for the images S and G. The overall weighed *style loss* (which we want to minimize) is represented as the following:

$$J_{style}(S,G) = \sum_l \lambda^{[l]} J^{[l]}_{style}(S,G)$$

Here, λ represents the weights for different layers. Bear the following in mind:

- The style of an image can be represented using the Gram matrix of a hidden layer's activations. However, we get even better results combining this representation from multiple different layers. This is in contrast to the content representation, where usually using just a single hidden layer is sufficient.
- Minimizing the style cost will cause the image G to follow the style of the image S.

Computing the overall loss

A cost function that minimizes both the style and the content cost is the following:

$$J(G) = \alpha J_{content}(C,G) + \beta J_{style}(S,G)$$

Sometimes, to encourage spatial smoothness in the output image G, a total variation regularizer TV(G) is also added to the RHS convex combination.

In this section, however, we shall not use transfer learning. If you are interested, you can follow the link provided in the further reading and references section. Instead, we are going to use a pre-trained Torch model (Torch is yet another deep learning library) with a particular image style, namely, the Starry Night painting by Van Gogh.

Neural style transfer with Python and OpenCV

Let's first download the pre-trained Torch model from `https://github.com/DmitryUlyanov/online-neural-doodle/blob/master/pretrained/starry_night.t7` and save it in the current folder (where we are planning to run the following code from). Create a folder named `output` on the current path to save the generated image by the model.

The next code block demonstrates how to perform an NST (with Starry Night style) to an input *content* image. First, use the `cv2.dnn.readNetFromTorch()` function to load the pre-trained model.

Next, create a 4-dimensional blob from the image with the `cv2.dnn.blobFromImage()` function by subtracting the mean values from the RGB channels. Finally, perform a forward pass to obtain an output image (that is, the result of the NST algorithm):

```python
import cv2
import matplotlib.pyplot as pylab
import imutils
import time

model = 'neural-style-transfer/models/eccv16/starry_night.t7' # assumes
                 the pre-trained torch file is in the current path
print("loading style transfer model...")
net = cv2.dnn.readNetFromTorch(model)

image = cv2.imread('../images/monalisa.jpg') # the content image path
image = imutils.resize(image, width=600)
(h, w) = image.shape[:2]
b, g, r = np.mean(image[...,0]), np.mean(image[...,1]),
          np.mean(image[...,2])

# construct a blob from the image, set the input, and then perform a
# forward pass of the network
blob = cv2.dnn.blobFromImage(image, 1.0, (w, h), (b, g, r), swapRB=False,
crop=False)
net.setInput(blob)
start = time.time()
output = net.forward()
end = time.time()

# reshape the output tensor, add back in the mean subtraction, and
# then swap the channel ordering
output = output.reshape((3, output.shape[2], output.shape[3]))
output[0] += b
output[1] += g
output[2] += r
#output /= 255.0
output = output.transpose(1, 2, 0)

# show information on how long inference took
print("neural style transfer took {:.4f} seconds".format(end - start))

#pylab.imshow(output / 255.0)
#pylab.show()
# show the images
cv2.imwrite('output/styled.jpg', output)
```

The following is the input content image of the Mona Lisa:

The following is the input style image, Van Gogh's Starry Night:

The following is the output image generated by the deep learning model, with the style of the Starry Night image being transferred over the content input image of the Mona Lisa:

Summary

In this chapter, we discussed a few advanced deep learning applications to solve a few complex image processing problems. We started with basic concepts in image classification with localization and object detection. Then we demonstrated how a popular YOLO v2 FCN pre-trained model can be used to detect objects in images and draw boxes around them. Next, we discussed the basic concepts in semantic segmentation and then demonstrated how to use DeepLab v3+ (along with a summary on its architecture) to perform semantic segmentation of an image. Then we defined transfer learning and explained how and when it is useful in deep learning, along with a demonstration on transfer learning in Keras to classify flowers with a pre-trained VGG16 model. Finally, we discussed how to generate novel artistic images with deep neural style transfer, and demonstrated this with Python and OpenCV and a pre-trained Torch model. You should be familiar with how to use pre-trained deep learning models to solve complex image processing problems. You should be able to load pre-trained models with Keras, Python, and OpenCV, and use the models to predict outputs for different image processing tasks. You should also be able to use transfer learning and implement it with Keras.

In the next chapter, we'll discuss a few more advanced image processing problems.

Questions

1. Use pre-trained Fast-RCNN and MobileNet models for real-time object detection with Keras.
2. We used a YOLO v2 pre-trained model to implement object detection. Try to use a YOLO v3 pre-trained model to implement object detection.
3. What is fine-tuning, and how does it differ from transfer learning? Demonstrate with an example.
4. We have trained the FC layers of VGG16 only for transfer learning. Use VGG19, Resnet50, and Inception V3 models instead, with Keras. Does the accuracy improve?
5. For transfer learning with Keras, we used 500 images for training and 50 images for validation for each of the flower classes, with a non-standard 91:9 training to validation dataset ratio. Change it to standard 80:20 validation—how much does it affect the accuracy in the validation dataset?
6. Follow this link, https://cs.stanford.edu/people/jcjohns/papers/eccv16/JohnsonECCV16.pdf, and implement the NST algorithm to transfer the style of image (except Starry Night) to an input content image using transfer learning.

Further reading

- http://www.deeplearning.ai
- http://www.learnopencv.com
- http://pyimagesearch.com
- https://arxiv.org/abs/1506.02640
- https://arxiv.org/abs/1612.08242
- https://pjreddie.com/darknet/yolo/
- https://arxiv.org/pdf/1506.02640.pdf
- https://sandipanweb.wordpress.com/2018/03/11/autonomous-driving-car-detection-with-yolo-in-python/
- https://arxiv.org/abs/1706.05587
- https://arxiv.org/pdf/1802.02611.pdf
- https://arxiv.org/pdf/1508.06576.pdf
- https://cs.stanford.edu/people/jcjohns/papers/eccv16/JohnsonECCV16.pdf
- https://sandipanweb.wordpress.com/2018/01/02/deep-learning-art-neural-style-transfer-an-implementation-with-tensorflow-in-python/

12
Additional Problems in Image Processing

In this chapter, we will discuss a few more advanced problems in image processing. We'll start with the seam carving problem and demonstrate a couple of applications, the first one being the content-aware image resizing, and the second one being object removal from images. Next, we'll discuss seamless cloning, which can be used to seamlessly copy one object from an image to another image. Then we'll discuss an inpainting algorithm that can be used to restore damaged pixels in an image. After that, we'll look at variational methods in image processing with an application in image denoising. Next, we'll discuss the image quilting algorithm and its applications in texture synthesis and the transfer of images. We shall end our discussion with a sophisticated face morphing algorithm.

The topics to be covered in this chapter are as follows:

- Seam carving
- Seamless cloning and Poisson image editing
- Image inpainting
- Variational image processing
- Image quilting
- Face morphing

Seam carving

Seam carving is a content-aware image resizing technique where the image is reduced in size by one pixel in height (or width) at a time. A vertical seam in an image is a path of pixels connected from the top to the bottom with one pixel in each row. A horizontal seam is a path of pixels connected from the left to the right with one pixel in each column. Although the underlying algorithm is simple and elegant, it was not discovered until 2007.

Now it is now a core feature in Adobe Photoshop and other computer graphics applications. Unlike standard content-agnostic resizing techniques, such as cropping and scaling, seam carving preserves the most interesting features of the image, such as aspect ratio, set of objects present, and so on. Finding and removing a seam involves three parts:

1. **Energy calculation**: The first step is to calculate the energy of a pixel, which is a measure of its importance—the higher the energy, the less likely that the pixel will be included as part of a seam. For example, the dual-gradient energy function can be used for energy computation.

2. **Seam identification**: The next step is to find a vertical or horizontal seam of minimum total energy. This is similar to the classic shortest path problem in an edge-weighted digraph, with the important difference that the weights are on the vertices instead of the edges. The goal is to find the shortest path from any of the W pixels in the top row to any of the W pixels in the bottom row. The digraph is acyclic, where there is a downward edge from pixel (x, y) to pixels (x − 1, y + 1), (x, y + 1), and (x + 1, y + 1), assuming that the coordinates are in the prescribed ranges. Also, seams cannot wrap around the image. The optimal seam can be found using dynamic programming. The first step is to traverse the image from the second row to the last row and compute the cumulative minimum energy, M, for all possible connected seams for each pixel (i, j), as follows:

$$M(i,j) = e(i,j) + min(M(i-i,j-1), M(i,j-1), M(i-1,j))$$

3. **Seam removal**: The final step is to remove from the image all of the pixels along the vertical or horizontal seam.

In the following two subsections, we'll discuss a couple of applications of the seam carving technique, the first one being content-aware image resizing, and the second one being object removal from images. The implementations of these will be done with `scikit-image` library's `transform` module's functions.

Content-aware image resizing with seam carving

The following code demonstrates how the `scikit-image` library's `transform` module's `seam_curve()` function can be used for content-aware image resizing. Let's first import the required packages, load the original input airplane image, and display the image using the following code block:

```
% matplotlib inline # for jupyter notebook
from skimage import data, draw
```

```
from skimage import transform, util
import numpy as np
from skimage import filters, color
from matplotlib import pyplot as pylab
image = imread('../images/aero.jpg')
print(image.shape)
# (821, 616, 3)
image = util.img_as_float(image)
energy_image = filters.sobel(color.rgb2gray(image))
pylab.figure(figsize=(20,16)), pylab.title('Original Image'),
pylab.imshow(image), pylab.show()
```

The following shows the output of the preceding code block:

Additional Problems in Image Processing

Let's make this image smaller with the `resize()` function, shrinking the width of the image using the usual downsampling, as in the following code snippet:

```
resized = transform.resize(image, (image.shape[0], image.shape[1] - 200), 
mode='reflect')
print(resized.shape)
# (821, 416, 3)
pylab.figure(figsize=(20,11)), pylab.title('Resized Image'), 
pylab.imshow(resized), pylab.show()
```

The following shows the output of the preceding code block. As can be seen in the following output, there is a considerable reduction of size of the airplanes, but they have been distorted too, as simply resizing to a new aspect ratio distorts image contents:

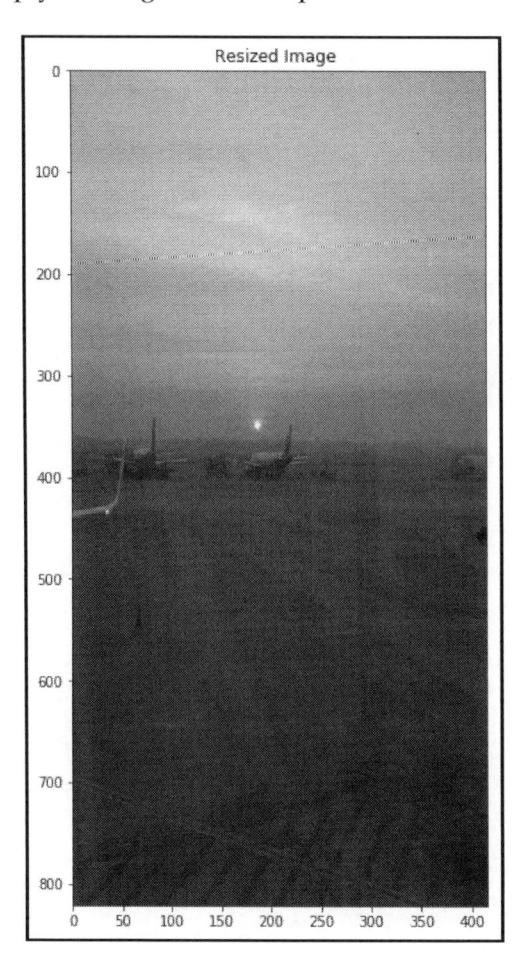

Now let's resize the image with the `seam_carve()` function. Here, a the `sobel` filter is used as the `energy` function, to signify the importance of each pixel:

```
image = util.img_as_float(image)
energy_image = filters.sobel(color.rgb2gray(image))
out = transform.seam_carve(image, energy_image, 'vertical', 200)
pylab.figure(figsize=(20,11)), pylab.title('Resized using Seam Carving'),
pylab.imshow(out)
```

The following shows the output of the preceding code block. As can be seen, seam carving attempts to resize without distortion by removing regions of an image that it deems less important (that is, with low energy). As a result, the airplanes do not have any visible distortion:

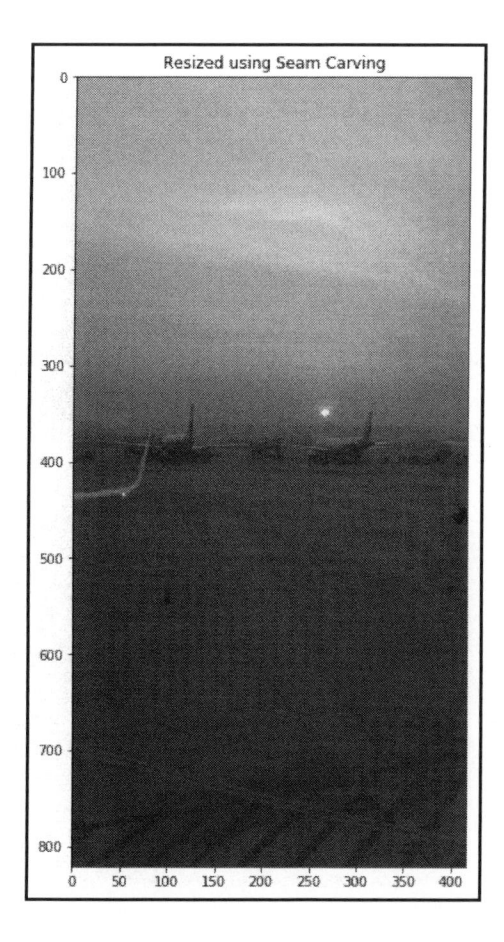

Additional Problems in Image Processing

Object removal with seam carving

You can use seam carving to remove objects or artifacts from images too. This requires weighting the object region with low values, since the lower weights are preferentially removed in seam carving. The following code block uses a mask image of the same shape as the original input photo that masks the region of the photo containing the dog with a low weight, indicating that it should be removed:

```
image = imread('man.jpg')
mask_img = rgb2gray(imread('man_mask.jpg'))
print(image.shape)
pylab.figure(figsize=(15,10))
pylab.subplot(121), pylab.imshow(image), pylab.title('Original Image')
pylab.subplot(122), pylab.imshow(mask_img), pylab.title('Mask for the
object to be removed (the dog)') pylab.show()
```

The following shows the input photo and the mask image used in the preceding code block:

Chapter 12

The next code block uses the `seam_carve()` function, along with the mask, and removes the dog from the image seamlessly:

```
pylab.figure(figsize=(10,12))
pylab.title('Object (the dog) Removed')
out = transform.seam_carve(image, mask_img, 'vertical', 90)
resized = transform.resize(image, out.shape, mode='reflect')
pylab.imshow(out), pylab.show()
```

The following shows the output of the preceding code block—now the dog object has been seamlessly removed from the photo:

[447]

Additional Problems in Image Processing

Seamless cloning and Poisson image editing

The goal of Poisson image editing is to perform **seamless blending** (cloning) of an object or a texture from a source image (captured by a mask image) to a target image. We want to create a photomontage by pasting an image region onto a new background using Poisson image editing. This idea is from the SIGGRAPH 2003 paper, *Poisson Image Editing*, by Perez et alia. The problem is first expressed in the continuous domain as a constrained variational optimization problem (the Euler-Lagrange equation is used to find a solution), and then can be solved using a discrete Poisson solver. The main task of the discrete Poisson solver is to solve a huge linear system. The central insight in the paper is that working with image gradients, instead of image intensities, can produce much more realistic results. After seamless cloning, the gradient of the output image in the masked region is the same as the gradient of the source region in the masked region. Additionally, the intensity of the output image at the boundary of the masked region is the same as the intensity of the destination image.

In this section, we shall demonstrate seamless cloning with Python and OpenCV (with the `seamlessClone()` function introduced in OpenCV 3.0). Let's use this function to copy the bird from the sky in the source image (with the help of a mask image) to the sky in the destination `sea-bird` image. These are the photos that we'll be using:

Destination image:

The next code block shows how to implement seamless cloning by invoking the function with the right arguments. In this example, the cloning type flag used is NORMAL_CLONE, where the texture (gradient) of the source image is preserved in the cloned region:

```
import cv2
print(cv2.__version__) # make sure the major version of OpenCV is 3
# 3.4.3
import numpy as np

# read source and destination images
src = cv2.imread("bird.jpg")
dst = cv2.imread("sea.jpg")

# read the mask image
src_mask = cv2.imread("birds_mask.jpg")
print(src.shape, dst.shape, src_mask.shape)
# (480, 698, 3) (576, 768, 3) (480, 698, 3)

# this is where the CENTER of the airplane will be placed
center = (450,150)

# clone seamlessly.
output = cv2.seamlessClone(src, dst, src_mask, center, cv2.NORMAL_CLONE)

# save result
cv2.imwrite("sea_bird.jpg", output)
```

The following shows the output of the preceding code block, with the bird from the source image having been seamlessly cloned to the destination image:

Image inpainting

Inpainting is the process of restoring damaged or missing parts of an image. Suppose we have a binary mask, *D*, that specifies the location of the damaged pixels in the input image, *f*, as shown here:

$$D(x,y) = \begin{cases} 0 \text{ if } pixel(x,y) \text{ is damaged in image } f \\ 1 \text{ if } pixel(x,y) \text{ is not damaged in image } f \end{cases}$$

Once the damaged regions in the image are located with the mask, the lost/damaged pixels have to be reconstructed with some algorithm (for example, **Total Variation Inpainting**). The reconstruction is supposed to be performed fully automatically by exploiting the information presented in non-damaged regions.

In this example, we shall demonstrate an image inpainting implementation with scikit-image restoration module's inpaint_biharmonic() function. Let's apply a mask to create a damaged image from the original Lena colored image. The following code block shows how the masked pixels in the damaged image get inpainted by the inpainting algorithm based on a biharmonic equation assumption:

```
import numpy as np
import matplotlib.pyplot as pylab
from skimage.io import imread, imsave
from skimage.color import rgb2gray
from skimage import img_as_float
from skimage.restoration import inpaint

image_orig = img_as_float(imread('../images/lena.jpg'))
# create mask from a mask image
mask = rgb2gray(imread('../images/lena_scratch_mask.jpg'))
mask[mask > 0.5] = 1
mask[mask <= 0.5] = 0
print(np.unique(mask))
# defect image over the same region in each color channel
image_defect = image_orig.copy()
for layer in range(image_defect.shape[-1]):
  image_defect[np.where(mask)] = 0
image_result = inpaint.inpaint_biharmonic(image_defect, mask,
multichannel=True)

fig, axes = pylab.subplots(ncols=2, nrows=2, figsize=(20,20))
 ax = axes.ravel()
ax[0].set_title('Original image', size=30), ax[0].imshow(image_orig)
ax[1].set_title('Mask', size=30), ax[1].imshow(mask, cmap=pylab.cm.gray)
ax[2].set_title('Defected image', size=30), ax[2].imshow(image_defect)
ax[3].set_title('Inpainted image', size=30), ax[3].imshow(image_result)
for a in ax:
 a.axis('off')
fig.tight_layout()
pylab.show()
```

Additional Problems in Image Processing

The following shows the output of the preceding code block. As can be seen, the restored photo looks the same as the original photo:

Variational image processing

In this section, we shall very briefly discuss variational methods in image processing, with an example application in denoising. Image processing tasks can be viewed as function estimation (for example, segmentation can be thought of as finding a smooth closed curve between an object and the background). Calculus of variations can be used for minimization of the appropriately defined energy functionals (with the Euler-Langrange method) for a specific image processing task, and the gradient descent method is used to evolve towards the solution.

The following diagram describes the basic steps in an image processing task, represented as a variational optimization problem. First, we need to create an energy functional E that describes the quality of the input image u. Then, with the Euler-Lagrange equation, we need to calculate the first variation. Next, we need to set up a **partial differentail equation (PDE)** for the steepest descent minimization and discretize it and evolve towards the minimum:

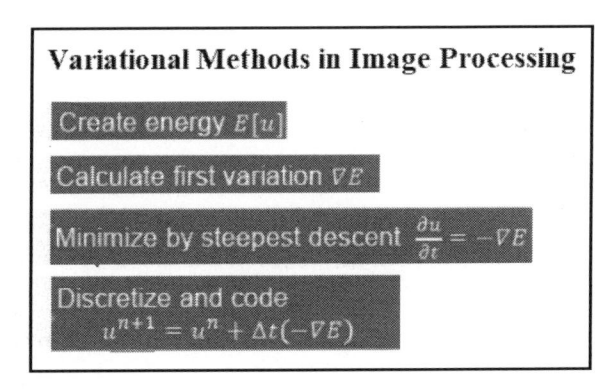

Variational Methods in Image Processing

- Create energy $E[u]$
- Calculate first variation ∇E
- Minimize by steepest descent $\frac{\partial u}{\partial t} = -\nabla E$
- Discretize and code
  $u^{n+1} = u^n + \Delta t(-\nabla E)$

Total Variation Denoising

The following shows the linear and non-linear **Total Variation Denoising** algorithms. As can be observed in the following, the energy functional is the only difference:

Total Variation Denoising

The Variational Approach

Linear

$$\min E[u|f] = \int_\Omega ||\nabla u||^2 d\vec{x} + \lambda \int_\Omega (u-f)^2 d\vec{x}$$

- The first variation is easy to modify.
$$\nabla E = -2\Delta u + 2\lambda(u-f)$$
- So the PDE becomes
$$\frac{\partial u}{\partial t} = \Delta u - \lambda(u-f)$$

Nonlinear

- *(Rudin-Osher-Fatemi, 1992)* proposed the Total Variation (TV) denoising model.

$$\min E_{TV}[u|f] = \int_\Omega ||\nabla u|| d\vec{x} + \lambda \int_\Omega (u-f)^2 d\vec{x}$$

- The first variation of energy is
$$\nabla E = -\nabla \cdot \left(\frac{\nabla u}{|\nabla u|}\right) + 2\lambda(u-f)$$

Let's demonstrate an implementation of total variation denoising using the `scikit-image` library's `restoration` module. The principle of total variation denoising is to minimize the total variation of the image, which can be roughly described as the integral of the norm of the image gradient. First, let's create a noisy input image by adding random Gaussian noise with the original input image. Next, let's use the `denoise_tv_chambolle()` function to do the denoising. Since we are using a grayscale input image, we do not need to set the `multichannel` parameter (by default it is set to `False`) to this function:

```
from skimage import io, color, data, img_as_float
from skimage.restoration import denoise_tv_chambolle
image = color.rgb2gray(io.imread('../my images/me12.jpg'))
pylab.figure(figsize=(12,9))
noisy_img = image + 0.5 * image.std() * np.random.randn(*image.shape)
```

```
pylab.subplot(221), pylab.imshow(image), pylab.axis('off'),
pylab.title('original', size=20)
pylab.subplot(222), pylab.imshow(noisy_img), pylab.axis('off'),
pylab.title('noisy', size=20)
denoised_img = denoise_tv_chambolle(image, weight=0.1)
pylab.subplot(223), pylab.imshow(denoised_img), pylab.axis('off'),
pylab.title('denoised (weight=0.1)', size=20)
denoised_img = denoise_tv_chambolle(image, weight=1) #, multichannel=True)
pylab.subplot(224), pylab.imshow(denoised_img), pylab.axis('off'),
pylab.title('denoised (weight=1)', size=20)
pylab.show()
```

The following shows the output of the preceding code block. As can be seen, the greater the denoising weight, the more denoised is the output image (at the cost of the fidelity to the input, it gets more blurred):

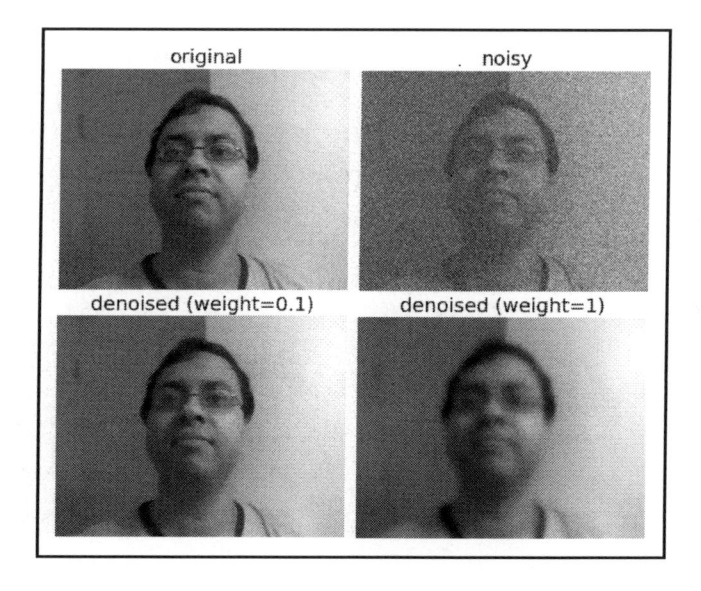

Creating flat-texture cartoonish images with total variation denoising

Total variation denoising can be used to produce cartoonish images; that is, piecewise-constant images, as demonstrated. The more we increase the weight, the flatter the textures (at the expense of fidelity to the input image):

```
image = io.imread('../my images/me18.jpg')
pylab.figure(figsize=(10,14))
pylab.subplot(221), pylab.imshow(image), pylab.axis('off'),
pylab.title('original', size=20)
denoised_img = denoise_tv_chambolle(image, weight=0.1, multichannel=True)
pylab.subplot(222), pylab.imshow(denoised_img), pylab.axis('off'),
pylab.title('TVD (wt=0.1)', size=20)
denoised_img = denoise_tv_chambolle(image, weight=0.2, multichannel=True)
pylab.subplot(223), pylab.imshow(denoised_img), pylab.axis('off'),
pylab.title('TVD (wt=0.2)', size=20)
denoised_img = denoise_tv_chambolle(image, weight=0.3, multichannel=True)
pylab.subplot(224), pylab.imshow(denoised_img), pylab.axis('off'),
pylab.title('TVD (wt=0.3)', size=20)
pylab.show()
```

The following image shows the output of the preceding code block, with the flat-texture images obtained with total variation denoising using different weights. The greater the weight, the flatter the texture becomes:

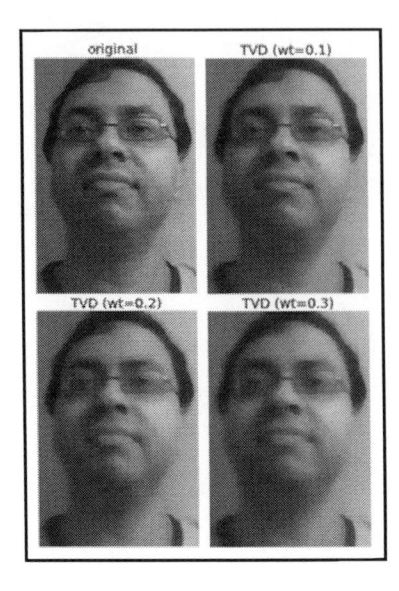

Image quilting

The image quilting algorithm is an algorithm used for texture synthesis and transfer in images, described in the *SIGGRAPH 2001* paper by Efros and Freeman. In this section, we shall touch upon the main idea behind the quilting algorithms for implementing texture synthesis and transfer, and show a couple of results obtained with an implementation of the algorithm. The code is left for the reader to implement (refer to `https://sandipanweb.wordpress.com/2017/10/24/some-computational-photography-image-quilting-texture-synthesis-with-dynamic-programming-and-texture-transfer-in-python/` for more information).

Texture synthesis

Texture synthesis refers to the creation of a larger texture image from a small sample. For texture synthesis, the main idea is to sample patches and lay them down in overlapping patterns, such that the overlapping regions are similar. The overlapping regions may not match exactly, which will result in noticeable artifacts around the edges. To fix this, we need to compute a path along pixels with similar intensities through the overlapping region, and use this path to select on which overlapping patch to draw each pixel. The following shows the output generated by the algorithm for texture synthesis:

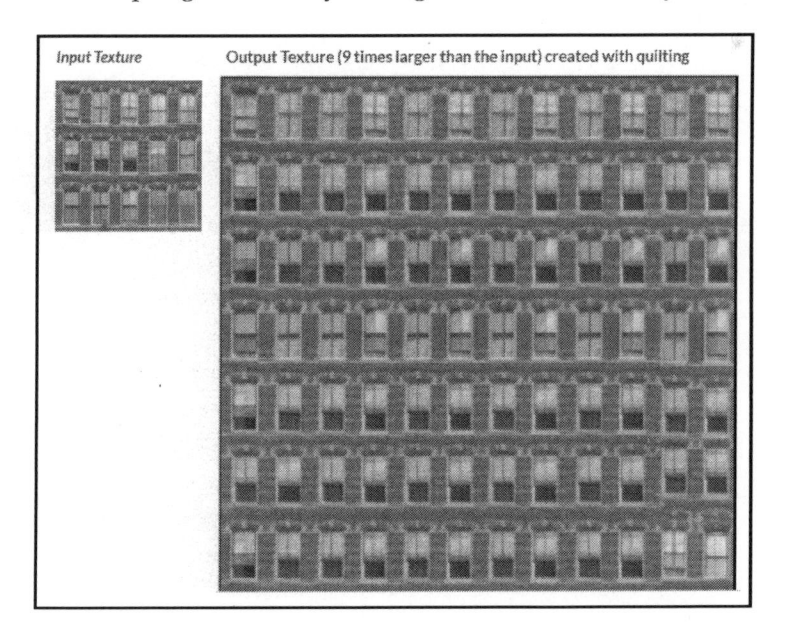

Texture transfer

Texture transfer refers to giving an object the appearance of having the same texture as a sample, while still preserving its basic shape. Texture transfer is achieved by encouraging sampled patches to have a similar appearance to a given target image, as well as matching overlapping regions of already sampled patches. The following screenshot shows the output generated by the algorithm for texture transfer:

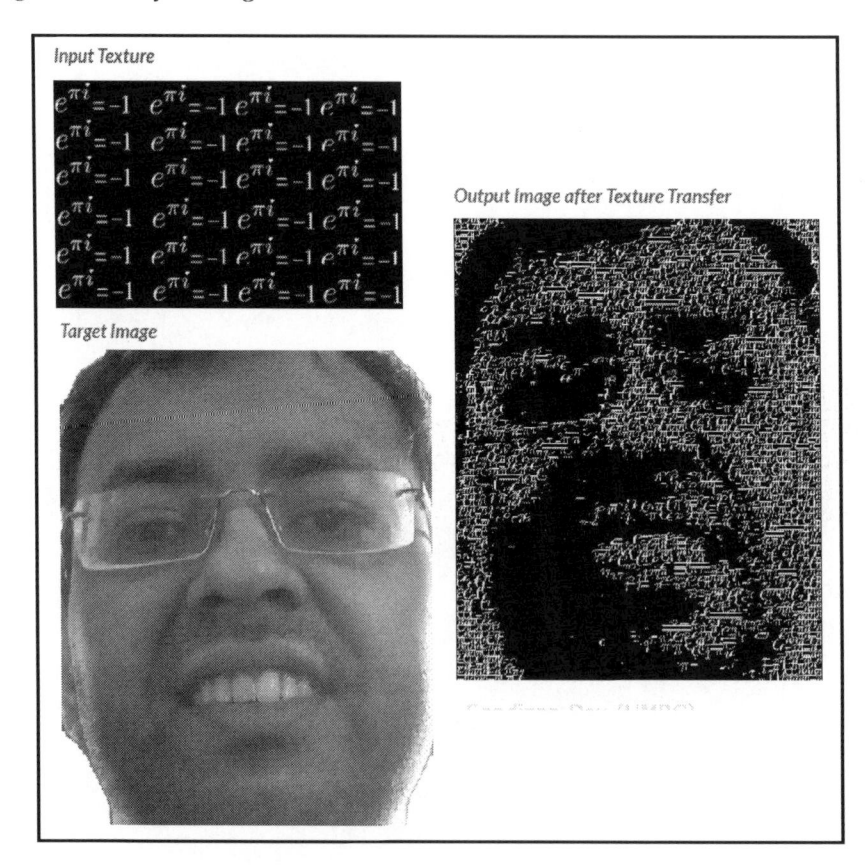

Face morphing

In Chapter 1, *Getting Started with Image Processing*, we discussed a naive face morphing technique based on simple α-blending, which looks terrible if the faces to be morphed are not aligned.

Let's conclude the last chapter by discussing a sophisticated face morphing technique, namely **Beier-Neely morphing**, which visually looks way smoother and better than α-blending for non-aligned faces. Here is the algorithm:

1. Read in two image files, A and B.
2. Specify the correspondence between source image and destination image interactively (by computing facial key points with PyStasm) using a set of line segment pairs. Save the line segment pair to lines file.
3. Read the lines file. The lines file contains the line segment pairs S_i^A, S_i^B.
4. Compute destination line segments by linearly interpolating between S_i^A and S_i^B by warp fraction. These line segments define the destination shape.
5. Warp image A to its destination shape, computing a new image A'.
6. Warp picture B to its destination shape, computing a new image B'.
7. Cross-dissolve between A' and B' by dissolve fraction α.
8. Save the resulting image to a file.

The implementation of this algorithm is left to the reader. The following figure shows a face morphing implementation with the PyStasm library. The images in the first row are the source and the target images, and the last row shows two intermediate average face images. As can be seen, using this implementation, the morphing is very smooth and visually pleasing:

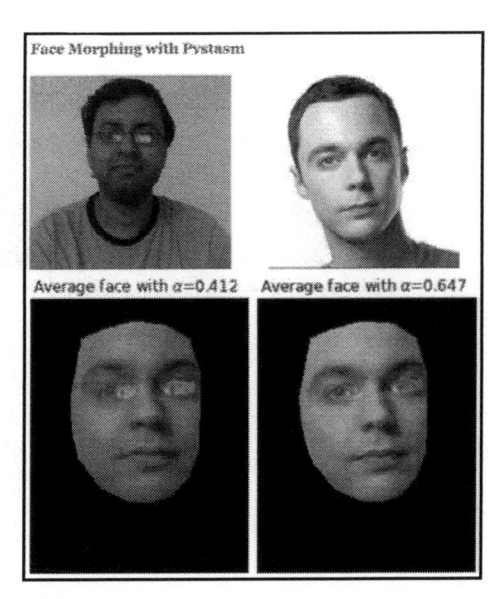

Summary

In this chapter, we discussed a few advanced image processing problems. We started with the seam carving algorithm and demonstrated a couple of applications of the algorithm in context-aware image resizing and object or artifact removal from images with the `scikit-image` library.

Next, we discussed seamless cloning with an application to copy one object from one image to another using Python and OpenCV. Then we discussed the biharmonic inpainting algorithm and applied it to restore damaged pixels in an image using the `scikit-image` library. After that, we discussed variational methods in image processing with an application in image denoising with `scikit-image` again. Next, we discussed the image quilting algorithm and its application in texture synthesis and transfer of images. Finally, we ended this chapter with a discussion on an advanced face morphing algorithm. By the end of this chapter, the reader should be able to write Python codes for all these tasks.

Questions

1. Use `MIXED_CLONE` as the clone type argument for seamless cloning with `python-opencv`. How does the output differ from the one obtained with `NORMAL_CLONE`?
2. Implement total variation inpainting with variational optimization using gradient descent (hint: refer to https://sandipanweb.wordpress.com/2017/10/08/some-more-variational-image-processing-diffusiontv-denoising-image-inpainting/).
3. Apply total variation denoising on an RGB image.

Further reading

- Shai Avidan and Ariel Shamir: *Seam Carving for Content-Aware Image Resizing* - http://www.cs.jhu.edu/~misha/ReadingSeminar/Papers/Avidan07.pdf
- Patrick Perez, Michel Gangnet and Andrew Blake: *Poisson Image Editing* - http://www.irisa.fr/vista/Papers/2003_siggraph_perez.pdf
- *Quilting for Texture Synthesis and Transfer*: http://www.merl.com/publications/docs/TR2001-17.pdf
- *Image inpainting by biharmonic functions*: https://arxiv.org/pdf/1707.06567.pdf

- *Feature-Based Image Metamorphosis*: https://www.cs.toronto.edu/~mangas/teaching/320/assignments/a4/Beier-SIG92.pdf
- https://sandipanweb.wordpress.com/2017/10/14/seam-carving-using-dynamic-programming-to-implement-context-aware-image-resizing-in-python/
- https://sandipanweb.wordpress.com/2017/10/03/some-variational-image-processing-possion-image-editing-and-its-applications/
- https://sandipanweb.wordpress.com/2017/10/08/some-more-variational-image-processing-diffusiontv-denoising-image-inpainting/

Other Books You May Enjoy

If you enjoyed this book, you may be interested in these other books by Packt:

Python Machine Learning - Second Edition
Sebastian Raschka, Vahid Mirjalili

ISBN: 9781787125933

- Understand the key frameworks in data science, machine learning, and deep learning
- Harness the power of the latest Python open source libraries in machine learning
- Master machine learning techniques using challenging real-world data
- Master deep neural network implementation using the TensorFlow library
- Ask new questions of your data through machine learning models and neural networks
- Learn the mechanics of classification algorithms to implement the best tool for the job
- Predict continuous target outcomes using regression analysis
- Uncover hidden patterns and structures in data with clustering
- Delve deeper into textual and social media data using sentiment analysis

TensorFlow Machine Learning Cookbook - Second Edition
Nick McClure

ISBN: 9781789131680

- Become familiar with the basic features of the TensorFlow library
- Get to know Linear Regression techniques with TensorFlow
- Learn SVMs with hands-on recipes
- Implement neural networks to improve predictive modeling
- Apply NLP and sentiment analysis to your data
- Master CNN and RNN through practical recipes
- Implement the gradient boosted random forest to predict housing prices
- Take TensorFlow into production

Leave a review - let other readers know what you think

Please share your thoughts on this book with others by leaving a review on the site that you bought it from. If you purchased the book from Amazon, please leave us an honest review on this book's Amazon page. This is vital so that other potential readers can see and use your unbiased opinion to make purchasing decisions, we can understand what our customers think about our products, and our authors can see your feedback on the title that they have worked with Packt to create. It will only take a few minutes of your time, but is valuable to other potential customers, our authors, and Packt. Thank you!

Index

2
2D projection 332, 333
2D visualization 332, 333

A
active contours 313
active contours model 313
Adam optimizer 383
aliasing 66
anti-aliasing 68, 209
artificial neural network (ANN) 368
Atrous Spatial Pyramid Pooling (ASPP) 422

B
band-pass filters 95
band-stop (notch) filter
  about 119
  used, to remove periodic noise from images 120
band-stop filters 95
Beier-Neely morphing 459
bilateral filter
  using 169, 170
binary operations
  black top-hat 236
  boundary, extracting 237
  convex hull, computing 232, 234
  dilation 229, 230
  erosion 228, 229
  fingerprint cleaning, with opening and closing 237
  grayscale operations 239, 240
  opening and closing 230, 231
  skeletonizing 232
  small objects function, removing 234
  white top-hat 236
black top-hat 236

Blob detectors
  with DoG 262
  with DoH 262
  with LoG 262
blurred version 187
BoundingBoxes
  computing, with HOG-SVM 362
box-kernel 95

C
canny edge detector
  with scikit-image 198
closing 230
color palette 325
Compact Watershed algorithm 299, 307, 308
contrast stretching
  about 141
  PIL ImageEnhance module, used 144
  PIL, used as point operation 142
  with scikit-image 151
convex hull
  about 232
  computing 232, 234
convolution theorem
  about 95
  application 96
convolution
  about 80, 95
  applying, to color (RGB) image 83, 85
  applying, to grayscale image 82
  boundary conditions 83
  modes 83
  on image 81
  pad values 83
  template, matching with cross-correlation between image 90
  versus correlation 87, 88, 89

with SciPy ndimage.convolve 85, 87
   with SciPy signal module's convolve2d() function 81
convolutional neural networks (CNN)
   about 367, 371, 393
   architecture 371
   classifying, with Keras 388
   convolutional layer 372
   dropout 374
   FC layer 374
   InceptionNet 404
   intermediate layers, visualizing 391
   MNIST, classifying 388
   non-linearity 374
   pooling layer 374
   Residual Network (ResNet) 405
   VGG-16/19 393
   working 371
correlation 95
cross-correlation 95

D

DC coefficient 75
deconvolution 123
deep learning
   about 368, 369, 371
   in image processing 368
   versus classical 369, 370
deep semantic segmentation
   semantic segmentation 421
   with DeepLab V3+ 421
DeepLab V3+
   about 422
   architecture 422
   model, used for semantic segmentation 423
   used, for deep semantic segmentation 421
degradation 122
derivatives 178
descriptors
   versus feature detectors 253, 254, 255
Determinant of Hessian (DoH) 263
Difference of Gaussian (DoG) 118, 263
dilation 229, 230
Discrete Cosine Transform (DCT) 74
Discrete Fourier Transform (DFT)
   about 59, 72, 73
   computing, Fast Fourier Transform (FFT) algorithm 74
   need for 73, 74
DoG filters 200
down-sampling, image formation
   anti-aliasing 67, 68, 69

E

edge detection
   derivatives, used 190
   filters, used 190
   gradient magnitude computed, with partial derivatives 190
   Hildreth's algorithm, zero-crossing computation 206
   Marr algorithm, zero-crossing computation 206
   with scikit-image 196, 198
edge-based segmentation 292, 293, 294, 295
edges
   enhancing, with PIL 207
   finding, with PIL 207
eigenfaces
   about 331, 337
   decomposition 339
   reconstruction 337, 339
   with PCA 333, 335, 336
entropy 243
erosion 228, 229

F

face morphing 458
Fast Fourier Transform (FFT)
   about 59, 74
   DFT, phase 76, 78, 79
   frequency spectrum, plotting 75, 76
   magnitude, computing 76, 78, 79
   with numpy.fft module 76
   with scipy.fftpack module 74, 75
feature detectors
   about 253
   versus descriptors 253, 254, 255
feature extractors 253
Felzenszwalb algorithm
   about 299

graph-based image segmentation 299, 300, 302
finite differences 178
Floyd-Steinberg dithering
  with error diffusion 149
frequency domain Gaussian blur
  about 95
  with numpy fft 97
  with scipy signal fftconvolve() 101
frequency domain
  band-pass filter (BPF), with DoG 118
  band-stop (notch) filter 119
  enhancement 105
  filtering 105
  high-pass filter (HPF) 106, 108
  image restoration 122
  low-pass filter (LPF) 112
  smoothing 105
  template matching 105
fully connected (FC) layer 371, 427
fully convolutional network (FCN) 410

G

Gaussian Bayes classifier
  about 347
  generative model, training 348, 349
  posterior probabilities, computing on model evaluation 350
  posterior probabilities, computing on test data 350
Gaussian kernel
  about 95
  fftconvolve(), runtimes comparing 103
  in 2-D plot 98
  in 3-D plot 98
  in frequency domain 98
  SciPy convolve(), runtimes comparing 103
Gaussian Pyramid
  about 209
  constructing, with scikit-image transform module's reduce function 214
  images, blending 220
  with scikit-image transform's pyramid module 210
generalization 368
GoogleNet (Inception v1) 404

GrabCut algorithms 313
GrabCut
  about 317
  with OpenCV 317, 318, 320, 321
gradient computation
  noise, effects 184
gradient
  about 178
  displaying, on image 181
gray-level quantization 8

H

Haar-like features
  about 277
  descriptor, with scikit-image 277, 278
  eye detection, with OpenCV using pre-trained classifiers with Haar-cascade features 279, 280
  face detection 279
  face detection, with OpenCV using pre-trained classifiers with Haar-cascade features 279, 280
  finding, for face classification with random forest ensemble classifier 358, 360
half-toning 148
Harris Corner Detector
  about 255
  image matching 258
  with scikit-image 255, 256
  with sub-pixel accuracy 256, 257
high-pass filters 95
histogram equalization
  about 150
  with scikit-image 151, 153, 155
histogram matching
  about 150
  for RGB image 158
  with scikit-image 156
Histogram of Oriented Gradients (HOG) 265, 360
HOG descriptors
  algorithm, computing 265
  computing, with scikit-image 265, 266
HOG training 360
holes
  filling, in binary objects 245, 246

Hough transform 286, 287, 288

I

image classification, supervised machine learning
  dataset, visualizing 342, 343
  Gaussian Bayes classifier 344
  kNN classifier, training 344
  MNIST dataset, downloading 341
  SVM model 344
image classification
  with Keras 375
  with TensorFlow 375
image denoising
  filter, in FFT 130
  final image, reconstructing 131
  with FFT 128, 129, 130
image derivatives
  gradient 178
  Laplacian 178
image formation
  about 60
  down-sampling 65, 66, 67
  quantization 60, 70
  sampling 60
image inpainting 450
image matching
  about 258
  Harris Corner features, used 258, 259, 261, 262
  RANSAC algorithm, used 258, 259, 261, 262
image processing libraries
  Anaconda distribution, installing 15
  installing, in Python 14
  Jupyter Notebook, installing 16
  pip, installing 14
image processing pipeline
  about 11
  acquisition and storage 11
  disk, saving 11
  enhancement 11
  image understanding/interpretation 12
  information extraction/representation 11
  manipulation 11
  memory, loading 11
  restoration 11
  segmentation 11

image processing
  about 8, 10
  applications 8, 11
  storing, on computer 8
image quilting
  about 457
  texture synthesis 457
  texture transfer 458
image restoration
  about 122
  deconvolution, with FFT 123
  image denoising, with FFT 128, 129, 130
  inverse filtering, with FFT 123
image sampling 8
image segmentation 285, 286
image
  Brute-force matching, with SIFT descriptors 275
  correct path, providing on disk 18
  displaying, Matplotlib used 18
  displaying, PIL used 17
  displaying, scikit-image used 21
  displaying, scipy misc used 23
  displaying, with Python 16
  I/O, with Python 16
  interpolating, while matplotlib imshow displayed 20
  matching, with binary descriptor using scikit-image 271
  matching, with BRIEF 269
  matching, with BRIEF binary descriptors with scikit-image 269
  matching, with ORB 269
  matching, with ORB feature detector using Brute-Force matching 273
  matching, with ORB feature detector using scikit-image 271
  matching, with python-opencv 273
  matching, with SIFT 269
  ratio test, with OpenCV 275
  reading, Matplotlib used 18
  reading, PIL used 17
  reading, scikit-image used 21
  reading, scipy misc used 23
  saving, Matplotlib used 18
  saving, PIL used 17

saving, scikit-image used 21
saving, scipy misc used 23
InceptionNet 404
inpainting 450
interference 120
inverse 95
Inverse Discrete Fourier Transform (IDFT) 73
isotropic derivative 182

J

Jupyter notebook
  about 16
  references 16

K

K-means clustering
  for image segmentation, with color quantization 325, 327
k-nearest neighbors (KNN) classifier
  about 344
  computing 345
  performance, evaluating 346
Keras
  network, visualizing 385
  used, for classifying CNN 388
  used, for classifying dense FC layers 383
  weights, visualizing in intermediate layers 386, 388
kernel 80, 372

L

Laplacian of Gaussian (LoG) 200, 263
Laplacian Pyramid
  about 209
  constructing, with scikit-image transform module's reduce function 214
  image, reconstructing 218
  images, blending 220
  with scikit-image transform's pyramid module 212
Laplacian
  about 177, 178, 182
  notes 183
linear noise smoothing
  about 160

averaging, with box blur kernel 162
comparing, with box filter 164
Gaussian kernels, SciPy ndimage used 164
with Gaussian blur filter 163
with ImageFilter.BLUR 160
with PIL 160
local entropy
  computing 244
LoG filter
  about 200
  used, for edge detection 205
  with SciPy ndimage module 204
log transform 137
LoG-convolved image 206
LoG-smoothed image 206
low-pass filter (LPF)
  about 95
  SNR changes, with frequency cutoff 118
  with fourier-gaussian 112
  with scipy fftpack 115, 116
  with scipy ndimage and numpy fft 112

M

Machine Learning (ML) 368
magnitude
  displaying 181
max pooling 374
Maximum Likelihood Estimates (MLE) 348
median filter
  using 166
MNIST
  classifying 388
morphological (Beucher) gradient
  computing 248
Morphological Active Contours without Edges (MorphACWE) 315
morphological contrast enhancement 241, 242
Morphological Geodesic Active Contours (MorphGAC) 315
morphological Laplace
  computing 249
morphological snakes 313, 315, 317
multiple images
  displaying 23
  reading 23

N

nearest neighbor classifier 344
neural style transfer (NST)
  about 432
  algorithm 432
  ensuring, with content loss 434
  implementing, with transfer learning 433
  loss, computing 435
  style cost, computing 434
  with cv2, pre-trained torch model used 432
  with OpenCV 436
  with Python 435
noise removal
  opening and closing used 246
  with median filter 242, 243
non-local means
  using 171
non-maximum suppression
  about 192, 363, 364
  algorithm 192
nonlinear noise smoothing
  about 165
  denoising, with scikit-image 168
  max and min filter, using 168
  median filter, using 166
  with PIL 166
  with scipy ndimage 173

O

object detection, supervised machine learning
  cascade classifiers, with AdaBoost 353, 354
  face classification, with Haar-like feature descriptor 354, 355, 357
  face detection, with Haar-like features 353, 354
  objects, detecting with SVM using HOG features 360
opening 230
Otsu's method 290
Otsu's segmentation 290, 291

P

padding 372
partial derivatives 178
partial differential equation (PDE) 453

pip installation
  reference link 14
pip
  about 14
  installing 14
pixel (pel) 8
point-wise intensity transformations
  about 136
  contrast stretching 141
  log transform 137
  power-law transform 139
  thresholding 145
poisson image editing 448
power-law transform 139
Principal Component Analysis (PCA)
  about 331
  dimension reduction 331, 332
  visualization 331, 332
pyvenv
  reference link 14

Q

quantization
  about 70
  with PIL 70, 72
QuickShift algorithm 299, 305, 306

R

Region Adjacency Graph (RAG) 304
Region Of Interest (ROI) 355
region-based segmentation
  about 292, 295
  morphological watershed algorithm 295, 296, 297, 298
Residual Network (ResNet) 405

S

same padding 372
sampling, image formation
  interpolation 62, 63, 64, 65
  up-sampling 61, 62, 63, 64, 65
scale-invariant feature transform (SIFT)
  about 266, 267
  images, matching with BRIEF 269
  images, matching with ORB 269

images, matching with SIFT 269
scikit-image filter.rank module
  about 241
  local entropy, computing 243, 244
  morphological contrast enhancement 241, 242
  noise removal, with median filter 242, 243
scikit-image morphology module
  about 228
  binary operations 228
scikit-image's astronaut dataset
  using 22
SciPy ndimage morphology module
  about 245
  holes, filling in binary objects 245, 246
  morphological (Beucher) gradient, computing 248
  morphological Laplace, computing 249
  opening and closing, used to remove noise 246
seam carving
  about 441
  content-aware image resizing 442, 445
  energy calculation 442
  object removal 446
  seam identification 442
  seam removal 442
seamless blending 448
seamless cloning 448
second-order partial derivatives 183
seed points 308
sharpening
  about 185
  with Laplacian 186
SIFT descriptors
  algorithm, computing 267
  keypoint descriptor computation 267
  keypoint localization 267
  orientation assignment 267
  scale-space extrema detection 267
  with opencv 267, 268
  with opencv-contrib 267, 268
signal to noise ratio (SNR) 111, 118
Signal-to-Noise Ratio (SNR) 70
SimpleITK
  region growing 308, 310
single-channel 8

skeletonizing 232
SLIC algorithm
  about 299, 303, 304
  RAG merging 304
small object function
  removing 234
SNR changes
  with frequency cut-off 111
Sobel edge detector
  with scikit-image 193
spectral clustering
  for image segmentation 328, 329, 330
spectrum of transform 75
squared Euclidean distance 344
stochastic gradient descent (SGD) 376
stride 372
superpixels 299
supervised machine learning
  about 324
  image classification 340
  object detection 352
  versus unsupervised machine learning 324
SVM classifier 350, 351, 352
SVM model
  classification 361

T

template 95
TensorFlow (TF)
  about 375
  classification 375, 376, 380, 382
texture synthesis 457
texture transfer 458
thresholding
  about 290, 291
  fixing 146
Total Variation Denoising 454
Total Variation Inpainting 450
transfer learning
  using 426
  with Keras 427, 430

U

unsharp masking
  about 185, 187

with SciPy ndimage module 187
unsupervised machine learning
  about 324, 325
  eigenfaces 331
  K-means clustering, for image segmentation with color quantization 325, 327
  Principal Component Analysis (PCA) 331
  spectral clustering, for image segmentation 328, 329, 330
  versus supervised machine learning 324
unsupervised Wiener filter 127

V

vanishing gradient problem 405
variational image processing
  about 453
  flat-texture cartoonish images, creating with Total Variation Denoising 456
  Total Variation Denoising 454
Vector Quantization (VQ) 325
VGG-16/19
  about 393
  testing phase 402
  training phase 395
  used, for classifying cat/dog images in Keras 395

Virtual Environment
  reference link 14
virtualenv
  reference link 14

W

white top-hat 236
wiener 95

Y

YOLO v2
  about 410
  images, classifying 410
  images, localizing 410
  objects, detecting 410
  objects, detecting CNN used 412
  objects, proposing CNN used 412
  pre-trained YOLO model, used for object detection 413, 419
  using 413
You Only Look On (YOLO) 409

Z

zero-crossings 182
zero-padded kernel 126